THE UNRECOGNIZABLE LANGUAGE OF OUR CHILDREN

Vol. 1

"Somebody Is Going to Miss This"

Natl. Evangelist Minister Lee Rice

Children From All Ethnicities Are Prey To A Predator
(A Sick-Minded Individual)

COPYRIGHT

The Unrecognizable Language of Our Children

Vol. 1: Somebody Is Going to Miss This

——————— ✦ ———————

FIRST EDITION

First Printing, 2026

Printed in the United States of America

ISBN: 979-8-9956104-1-0

——————— ✦ ———————

PUBLISHER INFORMATION

Published by:

Minister Lee Rice Ministries

www.MinisterLeeRice.com

For speaking engagements, training, or other events, please visit the website above.

TABLE OF CONTENTS

PART I—THE SACRED RESPONSIBILITY

CHAPTER ONE
The Sacred Duty of Protecting Our Children

CHAPTER TWO
The Watchtower of the Home
Establishing a Spiritually and Physically Secure Environment

CHAPTER THREE
The Role of the Watchman in the Family
Accountability, Discernment, and Authority

PART II—RECOGNIZING HIDDEN DANGER

CHAPTER FOUR
The Perils of Excessive Trust
The Danger of Over-Trust and Unrestricted Access

CHAPTER FIVE
Hidden Perils Within the Home
Invisible Influences and Digital Exposure

CHAPTER SIX
Identifying Signs of Abuse
Physical and Behavioral Indicators

CHAPTER SEVEN
Understanding Grooming and Predator Tactics
How Manipulation Gains Access

PART III—BUILDING PROTECTION

CHAPTER EIGHT
How to Talk to Children About Safety
Creating Open Dialogue and Trust

CHAPTER NINE
Creating a Nurturing Emotional Environment
Breaking the Power of Secrecy

CHAPTER TEN
Establishing Clear Boundaries
Practical Safeguards for Parents and Leaders

CHAPTER ELEVEN
Digital Vigilance
Guarding the Modern Gate

PART IV—HEALING AND RESTORATION

CHAPTER TWELVE
Emotional Healing for the Wounded Child

CHAPTER THIRTEEN
Trauma Awareness and Recovery

CHAPTER FOURTEEN
Restoring Safety After Breach
Rebuilding Trust and Stability

PART V—THE FINAL CHARGE

CHAPTER FIFTEEN
Spiritual Accountability
The Responsibility of Watchmen

THE FINAL WORD
A Solemn Warning

AUTHOR'S DISCLAIMER - 1

This book is not written to entertain a refined intellect but to carry a burden from the Spirit that will take root in the soul. Therefore, its language may not always suit the structure, elegance, or literacy that some might expect. Yet, if the message reaches the heart, stirs conviction, prompts repentance, encourages spiritual growth, and advances our shared faith journey in truth, then its purpose has been fulfilled and its mission before the Lord accomplished. Also, if you read something that seems redundant, it is intentional because it is ****layered reinforcement***.* The concerns in this book cannot be *overstated* or *understated* when it comes to a child's safety.

✝ BIBLICAL REINFORCEMENT ✝

This disclaimer stands in harmony with biblical truth, for Scripture itself often repeats divine realities so they will not merely pass through the mind, but take root in the heart. As seen in 1 Corinthians 15:16, Paul reinforces the same truth again, not because he lacked eloquence, but because the truth that carries eternal weight must be established firmly in the soul. In the same way, this book is not driven by literary polish for intellectual applause, but by spiritual burden for transformation. If its words convict, awaken, correct, and strengthen the reader in truth, then its repetition has served its holy purpose, for God often repeats what man too quickly overlooks.

DISCLAIMER - 2

This book is intended for educational, spiritual, and informational purposes only. It is not intended to replace professional legal, medical, psychological, or counseling services. If abuse is suspected or disclosed, readers are strongly encouraged to contact appropriate authorities and licensed professionals immediately.

The author and publisher assume no responsibility for the misuse or misapplication of the information provided herein.

Also, it is important to note that while many individuals commonly refer to the process of nurturing children as "raising" them, this text adopts the terminology of "child rearing."

CHILD PROTECTION NOTICE

If you suspect child abuse, contact your local child protective services agency or law enforcement immediately. In the United States, you may also contact:

National Child Abuse Hotline
1-800-4-A-CHILD (1-800-422-4453)
www.childhelphotline.org

If you are outside the United States, consult your national or local child protection authority.

ABOUT THIS BOOK

The Unrecognizable Language of Our Children is a spiritually grounded, biblically anchored call to vigilance, discernment, and proactive parental responsibility in an increasingly dangerous and deceptive world. The book unfolds as both a Servant Leader charge and a practical field manual, guiding parents in the sacred duty of protecting their children physically, emotionally, spiritually, and digitally. Rooted deeply in KJV Scripture, each chapter builds systematically—from establishing the home as a spiritual watchtower to identifying concealed dangers, understanding predator psychology, preventing grooming, and recognizing both physical and behavioral indicators of abuse. Minister Lee Rice frames parenting not merely as caregiving but as spiritual guardianship, emphasizing that children often communicate distress through behavior, silence, regression, fear, or withdrawal—forms of expression that require discernment rather than dismissal. The work confronts uncomfortable realities directly: predators disguise themselves behind trust, familiarity, and spiritual appearance; over-trust is dangerous; and silence is often the weapon that allows abuse to continue unchecked.

Beyond exposure and prevention, the book transitions to restoration—addressing emotional healing, trauma recovery, spiritual warfare in the home, and the evolving challenges teenagers face in digital and relational environments. It underscores that protection is not a one-time conversation but a lifestyle of consistency, prayer, boundary-setting, education, and open communication. Minister Lee Rice presents the home as a spiritual gate that must be intentionally guarded, where biblical truth, prayer, discernment, and parental presence serve as armor against unseen threats. Ultimately, the message is both urgent and empowering: awareness breeds preparedness, discernment closes doors to danger, and parents—through vigilance and spiritual clarity—serve as God-appointed protectors of their children's innocence.

The book stands as a comprehensive blueprint for safeguarding the next generation while offering hope, healing, and restoration for those already wounded.

If even one reader becomes more alert, if one parent becomes more courageous, if one church becomes more accountable, and if one child finds safety sooner because an adult finally "heard" what was being expressed—then this effort has not been in vain. Let this book serve as a turning point: moving from assumption to discernment, from silence to action, and from reaction to prevention. May we find the courage to confront discomfort, the humility to rectify carelessness, and the strength to create truly safe homes and ministries. While someone may overlook this message, it doesn't have to be you.

NOTE: This book leans toward the male perspective; be aware that it also applies to females. Because some females are predators, also do not be deceived. Use this as a starting blueprint to help protect your family, friends, and loved ones.

DEDICATION TO THE READERS

To you—the reader who chose not to look away.

This book is dedicated to parents, guardians, pastors, educators, and leaders who understand that protecting the vulnerable requires more than good intentions. It requires vigilance. It requires courage. It requires the willingness to confront uncomfortable truths rather than pretend danger does not exist.

This dedication is for those who understand that love must remain watchful, that trust must be guided by wisdom, and that silence must never become a shield that protects harm. It is for those who are willing to ask difficult questions, face difficult realities, and remain alert when others grow distracted or complacent.

It is also for those who refuse to confuse comfort with safety or familiarity with righteousness. You understand that discernment is not suspicion—it is stewardship. It is the responsibility of caring deeply enough to guard what has been entrusted to you.

If you approach these pages with humility, courage, and a sincere commitment to protect the lives God has placed within your care, then this work is written for you.

May you read with clarity.
May you lead with conviction.
May you protect with courage.
And may no warning sign under your watch ever go unheard.

A PERSONAL CONVICTION

Am I considered an expert in this field based on traditional educational credentials and the accumulation of degrees? While there is nothing inherently problematic with possessing degrees, the answer is No. But I know what I know, and I witness what I have witnessed.

The Bible teaches in John 3:11, "Verily, verily, I say unto thee, We speak that we do know, and testify that we have seen; and ye receive not our witness." Jesus Himself spoke these words. They reveal a powerful principle: truth often comes from what has been seen, witnessed, and experienced.

These words have shaped how I approach life and ministry. My journey has been one of witnessing the work of God's Spirit and observing realities that many would rather ignore. Over the years, I have listened to parents speak through tears about how their children became victims of predatory manipulation. I have heard friends from my college years share how predators entered their lives and left wounds that took years to confront and heal.

Even during my time in the military, I witnessed a sobering example. There was a man who appeared disciplined and respectable. Every day, he stood in formation, wearing a perfectly starched uniform, projecting an image of order and professionalism. Yet behind that public appearance, he was abusing his own daughters. Eventually, the truth surfaced, and he faced the consequences of his actions. But the experience revealed a painful truth: evil often hides behind appearances that seem respectable.

These experiences, along with many others, placed a deep conviction in my heart. I sensed that the Spirit of God was urging me not to remain silent about what I had witnessed from others and learned.

Yes, information about these dangers already exists in many places. But my prayer is that this book will offer something meaningful to someone who reads it. Perhaps it will be a single word, a single statement, or a single thought that awakens awareness, strengthens discernment, or prevents harm.

If even one life is protected, if even one parent becomes more watchful, if even one child is spared because someone recognized a warning sign in time, then the labor behind these pages will have been worthwhile.

May these words serve as a light where darkness tries to hide. And may every reader be strengthened to guard what God has placed within their care.

FOREWORD

There are books that inform, and there are books that awaken. The Unrecognizable Language of Our Children does both.

We live in a time when innocence is under pressure and vigilance has grown optional. Families are busier than ever, yet often less aware. Technology has expanded access while diminishing oversight. Cultural confusion has blurred boundaries that were once clearly defined. In such an environment, silence becomes dangerous.

Natl. Evangelist Minister Lee Rice writes with urgency—not alarmism, but conviction. He confronts the uncomfortable reality that children often communicate distress in ways adults overlook. Behavioral shifts, silence, regression, withdrawal—these are not inconveniences. They are signals.

This book does not promote paranoia. It promotes discernment.

Rooted firmly in Scripture (KJV), Minister Lee Rice calls parents, guardians, pastors, and community leaders back to the watchtower. He challenges excessive trust without accountability. He exposes the danger of spiritual complacency. He reminds us that protection is not fear—it is obedience.

What makes this work particularly valuable is its balance. It addresses hidden dangers while offering a practical structure. It warns, but it also equips. It confronts, but it restores. It reminds us that while evil may seek access, vigilance can deny it.

Every generation faces defining responsibilities. Ours is no different. The question is not whether children are communicating. The question is whether we are listening.

May this book sharpen discernment.
May it strengthen homes.
May it awaken watchmen.

Because someone will miss the signs.

Let it not be us.

OPENING CHARGE

There comes a moment in every generation when silence becomes complicity and awareness becomes responsibility. This is that moment. Children do not always speak in sentences. They speak in signals. They speak with hesitation. They speak in changes of temperament, in withdrawal, in regression, in defiance, in sudden fear. They speak in ways that require discernment rather than dismissal. The question is not whether children are communicating.

The question is whether we are listening.

We live in an era where danger does not always appear dangerous. It often presents itself as helpful, friendly, familiar, spiritual, trustworthy, or convenient. The modern predator understands access, psychology, technology, and secrecy. What once required physical proximity now requires only digital access. What once appeared suspicious now appears normal.

This book is crafted not to instill fear, but to illuminate the truths that lie before us. Its purpose is to foster clarity, enabling individuals to see the world and its complexities with greater understanding.

The intention here is not to place blame on parents, religious institutions, or communities. Rather, it aims to catalyze a profound awakening—a call to consciousness that invites reflection and action.

As you hold this book in your hands, recognize that it represents more than just a collection of pages; it embodies a weighty responsibility. With increased awareness comes a deeper sense of accountability. When the truth is brought to light, it becomes a force that demands attention and action—it cannot simply be dismissed or overlooked.

By continuing to engage with this text, you are accepting an important and sacred mission. This mission calls for you to become more discerning, more courageous, more disciplined, and deeply prayerful in the guardianship of those entrusted to your care.

Children are not only to be cherished—they must be vigilantly protected. The act of protection should not be misconstrued as paranoia; instead, it should be seen as a form of obedience—a duty that we owe to the most vulnerable among us. In doing so, we uphold their safety and well-being, ensuring they can thrive in a world that can often be challenging and unpredictable.

May you read with humility.
May you examine with honesty.
May you act with courage.

✝ CALL TO THE WATCHMAN ✝

"Son of man, I have made thee a watchman…"—Ezekiel 33:7 (KJV)

In Scripture, a watchman stood upon the wall. His task was simple, yet weighty: remain alert, observe carefully, and sound the warning when danger approached. If he failed to warn, he bore responsibility for the resulting harm.

The role of a watchman may not be glamorous, but it carries profound significance. This position demands unwavering discipline, consistent effort, and acute vigilance. It requires the ability to observe and acknowledge truths that many would rather ignore. The watchman must be willing to raise alarms—even at times when others might hope that such alarms are unnecessary.

In our lives, we find that every parent embodies the spirit of a watchman. Each guardian adopts this role with commitment. Pastors, teachers, and mentors who are entrusted with the care and guidance of children are all watchmen in their own right. Their responsibilities extend far beyond simple oversight; they are tasked with safeguarding the well-being and future of the young lives in their charge.

Consider the home, which should not be viewed merely as a place of residence; it serves as a critical gate. It is a threshold where influences and experiences converge to form a child's identity. Likewise, the church transcends its physical structure; it is also a gate, a sanctuary that shapes spiritual understanding and community values. Furthermore, the digital devices we constantly hold in our hands act as gates to the vast world of information, interactions, and influences that can significantly impact the lives of those we care for.

What enters these gates profoundly shapes not just personal identity but also aspects such as security, innocence, and destiny. This is why the role of a watchman is so vital.

To embrace the calling of a watchman is to commit to remaining spiritually alert at all times. It is crucial to establish clear boundaries that protect against harmful influences, ensuring a safe environment for growth and development. Refusing secrecy is also essential; transparency fosters trust and allows for healthy discussions about difficult topics. Confronting discomfort is part of the watchman's duty, as it often leads to necessary change and awareness of underlying issues. Moreover, acting swiftly when warning signs arise is imperative—being proactive can prevent larger problems from taking root.

Additionally, engaging in consistent prayer over the lives entrusted to us is a foundational practice that empowers the watchman and the individuals they watch over. This role demands much more than just good intentions; it requires a structured approach, disciplined habits, and the courage to challenge the status quo, especially when familiarity starts to pose risks.

If you find yourself reading these words, consider this a summons—not one rooted in fear, but rather one that calls for faithfulness and dedication to your responsibilities as a watchman in the lives around you. Embrace this challenge with resolve, understanding its essential role in nurturing and protecting those who depend on your vigilance.

You are being called to stand upon the wall of your household.

To observe without denial.
To question without apology.
To intervene without hesitation.
To protect without compromise.

May this book serve as both lantern and alarm.

May you never ignore what you now understand.

May you never choose comfort over courage.

And may every child under your watch find safety because you chose to remain awake.

THE PROTECTION MANDATE

A Generational Charge to the Reader

THIS IS NOT JUST A BOOK

IT IS A PROTECTION MANDATE RESOURCE

✦

Carry the mantle of a Spiritual Gatekeeper—preserve what is sacred, protect what is entrusted, and ensure that this truth does not end with you by passing this book into the hands of the next generation.

- The Guardian's Instruction Manual
- Divine Assignment
- Field Guide + Defense System

This statement carries prophetic weight because it is not presenting a book as information—it is declaring a transfer of responsibility. Scripture repeatedly shows that truth is never meant to terminate with one generation. In The Unrecognizable Language of Our Children, you will establish that "wisdom and knowledge are not meant to be hoarded; they must be passed on," and this aligns directly with the biblical mandate: "One generation shall praise thy works to another" (Psalm 145:4 KJV) and "Teach them diligently unto thy children" (Deuteronomy 6:7 KJV). Prophetically, this statement positions the reader as a watchman in succession, not just a reader of content. It declares that what is being received is not optional knowledge—it is protective revelation. Hosea 4:6 warns, "My people are destroyed for lack of knowledge," not because truth was unavailable, but because it was not received, retained, or passed on. When knowledge stops, vulnerability increases. When instruction is not transferred, exposure multiplies. Therefore, this book becomes more than a message—it becomes a defensive system against generational loss, equipping the reader to recognize, guard, and intercept what previous generations may have missed or what the current culture is attempting to normalize.

The prophetic force intensifies in the charge to "carry the mantle of a Spiritual Gatekeeper." This mirrors the watchman principle already established in your manuscript (Ezekiel 33:7 KJV), where responsibility is tied to awareness.

To read and not respond is to inherit knowledge without activating protection. To receive truth and not pass it on is to break the chain of preservation. Biblically, older generations are not just examples—they are instructors of survival, discernment, and covenant continuity (Titus 2:3–5 KJV). This insert calls the reader into that lineage: what you have learned must now become what you enforce, model, and distribute. It elevates the engagement level of the reader by shifting their posture from observer to participant, from consumer to guardian. This is where the book transforms into The Guardian's Instruction Manual—a living field guide that must be applied, shared, and multiplied. The implication is clear: if this truth stays with you, someone else remains unprotected; but if it passes through you, it becomes a shield for the next generation.

THE GUARDIAN'S ASSIGNMENT
READ THIS BOOK
PRAYERFULLY & MEDITATIVELY

A gatekeeper does not sleep through responsibility. A watchman does not ignore what he/she has been shown. In the same way, you will be accountable for what you have received. The role before you is not symbolic—it is active. It requires attentiveness, discipline, courage, and consistency. You are called to guard what enters your home, what influences your children, what shapes their thinking, and what attempts to access their lives.

This is your Instruction Manual—to guide your actions.
This is your Divine Assignment—to govern your responsibility.
This is your Field Guide and Defense System—to strengthen your response.

You are now positioned to see what others may overlook, to discern what others may dismiss, and to act where others may hesitate. What you do with this knowledge will determine what is protected under your watch.

Carry the mantle of a Spiritual Gatekeeper—
preserve what is sacred, protect what is entrusted,
and ensure that this truth does not end with you.

What you protect today…
will preserve a generation tomorrow.

PART I

RESPONSIBILITY

THE SACRED RESPONSIBILITY

CHAPTER ONE
THE SACRED DUTY OF PROTECTING OUR CHILDREN
The Silent Cry of the Innocent
When the Vulnerability of Children Reveals

The Responsibility of Adults

Children enter this world as a sacred trust. They arrive without defenses, without resources, and without the ability to protect themselves from the environments they are born into. They do not choose the homes they will live in, the conditions they will experience, or the adults who will shape their earliest understanding of life. Through the actions and decisions of others, they arrive here—innocent, dependent, and completely vulnerable. This reality alone should awaken a profound sense of responsibility within every parent, guardian, and community.

From the moment a child takes their first breath, they rely entirely upon the care and character of those entrusted with their upbringing. A newborn cannot provide for itself. They cannot feed themselves, defend themselves, or even articulate their needs beyond the cry that signals distress. Every aspect of their survival—nutrition, shelter, protection, affection, and instruction—must be provided by someone else. The early years of life are therefore not merely developmental stages; they are seasons of absolute dependency.

Yet despite this clear vulnerability, many children grow up in environments where their needs are overlooked, minimized, or completely ignored. The tragedy of neglect does not always appear in dramatic forms. Sometimes it hides behind busyness. Sometimes it disguises itself as exhaustion, distraction, or misplaced priorities. But regardless of its form, neglect leaves a lasting imprint on a child's heart and mind.

What makes this reality even more sobering is the example visible throughout the natural world. In the wild, creatures that humans often dismiss as unintelligent demonstrate remarkable dedication to the survival of their offspring. A mother animal recognizes the unique cry of her young even among hundreds of other sounds. She responds quickly to distress signals. She searches tirelessly for food to sustain them. She guards them from predators. When danger approaches, many animals will confront threats far greater than themselves to protect the life that came through them.

These animals do not attend parenting seminars. They do not read books about nurturing behavior. They operate primarily by instinct—yet their instinct compels them to care, defend, and sacrifice for their young. If creatures governed by instinct can display such devotion, the question must be asked: What does it say about humanity when children are abandoned emotionally, neglected physically, or abused intentionally?

Human beings were created with something far greater than instinct. We possess a soul, reasoning, conscience, moral awareness, and the ability to discern right from wrong. With those abilities comes responsibility. The care of children is not merely a biological function; it is a moral obligation and a spiritual assignment.

When a society begins to fail its children, it exposes a deeper problem within its moral foundation. A nation may advance technologically. It may grow economically. It may celebrate innovation and progress. Yet if its children are suffering neglect, instability, and abuse, those achievements become hollow. The true measure of a healthy society is not how powerful its adults become, but how protected and nurtured its children remain.

Children absorb far more from their environment than many adults realize. They may not fully understand every situation happening around them, but they feel the atmosphere of their surroundings. They sense tension. They notice the absence. They internalize words spoken carelessly. Over time, these experiences shape the lens through which they interpret the world.

When a child grows up surrounded by consistent care, encouragement, and stability, they begin to develop confidence. They learn that people can be trusted. They believe their voice matters. They feel safe enough to explore their identity and purpose. But when a child grows up surrounded by neglect, instability, or hostility, their internal framework begins to shift. Instead of learning trust, they learn caution. Instead of learning confidence, they learn survival.

The consequences of this emotional formation often surface later in life. Many adults struggle with insecurity, distrust, anger, or relational instability, not because they desire dysfunction, but because the foundations of their emotional development were fractured during childhood. What appears as adult behavior is often the echo of unresolved childhood experiences.

PARENTHOOD AS STEWARDSHIP

This is where discernment becomes essential. Without intentional awareness, broken patterns repeat themselves across generations. A person who experienced neglect as a child may unintentionally reproduce the same environment for their own children simply because it is the only pattern they have known. What was once endured becomes normalized.

Breaking these cycles requires courage and humility. It requires adults to examine their own upbringing honestly and determine which patterns must be rejected rather than repeated. True love for children does not simply continue the past—it improves it.

Parenthood, therefore, must be understood as stewardship. Children are not possessions because the Soul comes from God. They are not extensions of adult pride or instruments for fulfilling parental ambitions. They are individual lives entrusted to temporary guardianship. A parent's responsibility is to guide, protect, instruct, and nurture them until they are mature enough to walk wisely on their own.

This stewardship involves far more than meeting physical needs. Providing food, clothing, and shelter is essential, but children also require emotional presence, moral instruction, and consistent spiritual and physical guidance. They must see integrity modeled in the lives of the adults around them. They must experience discipline that corrects without crushing their dignity. They must hear words that build identity rather than diminish it.

THE FORMATION OF A CHILD'S EMOTIONAL FRAMEWORK

Children absorb far more from their environment than many adults realize, and that emotional absorption becomes the hidden architecture of their lives. A child's emotional framework is not formed only by major events, but by repeated atmosphere, repeated tone, repeated response, and repeated neglect or nurture. What is constant around them begins to define what feels normal within them.

When a child is met with tenderness, attentiveness, consistency, and truth, something stable begins to form within. That child learns that love can be trusted, that correction can coexist with safety, and that their inner world matters. But when a child is repeatedly exposed to volatility, indifference, fear, dismissal, or emotional absence, the framework forming inside them becomes fragile and defensive. They may still function outwardly, but inwardly, they are being trained not in peace, but in survival.

This is why childhood cannot be approached casually. Every home is teaching something. Every adult presence is shaping something. Every repeated response is planting something. A child's emotional world does not develop in isolation; it develops in reaction to what surrounds it. Stability teaches security. Chaos teaches vigilance. Nurture teaches belonging. Neglect teaches loneliness.

BREAKING GENERATIONAL CYCLES

This is where discernment becomes urgent. Without intentional awareness, broken patterns repeat themselves across generations. A person who experienced neglect as a child may unintentionally reproduce the same environment for their own children simply because it is the only pattern they have known. What was once endured becomes normalized.

Breaking these cycles requires courage and humility. It requires adults to examine their own upbringing honestly and determine which patterns must be rejected rather than repeated. True love for children does not simply continue the past—it improves it.

Every generation holds the power either to heal the wounds of the past or to repeat them. When adults choose attentiveness, wisdom, and compassion, they create environments where children can flourish. When they neglect that responsibility, the silence of children becomes the loudest testimony of failure.

Children are not merely the future of society—they are the present responsibility of every adult who influences their lives. Their safety, stability, and emotional well-being should never be treated as secondary concerns.

When children are neglected, the damage rarely remains confined to childhood. It spreads into families, communities, and generations yet unborn. But when children are protected, guided, and loved with intentional care, something extraordinary happens: the next generation grows strong enough to build a better world than the one they inherited.

And that, perhaps, is one of the most sacred responsibilities humanity has ever been given.

WORDS THAT SHAPE IDENTITY

Words spoken in childhood carry tremendous weight. A careless insult can echo in the mind of a child for decades. A moment of encouragement can become the seed of lifelong confidence. The tone, patience, and attentiveness of adults become the language through which children interpret their worth.

Children may forget exact dates, but they often remember how a home felt. They remember whether correction came with dignity or humiliation. They remember whether truth was spoken with love or with contempt. They remember whether their questions were welcomed or crushed. And long after the sound of a sentence fades, the meaning of it can remain lodged in the soul.

This is why adults must handle their words with reverence. Speech is never neutral around a child. It is either building or bruising, clarifying or confusing, strengthening or diminishing. A child's sense of self is often shaped in the echo of repeated words. If those words communicate worth, truth, and steadiness, identity grows stronger. If those words communicate annoyance, rejection, ridicule, or coldness, identity becomes unstable.

THE UNRECOGNIZABLE LANGUAGE OF CHILDREN

When adults fail to recognize the influence of their words and behavior, children often develop what might be called an "unrecognizable language." They may struggle to express their pain directly, so their hurt appears through behavior—withdrawal, anger, rebellion, or silence. These behaviors are often misinterpreted as defiance when they are actually the voice of unmet needs.

In many cases, children are not refusing to communicate. They lack the vocabulary to articulate what they feel. Their actions become the language they know how to speak. When adults respond only to the behavior without seeking the underlying message, the deeper issues remain unresolved.

Discernment allows adults to see beyond surface behavior. Instead of reacting only to what a child does, discernment asks what the behavior is trying to communicate. Is the child seeking attention because they feel unseen? Are they acting out because they feel insecure? Are they withdrawing because they feel misunderstood or unprotected?

Understanding this language requires patience and compassion. Children often communicate their deepest struggles indirectly. Their hearts speak through signals that must be interpreted with care. The responsibility for that interpretation belongs to the adults in their lives.

ADOLESCENCE: WHEN CHILDREN GROW TALLER BUT STILL NEED COVERING

Parenthood Does Not Expire When a Child Becomes a Teen

Let this be said with soberness and without apology: adolescence is not the end of parenthood's burden—it is the deepening of it. The teenage years do not signal a reduction in responsibility; they reveal how necessary that responsibility still is. Many parents make the dangerous mistake of assuming that because a child has grown taller, learned to speak with confidence, formed opinions, and begun pursuing independence, they no longer require the same intensity of covering, guidance, correction, and watchfulness. But that assumption is costly. A teenager may look strong on the outside while still being profoundly unformed on the inside. Height is not maturity. Vocabulary is not wisdom. Independence is not readiness. And exposure to the world is not the same as preparation for it.

Adolescence is one of the most fragile transitions in human development because it is the season where identity is forming, appetites are intensifying, emotions are deepening, and external influences are multiplying all at once. The teenager is no longer a small child, but is not yet a grounded adult. They stand in the narrow and dangerous space between dependence and self-direction. In that space, they are often deeply impressionable while fiercely resisting the idea that they are impressionable. They may crave freedom while lacking discernment. They may hunger for acceptance while pretending not to care what others think. They may speak with certainty while internally wrestling with confusion; they do not know how to name.

This is why adolescence requires more than supervision—it requires spiritual and emotional vigilance. Parents cannot afford to retreat during this stage. They cannot assume that because their son is quiet, he is healthy. They cannot assume that because their daughter is smiling, she is secure. They cannot assume that because grades are acceptable or outward behavior appears manageable, the soul is settled. Many teenagers have mastered the art of performing stability while silently drowning beneath pressure, temptation, identity confusion, rejection, comparison, hidden fear, or private shame. Their pain does not always come through tears. Sometimes it comes through sarcasm. Sometimes through isolation. Sometimes through rebellion. Sometimes through emotional numbness. Sometimes through overachievement. Sometimes through a smile that has learned how to hide.

Parents must understand that the teenage years are not merely years of management; they are years of shepherding. This is the season when a child begins testing boundaries, questioning values, evaluating examples, and deciding which voices they will allow to define them. If the parent becomes passive while the world becomes aggressive, the vacuum will be filled quickly. Culture is never silent. Entertainment is never neutral. Peer influence is rarely harmless. Digital environments do not merely expose teenagers to information; they disciple them in real time. If a parent is absent in discernment, another voice will take the lead in shaping the child's inner world.

And this must be stated with full conviction: provision alone is not parenting. Paying bills is not the same as building a soul. Buying clothes is not the same as clothing a child in wisdom. Providing a bedroom is not the same as creating refuge. A teenager can live in a furnished house and still feel emotionally homeless. They can be surrounded by devices, privileges, activities, and outward opportunities while starving inwardly for attention, instruction, affirmation, and presence. Some parents mistake access for a relationship. They give things when what is required is themselves. But teenagers do not only need resources—they need covering. They need parents who will notice shifts in tone, changes in appetite, new silences, strange friendships, altered patterns, hidden anger, and the subtle signs that something is moving in the heart beneath the surface.

PARENTHOOD IS A LIFETIME OCCUPATION

Parenthood is not seasonal employment. It is not a temporary contract that expires when a child reaches adolescence, graduates from school, or begins asserting independence. Parenthood is a lifetime occupation. Its expression may change with age, but its responsibility does not vanish. In childhood, the parent physically carries the child. In adolescence, the parent must carry them through intercession, discernment, instruction, consistency, and example. In adulthood, the parent may no longer control the child's choices, but the moral history of what was modeled, permitted, ignored, corrected, or neglected remains before God.

This is where the matter becomes deeply spiritual.

Children are not given to parents merely to be fed and released into society. They are entrusted with lives. To parent is to stand as a steward before God over a soul that did not create itself and cannot be treated as though it belongs exclusively to human preference. Every child is a divine trust placed in earthly hands. That trust carries accountability. The parent is not sovereign over the child; the parent is accountable for how they managed what heaven placed under their care.

And God is not casual about stewardship.

There is a terrifying comfort in knowing that God sees what others do not. He sees not only the bruises that human eyes can identify, but the neglect that leaves no visible mark. He sees the father who was present in body but absent in attention. He sees the mother who clothed the child outwardly but pierced them inwardly with contempt, coldness, or chronic dismissal. He sees the household where a teenager's emotional cries were mocked as attitude, where warning signs were called drama, where wounds were ignored because the family wanted appearance more than healing. God sees the moments when parents choose convenience over correction, silence over intervention, personal pleasure over parental duty, and image over truth.

And heaven keeps an accurate record. This is not written to condemn faithful parents who labor, pray, correct, and love with sincerity despite their imperfect human limitations. This is written to shake careless parents awake. Some have treated parenthood as though occasional concern is enough. Some have mistaken control for cultivation. Some have demanded outward obedience while never tending to inward pain. Some have handed their teenagers over to screens, trends, strangers, systems, and social currents while assuming they would somehow emerge morally intact. Some have been more attentive to careers than character, more invested in public reputation than private discipleship, more disturbed by embarrassment than by the actual condition of the child's soul.

But a day of divine reckoning stands over all stewardship.

The question will not merely be whether parents intended well. The question will be what they did with what was entrusted to them. Did they instruct? Did they protect? Did they correct? Did they pray? Did they discern danger? Did they create a home where truth could be spoken? Did they recognize when their child was slipping? Did they excuse what should have been confronted? Did they ignore what should have broken their heart? Did they wound the child they were assigned to nurture with their own mouth? Did they leave the teenager exposed in the name of "letting them figure it out," when what the child really needed was wise and holy covering?

Parents must understand that neglect is not always loud. Sometimes it is sophisticated. Sometimes it wears the face of busyness. Sometimes it hides behind the language of "I'm doing the best I can," while refusing to accept correction, reflection, or change. Sometimes it appears as material generosity without emotional presence. Sometimes it is the consistent failure to ask deeper questions, to listen carefully, to observe honestly, or to intervene courageously. Yet heaven is not deceived by polished explanations. God judges truthfully. He weighs motives, effort, tenderness, consistency, and responsibility in full light.

A teenager may challenge your authority, resist your rules, and misunderstand your intentions, but that does not release you from the assignment to cover them. Parenthood was never designed to be sustained only by the child's gratitude. It is sustained by covenantal duty. Real parenting continues even when the labor is inconvenient, when the child is moody, when communication is difficult, when discipline is exhausting, and when the emotional return is small. A faithful parent stays present in the hard season. They do not withdraw because adolescence has become uncomfortable. They do not abandon instruction because the child rolled their eyes. They do not stop watching because the child started driving. They do not stop praying because conversations have become shorter. They do not confuse resistance with irrelevance.

Teenagers need to be watched because temptation grows more sophisticated with age. They need covering because access increases before discernment is fully formed. They need instruction because they are being catechized daily by a world that profits from confusion. They need affection because hardness often grows where tenderness has been withheld. They need correction because love without boundaries leaves them vulnerable to their own impulses. They need truthful conversation because secrecy becomes fertile soil for destruction. They need parents who can say no with courage, yes with wisdom, and wait with discernment. They need adults who are not trying to be admired, but trying to be faithful.

And let every parent hear this clearly: the teenage years are not the years to disengage. They are the years to lean in with greater precision. Not with suffocating control, but with holy attentiveness. Not with suspicion toward everything, but with discernment about what is shaping the child's interior world. Not with ceaseless lectures, but with steady presence, firm boundaries, patient listening, truthful speech, and a life that models what righteousness looks like when nobody is performing.

For one day, every parent will answer not for perfection, but for stewardship. God will not ask whether parenting was easy. He will not ask whether the culture cooperated. He will not ask whether your teenager always appreciated your sacrifice. He will ask what you did with the soul placed under your roof. He will ask whether you covered what was vulnerable, corrected what was dangerous, nourished what was weak, and guarded what was impressionable. He will ask whether you parented as one aware that children belong first to Him and were only loaned to you for a season of formation.

That truth should shake the soul.

Because parenthood is more than biology, it is more than legality. It is more than shared DNA or household management. Parenthood is stewardship before God, and adolescence is one of its greatest tests. In that season, a child may look like they need less from you, while in truth, they need more wisdom, more prayer, more discernment, more consistency, more courage, and more love than ever before.

So let no parent grow lazy because the child grows older. Let no mother assume her work is done because her daughter now has a voice. Let no father imagine his assignment is complete because his son has become physically strong. Strength without guidance can self-destruct. Freedom without wisdom can corrupt. Exposure without covering can wound. And age without shepherding can leave a teenager vulnerable to everything except the people appointed to guard them.

Parenthood is a lifetime occupation. And every season demands its own obedience.

The crib required tenderness.
The childhood years required instruction.
The adolescent years require discernment, vigilance, and covering.
And through it all, the parent remains under God's watchful eye.

For the souls we shape in time will testify to the stewardship we offered them. And heaven does not forget what earth was too distracted to notice.

THE MANDATE TO TRAIN AND GUARD

The Sacred Responsibility of Parents Before God

Proverbs 22:6 (KJV) declares with remarkable clarity, "Train up a child in the way he should go: and when he is old, he will not depart from it." This command is not a casual suggestion offered to parents—it is a divine mandate. The language of training implies intention, structure, and consistency. Training is not accomplished through occasional correction or scattered advice. It is a deliberate process that shapes character through repeated instruction, steady guidance, and attentive presence. Just as a craftsman carefully shapes raw material into something useful and strong, parents are entrusted with the sacred task of shaping the moral and spiritual direction of their children.

Training requires proximity. A child cannot be trained from a distance. Instruction cannot be delegated entirely to institutions, schools, or religious programs. These may assist in development, but the primary responsibility rests upon the parent. Training happens through everyday interactions—the conversations held at the dinner table, the corrections offered in moments of misbehavior, the explanations given when a child asks difficult questions, and the quiet modeling of integrity when no audience is present. Children learn as much from what parents live as they do from what parents say. They observe attitudes, reactions, priorities, and values. Every day, whether consciously or unconsciously, parents are teaching their children how to interpret the world.

This is why Deuteronomy 6:7 (KJV) expands the parental calling beyond occasional moments of instruction: "And thou shalt teach them diligently unto thy children, and shalt talk of them when thou sittest in thine house, and when thou walkest by the way, and when thou liest down, and when thou risest up." The Scripture paints a picture of continual influence. Spiritual formation is not confined to a scheduled lesson or a weekly gathering; it is woven into the rhythms of daily life. When a family sits together, truth should have a place in the conversation. When they travel together, instruction should accompany the journey. When the day begins and when it closes, the awareness of God should frame the household atmosphere.

This passage dismantles passive parenting. It rejects the idea that children will naturally discover righteousness on their own if left to explore freely. Scripture recognizes that character does not develop by accident. Without guidance, the human heart tends to drift toward selfishness, impulsiveness, and imitation of whatever influences are loudest in the surrounding culture. Parents, therefore, function as guardians of influence. They must discern what voices shape their children's thinking, what environments mold their attitudes, and what examples capture their admiration.

Training involves both instruction and protection. It is not enough to teach truth if harmful influences are allowed unrestricted access to the child's mind and heart.

To guard a child is to recognize that vulnerability accompanies youth. Children enter the world without the experience necessary to recognize deception, manipulation, or destructive behavior. Their trust is easily given. Their curiosity is powerful. Their understanding of consequences is limited. Because of this, God has placed authority in the hands of parents as a protective boundary. That authority is not given for control or domination—it is given for stewardship. Parents are guardians of the atmosphere in which their children develop. They set the standards, enforce the boundaries, and correct the deviations that would otherwise lead a young life into harm.

Scripture provides a sobering example of what occurs when this responsibility is neglected. The account of Eli in 1 Samuel 3 reveals the consequences of passive authority. Eli served as a priest, a man familiar with the rituals of worship and the responsibilities of spiritual leadership. Yet within his own household, corruption was allowed to flourish. His sons behaved with open disregard for the sacred responsibilities entrusted to them, exploiting their positions and dishonoring the very service they were meant to uphold. The tragedy of the story is not merely their wrongdoing—it is Eli's failure to restrain them.

Eli knew their behavior was wrong. The record shows he spoke words of mild rebuke. But rebuke without correction is ineffective, and awareness without action becomes negligence. Authority that refuses to enforce righteousness creates an environment where wrongdoing grows unchecked. His silence, or rather his unwillingness to intervene decisively, allowed corruption to take root. Eventually, the consequences extended beyond his family and affected the wider community that depended upon the integrity of its spiritual leaders.

This account is not preserved in Scripture merely as historical documentation; it stands as a warning to every generation. Authority carries responsibility. When those entrusted with leadership refuse to confront destructive behavior, the damage rarely remains contained. What begins as tolerated misconduct within a household eventually spreads outward, influencing others and weakening the moral fabric of the community. Neglect in private spaces often produces consequences in public life.

The lesson is sobering: silence is not neutrality. Silence, when correction is required, becomes participation in the very harm it refuses to confront. To ignore wrongdoing is to permit its growth. To overlook corruption is to strengthen its foothold. Parents who avoid difficult conversations, who hesitate to enforce boundaries, or who fear the temporary discomfort of discipline may unknowingly allow patterns to form that will later produce painful consequences.

Yet the mandate to train and guard is not rooted in fear alone—it is rooted in love. Genuine love does not abandon a child to impulses that may lead to harm. Love intervenes. Love instructs. Love corrects. Love is willing to endure the momentary resistance of a child to secure the long-term stability of that child's character. Discipline, when administered with wisdom and compassion, communicates value. It tells a child that their life matters enough to be guided carefully.

Training and guarding also require patience. Character formation is not accomplished overnight. A child does not absorb wisdom in a single lesson. Understanding develops gradually through repeated experiences, corrections, explanations, and demonstrations of integrity. Parents must therefore remain consistent. One conversation about honesty does not establish honesty; it must be reinforced through example and expectation. One warning about respect does not guarantee respectful behavior; it must be reinforced through correction and affirmation.

The modern world presents parents with unprecedented challenges. Children today are exposed to voices, images, and influences that previous generations never encountered at such speed or intensity. Technology places entire worlds of information and ideology within immediate reach. Because of this, the mandate to guard becomes even more critical. Parents must remain vigilant about what enters the minds of their children. Influence is powerful, and repeated exposure gradually shapes perception. What children see often enough, they begin to accept as normal.

Guarding, therefore, involves more than restriction—it involves explanation. Children must be taught not only what to avoid, but why. They must understand the principles that guide moral decisions. When parents explain the reasoning behind boundaries, they help their children develop internal conviction rather than mere external compliance. A child who understands truth is better equipped to navigate environments where parental supervision is absent.

Ultimately, the mandate to train and guard reflects a profound truth about the nature of parenthood: rearing a child is not merely a biological event—it is a lifelong stewardship. From infancy through adolescence and into adulthood, the influence of parents continues to shape the direction of a child's life. Even as children grow older and gain independence, the foundations laid during their early years remain powerful anchors guiding their choices.

God does not assign this responsibility lightly. The formation of a human life is one of the most sacred trusts placed in human hands. Parents are not merely rearing children; they are cultivating future citizens, future leaders, future husbands and wives, future parents, and future servants of God. What is planted in childhood often becomes the harvest of adulthood.

For this reason, the call to train and guard must be approached with seriousness, humility, and devotion. It demands attentiveness. It demands courage. It demands the willingness to guide firmly while loving deeply. The parent who embraces this calling becomes more than a caretaker—they become a watchman over the destiny of a soul entrusted to their care.

HEARING THE CRY THAT IS NOT SPOKEN

The account of Hagar in Genesis 21 reveals something powerful about God's attentiveness. In the wilderness, abandoned and desperate, she wept for her son. Scripture says, "God heard the voice of the lad" (Genesis 21:17). The child's voice was heard even before words were spoken. Heaven discerns distress that others may overlook. God is not limited to articulated language. He is not waiting for a polished explanation before He recognizes pain. He hears what is carried in the cry, what trembles beneath fear, and what rises from helplessness before it ever becomes structured speech.

That truth should awaken something serious in every parent and guardian.

If God is attentive to the cry that has not yet become language, then those entrusted with children must not be careless with what is unspoken. Many adults expect children to communicate distress in mature, direct, and clearly interpreted ways. But children often do not possess that ability. Their emotional world may be overwhelmed long before their vocabulary is developed enough to describe it. They may feel fear they cannot explain, discomfort they do not understand, and confusion they do not know how to name. This is why parental attentiveness must go deeper than listening for words alone.

Children communicate long before they develop vocabulary. Their behavior is language. Their reactions are sentences. Their silence can be a paragraph of pain.

A newborn's cry carries meaning. An infant's sudden rigidity during routine care may signal discomfort or fear. A toddler who regresses, clings excessively, or develops sudden anxiety may be expressing something deeper than mood. An older child who withdraws, avoids eye contact, resists touch, becomes unusually fearful, or shifts dramatically in personality is speaking. The speech may be indirect, but it is not absent. It is being communicated through posture, pattern, instinct, expression, avoidance, and emotional change.

This is one of the most critical truths adults must learn: not all communication comes through words.

A child may scream because pain has found the only outlet available. A child may cling because insecurity is searching for safety. A child may become unusually aggressive because internal confusion has no other language. A child may go quiet because silence feels safer than saying something that they fear may not be received well. A child may suddenly resist a person, place, routine, or touch, not because they are being difficult, but because something inside them has already marked that space as threatening.

The tragedy is not that children fail to communicate. The tragedy is that adults sometimes fail to interpret.

And when adults fail to interpret, children may be left alone with experiences they do not understand how to carry. The wound becomes deeper when the signal is missed. The isolation grows heavier when the child senses something is wrong, but no one around them appears to notice. A child who is not interpreted carefully may begin to believe that their discomfort does not matter or that their fear must be hidden. In that silence, danger finds room to deepen.

This is why attentiveness must be cultivated as a discipline, not treated as an occasional instinct. A parent must learn the normal rhythm of their child well enough to notice when that rhythm changes. They must know how their child usually speaks, plays, sleeps, reacts, and relates so that disruption becomes visible sooner rather than later. Awareness is not obsession. It is stewardship.

Proverbs 29:15 (KJV) warns, "The rod and reproof give wisdom: but a child left to himself bringeth his mother to shame." A child left without attentive guidance becomes vulnerable to confusion, isolation, and exploitation. Discipline is not cruelty; it is structure. Structure is protection. Engagement is protection. Awareness is protection. This passage does not merely address correction—it addresses the danger of neglectful detachment. A child left to navigate discomfort, confusion, or hidden fear without attentive adult involvement becomes far more vulnerable to harm.

There is a world of difference between controlling a child and covering them. A child needs more than food and shelter. A child needs interpretation. They need adults who notice what changed, who ask why silence has grown heavier, who recognize that unusual fear, new withdrawal, or sudden distress may be a signal rather than a phase. A parent who is spiritually and emotionally present creates an environment where silent cries are more likely to be heard.

I thank God that my own childhood was free from abuse. I'm not saying that I never received physical discipline on my behind with a belt; that was my generation. I was blessed to have parents who kept their eyes on us. My parents instilled vigilance in us. They taught us to be aware. They did not assume safety; they established it. That watchfulness shielded not only our household but also others. I recognize that not every child was afforded that same covering.

That distinction matters.

Many children grow up under watchful love. Many others grow up in environments where adults are distracted, passive, emotionally unavailable, or too trusting to see what should be questioned. The difference between those two realities can shape a child's entire emotional world. A child who grows up under steady covering learns that safety is possible, that adults can be trusted, and that danger is not ignored when it appears. A child without that covering may learn the opposite: that discomfort must be carried alone, that fear may go unnoticed, and that silence is often safer than speaking.

This is why watchfulness must not be treated as extremism. It is not paranoia for a parent to pay attention. It is not overreaction to ask questions. It is not spiritual weakness to investigate what seems wrong. It is wisdom. It is love in disciplined form. It is stewardship refusing to sleep.

Parents must reject the dangerous assumption that harm only comes from strangers. Often, threats emerge from familiar spaces—extended family, trusted friends, neighbors, respected adults, even spiritual environments. Relationship does not equal righteousness. Familiarity does not equal safety.

These assumptions have silenced too many alarms and delayed too many interventions. A known face can still carry hidden intent. A trusted circle can still contain an unguarded opening. A respected position can still be occupied by a compromised heart.

Second Corinthians 11:14 (KJV) reminds us, "And no marvel; for Satan himself is transformed into an angel of light." If deception can wear the appearance of light, then predators can wear the appearance of trustworthiness. Evil often disguises itself in comfort. It does not always arrive through what is obviously threatening. It often enters through what seems harmless, familiar, and socially approved. That is why parents must not let outward appearance become the final measure of safety.

The child's cry may not come through a sentence.
It may come through a changed expression.
A fearful hesitation.
A rigid body.
A new silence.
A resistance that did not used to exist.
A sadness that appears without explanation.
A clinginess that suddenly intensifies.
A withdrawal that seems unlike the child you know.

These things must not be explained away too quickly.

A child may not say, "Something happened."
But their behavior may already be saying it.

A faithful parent learns to hear what is not being spoken. They ask questions without intimidation. They observe without mocking. They remain near without smothering. They notice what others overlook. They stay aware enough to discern when a child's inner world is trying to communicate distress through conduct rather than vocabulary.

Hearing the cry that is not spoken requires more than ears. It requires discernment. It requires patience. It requires the willingness to believe that discomfort may exist even when the child cannot yet name it. It requires adults who understand that children often reveal pain in fragments and who are willing to gather those fragments carefully rather than dismiss them because they are incomplete.

This is holy work.

To hear the cry that is not spoken is to participate in the mercy of God, who notices what others miss and who draws near to what others may overlook. Parents are called to reflect that attentiveness. They are called to create homes where silent pain does not remain undetected, where fear is not punished, and where the child's unspoken language is met with wise, protective love.

Because when a child's cry is heard early, isolation weakens.
When distress is interpreted wisely, danger loses ground.
And when adults learn to hear what is not yet spoken, children are less likely to suffer unseen.

RECOGNIZING BEHAVIORAL WARNINGS

Recognizing behavioral warnings requires more than occasional observation—it requires trained attentiveness, spiritual sobriety, and the willingness to take change seriously before it becomes a crisis. Children do not always have the language, confidence, or emotional clarity to explain what is happening within them. Very often, what they cannot yet speak with words begins to reveal itself through behavior. Because of this, a child's behavior should never be treated as mere noise. It must be examined with care, patience, and discernment.

When a child leaves home joyful and returns withdrawn, quiet, fearful, or unusually subdued, something has shifted. Do not dismiss it. Do not excuse it away. Do not silence it with impatience. A change in demeanor may not always point to abuse, danger, or trauma, but it always deserves attention. Healthy parental watchfulness does not wait for a pattern to become undeniable before asking questions. It leans in early. It notices tone, body language, mood, appetite, eye contact, sleep patterns, irritability, sudden silence, and unusual reluctance to return to places or people that once seemed ordinary.

Jesus instructed in Mark 4:24 (KJV), "Take heed what ye hear." That command extends beyond audible words. It includes the unspoken plea. The tightened shoulders. The sudden avoidance. The unexplained tears. The silence that feels heavy. Sometimes a child is speaking without speaking. Sometimes the body says what the mouth does not yet know how to form. Sometimes withdrawal is not moodiness—it is discomfort. Sometimes irritability is not rebellion—it is internal distress. Sometimes clinginess is not manipulation—it is fear searching for safety.

Infants scream when touched in sensitive areas because that is their language. Toddlers cling because that is their language. Teenagers isolate because that is their language. Behavioral change is communication. It may be fragmented communication. It may be indirect communication. It may be confused and inconsistent. But it is communication nonetheless. A wise parent learns to ask not only, "What is my child doing?" but also, "What might my child be trying to tell me through this?"

This kind of attentiveness matters because children often do not disclose discomfort immediately. They may lack vocabulary. They may fear consequences. They may not fully understand what has happened. They may be confused by the behavior of adults or peers. They may feel ashamed, guilty, or afraid they will not be believed. In those moments, behavior often becomes the first alarm. Nightmares, bedwetting, loss of appetite, extreme quietness, unusual aggression, emotional numbness, avoidance of a specific person, panic during routine care, reluctance to change clothes, new fear of being alone, sudden secrecy, or exaggerated startle responses—these signs should not be dismissed casually. They must be observed within context, but they must never be ignored.

Spiritual discernment must accompany parental observation. Protection requires attentiveness. A prudent parent does not live in paranoia but in awareness. Proverbs 14:15 (KJV) states, "The simple believeth every word: but the prudent man looketh well to his going." Blind trust is not biblical trust. Prudence examines environments. Prudence asks questions. Prudence verifies. Prudence understands that what appears small may not be small at all. It recognizes that repeated changes, emotional disruptions, and unexplained behavioral shifts may be indicators that something beneath the surface deserves immediate attention.

This is where many guardians fail. They do not always fail because they do not love the child; sometimes they fail because they normalize what should be investigated. They call it "a phase." They call it "attitude." They call it "teenage behavior." They call it "sensitivity." But repeated dismissal can train a child into silence. If a child senses that distress will always be minimized, they may stop attempting to communicate at all. What should have been investigated early then becomes buried more deeply.

Parents must therefore cultivate an environment where behavioral change is not merely corrected but also understood. Discipline has its place, but discernment must guide interpretation. A child acting out may need correction, but they may also need protection. A child withdrawing may need encouragement, but they may also be signaling fear.

A child suddenly attached to one adult or suddenly fearful of another may be revealing something through pattern rather than statement.

Awareness also requires comparison. Watchful parents know the normal rhythm of their child well enough to recognize when that rhythm changes. They notice when a once-talkative child becomes unusually guarded. They notice when a child who loved a certain activity now resists it. They notice when a child's play begins to reflect fear, secrecy, or confusion. They notice when emotional intensity feels disproportionate to what is visible on the surface. These shifts are not to be sensationalized, but they are to be respected.

Recognizing behavioral warnings also requires emotional steadiness in the parent. If a child begins to reveal distress and the parent immediately becomes explosive, dismissive, or panicked, the child may retreat again. A strong response is sometimes necessary, but it must be directed at the danger—not at the child who is trying to reveal it. Children need to feel that their pain will be taken seriously, not turned into a scene they must now manage emotionally.

A child's behavior should never be the only evidence a parent looks at, but it should also never be treated as meaningless. Patterns matter. Shifts matter. Repetition matters. Timing matters. Context matters. Discernment does not jump to conclusions without thought, but neither does it postpone concern until the evidence becomes catastrophic.

Parents are not called to obsessive fear. They are called to faithful attentiveness. There is a difference. Fear imagines danger everywhere and loses clarity. Discernment remains clear, observant, and responsive. It watches the child. It studies the environment. It listens closely. It asks careful questions. It pays attention to what is changing and refuses to call avoidable harm "normal" simply because it is uncomfortable to investigate.

The child who cannot explain clearly still deserves to be read carefully. The child whose behavior changes deserves more than frustration—they deserve discernment. And the parent who wishes to guard innocence faithfully must learn to recognize that behavior is often the first place where hidden trouble begins to surface.

For this reason, when behavior shifts, pay attention.
When silence grows heavy, pay attention.
When fear appears without explanation, pay attention.
When a child changes suddenly, pay attention.

Because behavioral warnings are often early mercy, they are the signals that something beneath the surface is asking to be seen before damage deepens. And the parent who learns how to recognize them is far more prepared to interrupt harm before it advances.

CONFRONTING CONCEALED DANGERS

Confronting concealed dangers requires parents to accept a difficult but necessary truth: danger does not always appear in unfamiliar places, through obviously suspicious people, or in settings that outwardly seem threatening. Often, the greatest risks emerge in environments we have already labeled safe. That is what makes concealed danger so dangerous—it thrives beneath the covering of normalcy. It hides inside routine. It settles into familiar spaces. It gains access through comfort, assumed trust, repeated exposure, and the quiet belief that because something feels ordinary, it must therefore be secure.

Dangers often reside where we are most comfortable—living rooms, playdates, school corridors, ministry programs, family gatherings. Safety is not guaranteed by familiarity. Parents must confront this reality without denial. Familiarity can lower guard faster than a visible threat. When a person is known, a place is common, or an atmosphere feels socially accepted, parents may unconsciously relax the very vigilance their children still require. But familiarity is not a shield against corruption. Regular exposure does not purify a dangerous influence. Repetition does not equal righteousness. A common environment can still contain uncommon harm.

This is why parents must reject the illusion that known places are automatically safe places. A child can be surrounded by smiling adults and still be vulnerable. A child can attend a structured program and still encounter inappropriate influence. A child can be among relatives, respected leaders, or long-time acquaintances and still face emotional pressure, unsafe access, or hidden manipulation. Denial becomes dangerous when it causes adults to protect assumptions more fiercely than they protect children.

When you pick up your child from an event, observe their demeanor. If they are unusually quiet, fearful, clingy, agitated, or withdrawn, investigate gently but firmly. Ask questions without intimidation. Create space for honesty.

Build an environment where truth is welcomed, not punished. The moment after an event often matters more than many parents realize.

Sometimes the first signal that something is wrong is not an obvious disclosure, but a changed posture, an altered voice, unusual silence, visible discomfort, or a resistance that seems deeper than simple tiredness.

Parents must learn to observe the child before they absorb the explanations of the environment. Watch the eyes. Watch the body language. Watch whether the child avoids naming certain people. Watch for over-eagerness to leave, or unusual reluctance to return. Watch whether their emotional tone shifts sharply compared to how they left. These are not details to overdramatize, but they are details to respect.

Children do not always reveal concealed danger directly. Sometimes the body signals what the mouth cannot yet form.

To investigate gently but firmly means refusing two dangerous extremes. One extreme is intimidation—questioning in a way that frightens the child into silence. The other is passivity—asking so casually that the child concludes the answer will not matter. Wise parents create a space where the child can speak freely without fear, yet still understand that the parent is serious, attentive, and prepared to act if necessary.

This requires emotional steadiness. If a child senses that the adult's response will become explosive, humiliating, panicked, or dismissive, they may withhold important information. But if the child senses calm strength, protective authority, and real interest, honesty becomes more possible. Safety in communication does not come from softness alone; it comes from steadiness. A child must feel, if I tell the truth, I will be protected—not blamed, not ridiculed, not ignored.

Open communication is preventative armor. When children know they will be believed, protected, and defended, they are more likely to speak. When they fear dismissal, shame, or anger, silence takes root. And once silence takes root, danger gains more room to operate. Predatory behavior and unhealthy influence often depend on this very silence. They count on the child's uncertainty.

They rely on the fear that telling the truth will create trouble. They take advantage of environments where children have learned that adults are too uncomfortable, too busy, too distracted, or too emotionally unstable to investigate what feels wrong.

That is why open communication cannot be occasional. It must become part of the rhythm of the household. Children should not be forced to wait for a crisis to discover whether truth is welcome. They should already know it. They should already feel it. They should already have evidence that difficult conversations will be handled with seriousness and care.

Protection requires a proactive structure.

Know where your child is.
Know who your child is with.
Know what environments your child enters.
Know behavioral changes immediately.
Know that your child's safety is your divine assignment.

These are not excessive standards. They are expressions of faithful guardianship. Protection is weakened when adults normalize unnecessary uncertainty.

A parent should not be content with vague answers about supervision, access, location, or who is present around their child. Clarity is not control—it is stewardship. A child's environment must not be left to casual assumption. Every environment carries influence, and every influence deserves examination.

Knowing where your child is means more than knowing an address. It means understanding the context, the supervision, the structure, and the atmosphere. Knowing who your child is with means more than knowing names. It means paying attention to character, patterns, access, and the nature of the relationship. Knowing what environments your child enters means evaluating not just the setting, but what that setting normalizes, permits, overlooks, or hides. Knowing behavioral changes immediately means refusing to wait until a pattern becomes undeniable before paying attention to its beginnings.

This kind of structure does not emerge automatically. It must be built intentionally. It requires parents to remain engaged rather than detached. It requires asking follow-up questions. It requires being willing to make others uncomfortable if a child's safety requires it. It requires the humility to admit that danger may exist where we had hoped it did not. And it requires enough courage to act when something feels misaligned, even before all the pieces are fully visible.

Guarding a child is not an overreaction. It is obedience to Scripture. Scripture never presents watchfulness as extremism. It presents it as wisdom. A prudent person does not wait until destruction is obvious before taking cover. A faithful guardian does not call vigilance "too much" simply because it disrupts convenience. Spiritual discernment and practical oversight are not opposed to trust—they are the very things that keep trust from becoming naïve.

There is a dangerous pressure in many environments to appear relaxed, agreeable, and untroubled by hard questions. But children are not protected by social ease. They are protected by attentive adults who understand that hidden danger often survives because too many people preferred comfort over confrontation. That mindset must be rejected.

To confront concealed dangers means being willing to see what others would rather ignore. It means refusing to let routine numb discernment. It means treating small signals seriously before they become large wounds. It means understanding that by the time danger becomes obvious to everyone, it may have already been working in secret for some time.

So watch closely.
Ask carefully.
Listen deeply.
Respond courageously.

Because concealed dangers do not become harmless through familiarity, they are interrupted by vigilance, exposed by truth, and defeated when faithful guardians refuse to abandon their post.

A WARNING AND A CALL TO CONVICTION

The sacred duty of protecting our children is not sentimental—it is spiritual warfare. It is not merely a tender subject for emotional reflection; it is a sobering matter of stewardship, vigilance, and accountability before God. Innocence is contested territory. The minds, hearts, bodies, and futures of children are not untouched spaces in a neutral world. They are being shaped constantly—by voices, by influences, by atmospheres, by relationships, by examples, and by access. Because of this, protection cannot be treated as optional, casual, or reactive. It must be intentional, watchful, and spiritually grounded.

Complacency invites compromise. Delay invites damage. What is ignored does not become harmless simply because it remains unaddressed. What is tolerated in its early form often grows in strength, boldness, and consequence. Many of the gravest harms do not begin with loud alarms. They begin with small dismissals. They begin with ignored discomfort, softened boundaries, delayed conversations, unchecked access, and the dangerous comfort of assuming that because something has not yet been exposed, it must therefore be safe. But hidden danger does not lose power through neglect. It gains room to operate.

Parents must decide now: will we be passive observers or vigilant guardians? That decision cannot be postponed until proof becomes undeniable. By then, the damage may already be deep. Guardianship requires action before certainty becomes public evidence. It requires moral courage to ask hard questions, spiritual sensitivity to notice subtle shifts, and disciplined love that is willing to disturb comfort in order to preserve innocence. The role of a parent is not to stand at a distance and hope for the best. It is to remain near enough to notice, wise enough to discern, and brave enough to respond.

God entrusted these lives to us. He hears what we may miss. He sees what we may overlook. He holds us accountable for what we ignore. This truth should not merely inspire affection; it should awaken reverence. Children are not casual assignments. They are sacred trusts.

They do not belong to culture, to convenience, to systems, or to the moods of distracted adults. They have been placed into our care under the eye of a God who does not treat stewardship lightly. Heaven pays attention to what Earth excuses. God sees the warning signs adults dismiss. He sees when fear goes unspoken, when discomfort is minimized, when patterns are tolerated, and when guardians choose ease over investigation.

This is not merely about rearing children. It is about guarding destiny. It is about shielding innocence. It is about honoring the sacred trust Heaven has placed in our hands. To protect a child is not only to preserve a moment—it is to defend a future. It is to guard the formation of trust, the shaping of identity, the health of emotional development, the strength of spiritual clarity, and the confidence that allows a child to grow without carrying avoidable wounds into later life. Every act of protection says to a child, Your life matters. Your safety matters. Your voice matters. Your future is worth defending.

This is why discernment must be sharpened. Love alone is not enough if it is not watchful. Concern alone is not enough if it does not act. Spiritual language alone is not enough if it does not translate into vigilance, structure, and courage. A household must not only sound righteous—it must be guarded. A parent must not only intend well—they must stand faithfully. A guardian must not only feel protective—they must be willing to interrupt what threatens the child under their care.

Let every parent rise to the wall. Let every guardian sharpen discernment. Let every household become a protected gate. Let the home no longer be treated as a casual dwelling but as a place of active covering. Let prayer become more than ritual. Let boundaries become more than suggestions. Let communication become more than occasional. Let truth be spoken clearly. Let discomfort be investigated early. Let secrecy find no refuge within the atmosphere of the home.

The sacred duty is clear. The responsibility is weighty. The time for vigilance is now.

Not later, when it becomes more obvious.
Not later, when the pattern becomes more severe.
Not later, when the damage demands attention.
Now.

Now is the hour to strengthen the wall.
Now is the hour to close unnecessary doors.
Now is the hour to listen more carefully, observe more soberly, pray more intentionally, and act more courageously.

Because innocence cannot defend itself against every threat, children cannot always identify danger, interpret manipulation, or advocate for themselves in time. They depend upon the watchfulness of those appointed to guard them. And when that watchfulness is faithful, danger loses ground. But when that watchfulness sleeps, exposure grows.

So let conviction rise where passivity once lived. Let courage replace hesitation. Let responsibility silence every excuse. And let every parent, guardian, and entrusted leader remember: to stand watch over a child is not a burden of fear—it is an assignment of love under the authority of God.

THE FINAL CHARGE OF CHAPTER ONE

Predators rarely introduce themselves as threats. They do not usually arrive wearing the appearance of danger. They come wrapped in familiarity. They speak softly. They serve willingly. They volunteer eagerly. They blend into environments where trust is abundant and suspicion is absent. Their strategy is not force—it is access. And access is often granted based on comfort, convenience, repeated exposure, and assumed safety. What appears helpful can be calculated. What appears generous can be strategic. What appears harmless can be studying the very house that has opened its door.

That is what makes this matter so serious. Many dangers do not begin with visible violence. They begin with tolerated proximity. They begin with an atmosphere where no one is asking questions, no one is verifying patterns, and no one wants to make the room uncomfortable. But a predator does not need a dramatic entrance if the environment is already welcoming him through carelessness. He only needs a gate that has been left too open, a family too relaxed in its oversight, or a guardian too eager to believe that familiarity is the same as safety.

Children, on the other hand, do not always cry aloud when harm approaches. They conceal pain in silence. They bury fear beneath obedience. They translate trauma into behavior—withdrawal, anger, regression, anxiety, unusual attachment, sudden isolation, emotional numbness, irritability, or a silence that feels heavier than ordinary quiet. What adults call "mood changes" may be distress signals. What appears to be rebellion may be survival. What looks like attitude may actually be confusion, fear, shame, or an attempt to make sense of what they do not yet know how to explain.

This is why the role of a parent is not passive. It is protective.

Parenthood is not merely the work of providing meals, paying bills, and making sure schedules are maintained. It is the sacred labor of watchfulness. It is the assignment of standing close enough to notice what has shifted, wise enough to interpret what is unusual, and courageous enough to intervene before what is hidden becomes deeply rooted. Children cannot be expected to identify every danger that moves toward them. They often do not know what they are seeing, what they are feeling, or why something that looked normal now feels wrong. They depend upon the alertness of the one appointed to guard them.

You may not control the world outside your door, but you absolutely control who crosses its threshold. You decide who has access to your home. You determine who gains proximity to your child's body, mind, emotions, and environment. You regulate the digital doors that open silently in bedrooms late at night.

You determine what atmosphere is normalized, what boundaries are enforced, what influences are tolerated, and what conversations are welcomed. Authority over access is authority over protection.

This must be understood with full conviction: your vigilance is not overreaction—it is stewardship. Your discernment is not suspicion—it is wisdom. Your presence is not control—it is covering. The culture may call watchfulness excessive. The careless may call boundaries unnecessary. The indifferent may call vigilance uncomfortable. But Heaven calls it responsibility. The God who entrusted children into the care of adults did not do so with the expectation that they would be guarded casually. He entrusted them to watchmen, not spectators.

Children cannot defend themselves against manipulation masked as kindness. They cannot detect motives hidden behind charm. They cannot always distinguish between healthy affection and strategic overfamiliarity. They often interpret adult behavior through trust long before they have the maturity to interpret it through discernment. That is why your alertness matters so deeply. When parents assume safety rather than establish it, vulnerability increases. When they rely on appearances rather than patterns, risk expands. When they ignore discomfort because the environment looks respectable, they create room for hidden harm to deepen.

Predators thrive where boundaries are blurred. They advance where oversight weakens. They persist where silence is tolerated. But protection rises where conviction lives. Conviction does not wait to see how far a dangerous pattern will go before taking it seriously.

Conviction responds early. It questions what seems misaligned. It interrupts what seems inappropriate. It is willing to make the room uncomfortable if that discomfort protects innocence.

You must resolve within yourself that no relationship, no social comfort, no family dynamic, and no ministry appearance will outrank your child's safety. If confrontation is necessary, confront. If access must be restricted, restrict. If environments must be changed, change them. If a conversation must be had, have it. If a pattern must be questioned, question it. Protection is not negotiable.

This is where many guardians fail—not because they do not care, but because they care more about avoiding tension than confronting what may require it. They fear appearing distrustful. They fear being misunderstood. They fear disrupting long-standing relationships. But what is social ease worth if innocence is compromised? What is reputation worth if a child carries silent wounds for years because someone wanted to keep the atmosphere pleasant?

Their innocence is not replaceable.

Once fractured, it cannot be restored to its original state. Once trust is broken, rebuilding requires years of healing. The damage that follows a violation does not remain in the moment where it happened. It often follows the child into later relationships, later choices, later fears, later identity struggles, and sometimes even into how they view authority, trust, or God Himself. This is why delayed protection is so costly. Harm that could have been interrupted early may leave consequences that echo far beyond the event itself.

The sacred calling of a parent is not merely to provide—it is to guard. It is to stand watch at the gate of your household. It is to examine what enters and what lingers. It is to discern shifts before they escalate. It is to act before damage deepens. It is to build a home where communication weakens secrecy, where boundaries reduce opportunity, where vigilance interrupts manipulation, and where the child knows with certainty: I am protected here.

Your child's safety is not an accidental outcome. It is the result of intentional vigilance. It is built through prayer, structure, boundaries, discernment, oversight, honesty, and courage. It is strengthened when parents remain teachable, watchful, and spiritually awake. It is weakened when those same parents become distracted, emotionally passive, overly trusting, or unwilling to confront what threatens the peace of the home.

Let your home be a fortress of clarity. Let your presence be constant. Let your children know that no threat—seen or unseen—will reach them without first meeting you. Let your atmosphere communicate that truth will be heard, that discomfort will be investigated, that secrecy will be challenged, and that safety will never be treated as secondary.

This is the final charge of this chapter:

Do not grow comfortable.
Do not grow distracted.
Do not grow silent.

Do not let routine dull discernment.
Do not let familiarity replace caution.
Do not let convenience outrank protection.
Do not let someone else's feelings become more important than a child's safety.
Do not wait until the evidence is undeniable before responding to what your spirit has already begun to notice.

Stand between your child and every threat. Stand without apology. Stand without hesitation. Stand with enough courage to confront, enough wisdom to discern, enough love to remain present, and enough conviction to refuse passivity.

Because their protection is not optional.

It is your sacred assignment.

And when Heaven measures stewardship, it will not ask how agreeable you remained while danger moved quietly near. It will ask whether you watched, whether you guarded, whether you responded, and whether you took seriously the life placed under your care.

So stand your post. Guard the gate. Strengthen the wall. And let no preventable threat pass easily through the house you were called to defend.

You must resolve within yourself that no relationship, no social comfort, no family dynamic, and no ministry appearance will outrank your child's safety. If confrontation is necessary, confront. If access must be restricted, restrict. If environments must be changed, change them. Protection is not negotiable.

Their innocence is not replaceable.
Once fractured, it cannot be restored to its original state.
Once trust is broken, rebuilding requires years of healing.

The sacred calling of a parent is not merely to provide—it is to guard. It is to stand watch at the gate of your household. It is to examine what enters and what lingers. It is to discern shifts before they escalate. It is to act before damage deepens.

Your child's safety is not an accidental outcome. It is the result of intentional vigilance.

Let your home be a fortress of clarity.
Let your presence be constant.
Let your children know that no threat—seen or unseen—will reach them without first meeting you.

This is the final charge of this chapter:

Do not grow comfortable.
Do not grow distracted.
Do not grow silent.
Stand between your child and every threat.

Stand without apology.
Stand without hesitation.
Because their protection is not optional.
It is your sacred assignment.

❖ SPIRITUAL WARNING ❖

There are moments in history when Heaven grows silent—not because God is absent, but because accountability has begun. Silence from Heaven is never indifference. It is not weakness. It is not surrender. It is the terrifying stillness that settles when responsibility has already been made clear, and those entrusted with it have continued as though warning were optional. There are seasons when God speaks with mercy, calling, correcting, and urging men and women to wake from spiritual carelessness. But there are also seasons when the weight of stewardship itself becomes the message. We are living in such an hour.

We live in an age where innocence is under assault, where distraction numbs discernment, and where comfort has replaced conviction. Children are not merely navigating a broken culture—they are being targeted within it. The pressures around them are not passive. They are strategic. They move through media, relationships, institutions, entertainment, unguarded conversations, digital access, emotional neglect, spiritual confusion, and environments where adults have grown too tired, too casual, or too trusting to remain alert. The tragedy is not only that evil exists. Evil has always sought access. The deeper tragedy is that watchmen have grown tired, guardians have grown comfortable, and some who were assigned to protect have mistaken silence for peace.

This is not a gentle reminder. It is a warning.

God does not overlook negligence. He does not excuse apathy disguised as trust. He does not bless denial masquerading as optimism. He does not call it faith when adults ignore what discernment has already placed before them. When responsibility is entrusted, expectation follows. When awareness increases, accountability intensifies. The more clearly a guardian understands the dangers surrounding children, the less innocent that guardian becomes if they continue in passivity. Knowledge deepens responsibility. Clarity strengthens obligation. To know and still ignore is not weakness alone—it is stewardship mishandled.

Every parent, guardian, and spiritual leader stands under divine examination. Not for perfection—but for vigilance. Not for control—but for courage. The question is not whether evil is present. The question is whether you are awake. The issue is not whether darkness exists in the world. It does. The issue is whether those assigned to stand at the wall are watching the gates, examining the atmosphere, listening to the unspoken cry, and responding before hidden danger becomes visible devastation.

Silence in the face of warning signs is not neutrality—it is surrender. Dismissing behavioral shifts as "phases" without investigation is not patience—it is risk. Blind trust without discernment is not faith—it is exposure. Calling concern "overreaction" does not make a child safer. Avoiding hard questions does not preserve peace. Protecting reputations at the expense of truth does not preserve righteousness. It preserves vulnerability. Too many wounds deepened because someone wanted the room to remain comfortable. Too many cries went unanswered because a child's changed behavior was treated as an inconvenience rather than communication. Too many doors remained open because no one wanted to appear suspicious.

Heaven hears what children cannot articulate. God records what adults overlook. Every tear shed in secrecy, every fear carried alone, every cry stifled by intimidation, rises before the throne of a righteous Judge. He sees what happened in hidden rooms. He sees what was tolerated in plain sight. He sees what was brushed aside with spiritual language while danger was quietly advancing. And He will require an answer. Not because He is cruel, but because children are sacred, and stewardship over them is holy.

The Scriptures declare that it would be better for a millstone to be fastened around the neck of one who harms a child than to face divine judgment. But there is another weight—the weight of entrusted oversight. To be given stewardship over a child's safety is to be handed a sacred assignment. That assignment demands alertness. It demands more than affection. It demands more than provision. It demands moral sobriety, spiritual watchfulness, and practical obedience.

A child's safety cannot be taken casually by adults who want all the privileges of guardianship without the burden of vigilance.

Do not assume that danger announces itself. It often whispers. It often hides beneath routine, friendliness, familiarity, service, humor, charisma, and environments that feel socially safe. Do not assume that familiarity equals safety. It often disguises itself. What is known is not always righteous. What is common is not always pure. What is respected is not always trustworthy. Do not assume that innocence protects itself. It does not. Innocence is beautiful, but it is vulnerable. It does not interpret danger well. It does not understand manipulation early. It depends on the watchfulness of those assigned to guard it.

Spiritual passivity is fertile ground for predatory boldness. Darkness advances where guardians are casual. Manipulation grows where adults are distracted. Secrecy strengthens where homes do not cultivate truth. Harm deepens where warning signs are delayed, rationalized, minimized, or explained away. Evil is emboldened when it learns that no one is asking questions, no one is reinforcing boundaries, and no one is willing to disturb comfort for the sake of protection.

If you sense something is wrong—act. If you see something shift—investigate. If you detect silence where joy once lived—lean in, not away. If a child's demeanor changes, if fear suddenly appears, if secrecy begins to grow, if discomfort settles in your spirit, do not numb it with politeness or postpone it with excuses. Investigate with wisdom. Ask with steadiness. Listen without intimidation. Respond without delay. Protection is not paranoia. It is obedience. It is watchfulness in motion. It is stewardship refusing to sleep.

This generation will not be judged solely by what evil did—but by what guardians failed to confront. History records collapses that began with ignored warnings. Homes, churches, ministries, schools, and communities have all learned too late that the cost of neglected vigilance is always heavier than the temporary discomfort of asking the right questions at the right time. Let it not be recorded that innocence was sacrificed because comfort was preferred over courage. Let it not be said that adults saw enough to ask but refused to do so because the truth threatened convenience, status, or social ease.

Let conviction rise where complacency once lived. Let discernment sharpen where distraction dulled. Let prayer become strategy, not ritual. Let protection become culture, not reaction. Let homes become places where truth is welcomed, where boundaries are clear, where children know they can speak, where adults know they must watch, and where spiritual attentiveness is not treated as extremism but as love in disciplined form.

You have been entrusted with a life. That life is not yours to risk through negligence. It is not yours to expose through laziness. It is not yours to leave uncovered because you feared tension more than harm. The child under your care is not a casual assignment. That child is a soul, a future, a destiny, a sacred trust placed in your hands under the eyes of God.

Stand watch. Remain awake. Guard what God has placed under your covering. Do not drift. Do not dull. Do not surrender the wall through distraction, emotional passivity, spiritual sleep, or the false peace of avoidance. Strengthen your post. Sharpen your sight. Reclaim your authority under God because Heaven is watching—not with indifference, but with holy expectation.

CHAPTER TWO
THE WATCHTOWER OF THE HOME

Establishing a Spiritually and Physically Secure Environment for Children Confronting Concealed Dangers

✦

A House vs. A Sanctuary

A house is not automatically a sanctuary simply because it has walls. A structure may provide shelter from the weather yet fail to protect against influence. A home becomes a watchtower only when it is intentionally guarded. Many dwellings are occupied, decorated, furnished, and maintained, yet remain spiritually careless, emotionally unstable, and structurally unguarded. The existence of a roof does not guarantee refuge. The presence of family members under one address does not automatically create safety. A house may hold people together physically while failing to protect what is happening within them spiritually, emotionally, and morally.

The home must function as both a sanctuary and a fortress. Sanctuary provides nurture, belonging, affirmation, and rest. Fortress provides boundaries, vigilance, and defense. One without the other creates an imbalance. A home with affection but no structure can become permissive and vulnerable. A home with rules but no tenderness can become cold and emotionally unsafe. Children need both. They need a place where they are loved deeply and guarded seriously. They need warmth without weakness and structure without cruelty. They need an environment where peace is felt, truth is spoken, and safety is actively protected.

Children develop their sense of identity within these walls. They interpret love, authority, safety, and trust by what they experience in their own household. Before they learn the world through institutions, peers, media, or culture, they first learn it through the atmosphere of home. They learn whether authority protects or intimidates. They learn whether love listens or dismisses.

They learn whether truth is welcomed or avoided. They learn whether discomfort is investigated or ignored. If the home lacks clarity and protection, confusion takes root early. And once confusion settles into the inner world of a child, it can shape how they respond to correction, relationships, danger, and even the presence of God.

This is why the condition of the home matters so deeply. The home is not merely where children sleep. It is where they are formed. It is where they learn what normal feels like. If chaos is normal, they will carry instability with them. If dismissal is normal, they may silence themselves. If secrecy is normal, they may fail to recognize danger when it hides.

But if truth is normal, safety is modeled, and protection is practiced, then strength begins to develop from within.

In a world saturated with spiritual opposition and moral instability, the home cannot be casual. It must be cultivated. It must be built with intention, governed with sobriety, and protected with vigilance. We are not rearing children in a neutral generation. We are rearing them in an hour where access is rapid, boundaries are often mocked, and confusion is marketed as freedom. Harm does not always arrive through force; often it enters through normalization.

It enters through repeated exposure, through passive routines, through unchecked influences, and through a household that slowly drifts from alertness into assumption.

Proverbs 24:3 (KJV) declares, “Through wisdom is an house builded; and by understanding it is established.” Brick and mortar construct a house. Wisdom establishes a home. Understanding fortifies it. Discernment guards it. This verse does not point merely to architecture; it points to spiritual and relational construction. A house can be purchased quickly. A home must be built carefully. Wisdom determines what is allowed to shape the atmosphere. Understanding recognizes what strengthens stability and what weakens it. Discernment identifies what must be confronted before it is permitted to remain.

A watchtower in ancient times was elevated, strategic, and alert. It was designed for visibility and defense. The guard stationed there did not sleep lightly. He observed approaching threats before they reached the gate. He watched not because he expected fear to rule the city, but because he understood that vigilance was the price of protection. He knew that danger seen early could be resisted more effectively than danger discovered late. His assignment was not decorative. It was essential.

In the same way, parents must rise above distractions and take their position, both spiritually and physically. They must see before harm advances. They must not wait until visible damage appears before becoming attentive. They must learn to notice patterns before patterns become crises. They must remain awake to the things that seem small but often grow silently: changes in tone, shifts in appetite, emotional withdrawal, unusual secrecy, inappropriate familiarity, digital overexposure, disrespect for boundaries, unfiltered entertainment, peer pressure, and subtle spiritual compromise.

This is part of what it means to serve as a watchman in the home. A watchman is not merely a responder to emergencies. A watchman is a discerner of movement. A watchman recognizes that the earliest stages of danger are often quiet. They rarely arrive with an announcement. They come by slow erosion, by softened standards, by delayed correction, by tolerated confusion, and by spiritual inattentiveness.

The modern home is under constant pressure—through media, digital access, cultural shifts, peer influence, and subtle spiritual compromise. If vigilance is absent, infiltration becomes easy. A spiritually unguarded door eventually becomes physically vulnerable. What is repeatedly allowed into the home through screens, conversations, attitudes, music, and unresolved conflict begins to shape the emotional and spiritual climate of that home. And when the atmosphere weakens, children often feel the shift long before they know how to explain it.

Parents must understand that the atmosphere is not accidental. Something is always shaping it. If truth does not shape it, confusion will. If peace does not govern it, agitation will. If prayer does not guard it, other influences will compete for authority.

If boundaries are not established clearly, access will expand carelessly. The home cannot remain spiritually neglected and still expect stability to thrive indefinitely.

The watchtower is not optional.

It is the sacred position of every parent.

This does not mean parents must live in panic. It means they must live in awareness. The watchtower is not built from fear but from responsibility. It is not maintained by suspicion of everything, but by discernment about anything that threatens what God has entrusted. It is a place of prayer, observation, structure, and courage. It is where adults stop assuming that safety preserves itself and begin understanding that safety must be cultivated, guarded, and reinforced.

A watchtower home is not loud in performance, but strong in posture. It builds routines that create predictability. It makes room for honest conversation. It treats discomfort seriously. It establishes clear boundaries without apology. It teaches children that love is not careless and that protection is not control. It refuses to let culture dictate the standards that should govern the household. It remains teachable before God and attentive to what is entering through both visible and invisible gates.

Such a home becomes more than a place of residence. It becomes a place of formation. It becomes a place where children learn that safety and truth belong together, that authority can be holy, that boundaries are loving, and that vigilance is an expression of care, not mistrust. In such a home, children are not merely kept—they are covered. They are not merely supervised—they are shepherded. They are not merely sheltered from weather—they are strengthened against influence.

Build with wisdom.
Establish an understanding.
Guard with vigilance.

For the strength of tomorrow is shaped by the protection of today. And a home that is spiritually alert, emotionally stable, and intentionally guarded becomes more than a house with walls—it becomes a sanctuary where innocence is protected, identity is strengthened, and darkness finds resistance at the gate.

ESTABLISHING THE HOME AS A WATCHTOWER

Positioning the Household for Protection, Discernment and Courage

---

A home that functions as a watchtower is not merely a place where children live—it is a place where children are guarded. It is a position of vigilance rather than passivity, awareness rather than assumption, and intentional protection rather than accidental safety. The imagery of a watchtower is ancient and instructive. In biblical times, watchmen were placed in elevated positions along city walls. Their task was not to wait for danger to strike, but to see it while it was still far away. Their responsibility was early detection, timely warning, and decisive response.

The same principle must guide the modern household.

When a home functions as a watchtower, protection becomes intentional rather than accidental. Parents are not merely reacting to problems after they appear; they are positioned to recognize danger before it reaches their children. They observe patterns, listen carefully to changes in tone or behavior, and remain attentive to the subtle signals that something may be shifting beneath the surface.

This kind of vigilance does not produce paranoia—it produces preparedness. It acknowledges a sober reality: danger rarely announces itself loudly at first. It often approaches gradually, quietly, and strategically. By the time a crisis becomes visible, the underlying pattern may have already been developing for some time.

A watchtower home disrupts that progression.

Parents who embrace this role do not wait for visible harm before they become attentive. They cultivate an atmosphere where awareness is part of everyday life. They ask questions. They remain present. They notice when something seems unusual, when a child withdraws emotionally, when secrecy begins to replace openness, or when a relationship introduces pressure rather than encouragement.

The watchtower is not built upon suspicion—it is built upon attentiveness.

Children flourish where consistency exists. Stability in daily life communicates safety to a child's heart and mind. Shared meals create communication pathways where conversation can flow naturally. These ordinary moments often become the places where children reveal what they might otherwise keep hidden. A casual conversation at the dinner table may uncover a troubling experience at school. A quiet moment during a car ride may open the door for a child to ask a question they were afraid to voice earlier.

Routine becomes a form of protection.

Family prayer builds spiritual sensitivity within the home. When families pray together regularly, children learn that their struggles, questions, and fears can be brought before God without shame. They see that their parents depend upon wisdom greater than their own. This example teaches humility, spiritual awareness, and the recognition that God is not distant from the everyday challenges of life.

Open dialogue fosters trust. A child who knows their voice will be heard without ridicule or immediate condemnation becomes far more willing to speak honestly. When children feel that their words will be dismissed or punished harshly, they often retreat into silence. But when parents respond with patience and steadiness—even when the conversation is uncomfortable—communication remains open.

When children are heard without judgment, they are more likely to speak before harm escalates.

A spiritually fortified home also teaches resilience. Children reared within clear boundaries learn that love and accountability belong together. They begin to understand that authority is not designed to control them but to protect them. Discipline becomes a form of guidance rather than humiliation. Boundaries become a framework within which freedom can operate safely.

Children who grow up within this structure often develop a deep sense of security. They know someone is watching over them. They know someone is paying attention. They know that their parents will act if something threatens their well-being.

That sense of covering produces confidence.

Emotional security becomes the soil from which courage grows. When children feel protected, they become more willing to speak the truth, resist pressure, and stand firm when something feels wrong. They learn that safety is not achieved through silence but through awareness and communication.

However, the watchtower of the home must guard not only against obvious danger but also against subtle compromise.

Not every threat is dramatic. Some dangers do not arrive with visible hostility. Instead, they creep in gradually through repeated exposure to unhealthy influences. An unfiltered stream of entertainment may slowly normalize attitudes that undermine moral clarity. Unmonitored devices may provide access to conversations and images that children are not emotionally prepared to process. Friendships that appear harmless on the surface may introduce pressure to conform to values that conflict with what the home has taught.

Subtle compromises are dangerous because they rarely provoke immediate alarm.

They appear small.
They seem manageable.
They often feel culturally acceptable.

But gradual exposure can reshape perception. What once seemed inappropriate may begin to feel ordinary. What once felt uncomfortable may begin to feel familiar. Over time, the boundaries of a child's thinking can shift quietly.

This is why vigilance requires awareness of both the obvious and the subtle.

Parents must remain attentive to the influences that surround their children—social, digital, relational, and spiritual. This does not mean attempting to control every aspect of a child's life, but it does mean refusing to abandon the responsibility of oversight.

Establishing a spiritually and physically secure environment demands intentionality. A watchtower home does not emerge by accident. It is built through consistent effort and deliberate choices.

It requires parents to reject passivity.
It requires discipline in routines.
It requires consistent oversight.
It requires courage to say "no" even when culture says "yes."

Culture often pressures parents to relax boundaries for the sake of convenience or acceptance. Yet wisdom sometimes requires the opposite. There will be moments when the responsible decision feels unpopular or uncomfortable. A watchtower parent understands that approval from others is never more important than the safety of a child.

Protection sometimes requires resistance.

It may require questioning a situation others assume is harmless.
It may require setting limits that others do not understand.
It may require slowing down where others rush ahead.

But a watchtower does not exist to mirror the comfort of the surrounding culture. It exists to guard what lies inside.

The goal of this vigilance is not to rear fearful children.

Fear weakens confidence and discourages exploration. The objective of the watchtower home is not to rear children who view the world with suspicion, but children who move through the world with discernment.

The goal is to rear aware children.

Awareness allows children to recognize danger without being paralyzed by it. Awareness equips them to identify manipulation, pressure, or unhealthy influence. Awareness helps them understand that their safety matters and that their instincts deserve attention.

Awareness is empowerment.

When children are equipped with awareness, they become participants in their own protection. They know when to ask questions, when to speak up, and when to seek help. They develop confidence in their ability to navigate complex environments with wisdom.

Protection, therefore, is not merely the act of shielding children from every possible risk. It is the process of preparing them to recognize and respond to danger when it appears.

Protection is preparation.

A watchtower home does not promise a life without challenge. What it provides is something far more valuable: a place where truth is spoken, vigilance is practiced, and children grow under the covering of intentional care.

When parents stand faithfully at the watchtower of the home, they create an environment where awareness thrives, trust remains strong, and protection becomes woven into the daily rhythm of family life.

And in such a home, children grow not only safer—but stronger.

THE ROLE OF PRAYER IN-HOUSEHOLD PROTECTION

Establishing Spiritual Authority Within the Home

✦

A home infused with prayer does more than express faith—it establishes spiritual authority. Prayer is not a decorative ritual reserved for ceremonial moments or religious appearances. It is an act of spiritual governance. It is the deliberate act of inviting God's authority into the atmosphere of the household and aligning the life of that home with truth rather than chaos.

When prayer is present consistently, it changes the climate of the home. Words spoken in prayer do not vanish into the air; they shape the environment in which children grow. They invite the presence of God, strengthen spiritual sensitivity, and reinforce the conviction that the home is not spiritually unguarded territory. In a world where confusion, deception, and harmful influences press constantly against the lives of children, prayer becomes a form of spiritual reinforcement that strengthens the walls of the household.

Parents must understand that the atmosphere of a home is never neutral. Something is always shaping it. Conversations shape it. Media influences shape it. Attitudes shape it. Emotional patterns shape it. If the atmosphere is not intentionally anchored in truth and prayer, it will eventually be shaped by whatever voices are most persistent. Prayer interrupts that drift. It re-centers the household on God's presence and reminds every member of the family that the home belongs under His authority.

When parents consistently pray over their children, they reinforce covering. Prayer becomes a declaration that the child is not navigating life unguarded. Each prayer offered over their life becomes an act of protection, asking God to guide their thoughts, guard their relationships, sharpen their discernment, and strengthen their character. These moments may appear quiet and ordinary, but their influence is profound.

Children who grow up hearing their names spoken before God begin to understand that their lives matter and that their family takes their spiritual well-being seriously.

Prayer also trains the heart of the parent. When parents pray regularly for their children, their awareness deepens. Concerns that might otherwise go unnoticed become clearer. Discernment becomes more responsive. The Holy Spirit often nudges attentive parents through prayer—prompting them to ask questions, investigate unusual behavior, or pay closer attention to subtle changes in their child's demeanor. In this way, prayer strengthens vigilance.

Scripture spoken within the home also shapes the spiritual environment. The Word of God provides language that anchors truth in the household. When biblical truth is spoken, repeated, and applied in everyday life, it trains the conscience of the family. Children learn to recognize the difference between what is healthy and what is destructive. They develop moral clarity. They begin to see that wisdom is not merely cultural opinion but divine instruction.

Teaching truth intentionally strengthens discernment within young hearts. Children who grow up hearing and understanding God's Word are less easily persuaded by deception. They become more capable of identifying manipulation, resisting unhealthy pressure, and recognizing when something violates the principles they have been taught.

Yet prayer must never be misunderstood.

Prayer does not replace responsibility—it strengthens it.

Some parents mistakenly treat prayer as a substitute for practical vigilance. They pray for protection while ignoring warning signs. They speak spiritual language while allowing unsafe access. They quote Scripture but fail to establish boundaries. This imbalance weakens protection rather than strengthening it.

Spiritual language without practical boundaries is incomplete protection.

A praying parent must also be a watchful parent. Prayer must be joined with attentiveness. Discernment must be joined with action. Faith must be joined with wisdom. A household that prays but refuses to confront harmful influences leaves its doors partially open.

A household that establishes boundaries but neglects prayer risks operating only in human strength. True protection grows where both are present.

When prayer becomes foundational rather than occasional, spiritual sensitivity grows within the household. Parents become more attentive to shifts in behavior, atmosphere, and influence. Children become more aware of right and wrong, not merely through rules but through spiritual conviction. Discernment becomes sharper because the family is consistently orienting itself toward truth.

Prayer also strengthens unity within the home. Families who pray together learn to face challenges collectively rather than individually. Children see that concerns are brought to God rather than buried in silence. They witness humility as parents acknowledge their need for divine guidance. This example teaches them that strength does not come from pretending to have all the answers—it comes from seeking wisdom from the One who does.

Ultimately, prayer reminds the household that God is not distant from daily life. He is present in decisions, conversations, conflicts, fears, and hopes. When prayer becomes part of the rhythm of family life, children grow up understanding that spiritual awareness is not confined to church services—it belongs in kitchens, living rooms, car rides, and quiet bedtime moments.

A home where prayer lives regularly is a home where the atmosphere is guarded intentionally. It is a place where truth is spoken, where vigilance is strengthened, and where the presence of God is welcomed rather than neglected.

Parents must therefore cultivate prayer not as an occasional reaction to crisis but as a daily foundation of leadership. Let prayer shape the rhythm of the household. Let Scripture guide conversations. Let truth govern decisions. Let discernment remain awake.

Because when prayer anchors a home, the atmosphere changes.
When truth fills the environment, deception loses ground.
When vigilance and prayer walk together, protection becomes stronger.

And a household governed by prayer is far less likely to drift into the confusion that silence and neglect create.

THE HOME AS A SPIRITUAL GATE

The home is not merely a physical dwelling—it is a spiritual gate. It is a threshold through which influences pass, shaping the atmosphere, attitudes, and direction of every life within its walls. A home is never just a place where people eat, sleep, and gather. It is a place where thoughts are formed, values are reinforced, sensitivities are trained, and identities are quietly shaped. What enters consistently will eventually establish authority. What is tolerated quietly will eventually take root openly. What is repeated often enough will no longer feel unusual; it will begin to feel normal. And what feels normal eventually starts to govern thought, speech, desire, and behavior.

This is why the home cannot be treated casually. A house may appear orderly on the outside while something corrosive is slowly shaping its inner climate. A home may look peaceful while confusion is being discipled into the hearts of those living there. A family may be busy, functional, and socially admired while spiritually vulnerable at its gates. External stability does not always mean internal protection. This is what makes spiritual oversight so necessary. Parents must learn to see the home not only as a place to maintain, but as an atmosphere to guard.

A gate is designed to regulate access. It determines what is allowed in and what is kept out. If the gate remains unguarded, intrusion becomes inevitable. Likewise, a home without intentional spiritual oversight becomes vulnerable—not necessarily through dramatic invasion, but through gradual infiltration. Spiritual decline rarely begins with a loud collapse. It often begins with small permissions, softened boundaries, delayed correction, and repeated exposure to what once would have been challenged. That is how gates weaken not always through open rebellion, but through tolerated compromise.

The adversary rarely storms through the front door. He enters subtly—through glowing screens, unchecked conversations, inappropriate media, toxic friendships, unmonitored devices, and an atmosphere of spiritual complacency. Distraction becomes the doorway. Normalization becomes the disguise.

Repetition becomes the strategy. What is dangerous is not always what appears violent or shocking at first glance. Often, it is what becomes acceptable by slow degrees. A household does not have to invite darkness for darkness to influence it openly. It only needs to stop guarding what enters, stop questioning what is repeated, and stop paying attention to what is quietly shaping the atmosphere.

Parents must understand this clearly: whatever consistently enters the home will eventually influence the heart.

That principle cannot be escaped. The human heart absorbs through repetition. What is seen repeatedly begins to shape imagination. What is heard repeatedly begins to shape language. What is laughed at repeatedly begins to shape conscience. What is tolerated repeatedly begins to shape standards. This is why influence must be taken seriously. A child does not need to understand the full meaning of everything entering their environment for that environment to begin shaping them. Repeated exposure can normalize things that they are not yet mature enough to resist.

Jesus warned in Matthew 26:41 (KJV), "Watch and pray, that ye enter not into temptation." Watching precedes resisting. Prayer fortifies awareness. Temptation often gains power where vigilance is weak. That order matters. Christ did not merely say pray. He said watch and pray. A family that prays but does not watch may remain spiritually sincere while becoming practically careless. A family that watches without prayer may become observant but spiritually exhausted. True protection requires both. Watching keeps the gate awake. Prayer keeps the gate strong.

Psalm 101:3 (KJV) declares, "I will set no wicked thing before mine eyes." This commitment extends beyond obvious immorality. It includes subtle corruption—content that trivializes sin, entertainment that normalizes sexualization, narratives that glorify rebellion, humor that mocks purity, and images that desensitize conscience. Wickedness does not always announce itself through what is openly grotesque. It often moves through what is culturally acceptable, aesthetically polished, emotionally persuasive, or widely celebrated. That is what makes spiritual discernment essential. A thing may be popular and still be poisonous. A thing may be common and still be corrupting.

A thing may be entertaining and still be forming the heart in ways that weaken holiness.

The eye gate and the ear gate are not passive channels. They are entry points.

What enters through the eyes enters the imagination. What enters through the ears enters the inner atmosphere. Long before outward behavior changes, inward desensitization may already be happening. Children and adults alike can be shaped by repeated visual and verbal exposure without fully realizing how deeply it is influencing them. This is why content cannot be evaluated only by whether it is explicit. It must also be evaluated by what it celebrates, what it minimizes, what it normalizes, and what it teaches the soul to tolerate.

A home where entertainment mocks purity, speech glorifies disrespect, music trains emotional instability, or constant noise replaces reflective peace will not remain spiritually unaffected. What enters repeatedly will not remain external. It will begin to settle into the language of the home, the tone of the home, the desires formed within the home, and the sensitivity or insensitivity of those who live there. The gate is not only breached by obvious wickedness. It is also worn down by tolerated subtlety.

This is why parents must think beyond whether something appears harmless in the moment. They must ask deeper questions. What is this teaching my child to admire? What is this teaching them to excuse? What is this training them to hunger for? What does this repeatedly entering my home make easier to accept later? Discernment is not only about rejecting what is clearly evil. It is also about recognizing what quietly erodes spiritual clarity.

The spiritual gate of the home also includes conversation. Words create atmosphere. Repeated sarcasm, cutting humor, sensual joking, constant criticism, angry speech, and careless language all train a household in something. They shape what feels acceptable. They influence whether the environment feels guarded or vulnerable. A child reared in a home where speech is consistently careless may struggle to distinguish conviction from condemnation, correction from shame, and truth from hostility. A spiritually guarded home watches not only what is played on screens, but what is practiced in conversation.

Relationships are gates as well. Not every friendship deserves access to the same level of influence. Not every person who enters a home should be allowed to shape its children. Not every voice should carry equal weight. Toxic friendships, morally careless influences, manipulative personalities, and emotionally unstable patterns do not remain harmless simply because they are relational. The home must discern not only what enters physically, but what enters relationally. Some influences weaken conviction one conversation at a time.

An atmosphere of spiritual complacency is one of the most dangerous breaches of all. A home may reject obvious wickedness and still become vulnerable through passivity. Prayer may become infrequent. Scripture may become decorative rather than central. Boundaries may become negotiable. Convictions may soften. Small discomforts may be ignored. Parents may become too busy to observe carefully, too distracted to listen deeply, or too tired to remain spiritually alert. In that condition, the gate is not forcefully taken—it is slowly neglected.

Spiritual neglect is often the quiet permission structure of later harm.

A guarded home, therefore, requires deliberate leadership. It requires parents who understand that they are not merely maintaining routines but regulating access. It requires adults who know that every screen, every conversation, every relationship, every media pattern, and every tolerated attitude is shaping something within the household. It requires enough courage to say no when culture says yes, enough discernment to challenge what seems small, and enough consistency to keep the gate guarded even when nothing dramatic appears wrong.

This is not paranoia. It is stewardship.

To guard the gate of the home is not to create an atmosphere of fear. It is to create an atmosphere of clarity. It is to ensure that what governs the household is not confusion, lust, rebellion, spiritual dullness, or emotional instability, but truth, peace, holiness, and watchful love. It is to build an environment where children can grow with a conscience that is not constantly being eroded by what enters unchallenged.

A spiritually guarded home does not become perfect. But it does become intentional. It does not become free from every pressure. But it becomes more resistant to infiltration. It does not guarantee that every external influence will be absent. But it ensures that what enters will not go unquestioned.

Guard the gate of the eyes.
Guard the gate of the ears.
Guard the gate of conversation.
Guard the gate of influence.
Guard the gate of the atmosphere.

Because the home will always be shaped by what is allowed to enter it, when the gate is watched carefully, truth remains stronger, discernment remains sharper, and darkness finds far less room to settle in what God intended to be a sanctuary.

GUARDING THE EYE GATE AND THE EAR GATE

Children's minds are impressionable. What they see repeatedly becomes familiar. What becomes familiar eventually feels acceptable. What feels acceptable often becomes adopted behavior. This is one of the most sobering realities of formation: repetition trains the heart long before a child is mature enough to recognize that training is taking place. The eye and the ear are not neutral passageways. They are instructors. They are influence channels. They are the roads by which ideas, images, values, attitudes, and appetites travel inward.

A child does not have to fully understand what they are seeing for it to begin shaping them. They do not have to agree with every message they hear for it to leave an impression. Exposure itself carries power. Repetition carries even more. A child who repeatedly sees disrespect framed as strength may begin to admire rebellion. A child who repeatedly hears impurity treated as humor may begin to lose sensitivity to holiness. A child who repeatedly absorbs content that celebrates vanity, aggression, lust, mockery, confusion, or emotional excess may begin to accept those things as ordinary features of life rather than distortions of it.

This is why guarding the eye gate and the ear gate is not a minor parental concern. It is part of spiritual stewardship.

Parents who fail to guard these gates unintentionally surrender influence to outside forces. They may still love their children deeply. They may still provide materially and care emotionally. But if they do not pay attention to what is feeding the inner world of the child, then other voices will help disciple that child in their place. And those voices will not ask permission before shaping desire, bending perception, dulling conscience, or weakening conviction.

Influence never waits for parental readiness. It is already speaking.

It speaks through entertainment.
It speaks through music.
It speaks through social media.

It speaks through jokes, trends, gaming culture, online personalities, peer conversations, and repeated images that normalize what God has called dangerous.

This is why a spiritually guarded home does not function in paranoia but in intentionality. It does not panic at every influence, but it does examine what is entering. It does not fear the existence of the world, but it refuses to let the world disciple its children without resistance. It is not erratic. It is deliberate. It is not driven by hysteria. It is governed by discernment.

Such a home asks important questions:

What messages are shaping our children's beliefs?
What conversations are molding their perceptions?
What digital spaces are influencing their identity?
What relationships are cultivating their values?

These are not excessive questions. They are responsible questions. The parent who refuses to ask them may feel less burdened in the moment, but that relief often comes at the cost of deeper vulnerability later. A child's worldview is always being formed by something. If parents do not examine what is entering through the eye and ear gate, then they may one day find themselves trying to uproot beliefs, appetites, and patterns that were quietly planted over time.

The eye gate is powerful because images linger. What a child sees can settle in imagination, shape expectation, and normalize what should have been challenged. Visual content bypasses many defenses because it does not always argue with the mind first—it imprints itself on the inner world. Over time, repeated images can train what the child admires, fears, laughs at, desires, or excuses. A single image may disturb the conscience briefly, but repeated exposure can desensitize it. That is why what is watched matters. It is not simply entertainment. It is formation.

The ear gate is equally serious because words shape the internal atmosphere. The language a child hears repeatedly becomes the language they begin to tolerate, adopt, and eventually speak. Speech teaches what is honorable and what is cheap. Music teaches emotional posture. Conversations train perspective. A child who constantly hears vulgarity, sensual suggestion, mocking humor, cynical speech, or rebellion dressed as empowerment is not merely being entertained. They are being instructed. They are learning what to honor and what to dismiss.

Parents must therefore understand that guarding the gates does not only mean blocking the obvious. It also means confronting the subtle.

Some things do not appear evil because they are packaged attractively. Some messages arrive through polished storytelling, humor, aesthetics, trendiness, or emotional appeal. Some influences do not openly oppose God while still gradually weakening reverence, reducing moral seriousness, and reshaping standards. That is why discernment must go deeper than simply asking, Is this explicit? It must also ask, What does this normalize? What does this celebrate? What does this make easier to accept over time?

A home may appear peaceful while a subtle compromise is quietly advancing. There may be no open rebellion, no visible collapse, no dramatic crisis. Yet something may still be eroding beneath the surface. Convictions may be softening. Sensitivity may be weakening. Entertainment may be training desires that Scripture calls dangerous. Humor may be making light of what should be handled with reverence. Conversations may be shifting the atmosphere from truth to casual compromise. A household can remain functional while its spiritual edge is slowly dulling.

Spiritual complacency is more dangerous than open opposition.

Open opposition is easier to recognize. Complacency is harder because it often feels normal. It does not always make a loud entrance. It arrives quietly through lowered standards, tired discernment, delayed correction, and an increasing willingness to tolerate what once would have been examined. It says, It's not that serious. Everyone watches this. Everyone says this. Everyone listens to this. Everyone talks like this. But the question for a household under God is never merely what everyone is doing. The question is what is shaping the spirit of the home and the soul of the child.

When prayer becomes occasional instead of foundational, the gate weakens. When Scripture becomes decorative instead of directive, the gate weakens. When discernment becomes secondary to convenience, the gate weakens. When the home is too busy to listen, too distracted to examine, or too passive to confront, the gate weakens. And once the gate weakens, influences that once would have been resisted begin to move in with little resistance at all.

This is why parents must not only monitor content—they must cultivate atmosphere.

A child needs more than blocked websites and screen rules. They need a home where truth has weight, where prayer is practiced, where Scripture is spoken with sincerity, where questions are welcomed, where influences are discussed rather than ignored, and where moral clarity is modeled in real life. Children learn not only by what is restricted, but by what is reinforced. They must see that holiness is not a relic, purity is not weakness, discernment is not extremism, and obedience to God is not something to be embarrassed by in a confused generation.

Guarding the eye gate and the ear gate also requires parental consistency. Children notice contradictions quickly. If parents warn against unclean speech but fill the home with careless words, the warning loses power.

If parents caution against digital corruption but consume media without restraint, the child receives confusion instead of clarity. What parents practice repeatedly becomes part of the atmosphere their children breathe.

Guarding these gates is therefore not only about external control. It is about internal leadership. It is about building a household where what enters is examined, where what influences is questioned, and where spiritual carelessness is not allowed to pose as harmless normal life.

A wise parent does not ask only, What am I keeping out? They also ask, What am I allowing in? What am I normalizing? What am I failing to challenge? What is training my child when I am not paying attention?

Those questions matter because the eye gate and the ear gate are never idle. Something is always entering. Something is always teaching. Something is always shaping.

So guard them with conviction.
Guard them with sobriety.
Guard them with awareness.
Guard them without apology.

Because what a child sees repeatedly will shape what they imagine. What they hear repeatedly will shape what they accept. And what they accept long enough may eventually shape who they become.

SPIRITUAL AND PHYSICAL BOUNDARIES

Defined boundaries are essential. They are not optional additions to wise parenting; they are part of the very structure that makes a home secure. A household without boundaries may still look loving from the outside, but love without structure can leave dangerous openings. Protection requires more than good intentions. It requires clearly established limits, visible lines of accountability, and a willingness to enforce them even when it feels inconvenient or unpopular.

Who enters the home must be intentional. A house should never function as an unrestricted passageway where familiarity alone grants access. Not everyone pleasant is safe. Not everyone who is known is trustworthy. Not everyone who is respected deserves unexamined proximity to a child. Parents must resist the cultural pressure to appear endlessly relaxed while their children's safety is on the line. Hospitality is a virtue, but careless access is not. The home is not a public field. It is a guarded space, and those who enter it should do so under the awareness that the gate is watched.

Who spends time alone with a child must be evaluated. Solitude creates opportunity, and opportunity can either be used for healthy mentorship or exploited for hidden harm. That is why parents must never treat one-on-one access casually. The issue is not assuming evil in every person; the issue is refusing to create unnecessary vulnerability. A wise parent asks, "Why is this access needed?" Under what conditions is it happening? Is there transparency? Is there accountability? Is the child comfortable? Is the adult respectful of oversight? These are not suspicious questions. They are responsible ones.

What devices are allowed in bedrooms must be monitored. A closed bedroom door and an unmonitored device can create a private world far larger than many parents realize. What once required physical access can now be entered through a screen in seconds. Conversations, images, videos, invitations, manipulation, comparison, pornography, and predatory contact can all arrive quietly while the home appears calm. Parents must understand that digital access is still access.

A phone in a bedroom is not merely a device—it is an open gate unless it is governed with wisdom. Boundaries around screens are not outdated or controlling. They are acts of practical stewardship in a generation where secrecy can be built silently and quickly.

What conversations are normalized must be guided. The spiritual and emotional tone of a home is shaped by what is repeated in it. If vulgarity, mockery, sexual carelessness, rebellion, bitterness, manipulation, or disrespect are allowed to become common speech, the atmosphere of the home will absorb those things. Language is not harmless. Repeated speech trains the conscience. What a child hears normalized, they often begin to accept.

Parents must therefore guide the conversation intentionally—both in what is allowed and in what is corrected. A home must be a place where truth has weight, where words are not weaponized, and where speech does not quietly erode holiness, dignity, or self-respect.

The watchtower does not merely feel safe—it functions safely. This distinction matters. Some homes feel warm but are structurally careless. Others appear orderly but are spiritually asleep. A guarded home does not rely on appearance alone. It builds systems of protection that are visible, consistent, and active. It understands that the absence of an obvious crisis does not prove safety. Safety is proven by the presence of wisdom, oversight, and intentional structure.

Boundaries are not restrictive. They are protective architecture. They are the framework that keeps freedom from becoming exposure. They are the walls that allow peace to remain peace rather than drift into permissiveness. They are the visible expression of love, taking responsibility seriously. Children do not suffer because a home has too much wise structure; they suffer when necessary lines are absent, blurred, delayed, or repeatedly ignored.

A spiritually secure home includes consistent prayer over children and over the atmosphere. Prayer is not a decorative routine to make a household appear religious. It is a spiritual act of covering. It acknowledges that children need more than rules—they need divine protection, wisdom, and discernment working around them and within them. Prayer over the home also trains the parents. It keeps them spiritually alert, softer toward God, and more sensitive to what may be shifting beneath the surface.

A spiritually secure home includes open dialogue about digital safety and moral clarity. Children must not be left to interpret the digital world on their own. They need ongoing conversation, not one-time warnings. They need parents who are willing to explain what is dangerous, why certain content matters, how manipulation works, and why personal dignity should never be traded for acceptance, curiosity, or pressure. Moral clarity must be taught calmly, repeatedly, and with enough depth that the child begins to internalize it.

A spiritually secure home includes clear guidelines regarding friendships and influences. Not every friendship builds. Not every influence strengthens. Some relationships flatter while eroding boundaries. Some friendships offer inclusion at the cost of conviction. Parents must guide children in learning that relationships are not to be evaluated by fun alone, but by fruit. A child must be helped to recognize whether a person draws them toward clarity, respect, and honesty—or toward secrecy, rebellion, shame, and confusion.

A spiritually secure home includes accountability for device usage. Accountability is not the enemy of trust; it is one of the ways trust is protected from naivety. Children and teenagers need boundaries around what they use, when they use it, how privately they use it, and what kind of access they are granted. Oversight is not an insult. It is stewardship. When handled with steadiness and explanation, it teaches the child that their inner world matters too much to be left unguarded.

A spiritually secure home includes immediate correction when boundaries are crossed. Delayed correction teaches dangerous lessons. It communicates that lines are optional, that discomfort can be ignored, and that repeated violations will eventually be tolerated. Immediate correction is not harshness. It is clarity. It says that the home takes safety, dignity, truth, and accountability seriously. A child needs to see that parents do not merely talk about boundaries—they uphold them.

Children reared in a guarded home develop internal discernment. They begin to sense when something is misaligned. They recognize unhealthy influences earlier. They learn that boundaries are expressions of love, not control. They begin to understand that discomfort deserves attention, that secrecy is not the same as privacy, and that a safe home is one where truth can be spoken without fear. Over time, these lessons become part of the child's internal framework. They no longer need every situation explained for them to sense that something is wrong. Their conscience becomes more awake. Their instincts become better trained. Their sense of worth becomes stronger.

This is one of the great gifts of consistent boundaries: they teach children to recognize what honors them and what threatens them. They learn that their body is not public property, that their voice matters, that adult authority is not absolute when it violates righteousness, and that love never demands silence in the face of danger.

If the gate is guarded, infiltration is resisted. If the gate is neglected, intrusion is invited. That is the sober reality. A gate does not remain neutral simply because no one is watching it. The absence of watchfulness is itself an invitation. Openings widen where no one is paying attention. Influence deepens where no one is asking questions. Harm becomes bolder where no one is willing to interrupt it.

So boundaries must be defined, spoken, modeled, and enforced. They must be reinforced through prayer, strengthened through consistency, and carried out with enough conviction that the child knows the home is not casually managed. It is guarded.

Because a spiritually and physically secure home does not happen by accident, it is built by adults who understand that love must have structure, vigilance must have action, and protection must be strong enough to withstand both the obvious threat and the subtle one.

ESTABLISHING PROTECTIVE HOUSEHOLD STRUCTURES

Establishing a watchtower requires structure. Vigilance cannot remain effective if it exists only as an emotion, an occasional concern, or a reaction to obvious danger. Protection that depends only on instinct will eventually become inconsistent. A household must therefore be built with rhythms, habits, and patterns that make safety normal rather than accidental. When protective structures are present, children are not left to navigate life by guesswork alone. They grow within an environment where order supports discernment, consistency strengthens trust, and daily life itself becomes part of the covering around them.

Children thrive when rhythms of protection become normal rather than reactionary. A child should not have to wait for a crisis to discover whether their home is safe, attentive, and engaged. They should experience that safety in the regular patterns of ordinary life. Stability is protective. Predictability is protective. Presence is protective. When the home has clear rhythms, children are more likely to notice when something feels wrong, because they have a healthy pattern against which they can measure what is unusual.

Protective household structures include family prayer and spiritual conversation. A home that prays together consistently is not merely maintaining a religious habit; it is building spiritual awareness into the rhythm of family life. Prayer teaches children that their lives are not detached from God's presence, that concerns can be brought into the light, and that spiritual covering is not occasional but intentional. Spiritual conversation also matters. Children need more than correction; they need interpretation. They need help understanding why truth matters, why boundaries exist, and how discernment operates in the real world. A household that speaks openly about God, holiness, wisdom, temptation, fear, and spiritual responsibility creates an atmosphere where truth is not ornamental—it is functional.

Protective household structures include shared meals that encourage communication. There is something powerful about repeated moments where the family gathers, not simply to eat, but to reconnect.

Shared meals provide natural opportunities for children to speak about their day, mention interactions that unsettled them, reveal emotional shifts, or ask questions that might never surface in more formal settings. The strength of these moments lies not in the meal itself but in the access they create. A child who regularly experiences calm, attentive conversation at the table is more likely to speak before secrecy grows too strong. In many homes, what is revealed casually in routine conversation becomes the very thing that prevents hidden harm from deepening.

Protective household structures include awareness of friendships and influences. Parents must know who is shaping their child, not only academically or socially, but also emotionally, morally, and spiritually. Friendships are never neutral. They teach language, values, responses, appetites, humor, and perspective. The same is true of mentors, teams, peer groups, leaders, online communities, and social spaces. Children and teenagers are deeply affected by repeated contact with those around them. That is why parental awareness must extend beyond simply knowing names. It must include understanding patterns. Is this friendship producing openness or secrecy? Is this influence strengthening honesty or increasing pressure? Is this relationship cultivating courage or confusion? A guarded home pays attention to these things because influence is one of the most powerful shaping forces in a child's life.

Protective household structures include clear expectations about digital devices. Technology cannot be treated as a minor household issue in a generation where devices often function as open doors to unfiltered influence. Clear expectations must exist regarding when devices are used, where they are used, what platforms are permitted, what privacy settings are allowed, what parental visibility remains in place, and what kind of communication requires accountability.

These expectations should not be vague. They should be direct, consistent, and reinforced without apology. A home that leaves digital life undefined will often find that secrecy grows faster than trust. But when digital boundaries are clear, the child understands that technology is not outside the reach of stewardship. It is part of it.

Protective household structures include parental presence in a child's daily environment. Presence does not mean surveillance without relationship; it means engaged awareness. It means parents know enough about the child's routines, environments, emotional tone, interests, pressures, and relationships that they are able to detect when something changes. Presence is not measured only by being physically in the same room. A parent may be physically near and still be mentally unavailable, emotionally distracted, or spiritually disengaged. True presence listens, notices, asks, follows up, and remains close enough to sense when something is shifting. Children need adults who are not merely around them, but tuned in to them.

When parents maintain involvement in their children's lives, the atmosphere of secrecy diminishes. Secrecy thrives in distance. It grows where no one is asking, no one is noticing, and no one seems emotionally available enough to handle the truth. But when parental involvement is steady, thoughtful, and relationally strong, secrecy loses one of its greatest advantages. A child who knows the adults in their life are engaged is less likely to believe they must carry fear alone. The more connected the household becomes, the less room hidden influence has to root itself quietly.

Trust grows where communication flows. Protection strengthens where observation is consistent. These are not separate realities—they work together. Communication without observation can become naïve. Observation without communication can become cold. But when both are present, the home becomes stronger. Children feel known. Patterns are noticed earlier. Concerns are addressed sooner. Boundaries make sense because they exist within a relationship rather than outside of it. The family becomes not only organized, but attentive.

Protective household structures also reduce the burden of last-minute decision-making. When a home already has clear rhythms, expectations, and lines of accountability, parents are less likely to be caught reacting blindly under pressure. Structure creates readiness. It means the family does not have to invent its standards in the middle of tension. It means children know what safety sounds like, what honesty feels like, and what family protection looks like before a crisis ever tests those realities.

This is especially important because danger often exploits disorder. Confusion creates openings. Inconsistency creates loopholes. Emotional unpredictability teaches children to hide rather than speak. A home with no rhythm, no structure, and no intentional communication may still love deeply, but that love may struggle to function protectively if the household environment remains undefined. Love must be organized into patterns strong enough to guard what it values.

The responsibility to guard the household environment rests with those entrusted to lead it. Parents are the watchmen. They are not merely participants in the atmosphere of the home; they are stewards of it. They set the tone. They establish patterns. They reinforce boundaries. They determine whether the home will drift into passivity or be built with intentional strength. Children should never be expected to create the structure that adults were assigned to provide. They need covering, not guesswork. They need guidance, not emotional vacancy. They need adults who understand that the condition of the household environment is not a small matter—it is one of the most powerful influences in their formation.

Parents are the watchmen.

That means they must remain awake.
They must remain observant.
They must remain spiritually alert.
They must remain emotionally available.
They must remain willing to build and maintain the structures that make the home safer, stronger, and clearer.

A watchtower without structure is only an idea.
A watchtower with structure becomes protection in motion.

And when protective household structures are established carefully, children grow in an atmosphere where truth is normal, communication is open, influence is examined, boundaries are clear, and safety is not left to chance.

THE MANDATE TO TRAIN AND GUARD

Proverbs 22:6 (KJV) declares, “Train up a child in the way he should go: and when he is old, he will not depart from it.” This command is not a casual suggestion—it is a divine mandate. It is not advice for parents to consider only when convenient, nor a gentle recommendation to be applied selectively. It is a charge from God concerning the shaping of a life. It speaks to responsibility, intentionality, and the holy seriousness of influence. A child’s development is never left untouched by what surrounds them. If truth does not shape them, something else will. If wisdom is not poured in, confusion will find room. If godly guidance is absent, competing influences will not remain idle.

Training requires intention, structure, and consistency. A child’s character does not develop by accident. Integrity is not inherited automatically. Discernment does not arise by chance. Moral clarity does not emerge simply because a child grows older. Without guidance, influence fills the vacuum. And whatever fills that vacuum will begin to form thought patterns, reactions, desires, loyalties, and beliefs. This is why parents cannot afford passivity. A child is always being taught by something—by what is modeled, what is tolerated, what is repeated, what is ignored, and what is celebrated. If the home does not disciple the child, the world will try to do it in its place.

Training is more than correction after wrongdoing. It is the patient, repeated shaping of the inner life. It is the work of forming conscience before crisis, wisdom before temptation, and conviction before compromise. It includes instruction, example, repetition, boundaries, explanation, correction, encouragement, and moral clarity. A parent is not merely managing behavior; a parent is cultivating direction. That means the work is deeper than getting a child to obey externally. The deeper work is teaching them why truth matters, why holiness matters, why discipline matters, why speech matters, why integrity matters, and why the fear of God is safer than the approval of people.

To train a child rightly, parents must understand that formation happens in ordinary moments. It happens at the table, in correction, during conflict, in routine conversation, through observed reactions, through answered questions, through repeated standards, and through the atmosphere of the home itself. Children are not shaped only by what they are formally taught. They are shaped by what they repeatedly experience. If parents preach self-control but model chaos, confusion enters. If they demand honesty but practice secrecy, trust weakens. If they teach holiness but normalize compromise, the child learns contradiction instead of conviction. Training, therefore, requires integrity between word and life. What is taught must be seen. What is commanded must be modeled. What is expected must be reinforced.

Parents are responsible not only for instruction but also for protection. This is where many fail by separating what Scripture keeps joined. Some focus on training while neglecting guarding. They give lessons but fail to regulate access. They speak the truth but do not examine influences. They teach values, but do not protect the environment in which those values must survive. But protection is not a lesser task than instruction. It is part of it. A child cannot be trained effectively while left exposed carelessly. The mind cannot retain a clear moral direction while the gates of the heart remain open to corrupting influence without oversight.

Authority within the home is not given for domination; it is given for stewardship. Biblical authority is not permission to control people harshly. It is our responsibility to serve, govern, protect, and guide what God has entrusted to us. A parent stands in authority not to crush the child's spirit, but to guard the child's development. Authority should create safety, not fear. It should provide structure, not intimidation. It should establish order, not oppression. When rightly exercised, authority becomes one of the child's greatest protections, because it keeps watch over what the child is not yet mature enough to discern for themselves.

To train is to guide. To guard is to protect. Both responsibilities belong to the parent.

To guide means to lead a child toward truth before falsehood becomes appealing. It means to direct them toward wisdom before foolishness becomes habitual. It means to walk with them through questions, pressures, temptations, disappointments, and decisions. It means helping them interpret life through righteousness rather than impulse. Guidance is not merely telling a child what not to do; it is helping them understand how to live. It is not enough to say no to danger if the child has never been shown the beauty of what is right.

To guard means to stand between the child and what seeks to corrupt, wound, confuse, seduce, or distort. It means regulating access. It means paying attention to friendships, environments, digital exposure, repeated patterns, and subtle shifts in atmosphere. It means recognizing that danger often enters gradually, not dramatically. It means refusing to leave children unguarded in places where their innocence, identity, or stability can be quietly eroded. Guarding is not suspicious of everything; it is vigilance about anything that threatens what God has assigned you to protect.

These two responsibilities—training and guarding—must remain joined. Training without guarding leaves instruction vulnerable. Guarding without training leaves the child externally protected but internally unprepared. A wise parent does both. They teach, and they watch. They instruct, and they regulate. They explain, and they intervene. They form, and they protect. They do not wait until a child is wounded to start building wisdom. They do not wait until compromise is visible to start setting boundaries.

This mandate also requires perseverance. Training is not a one-time conversation. Guarding is not a seasonal burst of concern. Children are not shaped by occasional seriousness. They are shaped by steady faithfulness. This means parents must resist the temptation to become lazy when things appear calm. Many dangers deepen during seasons when adults assume all is well. But a wise parent understands that the absence of a crisis is not a reason to sleep. It is an opportunity to build deeper strength.

There is also great hope in this mandate. The command of God reveals the value God places on early formation. It tells parents that their influence matters. Their consistency matters. Their prayers matter. Their words matter. Their boundaries matter. Their discernment matters. They are not powerless observers watching culture shape their children unchecked. They have been entrusted with real authority, real responsibility, and real opportunity to establish a stronger foundation than the surrounding world can provide.

This is why parenting must be approached with reverence. It is not merely the maintenance of childhood. It is the stewardship of destiny. It is the shaping of future men, future women, future marriages, future homes, future leaders, future disciples, and future generations. What is planted now may bear fruit long after the parent is no longer standing in the same daily role. This should not produce panic, but it should produce seriousness. Children must not be reared casually in a careless age.

So let every parent receive this command as sacred.

Train with patience.
Guard with vigilance.
Correct with love.
Lead with truth.
Protect with courage.
Stand with consistency.

Because a child's path will be shaped by what is planted, protected, and practiced in the years of formation. And when parents accept both halves of this mandate—to train and to guard—they become more than providers. They become watchful stewards of a life God has placed under their care.

HEARING THE CRY THAT IS NOT SPOKEN

Children communicate long before they possess the language to explain their pain. That is one of the most critical realities a parent, guardian, or caregiver must understand. A child may be wounded before they know the word wounded. They may feel fear before they can describe what frightened them. They may sense violation, discomfort, confusion, or dread long before they can organize those feelings into a sentence clear enough for an adult to understand. This is why listening to children requires more than hearing words. It requires discernment. It requires attentiveness. It requires adults who know how to listen beneath the surface.

Many parents themselves have not been taught how to tune in to that frequency. When I was a boy, I had a portable radio with a dial that had to be turned by hand. Today's generation knows little about that kind of listening. Back then, if I wanted to hear a particular station clearly, I had to tune in carefully. If I were off even a little bit, the transmission was not clear. There would be static, broken sound, interference, and distortion. The signal was there, but I could not hear it properly unless I found the right frequency.

That is the problem with many parents, guardians, and caregivers of children: they do not know how to tune in to the right frequency to hear the unspoken cry.

The signal is present.
The distress is real.
The communication is happening.
But the adult is listening at the wrong level.

Some adults only listen for words. Some only respond to obvious breakdowns. Some wait for a child to explain everything clearly, calmly, and directly, as though childhood pain arrives with adult vocabulary. But children do not always cry in language. Very often, they cry in behavior. They cry in tone. They cry in silence. They cry in avoidance. They cry in changed appetite, disrupted sleep, sudden fear, unusual clinginess, aggression, withdrawal, secrecy, or emotional shutdown. The signal is still there, but it must be interpreted.

Their behavior becomes their voice.

Genesis 21:17 records that God heard the child's voice even before Hagar fully understood what was happening. Heaven recognized distress that others might overlook. That should shake every attentive adult into deeper responsibility. God did not require polished speech before recognizing pain. He heard the cry beneath the crisis.

He discerned the need before anyone around the child could fully explain it. If Heaven is that attentive, then earthly guardians cannot afford to be careless.

Children communicate through signals.

A newborn cries.
A toddler clings.
A child withdraws.
A teenager isolates.

Behavior often reveals what words cannot express.

A newborn's cry may signal more than hunger. It may communicate discomfort, fear, overstimulation, or physical distress. A toddler who suddenly becomes excessively attached, regresses in behavior, or panics when separated may be communicating something deeper than simple mood. A child who once laughed freely but now avoids eye contact, resists touch, or becomes unusually guarded may be saying something with their body that they cannot yet say with their mouth. A teenager who isolates, becomes abruptly secretive, erupts in anger, or emotionally disappears may not be merely moody—they may be overwhelmed, confused, ashamed, or silently burdened.

The tragedy is not that children fail to communicate. The tragedy is that adults sometimes fail to interpret.

And when adults fail to interpret, children may remain trapped inside pain they do not yet know how to name. The silent cry becomes heavier when the child senses that their changes are being corrected but not understood, noticed but not explored, or dismissed as "just a phase."

That is how hidden suffering deepens. That is how fear learns to live underground. That is how children begin to believe that what they feel either does not matter or will not be heard correctly.

To hear the cry that is not spoken, a parent must become a student of their child. They must know the child's normal rhythm well enough to recognize when something shifts. They must pay attention to patterns, not just isolated moments. They must ask, What changed? What feels different? What is this behavior trying to say? A wise parent does not only ask, Why is my child acting this way? A wise parent also asks, What might my child be carrying that they cannot yet explain?

This kind of listening requires emotional maturity from the adult. If every troubling behavior is met only with irritation, punishment, or rushed correction, the deeper message may never be uncovered. Some behaviors do need discipline. But discernment asks whether discipline alone is enough.

A child may indeed need correction, but they may also need comfort, protection, reassurance, or investigation. Not every outburst is rebellion. Not every silence is peace. Not every withdrawal is an attitude. Some of what looks like disobedience is actually distress searching for language.

This is why tuning in matters.

A parent who is spiritually and emotionally present begins to hear things others miss. They notice when the child’s voice changes around certain people. They observe when joy disappears after a specific environment. They pay attention when fear appears without explanation. They recognize that clinginess, aggression, regression, avoidance, numbness, or sudden secrecy may all be frequencies of pain. The child is transmitting something. The question is whether the adult is tuned in carefully enough to hear it clearly.

This kind of attentiveness is not paranoia. It is stewardship.

Children need adults who do more than manage schedules and behavior. They need adults who notice when the signal is changing. They need adults who do not demand perfect articulation before offering protection. They need adults who understand that emotional pain often comes in fragments, and those fragments must be gathered with patience and discernment.

A child does not always say, "Something happened."
Sometimes they say it by not wanting to go back.
Sometimes they say it by growing quiet.
Sometimes they say it by clinging at the wrong moment.
Sometimes they say it by becoming angry, distant, or strangely fearful.

The signal is there.
The frequency is active.
The cry is being made.

The parents' responsibility is to tune in.

That means slowing down enough to notice. It means remaining near enough to observe. It means being wise enough to interpret. It means being humble enough to admit that a child's behavior may be carrying meaning deeper than what is visible at first glance. And it means being courageous enough to ask the next question rather than settle for the easiest explanation.

Because when a child's cry is heard early, harm can be interrupted sooner. When distress is interpreted wisely, isolation begins to weaken. When behavior is read with discernment, the child no longer has to carry pain alone while adults remain unaware.

To hear the cry that is not spoken is holy work. It is love made attentive. It is vigilance made compassionate. It is stewardship refusing to listen only to words while missing the voice of pain in everything else.

So tune in carefully.
Listen beyond the sentence.
Read the behavior.
Observe the shift.
Notice the silence.
Hear the child.

Because sometimes the most urgent cry in a home is the one no one has yet learned how to hear.

RECOGNIZING BEHAVIORAL WARNINGS

When a child leaves home joyful and returns withdrawn, quiet, fearful, or unusually subdued, something has shifted. Parents must not brush past that change as though it is meaningless. That change may be a warning. It may be a red flag blowing in the wind of abuse, pressure, manipulation, fear, or emotional distress. Just as a siren roars through a city or town, warning that trouble or a storm is coming, parents should have enough sense, sobriety, and spiritual attentiveness to recognize when something is different about their child. A wise parent does not need visible proof of disaster before taking a signal seriously. They understand that danger often announces itself through change before it ever reveals itself through confession.

Ignorance causes many children to suffer.

Not always because their parents do not love them, but because some adults do not know what to look for, do not know how to interpret what they see, or do not want to face what the signs may mean. A child's changed behavior is often the first alarm. It may be the earliest evidence that something has unsettled their inner world. Yet too many warning signs are minimized with phrases like "they're just tired," "they're being dramatic," "they're in a phase," or "that's just how teenagers are." But every change is not harmless, and every phase should not be accepted without discernment. Some of what adults casually dismiss as mood may actually be the child's only available signal that something is wrong.

Do not dismiss it.
Do not excuse it away.
Do not silence it with impatience.

Jesus said in Mark 4:24 (KJV), “Take heed what ye hear.” This includes the silent signals of distress. It includes what is communicated without a full explanation. It includes what shows up in body language, altered routine, emotional withdrawal, fear of certain people or places, unusual agitation, defensiveness, sudden secrecy, excessive clinginess, sleep disruption, appetite changes, and the heaviness that enters a child’s atmosphere when something has burdened them beyond what they can describe. To take heed means more than noticing. It means paying serious attention. It means refusing to let a warning pass by unexamined.

Behavioral change is communication.

Children often lack the vocabulary, confidence, or emotional maturity to describe pain directly. Many cannot yet separate fear from shame, discomfort from guilt, or confusion from danger. So what they cannot yet say with words, they may reveal through behavior. A child who suddenly avoids eye contact, no longer wants to be around a certain person, becomes uncharacteristically aggressive, starts wetting the bed again, cries more easily, stops laughing freely, or grows quiet in places where they were once open may be communicating something far deeper than attitude. A teenager who isolates, becomes unusually irritable, abruptly changes the way they dress, guards their phone obsessively, or shows distress in certain situations may also be signaling that something inside has shifted.

Parents must learn to see these things not as random interruptions but as possible indicators.

This does not mean every behavioral change proves abuse. It does mean every significant change deserves attention. Wisdom does not leap recklessly to conclusions, but neither does it relax carelessly into denial. A discerning parent understands that pattern matters. Timing matters. Context matters. A single hard day may not reveal much. But repeated changes, especially after contact with certain people, places, events, or environments, must not be ignored. The watchful parent asks, "What changed?" When did it change? What happened before the change? Why does this child seem unlike themselves?

Spiritual discernment must accompany parental observation.

Observation alone may notice the behavior, but discernment begins to ask what may be beneath it. Discernment helps a parent understand that children are not always disobedient when they are distressed. Sometimes fear looks like withdrawal. Sometimes confusion looks like anger. Sometimes shame looks like silence. Sometimes trauma looks like attitude. The spiritually attentive parent knows that outward behavior is not always the full story. They pray, they listen, they watch carefully, and they refuse to let discipline become a substitute for investigation when the signs suggest something deeper may be wrong.

A prudent parent does not live in paranoia but in awareness.

Paranoia imagines danger everywhere and loses clarity. Awareness notices what is real and responds with wisdom. Awareness does not panic at every change, but it does not ignore what is significant. Awareness learns the child's normal rhythms well enough to recognize when something has become abnormal. Awareness does not need perfect evidence to begin paying attention. It understands that the earlier a signal is taken seriously, the greater the chance of interrupting harm before it deepens.

Proverbs 14:15 (KJV) declares, "The simple believeth every word: but the prudent man looketh well to his going." Blind trust is not biblical trust. Scripture does not praise careless confidence. It praises prudence. Prudence observes. Prudence asks questions. Prudence verifies. Prudence understands that not everyone with a pleasant face has righteous intentions, not every familiar environment is safe, and not every child who says "I'm fine" is actually untroubled. Prudence does not insult trust; it protects trust from becoming naïve.

This is one of the great responsibilities of a parent: to know the child well enough to recognize when they are no longer moving within their normal emotional rhythm. A parent should know when their child's laughter sounds forced, when their silence feels heavy, when their eyes are carrying something they have not said, and when a change in behavior points to more than a temporary mood. That knowledge does not come from occasional interest. It comes from involvement. It comes from listening often, observing regularly, and staying close enough to notice the shift before the damage becomes more visible.

Ignorance is dangerous because it often cooperates with harm without intending to. A parent may say, “I didn’t know,” but the child may have been communicating all along—just not in a form the adult had trained themselves to hear. This is why awareness must be cultivated.

Parents must learn to recognize the warning signs, not after the crisis has broken open, but while the alarm is still sounding softly in the early stages. They must train themselves to hear what the behavior is saying before the child has words strong enough to explain it clearly.

So when a child returns differently, do not rush past it.
When a child becomes suddenly quiet, pay attention.
When fear appears where ease once lived, lean in.
When silence settles where joy once moved freely, investigate.

Because some of the earliest warnings of hidden harm do not come with a full explanation, they come through changed behavior, altered presence, and quiet signals that ask to be noticed before it is too late. And the parent who learns to recognize those warnings is far more prepared to protect what God has placed under their care.

❖ A WARNING AND A CALL TO CONVICTION ❖

Confronting Concealed Dangers

✦

The sacred duty of protecting our children is not sentimental. It is spiritual warfare. It is not a soft subject for shallow reflection, nor is it merely an emotional appeal to concerned parents. It is a matter of divine responsibility, holy stewardship, and urgent obedience. Innocence is contested territory. The heart of a child is not growing in a harmless world. It is being approached, shaped, tested, courted, and targeted by influences that do not fear God, do not honor purity, and do not value the soul of a child. This is why protection cannot remain casual, emotional, or occasional. It must become deliberate, watchful, and unflinching.

Complacency invites compromise. Delay invites damage. Silence invites darkness to stay longer than it should. Every time a warning sign is minimized, every time discernment is silenced to preserve comfort, every time a parent chooses ease over investigation, danger gains room to work. Harm does not always begin with a scream. Often it begins with what adults explain away. It begins with subtle shifts, quiet discomfort, repeated uneasiness, altered behavior, unusual attachment, unnecessary secrecy, and the dangerous habit of calling obvious warning signs "nothing serious." But what is ignored does not become harmless. What is tolerated does not remain small. What is left unchecked often grows teeth.

Parents must decide now: will we be passive observers or vigilant guardians? This is not a minor choice. It is a dividing line. Passive observers wait until the evidence is overwhelming, the wound is visible, the child is already carrying trauma, and the damage can no longer be hidden. Vigilant guardians move sooner. They pay attention when something feels wrong. They ask when others remain silent. They investigate what others excuse. They confront what others avoid. They do not need public consensus before they become privately alerted. They understand that by the time everyone can see the danger clearly, the child may already have suffered far too much.

God entrusted these lives to us. He hears what we may miss. He sees what we may overlook. He holds us accountable for what we ignore. That truth should shake every parent, guardian, and spiritual leader to the core. Children are not casual assignments. They are sacred trusts. They are not ours to neglect, expose, or mishandle through laziness, denial, fear of conflict, or emotional passivity. Heaven is not indifferent to the safety of children, and Heaven is not blind to the condition of those appointed to guard them. God is not measuring how calm a household appears on the outside. He is measuring whether the watchman is awake.

This is not merely about rearing children. It is about guarding destiny. It is about protecting what is still being formed. It is about shielding innocence before it is fractured, trust before it is violated, identity before it is distorted, and conscience before it is numbed. A child's future is shaped not only by what they are taught, but by what they are protected from, what is allowed near them, and whether the adults over them take their role seriously enough to stand watch without growing soft, sleepy, or careless.

Let every parent rise to the wall. Let every guardian sharpen discernment. Let every household become a protected gate. Let the home no longer be governed by assumption. Let it no longer be lulled by familiarity. Let it no longer be weakened by spiritual passivity, emotional inconsistency, or the fear of making others uncomfortable. Let the wall be reinforced with prayer. Let the gate be guarded with boundaries. Let the atmosphere be governed by truth. Let the child know by repeated evidence: I am not alone. I am seen. I am heard. I am protected here.

This responsibility is weighty because the consequences of neglect are weighty. A child should not have to carry wounds because the adult assigned to protect them was too trusting to question, too distracted to notice, too intimidated to confront, too lazy to follow through, or too eager to preserve relationships at the expense of safety. That is not a light failure. That is grievous negligence. No child should suffer because a guardian chose comfort over courage. No child should bleed inwardly because an adult refused to disturb the peace of a room where danger was quietly growing.

The time for vigilance is now, before the pattern deepens, before the silence hardens. Now, before the wound becomes hidden history. Now, before the child learns to stop trying to communicate. Now, before the parent becomes so used to compromise that discernment no longer stirs. This is the hour to wake up. This is the hour to pay attention. This is the hour to stop calling passivity peace. This is the hour to stop calling delay wisdom. This is the hour to stop mistaking blind trust for faith.

Faithful parents watch. Faithful guardians pray. Faithful watchmen listen. Faithful stewards act. So let conviction rise where complacency once lived. Let holy courage overtake emotional laziness. Let every excuse die under the weight of what is at stake. Let no title, no family connection, no ministry image, no social ease, and no human relationship outrank the protection of a child. Stand watch. Stand sober. Stand firm. Stand without apology. Stand before God as one who understands that innocence is sacred, children are entrusted, and watchmen will answer because this is not merely about whether evil exists. It does. The question is whether you are awake enough, brave enough, and faithful enough to confront it before it reaches what God placed under your care.

Dangers often reside where we feel most comfortable. That is what makes them concealed. They do not always emerge from dark alleys, unfamiliar streets, or visibly threatening environments. They often sit in settings that people have already labeled safe. They move through familiarity. They hide inside routine. They pass beneath social comfort, family connection, religious appearance, and repeated access. This is why parents must not confuse what is common with what is secure. A place can be familiar and still be dangerous. A person can be known and still be unsafe. Others can trust an environment and still contain a hidden threat.

Living rooms. Playdates. Family gatherings. School corridors. Ministry environments. These are the very places where many parents lower their guard because the surroundings feel normal. Yet concealed danger often persists in seemingly normal spaces because adults stop asking questions once familiarity settles in. Familiarity does not guarantee safety. Repeated exposure does not prove righteousness. Relationship does not cancel the need for discernment. Some of the deepest wounds children carry began in environments that adults called harmless, simply because they felt socially comfortable.

This is one of the hardest truths for many adults to accept: danger does not always come from strangers. Sometimes it comes from people whose names are already in the family conversation. Sometimes it comes from those whose presence has been normalized for years. Sometimes it comes from those whose position, title, history, or blood connection causes others to lower their guard. Some fathers violate their daughters. Some mothers violate their sons. Some uncles violate family members. Some cousins, siblings, stepparents, grandparents, family friends, church workers, mentors, and trusted adults misuse access that should have been more carefully guarded. These realities are grievous, but they must be faced honestly. Protection cannot be built on fantasy. It must be built on truth.

Many children have suffered not because no one loved them, but because the adults around them could not imagine danger wearing a familiar face. They believed a relationship guaranteed safety. They believed family status guaranteed purity. They believed religious involvement guaranteed moral restraint. But wickedness does not always stand outside the circle. Sometimes it hides within it. That is why parents must never surrender discernment to titles, traditions, long history, shared blood, or public respectability. Relationship does not equal righteousness. Familiarity does not equal safety. Repeated access does not equal innocence.

Concealed danger thrives where adults refuse to think soberly. It survives where people protect the comfort of the family image more fiercely than the child's actual safety. It deepens where hard questions are considered offensive, where patterns are ignored because "that's family," and where discomfort is silenced because no one wants to expose what might disturb the household's structure or the community's reputation.

But a child's body is not the price that should ever be paid to preserve appearances. A child's safety must outweigh family pride, social comfort, ministry image, and every other human concern that tempts people to stay silent.

This is why concealed danger is so dangerous: it often lives in plain sight while the adults around it keep calling it normal. A child may feel afraid around a relative while the family keeps inviting that relative into unrestricted access. A teenager may become withdrawn after a gathering while everyone else praises how "wonderful" the environment was. A small child may resist being left with a certain adult while the people around them keep saying, "Stop acting strange," because they trust the adult more than they are willing to study the child. This is where failure becomes devastating. Adults often assume the child is misreading the situation while refusing to consider that the child may actually be detecting something the adults have normalized.

Parents must confront this reality without flinching. A hidden threat is not made harmless because it shares your last name. It is not purified because it attends church. It is not made trustworthy because it has been around for years. Evil has never required unfamiliarity to operate. Sometimes it hides best where no one wants to believe it could be present.

That is why the role of the parent requires both love and sober judgment. Love must not become blind. Compassion must not become careless. A parent who says, "I know them," but refuses to evaluate patterns may be opening the door to unnecessary harm. The issue is not whether a person is known. The issue is whether access is being governed wisely. Every person who gains proximity to a child should remain subject to boundaries, transparency, and accountability. No one should be above examination. No one should be beyond question. No one should have automatic, unquestioned access simply because the adults in the room feel comfortable.

Children depend on adults to do what they cannot yet do for themselves. They cannot always identify predatory intent. They cannot always interpret manipulation. They cannot always explain why someone makes them uncomfortable. They often only know that something feels wrong. That is why adults must not train children to ignore discomfort for the sake of politeness. Nor should adults ignore a child's resistance simply because the environment appears familiar. A child's discomfort should be investigated, not mocked.

Their hesitation should be noticed, not overridden. Their behavioral changes should be interpreted, not dismissed.

Confronting concealed dangers also means confronting the lies adults often tell themselves. "It could never happen here." "They would never do that." "We've known them too long." "They're family." "They're in leadership." "They're respected." These are the kinds of phrases that have protected abusers and exposed children. These phrases may feel reassuring to adults, but they have often become shields behind which harm was allowed to continue. Wisdom must be stronger than emotional denial.

A spiritually sober parent understands that concealment is part of how evil works. Darkness survives by hiding. It depends on silence, confusion, fear, and disbelief. It prefers environments where no one asks follow-up questions, where warning signs are minimized, and where children are expected to adjust rather than adults being required to answer. That is why confronting concealed dangers requires more than concern—it requires courage. It requires adults who are willing to inspect what others excuse, question what others defend, and interrupt what others prefer to leave untouched.

Parents must therefore build a home where hidden things lose their power. A child should know that no relationship outranks their safety. No adult's feelings outrank their voice. No family connection outranks truth. No title outranks accountability. No ministry appearance outranks protection. These convictions must not merely be felt inwardly; they must be demonstrated through boundaries, presence, questions, and action.

This must be said with force and without apology: if a child cannot depend on the parent—the one appointed by God to protect them—then something foundational has failed. A child should not have to suffer because the adult assigned to guard them was too passive, too distracted, too intimidated, too trusting, or too emotionally careless to do what protection required. If a parent consistently ignores warning signs, refuses to investigate what feels wrong, protects the comfort of adults over the safety of the child, or repeatedly leaves the child exposed to preventable harm, that is not merely poor judgment. That is a failure of stewardship. And until that parent repents, wakes up, and does the work protection demands, they remain in dangerous neglect.

That language is weighty because the matter is weighty. Parenthood is not a decorative role. It is not a sentimental title. It is not fulfilled by provision alone. It is not enough to feed a child, house a child, and claim love for a child while remaining careless with their safety. A parent is called to more than affection. A parent is called to guardianship. To neglect that duty is not minor. It is serious. It is destructive. It leaves the child to bear burdens the adult was supposed to help prevent. No child should have to live with wounds that could have been interrupted if the parent had been watchful, sober, and willing to act.

Parents must carefully examine their child's emotional state. The child's emotions often reveal what the child's words cannot yet explain. If a child becomes unusually quiet, fearful, withdrawn, or agitated after being somewhere, investigate gently but firmly. Do not wave it away. Do not excuse it because the people involved are known. Do not call it moodiness without paying attention. Do not label it an attitude before asking what may have unsettled the child. Emotional change is often the earliest surface sign of hidden pressure, hidden fear, or hidden injury.

Ask questions without intimidation. Create space for honesty. A child who is afraid of the parent's reaction may bury what should be revealed. A child who feels rushed, mocked, or dismissed may retreat into silence even if danger is already near. This is why the tone of the parent matters. Protection does not require a parent to become soft in conviction, but it does require steadiness. The child must sense: If I tell the truth here, I will be heard. I will be taken seriously. I will be protected.

Children speak more freely where they feel safe to be believed. That safety does not come from speeches alone. It comes from a pattern. It comes from repeated evidence that the parent listens, notices, follows up, and does not make the child regret telling the truth. The home must become a place where honesty does not create danger for the child, but relief. A child should know that speaking up will bring help, not humiliation.

Protection requires proactive awareness. Know where your child is. Know who your child is with. Know the environments they enter. Know behavioral changes immediately. These are not excessive demands. They are baseline responsibilities. A parent does not honor their role by remaining vague about their child's whereabouts, influences, or emotional condition. A child is not protected by parental assumption. They are protected by parental awareness. A wise parent does not surrender oversight in the name of convenience, social ease, or false trust. They remain involved enough to notice what has shifted and alert enough to respond before hidden danger deepens.

Know where your child is means more than knowing a location. It means understanding the structure, supervision, and atmosphere of the place. Know who your child is with means more than knowing names. It means paying attention to character, boundaries, patterns, and access. Know the environments they enter means evaluating what those spaces normalize, permit, and conceal. Know behavioral changes immediately means refusing to wait until the child breaks down publicly before taking privately visible signals seriously.

Guarding a child is not an overreaction. It is obedience. It is obedience to the responsibility God placed on the adult. It is obedience to the call to watch, to discern, to stand at the gate of the home, and to refuse passivity while innocence is at stake. The world may call vigilance extreme. Careless people may call it unnecessary. Comfortable people may call it disruptive. But when Heaven entrusts a child to a parent, protection is not a negotiable style of parenting. It is a sacred duty.

Confronting concealed dangers means being willing to see what others prefer to ignore. It means refusing to let relationship, familiarity, or appearance dull the edge of discernment. It means being willing to ask the second question, make the awkward call, restrict access, change the environment, or confront the pattern when something feels wrong. It means understanding that by the time danger becomes obvious to everyone, it may already have been quietly at work for some time.

A home that confronts concealed dangers refuses naïveté. It refuses emotional laziness. It refuses the false peace that comes from pretending what is possible could never happen nearby. Instead, it chooses the harder and holier path: to stay awake, to stay discerning, and to remain willing to protect a child even when doing so disrupts assumptions, relationships, and appearances.

Because concealed dangers are not defeated by comfort. They are exposed by truth. They are interrupted by vigilance. They are confronted by adults who love children enough to believe that safety must be established—not assumed.

So let the parent hear this plainly: wake up, pay attention, and do your job. Not with panic, but with conviction. Not with cruelty, but with courage. Not with denial, but with disciplined awareness. The child under your care should not have to suffer because the adult assigned to protect them refused to stand watch.

Stand up.
Look closely.
Ask carefully.
Listen deeply.
Act quickly.

Because concealed danger is interrupted not by wishful thinking, but by faithful guardians who refuse to abandon their post.

❖ SPIRITUAL WARNING ❖

A Warning From The Wall

Confronting Concealed Dangers

✦

There is a difference between being informed and being awakened. Many have heard the statistics. Many have read the reports. Many have listened to testimonies. Many can repeat the language of concern, quote the dangers, and acknowledge that the world is changing. Yet awareness without action is deception. Information alone does not protect a child. Concern alone does not guard a household. Knowledge that does not move the heart becomes hardened ground. It produces the illusion of responsibility without the fruit of obedience. A person may know much and remain asleep at the gate.

This is not merely a cultural issue. It is a spiritual confrontation. It is not only about trends, policies, technologies, or social decay, though all of those matter. It is about the unseen battle surrounding access, innocence, identity, and influence. It is about whether the gates of the home, the heart, the mind, and the atmosphere are being watched with sobriety or neglected through comfort. There are forces in every generation that seek access to innocence. They study weakness. They exploit distraction. They search for openings where vigilance has grown casual and where guardians have become more reactive than watchful.

Evil does not require an invitation. It only needs an unattended gate. It does not need to be welcomed ceremonially. It only needs a door left unwatched, a boundary left vague, a pattern left unexplored, a warning sign left unanswered, or a parent too tired, too busy, too trusting, or too emotionally disengaged to take the shift seriously. Darkness often advances not because adults desired it, but because they underestimated how quietly it can move when no one is standing at the wall with clear eyes and a sober spirit.

And unattended gates often result from spiritual fatigue.

Parents become busy. Leaders become distracted. Communities become comfortable. Routines multiply. Demands increase.

Screens consume attention. Emotional exhaustion lowers spiritual alertness. Prayer becomes rushed. Discernment becomes dulled. Hard questions are postponed. What once would have caused immediate concern is being explained away because people are too tired to investigate, too uncomfortable to confront, or too accustomed to the atmosphere to notice it has changed.

And in that subtle shift, the watchtower grows quiet.

That quietness is dangerous. Not because silence is always sinful, but because there is a kind of silence that signals neglect. There is a silence that means no one is watching closely enough, praying deeply enough, or listening carefully enough. There is a silence on the wall that allows subtle compromise to keep moving without interruption. And silence on the wall invites intrusion. What is not challenged often continues. What is not inspected often deepens. What is not guarded often becomes exposed.

This is why spiritual fatigue must be taken seriously. A tired watchman is still a watchman. A weary guardian is still accountable for the post. Fatigue may explain why alertness weakened, but it does not make the child less vulnerable. Busyness may explain distraction, but it does not reduce the seriousness of what slips through neglected gates. Comfort may explain why discernment softened, but it does not make concealment harmless. This is why renewal is not optional for those called to guard others. Parents and guardians must fight to remain spiritually awake. They must refuse the drift into casual oversight. They must recognize that a household does not remain guarded by accident. It stays guarded because somebody keeps standing watch.

Protection requires courage. Not theoretical courage. Not emotional language about being strong. Real courage. The courage to ask what others would rather leave alone. The courage to restrict access when others say you are doing too much. The courage to question what has become normal.

The courage to believe a child's discomfort over an adult's polished appearance. The courage to challenge the atmosphere of the home, the family, the ministry, the friendship circle, or the digital world when something feels spiritually wrong. Courage in this context is not loudness. It is faithfulness with a backbone.

You may be misunderstood. You may be labeled extreme. You may be accused of overreacting. People who do not understand vigilance often resent it because it disrupts ease. It interrupts convenience. It questions assumptions. It refuses to let appearances settle the matter. But better to be called vigilant than to live with regret. Better to be criticized for watchfulness than to sit later with the crushing knowledge that a warning was felt, a signal was seen, and action was delayed because someone feared looking too serious.

Parents and guardians must settle this within themselves now: protecting a child will sometimes require making others uncomfortable. It may strain relationships. It may disturb social routines. It may expose hidden things. It may require saying no when others expected yes. It may require reevaluating people, environments, programs, habits, and access points that others assumed were safe. But discomfort is a small price compared to the devastation of neglected warning.

You are not merely rearing children. You are guarding destinies. You are not simply managing schedules, meals, moods, and milestones. You are standing in stewardship over lives that are still being formed. You are guarding trust before it is fractured, identity before it is distorted, innocence before it is exploited, conscience before it is numbed, and future stability before it is burdened with preventable wounds. This is why your role cannot be casual. The stakes are too high, the influences too active, and the consequences too lasting.

To guard a destiny means to understand that what is allowed now may echo later. What is ignored now may surface later. What is protected now may strengthen later. A child who grows up under clear covering, honest communication, consistent boundaries, and spiritually awake guardians is being given more than safety in the moment. That child is being given strength for the future. That is why the wall matters. That is why the watchtower matters. That is why this warning matters.

Stand on the wall. Not occasionally, but consistently. Not fearfully, but faithfully. Not as one performing suspicion, but as one carrying responsibility before God. Remain alert. Guard relentlessly. Watch the atmosphere. Watch the access points. Watch the changes in the child. Watch the drift in the home. Watch your own spiritual condition.

Watch what enters through the eye gate, the ear gate, the digital gate, the relational gate, and the emotional gate. Keep the wall active. Keep the gate guarded. Keep the house covered.

Heaven is watching the watchmen.

That is the part many forget. God is not only observing what evil attempts. He is also observing how those entrusted with children respond to what they see, sense, excuse, confront, and allow. Heaven watches whether the guardian is awake. Heaven watches whether the watchman is sober. Heaven watches whether the one assigned to the wall has grown passive, prayerless, distracted, or numb. And Heaven also watches when a parent rises in courage, strengthens the gate, sharpens discernment, and refuses to let comfort replace conviction.

So let this warning do more than stir emotion. Let it awaken posture. Let it call the weary watchman back to the wall. Let it confront the comfortable guardian. Let it strengthen the praying parent. Let it shake loose every excuse that has made negligence feel acceptable.

Because children are listening.
Because danger is patient.
Because access is active.
Because the wall must not go quiet.
And because the watchman who stays awake may interrupt what others would only mourn later.

CHAPTER THREE
THE ROLE OF THE WATCHMAN IN THE FAMILY

Accountability, Discernment, and Authority in the Family

The Biblical Watchman

In Ezekiel 33:7 (KJV), the Lord declares, "So thou, O son of man, I have set thee a watchman unto the house of Israel." This was not a symbolic position or a decorative title. It was a serious appointment carrying moral weight, immediate responsibility, and grave consequences. The watchman stood on the wall, scanning the horizon, discerning approaching danger before it reached the gates. He did not wait for the enemy to enter the city before responding. He watched early. He warned clearly. He remained alert while others slept. If he saw the threat and failed to sound the alarm, the blood of the people would be required at his hand. Scripture presents that role with soberness because God intended it to be understood as a matter of accountability, not convenience.

The role of the watchman was not passive observation. It was an active responsibility. He was not assigned to admire the view from the wall. He was assigned to protect what lay behind it. His eyes were not for curiosity; they were for discernment. His position was not for status; it was for service. A watchman was valuable not because he stood high, but because he stayed awake. He recognized that danger often first appeared as movement in the distance, a subtle shift on the horizon, a pattern that seemed small until it drew closer. That is why his work required sobriety, endurance, and an unwillingness to be lulled by temporary quiet.

In the family, parents occupy that sacred position. They are not merely caregivers—they are guardians. They are not simply providers—they are protectors. God has placed them at the spiritual gate of their household, and with that placement comes accountability. Parenthood is not merely the management of daily needs. It is not exhausted by food on the table, clothes on the back, and bills paid on time. A parent is called to watch over atmosphere, access, influence, relationships, speech, patterns, and the unseen pressures that gather around the formation of a child. To parent biblically is to accept that someone must stand at the wall of the home, and God has not assigned that task to the child.

A watchman does not assume that peace guarantees safety. He does not relax because danger is not immediately visible. He remains alert. He studies patterns. He pays attention to shifts. He understands that threats often appear gradual before they become obvious. What is dangerous does not always arrive dramatically.

Sometimes it advances through repetition, normalization, and tolerated compromise. Sometimes it moves through relationships that feel familiar, media that appears harmless, emotional changes that seem temporary, and influences that do not raise alarm until they have already gained ground. A watchman knows that what is subtle can still be serious. He is not waiting for panic to tell him something is wrong. He is trained to observe before panic becomes necessary.

Likewise, parents must reject complacency. The absence of a visible crisis does not equal the absence of danger. Cultural pressures, digital influences, relational manipulation, and subtle moral compromise approach quietly. If the watchman is distracted, infiltration becomes easy. The family can remain busy, outwardly functional, and socially active while something corrosive is slowly entering the atmosphere of the home. A child can still smile while confusion grows. A routine can still continue while hidden influences deepen. This is why biblical watchfulness must be deeper than surface peace. Some homes are quiet but not guarded. Some families are active but not attentive. Some parents are loving but not watchful. Scripture does not call the watchman merely to care. It calls him to discern.

This discernment must be developed, not assumed. A biblical watchman learns to ask not only what is happening, but what is emerging. He notices patterns in behavior. He tracks shifts in emotional tone. He pays attention to what repeatedly enters the home through screens, relationships, language, and environment.

He understands that the enemy often works through gradual erosion rather than instant collapse. The wall is not only threatened by obvious attackers; long neglect, small breaches, and overlooked compromise also weaken it.

In the same way, a family is not only endangered by dramatic crises, but also by what is repeatedly excused, tolerated, or left unexplored.

To be a watchman in the family also means understanding that authority is not given for domination but for stewardship. Biblical authority is not permission to control harshly. It is a burden to guard faithfully. The parents' authority should create safety, not intimidation. It should establish order, not fear. It should protect the vulnerable, not silence them. When authority functions rightly, it becomes a shield. When it is absent, passive, or careless, the child is left exposed to voices and influences they are not yet mature enough to interpret. A child should not have to become their own watchman while the adult appointed by God to guard them remains emotionally absent, spiritually dull, or chronically distracted.

There is also a relational dimension to watchfulness that many overlook. A parent cannot watch well from a distance. Watchfulness requires nearness. It requires enough involvement to notice what has changed, enough presence to recognize when something feels misaligned, and enough trust in the relationship so that the child does not feel alone with what they are carrying.

The watchman is not only scanning the outside horizon; he is also paying attention to what is happening inside the gates. In family life, that means a parent must learn the child's rhythms well enough to recognize when silence is heavier than usual, when behavior communicates more than attitude, and when fear is trying to speak through patterns rather than words.

This is where accountability becomes deeply personal. God does not merely ask whether parents loved their children emotionally. He also asks whether they guarded what was entrusted to them. Did they pay attention? Did they act when something felt wrong? Did they question what others excused? Did they remain awake at the wall, or did they surrender the post to busyness, distraction, convenience, and the false comfort of assuming all was well? The office of the watchman is not honored by intention alone. It is honored by faithfulness.

The Biblical watchman teaches us that a quiet horizon is not permission to sleep. It is a call to remain prepared. He teaches us that responsibility increases with assignment. He teaches us that discernment is not suspicion but spiritual intelligence under God. He teaches us that warning is an act of love, not extremism. And he teaches us that what is behind the wall is precious enough to require someone willing to stand between it and whatever may be moving toward it.

For this reason, parents must not treat watchfulness as optional or seasonal. It is part of the sacred office of family leadership. The home needs someone who sees, someone who listens, someone who discerns, someone who acts, and someone who refuses to abandon the wall simply because the day looks calm. The watchman does not wait for disaster to prove the value of vigilance. His value is proven in what never reaches the gates because he was awake enough to see it coming.

That is the biblical watchman.
And that is the calling resting upon the family.

To watch is to love with eyes open.
To guard is to care with responsibility attached.
To stand at the wall is to accept that the peace of the household must be protected, not presumed.

So let every parent take their place with sobriety. Let every guardian understand that their role is not symbolic. Let every household recognize that someone must remain alert at the gate. Because if the watchman sleeps, danger does not stop moving. But if the watchman stays awake, what approaches can be recognized early, resisted wisely, and kept from reaching what God has placed behind the wall.

PARENTS AS GUARDIANS OF THE HOUSEHOLD WALL

Parents stand on the wall of their household. Their presence establishes protection, and their vigilance preserves stability. A child may not understand the language of guardianship, but they live beneath its effects every day. They feel the difference between a home that is being watched and a home that is merely being occupied. They sense when boundaries are strong, when adults are attentive, when truth is taken seriously, and when their environment is being governed with care rather than left to drift. When the watchman stands faithfully, the family remains secure—not because danger ceases to exist, but because danger is less free to move unchallenged.

Children depend upon the alertness of the one assigned to guard them. They rely upon the awareness, judgment, and discernment of the parent. They are not yet mature enough to interpret every influence, question every motive, or identify every hidden threat. Much of what adults take for granted as obvious is still unclear to a child. What seems harmless may not be. What appears kind may not be safe. What feels uncomfortable may be real, even if the child cannot explain why. This is why the parents' alertness matters so deeply. The child is not meant to carry the burden of watchfulness alone. God assigned that weight to the adult.

The watchman's responsibility is not to control every circumstance but to observe, discern, and respond before harm gains access. This is an important distinction. Parents are not called to become fearful tyrants trying to dominate every movement in the child's life. They are called to remain attentive enough to recognize patterns, sober enough to evaluate what is approaching, and courageous enough to act when something is misaligned. Watchfulness is not control. It is stewardship with open eyes. It understands that protection often happens in the early stages—before the door is opened too wide, before the influence settles too deeply, before the child learns to normalize what should have been interrupted.

The safety of a household does not depend upon wishful thinking. It depends upon watchfulness. A guarded home is not accidental; it is the result of intentional leadership. It is built by adults who know that love must be organized into boundaries, prayer, observation, consistency, and follow-through. Hope alone does not guard a family. Good intentions alone do not preserve innocence. A parent may sincerely want the best for the child and still leave them vulnerable through passivity, distraction, overconfidence, or the refusal to examine what feels wrong. Safety does not come from assuming that all is well. It comes from staying awake enough to know when something is not.

When parents embrace this responsibility, the household environment becomes stable. Stability is one of the great fruits of faithful guardianship. Children live differently when they know the wall is being watched. They become more confident because structure communicates safety. They speak more freely because they know someone is listening. They rest more deeply because they sense that protection is not random or occasional. In such a home, boundaries remain clear. Influences are filtered. Access is examined. Correction has purpose. Communication has space. Protection becomes normal rather than reactionary.

That phrase matters: protection becomes normal rather than reactionary.

A reactionary home waits until the crisis appears. A guarded home builds in advance. It does not wait until secrecy has already deepened before talking about honesty. It does not wait until digital corruption has already begun to shape the child before establishing oversight. It does not wait until an unhealthy relationship has already gained emotional leverage before asking questions. It does not wait until a child breaks down visibly before paying attention to emotional changes. Watchful parents understand that the wall is strengthened long before the attack becomes obvious. That is why daily attentiveness matters. That is why routines matter. That is why presence matters. That is why follow-up matters.

A household wall is not only weakened by obvious rebellion. It is also weakened by subtle neglect. When parents stop observing, access expands. When they stop asking questions, patterns go unexamined.

When they stop maintaining boundaries, lines blur. When they stop tending the home's atmosphere, outside influences begin to shape it more than the truth within it. This is often how vulnerability grows—not through one dramatic collapse, but through a long series of unattended moments.

But when the watchman grows inattentive, the wall weakens.

Boundaries blur.
Influences enter unchecked.
Confusion grows quietly.

These things rarely happen all at once. Boundaries blur first in small ways—exceptions become habits, oversight becomes irregular, conversations become shallower, discomfort goes unexplored, and spiritual sensitivity dulls beneath routine. Then influences enter unchecked. Voices begin shaping the child that the parent has not examined. Digital content, friendships, attitudes, emotional patterns, and quiet distortions begin to take up space within the child's inner world. And then confusion grows quietly. The child may no longer know what is safe, what is normal, what is true, or what can be trusted. That confusion is dangerous because it often develops before anyone names it.

The difference is vigilance.

Vigilance keeps lines clear before they blur.
Vigilance notices influences before they settle in.
Vigilance interrupts confusion before it becomes a culture in the home.

This is why the wall matters so much. Parents as guardians of the household wall are not merely standing against threats; they are preserving clarity within the home. They are maintaining an atmosphere where a child knows what truth sounds like, what safety feels like, and where help can be found when something feels wrong. They are making it more difficult for hidden things to thrive and more likely that small warning signs will be noticed before they become major wounds.

A parent guarding the wall must therefore remain spiritually awake, emotionally available, mentally engaged, and morally steady. Children need more than parents who are physically present.

They need parents who are present enough to notice. Presence without attentiveness can still miss danger. But a watchful parent studies the household's condition. They pay attention to the atmosphere. They notice shifts in the child. They regulate access. They ask follow-up questions. They remain involved in the environments, patterns, and relationships that shape the family's life.

Parents must also understand that the wall is not guarded once and for all. It must be guarded continually. Every season of childhood brings different threats, different pressures, and different forms of access. What guards a toddler is not the same as what guards a teenager, but the principle remains the same: someone must stay at the wall. Someone must remain aware. Someone must filter what comes near. Someone must resist the temptation to assume that because one season passed safely, the next requires less watchfulness.

That someone is the parent.

To be the guardian of the household wall is to accept that the child's stability is tied, in part, to your steadiness. It is to understand that your vigilance helps preserve their peace. Your discernment helps preserve their clarity. Your courage helps preserve their safety. And your willingness to remain awake at the post may keep danger from ever gaining the access it sought.

So let the parent not grow casual.
Let the guardian not grow dull.
Let the wall not go unwatched.

Because families remain stronger where watchmen stay faithful, and when parents stand seriously in their God-given role as guardians of the household wall, the home becomes more than a place of residence—it becomes a place of ordered protection, stable truth, and intentional covering.

DISCERNMENT VS SUSPICION

The parental watchman must develop spiritual discernment. Without it, a parent may either become careless and miss danger or become fearful and misread everything. Discernment is not suspicion—it is sensitivity guided by wisdom. It is the ability to recognize misalignment before damage becomes visible. It is not driven by panic, prejudice, or imagination. It is shaped by prayer, sharpened by truth, steadied by observation, and governed by responsibility.

This distinction matters deeply because many parents struggle at one of two extremes. Some are so relaxed that they explain away every warning sign until the situation has already deepened. Others become so anxious that every discomfort is treated as proof of the worst. Neither extreme protects well. Suspicion without wisdom can create confusion, fear, false accusation, and emotional instability. But the absence of discernment creates exposure. The watchman must therefore learn the difference between reacting out of fear and responding out of spiritual clarity.

Suspicion assumes guilt without evidence. Discernment observes carefully and seeks clarity. Suspicion rushes to conclusions because it is often driven by anxiety, unresolved fear, or personal projection. Discernment is slower, steadier, and more anchored. It pays attention to patterns. It notices inconsistencies. It weighs tone, timing, behavior, atmosphere, and repeated signals. It does not deny concern, but neither does it abandon sobriety. It asks, "What is happening here?" What has shifted? What am I seeing repeatedly? What needs further attention? Discernment is not careless, but it is also not reckless.

Discernment listens. Discernment watches. Discernment responds wisely.

To listen with discernment means hearing more than words. It means recognizing when a child's answer sounds forced, when silence feels heavy, when a laugh feels unnatural, or when a child says "nothing" in a way that suggests something is present beneath the surface. Discernment pays attention not only to what is said, but to what is avoided, delayed, softened, or emotionally carried. It understands that children do not always communicate distress directly, and that adults who are spiritually awake must learn how to hear beyond the sentence.

To watch with discernment means noticing patterns rather than isolated fragments alone. It means recognizing that one unusual moment may be nothing—or it may be the beginning of something deeper. Discernment watches over time. It compares present behavior with known patterns. It studies shifts in appetite, fear, secrecy, emotional tone, interest in certain places or people, resistance, unusual attachment, and subtle changes in the child's atmosphere. It understands that danger often reveals itself first through pattern before it ever reveals itself through confession.

To respond wisely means acting neither too quickly out of fear nor too slowly out of denial. Wisdom does not freeze when something feels wrong. It investigates. It asks careful questions. It increases oversight. It adjusts access. It slows down trust where trust has become too casual. It moves with enough seriousness to protect the child, but enough steadiness to avoid creating confusion through panic. Discernment does not mean doing nothing until proof becomes undeniable. It means taking what is seen seriously enough to seek clarity before harm has more room to grow.

This kind of discernment requires prayer. A parent cannot live on instinct alone. Human perception is limited. Fatigue, past wounds, assumptions, or emotional pressure can influence personal feelings. Prayer helps purify discernment. It quiets emotional noise. It brings the heart under God's authority. It helps the watchman separate fear from wisdom, reaction from revelation, and imagination from genuine warning. A praying parent is not automatically perfect, but they are far more likely to remain spiritually sensitive than a parent who moves only by natural impulse.

It also requires attentiveness. Discernment is not granted to the absent. A parent who is always distracted, disconnected, rushed, or emotionally unavailable will often miss the subtle shifts that require wise response. Attentiveness is part of discernment's training ground. The more a parent knows the child's normal emotional rhythm, the more quickly, they can detect when something is no longer normal. Discernment grows stronger where presence is steady, observation is thoughtful, and the relationship is close enough for change to be noticed.

It requires courage as well. Discernment that is never acted upon becomes wasted light. There are moments when a parent senses misalignment but does not want the inconvenience of following through. They fear being wrong. They fear offending someone. They fear making the room uncomfortable. But discernment often requires confrontation—not always dramatic confrontation, but at minimum the courage to question what others would rather excuse, to interrupt what others would rather leave alone, and to investigate what others would rather explain away. Discernment without courage becomes silent concern. Silent concern does not guard children well.

The watchman who refuses discernment risks overlooking danger simply because it appears subtle or familiar. This is one of the most dangerous failures of family guardianship. Some parents are not blind because there were no signs. They are blind because the signs came wrapped in normalcy. The person was known. The environment was routine. The access had been repeated. The behavior was explained. The discomfort was minimized. Because the danger did not appear dramatic, it was treated as harmless. But subtle danger is still danger. Familiar danger is still danger. Unquestioned access is still access. Discernment is what keeps the watchman from mistaking normality for safety.

Discernment also protects against unjust suspicion. It prevents a home from becoming governed by instability, accusation, and fear. A discerning parent does not teach children to be terrified of everyone. They teach them to be aware. They do not create a culture of panic. They create a culture of clarity. They do not assume every person is dangerous. They understand that every person with access must remain under the guidance of wisdom, within boundaries, and subject to accountability. That is not suspicion. That is stewardship.

There is also a spiritual dimension to this distinction. The flesh can fuel suspicion. The Spirit strengthens discernment. Suspicion often arises from personal agitation. Discernment flows from cultivated awareness under God. Suspicion can turn a parent into someone chronically unstable, emotionally led, and relationally disruptive. Discernment makes a parent sober, measured, and difficult to deceive. It helps them see beneath appearances without becoming controlled by fear of appearances.

In practical life, discernment may sound like this: Why has my child changed around this person? Why is this adult pushing for unnecessary privacy? Why does this setting feel increasingly misaligned? Why am I noticing repeated discomfort after the same environment? Why is this influence weakening peace rather than strengthening it? These questions do not condemn automatically, but they do refuse carelessness. Discernment is willing to ask what others avoid asking, because it understands that clarity is often born on the other side of uncomfortable questions.

Parents must therefore ask God for discernment, cultivate it in daily watchfulness, and refuse both extremes of naïve passivity and reckless suspicion. The home needs neither panic nor blindness. It needs sober eyes. It needs ears tuned to subtle shifts. It needs a guardian whose spirit is awake enough to sense misalignment and wise enough to pursue truth carefully.

Discernment is not suspicion.
It is disciplined awareness under God.
It is prayer with open eyes.
It is love that refuses to sleep.
It is wisdom standing at the wall, unwilling to let subtle danger pass unnoticed simply because it arrived wearing a familiar face.

GUARDING THE PARENTS' OWN HEART

Before a watchman guards the wall, he must guard himself. This is one of the most neglected truths in family leadership. Many parents want to protect their children from external threats while ignoring the internal condition of their own hearts. But a parent cannot stand effectively at the gate of the home while spiritually dull, emotionally unstable, morally compromised, or inwardly undisciplined. What is unguarded within the parent will eventually weaken what is guarded around the child.

Proverbs 4:23 (KJV) commands, "Keep thy heart with all diligence; for out of it are the issues of life." This is not casual counsel. It is a warning tied to a consequence. The heart is not a private space with no effect on others. It is a wellspring. It shapes tone, judgment, reactions, appetite, patience, perception, and discernment. If that well is polluted, the effects do not remain contained within the parent. They spill into the home's atmosphere. They influence the child. They alter the way protection is carried out. They weaken clarity where strength should have lived.

A spiritually careless parent cannot effectively guard a child's spiritual development. If the parent's heart is clouded by distraction, bitterness, compromise, or exhaustion, discernment weakens. A distracted parent may miss what should have been noticed. A bitter parent may interpret everything through wounded emotion rather than wisdom. A compromised parent may normalize what should be confronted. An exhausted parent may become too passive to follow through, too numb to ask questions, or too impatient to listen well. In all of these conditions, the home's wall becomes more vulnerable because the watchman himself is not standing strong.

This is why guarding one's heart is not selfish. It is part of stewardship.

Parents often think first of schedules, rules, environments, friends, schools, and digital boundaries—all of which matter. But there is another question that must be asked with equal seriousness: What is governing me? What is shaping my reactions?

What am I feeding my own inner life? What unresolved issues are affecting the tone of my household? What habits are dulling my spiritual sensitivity? What private compromises are weakening my public authority? The parent who refuses to answer these questions may continue functioning outwardly while slowly losing inner sharpness.

Guarding one's heart involves intentional discipline. It is not maintained by accident. It includes monitoring personal influences, protecting one's spiritual life, maintaining integrity in relationships, and cultivating emotional stability. A parent must pay attention to what they themselves are consuming—what they watch, what they listen to, what they entertain mentally, what they normalize emotionally, and what they excuse spiritually.

If they allow their own eye gate and ear gate to be shaped carelessly, they should not be surprised when their discernment toward the child's environment grows weaker as well.

It also includes protecting one's spiritual life. Prayer cannot be decorative for the parent. Scripture cannot be occasional. Repentance cannot be delayed. A parent who neglects personal communion with God may still know religious language, but the edge of spiritual alertness will gradually fade. It is possible to speak about protection while living inwardly dry. It is possible to warn children about compromise while allowing compromise to live unchallenged in the parent's own heart. But hypocrisy weakens authority. Children may not be able to explain it, but they often feel that the home's atmosphere is inconsistent with the words spoken there.

Maintaining integrity in relationships is also part of heart-guarding. A parent who lives with hidden dishonesty, unresolved resentment, flirtation with unhealthy ties, double standards, or emotional chaos is not simply affecting themselves. Those fractures shape the home. They weaken trust. They introduce tension. They distort the child's understanding of love, security, and truth. A parent's relational integrity becomes part of the child's environment, whether spoken about or not.

Cultivating emotional stability is just as necessary. This does not mean parents never feel tired, overwhelmed, or wounded. It means they do not surrender leadership of their inner life to those conditions. Children need adults whose moods do not make honesty unsafe. If a parent is chronically explosive, reactive, sarcastic, dismissive, emotionally absent, or unpredictable, a child may stop bringing important things to them—not because the child has nothing to say, but because the parent's heart has become a difficult place to approach. An unstable parent can unintentionally become a closed gate to the very truth they need to hear.

Children absorb not only instruction but atmosphere. They learn from what their parents practice. They watch how conflict is handled. They notice whether the correction is just or emotional. They sense whether prayer is real or performative. They learn what peace feels like—or what tension feels like. They learn whether repentance happens in the home. They learn whether truth is lived or only demanded. This is why a parent's inner condition cannot be treated as a private side issue. It becomes part of the child's formation.

A guarded parent produces a guarded home.

That does not mean a perfect parent. It means a parent who stays honest before God, is attentive to their own weaknesses, is willing to repent, is eager to stay spiritually awake, and is unwilling to let private disorder quietly shape the household atmosphere. A guarded parent notices when bitterness is rising and deals with it.

They notice when fatigue is turning into passivity and seek renewal. They notice when compromise is creeping in and cut it off. They notice when distraction is weakening attentiveness and make adjustments. They do not defend their own dullness. They confront it.

This kind of self-guarding is an act of love. It says, I will not let my private neglect become my child's public vulnerability. It says, I understand that if I am to watch well, I must live soberly. It says, I cannot stand at the wall faithfully while refusing to examine the condition of the one standing there.

Before asking whether the child's environment is guarded, the parent must ask whether their own heart is guarded.

Is prayer alive there?
Is bitterness being dealt with there?
Is compromise being tolerated there?
Is distraction ruling there?
Is integrity strong there?
Is spiritual sensitivity still active there?

These are not secondary questions. They are foundational questions. Because the watchman who does not guard his own heart will eventually bring confusion to the wall. But the parent who stays guarded inwardly becomes harder to deceive outwardly. They hear more clearly. They see more soberly. They respond more wisely. And their very presence begins to strengthen the atmosphere of the home.

So before you guard the child's gate, guard your own heart with diligence. Keep it clean. Keep it watchful. Keep it honest before God. Keep it free from tolerated bitterness, private compromise, careless distraction, and emotional disorder.

Because what flows from the parent will help shape the household. And when the parent is guarded, the home becomes stronger at every wall.

OBSERVING INFLUENCES AROUND THE CHILD

The watchman must also observe the environment surrounding the child. Protection is not only about responding to obvious threats after they surface. It is about paying close attention to the influences already shaping the child long before harm becomes visible. A parent cannot guard a child well while remaining indifferent to the atmosphere around them. Children do not grow in isolation. They are formed in context. They are repeatedly shaped by what surrounds them—people, voices, habits, language, digital content, expectations, emotional climates, and relational patterns. If those influences are not examined, then formation is being left to chance.

Who has access to the child? What conversations are shaping identity? What digital influences are forming perspective? What friendships are strengthening or weakening values? These are not small questions. They are essential questions. A child may spend only a few hours in a certain setting, but repeated exposure can still carry significant influence. Sometimes what appears harmless in short moments becomes deeply formative over time. It is not always the loudest force that shapes a child most powerfully. Often, it is the most consistent one.

Watchfulness is not controlling behavior—it is protecting formation. A wise parent understands that behavior is often the fruit of influence. If a child's environment feeds confusion, compromise, fear, sensuality, mockery, rebellion, or secrecy, those influences may begin to shape the child long before obvious outward problems appear.

This is why the watchman studies the environment, not merely the child's visible conduct. By the time troubling behavior becomes obvious, some shaping has often already been underway in the background.

Children are shaped by what consistently surrounds them. If influences are healthy, character strengthens. If influences are corrosive, confusion grows. Repeated exposure matters. The values children hear repeatedly begin to sound normal.

The attitudes they see repeatedly begin to feel acceptable. The emotional patterns they live around begin to shape how they interpret love, authority, correction, truth, conflict, and self-worth. A child who lives near honesty is strengthened by it. A child who lives near manipulation may become confused by it. A child who is surrounded by reverence learns reverence more naturally. A child surrounded by mockery may begin to treat sacred things casually.

This is why parents must observe not only dramatic influences, but subtle ones. The most dangerous shaping is not always obvious. A friendship may not immediately lead a child into open rebellion, yet it may steadily weaken modesty, humility, self-respect, or honesty. A digital platform may not instantly produce visible collapse, yet it may quietly distort beauty, sexuality, identity, and the value of attention. A mentor may not say anything openly wicked, yet they may subtly create emotional dependency, blurred boundaries, or misplaced loyalty. A family environment may appear peaceful, yet repeated sarcasm, criticism, tension, or emotional neglect may still be shaping the child's inner life. Subtlety must never be mistaken for harmlessness.

The watchman studies the environment carefully, knowing that subtle influences often shape a child long before obvious problems appear. This requires more than casual awareness. It requires parents to notice patterns. What tone does this environment leave on my child? Do they return from certain places heavier, sharper, more secretive, more disrespectful, more anxious, more withdrawn? Do they sound different after certain relationships? Are they becoming more truthful, or more evasive? More grounded, or more unstable? More respectful, or more resistant? These kinds of questions help the parent discern not only what the child is doing, but also what may be being done to the child.

Parents must also understand that access is influence. Every person who gains repeated access to the child gains some opportunity to shape the perspective. This does not mean parents should treat every relationship with fear, but they must take repeated proximity seriously. Access includes physical presence, emotional closeness, digital contact, private communication, social environments, and recurring conversations.

Children are impressionable, not because they are foolish, but because they are still forming. They are learning how to interpret the world. That is why the voices nearest to them matter so much.

Observing influences also means paying attention to language. Conversations shape identity more than many adults realize. Repeated jokes, suggestive comments, cynical attitudes, degrading labels, careless speech, and subtle affirmations of compromise all leave marks. Words can normalize what should be challenged. They can make confusion feel sophisticated, and rebellion feel courageous. They can slowly teach a child to laugh at what should grieve them, excuse what should trouble them, or admire what should concern them. A watchful parent, therefore, listens not only for explicit danger but for the tone of what is shaping the child's emotional and moral imagination.

Digital influence deserves special attention because it often bypasses traditional boundaries. A child may be physically at home while mentally and emotionally being discipled by strangers through videos, feeds, chats, games, influencers, or endless content streams. What repeatedly enters through the screen can form perspective, appetite, insecurity, fantasy, comparison, and desire. A child may begin to adopt attitudes they never heard directly in the home because digital environments have trained them quietly over time.

This is why a parent cannot separate digital oversight from spiritual stewardship. To ignore digital influence is to leave a major channel of formation unguarded.

Friendships must also be observed with wisdom. Not every friendship deserves panic, but every friendship deserves attention. Some friends sharpen character. Others erode it. Some strengthen honesty, restraint, courage, and godly sensitivity. Others normalize disrespect, secrecy, pressure, impurity, and divided loyalty. The watchman does not simply ask, Does my child enjoy this friendship? The deeper question is, What is this friendship producing? Fruit matters. A child may like a person deeply and still be quietly shaped in harmful ways by that relationship. That is why parental observation must go beyond surface-level compatibility and consider the moral and emotional effects.

A parent who observes influences well is not trying to dominate the child's every thought. They are trying to keep the child's formation from being surrendered to whatever voice is loudest, nearest, or most emotionally persuasive. This kind of watchfulness requires humility, prayer, and consistency. Parents must remain close enough to the child to notice change, wise enough to interpret influence, and courageous enough to intervene when something surrounding the child is weakening what should be strengthened.

Observing influences around the child also means admitting that some environments may need to change. Some access must be reduced. Some platforms must be restricted. Some relationships must be questioned. Some routines must be interrupted. Some repeated exposures must not continue simply because they are common or socially accepted. A faithful watchman is not governed by convenience. They are governed by what protects formation.

Because this is the deeper issue: the child is always being formed by something.

The question is whether the parent is paying enough attention to know what that something is.

A wise watchman does not wait for obvious destruction before studying the atmosphere. They watch early. They ask deeply. They observe repeatedly. They protect what is being formed while it is still forming.

And that is not control.
That is stewardship.
That is discernment.
That is love with open eyes.

SOUNDING THE ALARM

When danger appears, the watchman does not remain silent. He does not stand on the wall, see movement in the distance, and tell himself that perhaps it will fade on its own. He does not wait for proof so overwhelming that everyone else finally agrees. He does not protect appearances while risk continues to move. He sounds the alarm. That is the duty of the watchman. Not because he enjoys disruption, but because he understands that silence in the presence of danger is not calmness—it is failure.

Silence is not protection.

This is one of the most dangerous misunderstandings in families, ministries, and communities. Many adults think they are preserving peace when they stay quiet, delay action, or avoid hard conversations. But what they often call peace is only a postponed confrontation. And a postponed confrontation frequently gives harm more time to deepen. A boundary crossed in silence becomes easier to cross again. A warning sign ignored becomes easier to minimize the next time. An unsettled atmosphere left unchallenged often grows more settled in the wrong direction. What is tolerated quietly may begin to feel normal simply because no one interrupted it early.

If a boundary is crossed, address it. If behavior shifts, investigate it. If the atmosphere feels unsettled, confront it. These responses are not signs of overreaction. They are the necessary movements of faithful guardianship. A parent does not need permission from a crowd to respond to what wisdom has already made plain. If an adult seeks access that feels inappropriate, address it. If a child's demeanor changes after contact with a person or place, investigate it. If secrecy begins growing where openness used to live, confront it. If something in the home, relationship, or environment repeatedly disturbs peace, do not baptize your discomfort with excuses and call it patience. Address it.

Parents need to understand that early intervention is one of the best forms of protection. Waiting increases danger. Acting quickly reduces harm. This isn't because every worry becomes the worst case, but because acting fast limits opportunities for problems to grow. Harm often increases when adults leave certain issues unaddressed while they wait, wonder, hope, or avoid. The longer an unhealthy pattern goes unchallenged, the more it can become fixed. The longer secrets are kept, the more confident manipulation becomes. The longer a child's distress remains unexplored, the lonelier they may feel. Early action doesn't guarantee all dangers are gone instantly, but it significantly reduces the risk of hidden issues worsening without interruption.

The purpose of an alarm is not to create panic but to initiate protection. Alarms are not acts of chaos; they are acts of mercy. They interrupt the routine because the routine has become unsafe. They disturb the room because the room needs to be disturbed. They call attention to what others might prefer to overlook because what is being overlooked may carry serious consequences. In the same way, a parent who sounds the alarm is not trying to create drama. They are trying to prevent damage. They are saying, This will not continue unchecked. This must be looked at now. This child's safety is worth the discomfort this conversation may bring.

There is a holy urgency in parents who know when to act. Not panic. Not hysteria. Urgency. The difference matters. Panic loses clarity. Urgency preserves it. Panic is ruled by fear. Urgency is ruled by responsibility. Urgency does not wait for absolute certainty when enough warning exists to justify wise intervention. It knows that there are moments when the cost of moving too slowly is far greater than the cost of asking a hard question early.

This is where many guardians fail. They see the sign, but they talk themselves out of responding. They notice the shift, but tell themselves it is probably nothing. They feel unsettled, but fear being misunderstood. They recognize misalignment, but hesitate because confrontation may be awkward. Yet the watchman who sees and says nothing has not protected the city. The parent who notices and does nothing has not fulfilled the assignment. The issue is not whether they cared inwardly. The issue is whether their care moved into action before the harm deepened.

Sounding the alarm also requires moral clarity. A parent must settle within themselves that a child's safety outranks politeness, convenience, image, and social ease. If the cost of speaking up is an awkward conversation, then let the conversation be awkward. If the cost of asking questions is someone becoming offended, then let offense come. If the cost of restricting access is others' misunderstanding, then let misunderstanding happen. Better to endure temporary discomfort than to leave a child unguarded because an adult was unwilling to disturb the atmosphere.

A child must never have to pay for an adult's hesitation.

That is why parents must not only learn to hear warning signs but also learn to honor them. A child's sudden fear, unusual silence, change in behavior, emotional withdrawal, guardedness, or unexplained agitation may be the first alarm. It is not enough to notice it. The watchman must respond to it. The response may begin with questions, increased observation, tightened boundaries, restricted access, more direct conversation, or immediate removal from an environment. But whatever the case, silence must not be the answer.

There is also a spiritual dimension here. Sometimes the alarm sounds first in the spirit before it is fully visible in the natural. A parent may feel unsettled, unable to explain completely why something feels off, why a relationship seems misaligned, why an atmosphere has shifted, or why a child's interaction with a certain environment leaves a troubling impression.

That spiritual stirring should not be ignored lightly. It must be tested, prayed through, and followed up with wisdom. God often gives the watchman discomfort before He gives the whole explanation. The purpose is not to create confusion but to alert the guardian to the danger before it becomes more visible.

Parents who act early prevent greater damage later. That is one of the simplest and strongest truths of watchfulness. They prevent access from becoming an attachment. They prevent secrecy from becoming control. They prevent discomfort from becoming trauma. They prevent subtle shifts from becoming settled patterns. They prevent hidden things from gaining the advantage of time.

Taking action in the early stage often prevents the child from having to recover from something much deeper later on.

So when danger appears, do not grow quiet.
When misalignment surfaces, do not retreat into an excuse.
When the alarm sounds, do not smother it with politeness.

Speak.
Question.
Interrupt.
Confront.
Protect.

Because the watchman was never called to preserve comfort.
He was called to preserve what was behind the wall.

BUILDING COMMUNICATION IN THE FAMILY

A watchman must also cultivate communication within the household. Protection is not built by observation alone. A parent may notice much, suspect much, and care deeply, but if the atmosphere of the home does not make it safe to speak the truth, then many important things will remain hidden until they have already deepened. Watchfulness requires more than looking outward toward possible threats. It also requires creating an environment of trust where children know they can speak honestly without being punished.

Communication in the family must therefore be intentional. It does not happen merely because people live under the same roof. Shared space is not the same as shared openness. Many households are busy but not connected. Many families talk often yet say little that is emotionally or spiritually safe. Real communication is more than exchanging information about schedules, responsibilities, and daily routines. It is the steady cultivation of trust, clarity, listening, and emotional accessibility. It is the kind of relational structure that tells a child, Your words matter here. Your concerns matter here. Your confusion will not be mocked here. Your fear will not be brushed aside here.

When children feel heard, they speak sooner. When they know questions are welcome, they disclose earlier. That timing matters. A child who feels secure enough to bring concerns forward early is far less likely to suffer alone in silence while a problem grows. Communication becomes a defense mechanism. It allows hidden things to surface before they become deeply rooted. It weakens secrecy before secrecy becomes control. It creates a relational pathway through which discomfort, fear, confusion, and warning signs can reach the adults who are assigned to protect the child.

This is why parents must build more than rules—they must build access.

Children should not have to guess whether difficult conversations are safe. They should not have to calculate whether honesty will result in understanding or humiliation. They should not have to weigh whether telling the truth will create more danger for them than remaining silent. A wise parent understands that the child's willingness to speak is determined not only by the seriousness of the issue but also by the trustworthiness of the environment to which it is addressed. Even a child who knows something is wrong may remain quiet if they believe the parent will react with mockery, explosive anger, impatience, emotional collapse, or dismissal.

A child who trusts the parent's response will bring concerns forward before problems escalate. But if the child fears dismissal, shame, or anger, silence becomes their refuge. And silence is a dangerous refuge.

It may feel safer in the moment, but it often becomes the shelter under which fear, confusion, and manipulation continue to grow. This is why the tone of the parent matters as much as the content of the conversation. A child is not only listening to what the parent says; they are studying how the parent receives what is said.

Parents must therefore discipline their own reactions. If every difficult disclosure is met with immediate accusation, panic, ridicule, emotional intensity, or harsh interruption, the child may learn that truth is too costly to tell. But when the parent responds with steadiness, attentiveness, and seriousness, the child learns that honesty has somewhere to go.

This does not mean the parent becomes weak, vague, or passive. It means the parent becomes safe enough to approach and strong enough to handle what is brought forward.

Healthy communication builds internal security. It assures children that they are protected, believed, and supported. Internal security is one of the strongest defenses a child can carry. A child who feels secure at home is less likely to be easily manipulated from the outside. A child who knows their voice has value is less likely to believe they must submit to secrecy to preserve peace.

A child who has seen truth handled well at home is more likely to bring troubling things to light while there is still time for intervention.

Communication also trains discernment within the child. When parents explain, listen, answer, and revisit important subjects, children begin learning how to interpret the world with greater clarity. They learn what healthy behavior looks like. They learn how to identify discomfort. They learn the difference between secrecy and privacy, between correction and abuse, between kindness and manipulation, between attention and inappropriate attachment. This kind of communication does more than keep a child talking—it helps form the child's understanding.

For this reason, parents must not reserve meaningful conversation only for a crisis. If communication only appears when something is wrong, children may begin to associate serious conversation with trouble. But when communication is part of the normal rhythm of family life, it becomes easier for the child to speak before a crisis forms. Shared meals, car rides, bedtime conversations, moments after school, ordinary check-ins, and patient follow-up questions all help build a culture where children know they are not being interrogated—they are being cared for.

A family that communicates well does not merely ask, What happened today? It also learns to ask, How did that make you feel? Did anything feel uncomfortable? Is there anything you have been carrying that you have not known how to say? Is there anyone or anything that has been troubling your spirit? These kinds of questions open doors.

They tell the child that the parent is interested not only in behavior but also in the inner world that shapes that behavior.

Parents must also learn to listen beneath the first answer. Many children do not say the deepest thing first. Some test the waters with partial truth. Some speak indirectly. Some mention something casually that is actually more serious than it sounds. A watchful parent does not always stop at the surface answer. They remain gentle enough to keep the child talking and attentive enough to know when there is more beneath the surface of what has been said.

The watchman who fosters trust strengthens the wall from within.

That phrase matters because the strongest wall in a family is not built only from rules and restrictions. It is also built on relationships. Boundaries matter. Oversight matters. Accountability matters. But when those things are joined to trust-filled communication, the child is not simply being guarded from the outside. They are becoming safer from the inside as well. They begin to understand that protection is not merely something done to them; it is something that surrounds them, supports them, and invites them to speak when something is wrong.

A home with healthy communication becomes harder for darkness to operate in. Manipulation struggles where truth is welcome. Secrecy loses leverage where questions are normal. Confusion weakens when children know they can ask without shame. Harm is more likely to be interrupted when the child has already learned: My parents listen. My voice matters. I do not have to hide what burdens me.

This kind of communication takes work. It takes patience when answers are slow. It takes humility when parents realize they have not always listened well. It takes restraint when emotions are high. It takes consistency when children seem distant or hesitant. But the labor is worth it. Because many of the most important warnings in a child's life will not come through an obvious crisis first, they will come through fragments of speech, half-formed questions, emotional hesitations, a changed tone, or subtle disclosures that only a listening home can properly receive.

So build communication deliberately.
Make room for honesty.
Welcome questions.
Follow up carefully.
Listen without mockery.
Respond without carelessness.
Stay near enough for truth to surface.

Because when trust lives in the home, children speak sooner. When children speak sooner, danger is interrupted earlier.

And when a watchman strengthens the wall from within, the family becomes harder to penetrate from without.

MODELING INTEGRITY

The role of the watchman extends beyond instruction. It includes an example. A parent can teach truth with their mouth and weaken it with their life if conduct and conviction do not agree. Children are not shaped only by what they are told; they are shaped by what they repeatedly witness. They study consistency. They observe how authority is exercised, how boundaries are enforced, how integrity is practiced, how pressure is handled, how apologies are made, and how truth is lived when no one is performing for an audience. In this way, the parents' daily life becomes part of the child's moral curriculum.

This is why an example carries such weight. Children are skilled observers. They notice when a parent demands honesty but speaks deceptively. They notice when a parent preaches restraint but lives impulsively. They notice when a parent warns them about compromise while privately tolerating it in their own habits. They notice when spiritual language is used publicly but ignored in the private atmosphere of the home. A child may not always know how to explain these contradictions, but they absorb them. And what they absorb shapes how seriously they will take instruction later.

When they see vigilance practiced, they learn vigilance. When they observe discipline maintained, they learn discipline. When they witness courage in leadership, they learn courage. An example gives flesh to the instruction. It shows the child what truth looks like under pressure, what conviction looks like in real time, and what faithfulness looks like in ordinary life. A parent who remains alert, follows through on concerns, asks hard questions without flinching, and refuses to be controlled by social discomfort is quietly teaching the child how to value what is right above what is easy.

The watchman teaches not only through words but through conduct. That conduct matters in moments that seem small. It matters when a parent admits fault instead of defending pride. It matters when a parent keeps their word. It matters when a parent says no to something popular because it is not wise. It matters when a parent protects boundaries, even when others do not understand. It matters when a parent refuses to laugh at what degrades holiness, refuses to excuse what threatens safety, and refuses to call compromise harmless simply because it has become common.

Leadership within the family is demonstrated daily. It is not proven by how loudly a parent speaks, but by how steadily they live. True leadership is seen in the repeated choices that shape the household atmosphere. It is seen in whether the parent is emotionally stable enough to be approached, spiritually grounded enough to discern wisely, morally clean enough to lead without hypocrisy, and disciplined enough to remain watchful when routine tempts carelessness.

The child is learning from all of it.

Integrity is especially powerful because it creates trust. A child is far more likely to receive correction from a parent whose life reflects the same truth the parent is teaching. But when instruction and conduct collide, confusion enters. Children may begin to question not only the parent's authority, but the value of the principles being taught. That is why integrity is not a decorative virtue for parents. It is structural. It helps hold up the moral framework of the home. Without it, the wall may still appear to be standing, but it is already weakening beneath.

Modeling integrity also means showing children that leadership is accountable. Parents who model integrity do not act as though authority places them above self-examination. They understand that a watchman who cannot correct himself will eventually confuse those he is trying to guard. So they repent when wrong. They make amends when needed. They do not hide behind titles, age, or position. They let the child see that righteousness is not the absence of humility, but the presence of it. This teaches the child that strength and repentance are not opposites.

A parent's consistency also helps children understand the true purpose of authority. Many children grow up confused about authority because they have seen it used inconsistently, emotionally, or selfishly. But when a parent models integrity, authority begins to make sense. The child sees that rules are not random, boundaries are not cruel, and correction is not personal hostility.

They begin to understand that authority can be trustworthy when it is governed by principle rather than mood. That understanding becomes a safeguard for their future, because it helps them recognize the difference between righteous leadership and manipulative control.

Integrity in the parent also stabilizes the home atmosphere. Children feel safer where there is congruence between what is spoken and what is lived. They rest more deeply where promises are kept, standards are clear, and responses are not ruled by emotional chaos. They learn to trust instruction because they have seen it embodied. They learn to value truth because truth has been practiced, not merely quoted. They learn that conviction is not a sermon for special moments, but a way of life.

This is especially important in a generation flooded with performance, image, and contradiction. Children do not need parents who only know how to sound right. They need parents who live right with sincerity, steadiness, and reverence. They need to see what courage looks like when it protects rather than intimidates. They need to see what discipline looks like when it is consistent rather than harsh. They need to see what watchfulness looks like when it is loving rather than controlling. They need to see what holiness looks like when it is practiced in daily choices, not merely spoken from the lips.

Parents who model integrity strengthen the moral foundation of the household. They give the child something stable to stand on. They make truth believable. They make discipline understandable. They make courage visible. They make vigilance normal. And in doing so, they do more than guard the child for the moment—they help form the kind of inner character that the child may carry into future relationships, future decisions, future leadership, and future homes.

So let the watchman remember: the wall is strengthened not only by warning, but by witness. The household becomes stronger not only because truth is spoken, but because truth is lived. And the child learns most deeply when the parent's life confirms what the parent's mouth declares.

Because an example has weight.
Conduct has power.
And integrity lived daily becomes one of the strongest forms of protection a parent can give.

STANDING FAITHFULLY ON THE WALL

The position of watchman demands foresight. It anticipates rather than reacts. It prepares rather than panics. It creates structure before a crisis emerges and establishes expectations before confusion arises. A faithful watchman does not wait for visible collapse before becoming serious. He understands that wisdom is strongest before damage, not after it. He knows that many of the gravest wounds in a family do not begin with a public emergency but with a private negligence—a boundary that was never clearly set, an atmosphere that was never properly guarded, an influence that was allowed to settle in unchecked, or a warning that was noticed but not pursued.

This is why standing on the wall requires more than sincerity. It requires discipline. It requires a parent to think ahead, to ask what could happen if access is left loose, if routines are left undefined, if the child is left emotionally unheard, if the atmosphere is left spiritually unattended, if the home is left governed by assumption instead of intentional leadership. Foresight does not mean expecting evil at every turn. It means understanding that safety must be built before it is tested. It means a wise parent does not wait for a child to be harmed before deciding that clearer boundaries, closer observation, stronger communication, and firmer oversight were necessary all along.

This role may feel weighty—and it is. The burden is real because what is being guarded is precious. Children are not light assignments. Their trust is fragile. Their formation is ongoing. Their discernment is still developing. Their safety is too valuable to be left to weak structure, shallow attention, or emotional laziness. The weight of the role comes from the reality that what parents do not guard may eventually shape the child just as much as what they intentionally teach.

But it is also sacred.

To be appointed as a watchman for a family is an honor entrusted by God. It is not driven by fear but by love. It is not fueled by paranoia but by responsibility. It is not motivated by control but by stewardship. A faithful watchman does not stand at the wall because he is obsessed with danger. He stands there because he understands the value of what is behind him. He is not guarding a structure alone. He is guarding innocence, identity, stability, conscience, and future. He is guarding souls still being formed, hearts still learning to trust, and lives that will bear the effects of present protection or neglect long after childhood has passed.

This is what gives the role its sacred character. The watchman stands not merely as a parent fulfilling routine duties, but as a steward before God. The home is not only a place of residence; it is a sphere of formation.

The children within it are not merely members of a household; they are lives entrusted by Heaven. To stand on the wall faithfully is to understand that your vigilance is part of your worship. Your attentiveness is part of your obedience. Your refusal to sleep at the gate is part of your answer to God.

When the watchman stands faithfully, children grow secure. Not because they are told repeatedly that they are safe while the home remains careless, but because they live in the consistent evidence of protection. Security grows where children know the adults around them are attentive, where discomfort is not mocked, where truth is welcome, where boundaries are clear, and where the home's atmosphere communicates steadiness rather than confusion. A faithful watchman gives a child something more powerful than reassurance alone—he gives them living covering.

When the watchman stands faithfully, boundaries remain strong. Strong boundaries do not emerge from a single stern conversation. They are maintained by repetition, clarity, follow-through, and conviction. A watchman who stays awake does not allow lines to blur simply because life is busy or others are uncomfortable. He knows that blurred boundaries create openings, and openings create risk. So he holds the line. He reinforces what matters.

He does not let discipline become occasional, access become casual, or standards become negotiable whenever pressure rises.

When the watchman stands faithfully, influences are filtered. Not every voice deserves equal access. Not every relationship deserves unquestioned proximity. Not every trend deserves a place in the home. Not every digital environment should be allowed to shape the child without examination. The faithful watchman understands that formation is happening constantly, and because of that, filtering is not extremism—it is wisdom. He studies what surrounds the child, what is discipling the child, what is undermining peace, and what is quietly competing for moral and spiritual influence.

When the watchman stands faithfully, threats are detected early. This may be one of the greatest blessings of consistent vigilance. The watchman often sees what others miss because he has remained close enough, alert enough, and prayerful enough to notice subtle shifts. He detects misalignment before it fully matures. He hears a strain in the atmosphere before conflict becomes an open fracture. He sees behavioral changes before they become settled patterns. He notices access becoming too familiar, secrecy becoming too comfortable, or emotional heaviness becoming too repeated. Early detection does not solve everything instantly, but it can interrupt much that would otherwise deepen.

When the watchman stands faithfully, the atmosphere remains guarded. This matters because children do not grow merely in physical spaces; they grow in atmospheres. The emotional and spiritual climate of the home teaches them what normal feels like. A guarded atmosphere teaches that truth can be spoken, that prayer is real, that holiness matters, that boundaries protect, and that adults take safety seriously. An unguarded atmosphere teaches very different lessons—sometimes without words. It teaches that confusion can remain unchallenged, that discomfort can be overlooked, that compromise can blend in unnoticed, and that children may have to carry more than they should. The watchman's faithfulness helps determine which atmosphere prevails.

The family becomes stable because the wall remains secure. Stability does not mean life is free of challenges. It means the family is not left exposed to every pressure without covering. It means there is a structure strong enough to hold truth, communication open enough to surface concern, leadership steady enough to preserve clarity, and spiritual attentiveness strong enough to resist what seeks to enter quietly. Stability is one of the fruits of faithful watchman-ship.

Every parent must decide: Will I stand on the wall? Or will I assume the wall will guard itself?

That question cannot be ignored. The wall does not guard itself. Boundaries do not maintain themselves. The atmosphere does not preserve itself. Discernment does not sharpen itself. Communication does not deepen by accident. Vague hope, good intentions, or sentimental affection alone will not secure the child's safety. Someone must stand at the wall. Someone must remain awake. Someone must bear the holy responsibility of seeing, listening, discerning, and acting.

And if the parent does not take that place seriously, other forces will not hesitate to take advantage of the vacancy.

That is why passive parenting is so dangerous. It assumes the child will somehow remain safe without intentional guardianship. It assumes the home will remain spiritually strong without deliberate covering. It assumes that because nothing obvious has happened yet, nothing requires attention. But the wall does not guard itself, and what is left unattended does not remain neutral. It becomes vulnerable.

So stand alert. Guard intentionally. Lead courageously.

Stand alert enough to notice what changes. Guard intentionally enough to build protection before a crisis. Lead courageously enough to make decisions that others may not understand, but that wisdom requires. A careless world may not always praise this kind of leadership, but it will be honored by God and felt by the children who live beneath its covering.

Because the safety of your household depends not on hope, but on the faithfulness of the watchman.

Hope is not enough without vigilance. Concern is not enough without structure. Love is not enough without watchfulness. The faithful watchman understands that the wall must be inhabited, not admired from a distance. It must be stood upon daily, soberly, prayerfully, and with conviction.

So remain at your post.
Do not sleep through peace.
Do not drift through routine.
Do not grow casual where God called you to be watchful.

The family behind the wall is worth the weight of the assignment. And the watchman who stands faithfully may prevent the very things others only recognize after it is too late.

❖ SPIRITUAL WARNING ❖

A Warning To The Unwatchful

There is a danger more terrifying than visible evil—it is invisible negligence. Visible evil can at least be recognized, named, confronted, and resisted. Invisible negligence is more dangerous because it disguises itself as normal life. It hides behind routine. It wears the face of busyness, fatigue, overconfidence, and misplaced ease. It does not look like rebellion at first. It looks like a delay. It looks like an assumption. It looks like a parent who still cares, but no longer watches carefully enough to guard what care alone cannot protect.

The greatest threats to innocence do not always begin with violence. They begin with distraction. They begin with overconfidence. They begin with the quiet assumption that everything is fine. They begin when adults stop asking follow-up questions because the environment feels familiar. They begin when routine numbs discernment, when warning signs are explained away, when access becomes too casual, and when the atmosphere of the home is no longer being examined with spiritual sobriety. Many tragedies do not start with a loud alarm. They start with a gate left unwatched because someone believed peace on the surface meant safety beneath.

But everything is not always fine.

This is one of the hardest truths for the unwatchful to accept. Some homes look stable while vulnerability is quietly growing. Some children appear outwardly compliant while inwardly carrying confusion, fear, or hidden distress. Some environments appear respectable, while a subtle compromise is already at work in the background. The problem is not only the presence of evil. The problem is that evil often operates most effectively where no one expects to find it. It thrives where adults have mistaken familiarity for security and calm appearance for actual protection.

There are moments when Heaven observes not only the wicked, but the watchmen. Not only the offender, but the overseer. Not only the act, but the inaction. This is what makes the matter so weighty. Children are not self-appointed. Guardians are. Parents, caregivers, and leaders stand under divine responsibility because God entrusted vulnerable lives into their hands. Heaven does not merely record who caused harm. It also examines who was standing at the wall when warning signs began to move and whether that watchman remained awake enough to act. Accountability does not begin only after the crisis. It begins at the first ignored signal.

Spiritual negligence rarely announces itself loudly. It creeps. It settles. It whispers, "You're overthinking." It persuades, "It's probably nothing." It comforts, "Don't make this uncomfortable." It suggests, "You don't want to accuse the wrong person." It reasons, "You've known them too long for that." It soothes the conscience with delay while risk quietly expands. And in that subtle persuasion, vigilance relaxes. The wall is still standing, but the watchman is no longer fully awake.

When vigilance relaxes, vulnerability expands.

That expansion may not be visible at first. It may begin with small things—loose boundaries, unguarded access, emotional distance, tolerated secrecy, weakened follow-through, prayer becoming occasional, spiritual sensitivity becoming dull, and discomfort being repeatedly rationalized. But what begins small does not always remain small. What is not confronted often becomes bolder. What is left unchecked often learns how much room it has to move.

Children do not choose their protectors. God appoints them. That appointment carries weight. It carries expectation. It carries accountability. A child should not have to suffer because the adult assigned to guard them was too passive to pay attention, too fearful to confront, too distracted to notice, or too comfort-driven to disturb what needed disturbing. Protection is not a decorative part of parenting. It is one of its most sacred demands.

You cannot claim love while neglecting watchfulness. You cannot claim faith while ignoring discernment. You cannot claim protection while refusing confrontation. Love that will not watch is incomplete. Faith that refuses to examine what feels wrong is not biblical confidence—it is dangerous presumption. Protection that exists only in words but disappears in practice is not protection at all. A child needs more than verbal reassurance. They need adults whose vigilance has substance, whose discernment has backbone, and whose love is strong enough to act.

If warning signs surface and are dismissed…
If intuition stirs and is silenced…
If behavior shifts and is ignored…
A door is opened.

That door may not look dramatic in the beginning. It may open through one excuse, one delayed conversation, one unchallenged environment, one unnecessary access point, one adult the family refuses to question, one child's discomfort being called attitude, one pattern left uninterpreted. But once harm passes through that door, regret cannot rewind it. Regret can grieve it. Regret can confess it. Regret can wish for another chance. But it cannot go backward and restore what faithful watchfulness might have interrupted earlier.

The soul must be shaken because complacency has become comfortable. Many would rather preserve social harmony than disturb a potential threat. Many would rather keep a room peaceful than make it honest. Many would rather avoid embarrassment than investigate what their spirit is already unsettled about. But what will comfort matter if innocence is compromised? What will social ease matter if a child carries hidden wounds because an adult chose emotional convenience over protective courage? What will reputation matter if the truth was delayed until the damage was already serious?

You are either alert, or you are exposed. There is no faithful middle ground where a watchman can remain half-awake and still expect the wall to stay strong. A dull watchman weakens the gate. A distracted guardian increases opportunity. A passive parent makes it easier for danger to move around.

The watchman who sleeps during peace awakens during a crisis. By then, the urgency is no longer about prevention. It is about damage control. That is why spiritual wakefulness matters most before the emergency becomes visible.

This warning is not written to instill panic—it is written to awaken conviction. Panic confuses. Conviction clarifies. Panic imagines danger everywhere. Conviction teaches the guardian to remain spiritually awake, emotionally steady, and practically engaged. It says: Do not dismiss what unsettles you. Do not mock what needs to be examined. Do not mistake silence for peace. Do not call delay wisdom when wisdom has already been asking you to move.

If something unsettles your spirit, investigate. If something feels misaligned, address it. If something changes in your child, lean closer—not away. Do not back off when the signs begin to surface. Do not let your discomfort become your child's increased vulnerability. Do not wait until every question is answered before taking the first faithful step. Tighten the boundary. Ask the question. Watch the pattern. Change the environment. Restrict the access. Pray with urgency. Listen with sobriety. Act with courage.

Because the cost of vigilance is temporary discomfort, the cost of negligence may echo for a lifetime.

Stand awake.
Stand unafraid.
Stand unwavering.

You have been assigned to guard what cannot guard itself. That assignment is not casual, and it is not transferable to culture, institutions, appearances, or wishful thinking. It belongs to the watchman God placed at the wall. Heaven will not ask whether you were comfortable. Heaven will ask whether you were faithful. It will ask whether you watched when you should have watched, whether you listened when you should have listened, whether you acted when you should have acted, and whether you treated the protection of innocence as sacred enough to interrupt whatever needed interrupting.

And faithfulness requires watchfulness.

PART II

AWARENESS

RECOGNIZING HIDDEN DANGER

CHAPTER FOUR

THE DANGER OF BLIND TRUST

The Perils of Excessive Trust

The Danger of Over-Trust and Unrestricted Access

One of the most underestimated dangers facing families today is not open hostility—it is misplaced trust. It is the quiet assumption that familiarity equals safety. The belief is that a good reputation guarantees good character. It is the habit of granting access without maintaining oversight. Many parents are not undone by what they feared; they are undone by what they never thought to question. They prepare for obvious threats yet leave the door open to subtle ones. They watch for strangers while lowering their guard around the familiar. And in that misplaced confidence, vulnerability quietly increases.

Jeremiah 17:5 (KJV) delivers a sobering warning: "Cursed be the man that trusteth in man, and maketh flesh his arm." This scripture does not forbid trust altogether, but it exposes the danger of blind reliance. Human judgment, human reputation, and human appearance are not sturdy enough foundations upon which to rest a child's safety. When trust replaces discernment, vulnerability increases. When emotional comfort overrides spiritual caution, protection weakens. When parents feel too reassured to remain watchful, they may unknowingly create the very openings through which harm advances.

Excessive trust is not love—it is exposure.

Trust becomes dangerous when it is detached from vigilance. Trust, by itself, is not the problem. The danger appears when trust is treated as a substitute for oversight. Some parents assume that because a person is known, they are safe; because a person is pleasant, they are harmless; because a person has been around for years, they are beyond suspicion. But blind trust is not wisdom.

Blind trust is the removal of protective thought. It is comforting to take the place of caution. It is the suspension of sober evaluation because a relationship feels established, a title feels respectable, or a history feels reassuring.

That is where many families become vulnerable. The threat is not always the obviously suspicious person. Often, it is the one who has learned how to appear trustworthy, helpful, stable, or spiritually acceptable. Some people gain unrestricted access not because they have proven deep integrity, but because no one wanted to keep asking questions.

They were familiar enough to be welcomed, respectable enough to avoid scrutiny, and close enough to be assumed safe. Yet assumption is one of the most dangerous foundations upon which a child's protection can rest.

A child's safety must never rest upon assumption alone. No parent can afford to believe that familiarity eliminates risk. No guardian can afford to conclude that access should be granted simply because someone feels trustworthy. The moment trust becomes unquestioned, the wall of protection begins to weaken. Once an individual is treated as beyond evaluation, beyond boundaries, or beyond accountability, access expands in ways that can quickly become dangerous. The issue is not whether people should ever be trusted. The issue is whether trust is being governed wisely or has grown careless enough to stop asking what should still be asked.

Blind trust often grows in emotionally comfortable environments. People feel rude for maintaining boundaries. They fear offending others by clarifying expectations. They feel it is unnecessary to ask follow-up questions. They do not want to appear suspicious, difficult, or overprotective. But wisdom does not measure safety by whether others feel affirmed. Wisdom measures safety by whether a child remains protected. Adults must never confuse politeness with prudence. They must never conclude that because someone is offended by boundaries, those boundaries were unnecessary.

In many cases, the very resistance to healthy oversight reveals why oversight must remain in place.

Families must also understand that reputation is not righteousness. A person may be admired publicly and still be unsafe privately.

They may be helpful, charming, articulate, generous, or spiritually expressive while still lacking the moral integrity required for unrestricted proximity to children. This is why parents must evaluate patterns, not merely presentation. Do they honor boundaries willingly? Do they welcome transparency? Do they avoid secrecy? Do they respect parental oversight without pressure or irritation? Healthy people do not resent appropriate accountability. They understand it. Unsafe people often try to move around it.

Over-trust also creates a false sense of peace. Parents may feel relieved because someone else seems dependable, but relief is not the same as protection. A wise parent does not hand over vigilance simply because another adult appears capable. Delegation of care never removes parental responsibility. The guardian must remain the guardian. Access may be shared in limited, appropriate ways, but oversight must remain active.

The wall must still be watched. The child must still be observed. The atmosphere must still be examined. The relationship must still be evaluated over time.

This is especially critical because children themselves are often taught to trust adults reflexively. They may assume that if the family welcomes a person, they must be safe. If a person serves in the church, they must be safe.

If a person is older, kind, funny, or respected, they must be safe. But children are not mature enough to consistently discern hidden motives. That is why adults must not foster a culture in which the child feels obligated to override their discomfort simply because the family trusts the other person. A child should know that even in the presence of familiar people, their discomfort still matters, their voice still matters, and access is never above question.

Over-trust is especially dangerous because it often makes warning signs easier to dismiss. When a child changes after being around someone well-liked, adults may explain the change away because they do not want to rethink the person. When a child resists someone they trust, adults may correct the child rather than investigate the pattern. When something feels unsettled, the adult may suppress discernment because acknowledging concern would disrupt an established relationship. But that is precisely how hidden danger survives. It hides behind the adults' unwillingness to revisit their assumptions.

A faithful parent must therefore learn to hold trust and vigilance together. Healthy trust does not erase boundaries. Healthy trust does not remove accountability. Healthy trust does not resent observation. The wisest homes are not those that trust no one, but those that trust carefully, govern access clearly, and refuse to let familiarity become a substitute for discernment.

This requires a renewed understanding of love. Love does not mean unlimited access. Love does not mean unquestioned permission. Love does not mean handing children into environments simply because the adults there are known. Love protects. Love filters. Love watches. Love remains willing to ask again what it has already asked before, because love understands that a child is too valuable to be placed beneath the weight of an adult's unexamined confidence.

Parents must reject the lie that vigilance is a lack of faith. It is not. Vigilance is how love behaves when it understands the world is fallen, access matters, and innocence is sacred. Faith does not call parents to sleep at the gate. Faith calls them to stand there with sobriety, prayer, and wisdom. Faith does not say, "I know them, so I no longer need to watch." Faith says, "I trust God enough to remain awake, honest, and responsible in what He has entrusted to me."

So let every parent hear this clearly: trust is safest when it remains accountable. Trust is healthiest when it remains visible. Trust is strongest when it is joined to discernment. But when trust becomes excessive, unquestioned, and detached from oversight, it stops protecting and starts exposing.

Guard the gate.
Question the assumption.
Keep the boundary.
Maintain the oversight.

Because a child's safety should never depend upon how trustworthy someone feels, it must rest on wisdom strong enough to remember that access without vigilance is not peace. It is risk dressed in comfort.

REPUTATION VS. CHARACTER

Those who intend harm rarely appear threatening. They often appear helpful. They volunteer eagerly. They serve generously. They offer assistance during busy seasons. They present themselves as spiritual, responsible, and dependable. They position themselves where access is abundant, and suspicion is minimal. They understand that in many homes, churches, schools, and community settings, people are often granted trust not because they have been thoroughly examined, but because they have learned how to appear useful, familiar, and safe.

Predatory behavior thrives on over-trust.

A person may be respected publicly and harmful privately. They may hold titles, credentials, and influence. They may be well-liked, charismatic, and trusted within community settings—schools, churches, sports programs, and neighborhoods. Yet reputation is not immunity from wrongdoing. Public affirmation does not purify private motive.

A respected name does not guarantee a righteous nature. A visible role does not prove invisible integrity. This is why parents must never allow a polished image to do the work that discernment was meant to do.

This is one of the great errors of careless discernment: confusing a public image with private integrity. Reputation is what people have heard. Character is who a person is when oversight is absent. Reputation may be polished. Character may still be corrupt. Reputation may be celebrated. Character may still be predatory. Parents must understand this difficult truth: a trusted image does not guarantee a trustworthy soul. Some individuals become skilled in managing perception. They know how to be seen. They know how to speak the right language, perform the right gestures, and occupy the right spaces in order to disarm concern. But presentation is not proof.

Public admiration can become a dangerous shield when it causes adults to silence their questions. Some people are trusted not because they have been carefully verified, but because they are impressive, influential, articulate, or familiar. But charm is not proof of purity.

Consistency in public does not automatically mean safety in private. Many harmful people survive behind the protection of their reputation because the adults around them would rather defend the image than investigate the pattern. This is how danger stays hidden in plain sight—under the cover of admiration.

Parents must therefore train themselves to look beneath the surface. A person's ability to inspire confidence in a room does not answer the deeper questions that matter for a child's safety. Do they honor boundaries when no one praises them for it? Do they welcome transparency, or do they quietly push against it? Do they seek excessive access to children, private communication, special exceptions, or situations where oversight is thin? Do they become offended when reasonable limitations are placed on their involvement? These are the kinds of questions that a character must answer—because reputation alone cannot.

There is also a sobering reality that many adults do not want to face: the very people most publicly trusted are sometimes given the least accountability. Their title becomes their shield. Their service becomes their cover. Their long history in the community becomes the reason no one wants to ask a hard question. But no title should ever outrank transparency. No role should ever remove scrutiny. No reputation should ever place a person beyond wise boundaries when children are involved. The more access a person has, the more accountability should surround that access—not less.

Children are especially vulnerable to this confusion because they are often taught to trust adults whom other adults trust. If the parent admires the person, the child may assume the person is unquestionably safe. If the church honors the person, the child may assume their position means purity. If the school recommends the person, the child may assume there is no reason for concern. This is why parents must be careful not to teach children that public respectability is the same as private righteousness. Children must learn that no matter how admired a person may be, boundaries still matter, discomfort still matters, and access should never be treated as unquestionable.

A wise parent also understands that character is tested most clearly where there is no spotlight. Character shows itself in restraint, humility, accountability, and consistency when there is nothing to gain from being seen. Character accepts oversight without resentment. Character respects limits without maneuvering around them. Character does not require secrecy, special treatment, emotional dependency, or hidden access to operate. Character remains clean in private because it is rooted in truth rather than maintained by image.

This is why discernment must go beyond what a person looks like, sounds like, or is known for. Parents must not simply ask, Is this person respected? They must ask, How does this person behave around boundaries? How do they respond to accountability? What kind of access do they seem to want? Does their conduct remain healthy when supervision is present and when it is not? These questions help separate reputation from character.

It must also be said that adults often feel pressure to protect the admired. The more celebrated a person becomes, the harder some people find it to imagine wrongdoing in them. Their minds resist the possibility because the reputation feels too established to question. But that resistance is dangerous. It is one thing to honor service, leadership, or consistency. It is another thing entirely to let admiration dull discernment. A parent must be willing to question what others are too impressed to examine. A child's safety must never be sacrificed on the altar of somebody else's good image.

This does not mean parents must become cynical toward every respected person. It means they must become wiser than appearances. Healthy discernment does not treat everyone as guilty. It treats no one as beyond accountability. That is the balance. A wise home is not governed by paranoia, but it is also not ruled by naïve admiration. It does not surrender its protective boundaries simply because a person is liked, applauded, trusted, or spiritually expressive.

Reputation can open doors.
Character determines whether access should remain.

And when children are involved, no wise parent can afford to confuse the two.

So let parents remember: what people say about someone may be true as far as they have seen, but it may not be the whole truth. The issue is not whether others admire them. The issue is whether their life has been proven safe enough, accountable enough, and transparent enough to be entrusted with meaningful proximity to a child. Reputation may impress a crowd. Character is what should be trusted near innocence.

Because a public image may be polished for many eyes.
But a child's safety requires more than polish.
It requires truth.
It requires verification.
It requires discernment strong enough to look past reputation and ask what kind of character is actually standing at the door.

HOW PREDATORS GAIN ACCESS

How predators gain access is rarely through force at the beginning. It is usually through positioning. They study families. They observe routines. They identify where parents are tired, busy, distracted, overextended, emotionally drained, or eager for help. They watch for gaps in structure, not merely gaps in schedule. They notice when oversight is inconsistent, when boundaries are loosely defined, when a child appears emotionally needy, and when a household is functioning in trust without verification. They do not always press at once. They often build comfort first. They understand that access is easiest to gain when it feels earned rather than requested.

This is what makes their strategy so dangerous. Many people imagine danger as something that arrives aggressively, but in reality, predatory access is often cultivated slowly. It grows through familiarity, repeated presence, emotional usefulness, and the careful reduction of adult vigilance. A predator often understands that if they can fit into the family's routine, they will be less questioned in the family's decisions. Once their presence feels ordinary, their access is more easily expanded. Once access is expanded, secrecy becomes easier to develop. Once secrecy develops, manipulation gains ground.

They may present themselves as dependable. They may offer support, assistance, transportation, childcare, mentorship, ministry help, or educational attention. They make themselves useful. They make themselves seem safe. They understand that access is often granted to people who appear cooperative, sacrificial, and available. They do not always begin by trying to win the child. Often, they begin by winning the adults' confidence. If they can become the person the family leans on, the person who always shows up, the person who seems willing to help when others are unavailable, then their presence may begin to feel like a blessing rather than a possible risk.

This is why usefulness must never be confused with trustworthiness. Help can be genuine, but help can also be strategic. Availability can be kind, but availability can also be calculated.

Some people do not offer assistance merely because they care; they offer assistance because usefulness lowers suspicion. The more indispensable they appear, the less likely they are to be examined carefully. That is why wise parents must ask not only, What is this person offering? But also, what kind of access is this offer creating?

Predatory behavior thrives where access is abundant and oversight is minimal.

That sentence must be taken seriously. Access is not a small matter. Access is the pathway through which influence, grooming, manipulation, and harm often begin. It is far easier to protect a child by regulating access early than to repair damage after access has already been misused. A predator does not need an immediate private opportunity to begin moving closer. Sometimes all they need is repeated inclusion, emotional trust from the adults, and enough comfort within the family's rhythm that boundaries start to feel unnecessary.

This is why parents must look beyond the helpful gesture and examine the structure surrounding it. Who is spending time alone with the child? Under what conditions? With what level of transparency? With what accountability? If access is granted repeatedly without visible boundaries, vulnerability increases.

Harm often develops not because a predator was unknown, but because they were allowed to become comfortable inside the family's patterns. Once a person becomes woven into the normal functioning of the home, adults may stop examining them with the same sobriety they would have used at the beginning. But danger does not become safer simply because it has become familiar.

There is also a deeper reality parents must recognize: predators often prefer households where questions are few, gratitude is high, and boundaries are weak. They look for places where adults are so relieved by the help that they don't scrutinize the helper. They notice when a family is overwhelmed enough to welcome assistance without evaluating the long-term structure around that assistance. They study who can be emotionally won over, who can be disarmed by kindness, and who is too exhausted to remain fully watchful. This is not accidental behavior. It is a strategic observation.

Parents who surrender vigilance in exchange for convenience unintentionally weaken the protective wall around their children.

Convenience is one of the most dangerous trade-offs in family protection. A busy parent may welcome transportation help because it relieves pressure. An overwhelmed parent may welcome childcare support because it creates breathing room. A strained household may welcome emotional investment from another adult because it feels like a needed source of reinforcement. But any help that increases private access to the child must be governed with wisdom. Relief is never a reason to remove oversight. Gratitude is never a reason to suspend discernment. A child's safety must never become the hidden cost of an adult's convenience.

Trust should never eliminate supervision.

That principle should remain fixed in the mind of every parent and guardian. Supervision is not an insult to trustworthy people; it is a safeguard for children and a protection against unnecessary vulnerability. Healthy adults do not resent appropriate structure. They understand it. They do not push for private exceptions. They do not need exclusive access to be helpful. They do not resist transparency. The moment a person seems to require less accountability to stay involved, that requirement itself should raise concern.

No adult should have unrestricted access to a child without visibility. No environment should be assumed safe without evaluation. No relationship should be beyond question simply because it is familiar. These are not harsh principles. They are necessary ones. A child should never be placed into repeated one-on-one access simply because the adult is liked, admired, spiritual, generous, or already woven into the family's life. Familiarity does not remove the need for wisdom. Repetition does not remove the need for structure. Access must always remain governed.

Parents must also understand that predators often test boundaries in small ways before moving on to larger ones. They may seek extra time with the child, offer special attention, create little exceptions, or gradually become more integrated into routines that place them near the child with less oversight. These small expansions of access may not seem alarming when viewed individually.

That is exactly why they are dangerous. What appears small in isolation may be significant in pattern. Wise parents watch for progression, not only isolated actions.

They ask: Is this access increasing? Is transparency decreasing? Is this person becoming unusually comfortable around the child? Are family routines shifting in ways that make their involvement more normalized and less questioned?

The issue is not whether every helpful person is dangerous. The issue is whether parents are awake enough to ensure that help never outruns healthy boundaries. A wise home can receive support without surrendering oversight. It can appreciate generosity without abandoning discernment. It can welcome the community without allowing the community to replace the parents' role as watchmen at the gate.

This is where many families become vulnerable—not because they wanted harm, but because they mistook access for safety, usefulness for integrity, and familiarity for protection. But a faithful parent must learn to think more deeply. Not everyone who gets close should remain close without accountability. Not everyone who offers support should receive expanded proximity to the child. Not every open door should stay open simply because the person on the other side feels helpful.

How predators gain access is rarely by announcing harmful intent. It is usually by becoming normal enough not to be questioned, useful enough not to be resisted, and familiar enough not to be examined. That is why the wall of protection must be maintained not only against the obvious threat, but also against the quiet expansion of access that others may call harmless.

So watch the pattern.
Measure the access.
Examine the structure.
Keep the boundary visible.
Keep the oversight active.
Keep the child protected.

Because what enters gradually can still wound deeply. And the parent who understands how access is gained will be far more prepared to interrupt it before comfort becomes vulnerability and familiarity becomes a doorway to harm.

❖ SPIRITUAL DECEPTION ❖

Parents must understand a difficult truth: proximity does not equal purity. Nearness does not prove righteousness. Repeated presence does not guarantee a clean heart. Access to a child is not evidence of trustworthiness; it is simply access. This is where many families become vulnerable. They mistake closeness for character, familiarity for safety, and religious or social comfort for spiritual integrity. But the home must never be guarded by assumption. It must be guarded by discernment.

Second Corinthians 11:14 (KJV) reminds us, "And no marvel; for Satan himself is transformed into an angel of light." If darkness can appear as light, then harm can appear as kindness. Evil rarely announces its intention—it conceals it behind normalcy. It does not always arrive wearing ugliness. Sometimes it comes dressed in helpfulness, respectability, attentiveness, spiritual language, and apparent concern. This is what makes spiritual deception so dangerous. It does not ask to be admitted as evil. It seeks entrance by appearing harmless enough not to be questioned.

Spiritual deception is dangerous precisely because it does not present itself honestly. It wears the garments of safety. It borrows the language of care. It hides behind familiarity, helpfulness, service, and outward decency. It may speak softly, serve faithfully, show up consistently, and appear emotionally invested in the well-being of a child or family. Yet appearance is not revelation. A person may know how to perform correctly without possessing moral purity. They may know how to mirror compassion without having a righteous motive. They may learn the tone of trustworthiness while carrying intentions that should never be granted free access to innocence.

This is why discernment must be spiritual and not merely emotional. If parents respond only to what feels good, looks kind, or sounds respectable, they may miss what lies beneath the surface. Emotions can be moved by personality. Eyes can be persuaded by presentation. Ears can be softened by polished speech. But spiritual discernment listens deeper. It watches patterns. It notices inconsistencies.

It pays attention not only to what is said publicly, but to how boundaries are handled privately, how accountability is received, how access is pursued, and whether transparency is welcomed or quietly resisted.

Deception works best where people assume appearances are enough. That is why families who rely too heavily on outward impressions become easier to deceive. A person's smile, title, generosity, involvement, or religious vocabulary may calm the room while concealing what should still be carefully examined. Scripture warns us that what appears bright is not always holy, and what appears gentle is not always harmless.

This does not mean parents must become cynical toward everyone. It does mean they must become deeper than surface judgment. They must refuse to let niceness replace scrutiny, and they must not allow a polished image to silence legitimate questions.

The danger of spiritual deception is that it often imitates the very qualities people are taught to trust. It can sound compassionate while slowly violating boundaries. It can seem supportive while quietly creating emotional dependence. It can appear spiritually mature while subtly moving outside proper accountability. It can present itself as a service while seeking access. It can behave with enough patience to earn the confidence of adults before ever revealing the depth of its corruption.

That is why a parent must not only ask, Does this person seem kind? But also, how do they handle limits? Do they respect visibility? Do they welcome accountability? Does their presence strengthen clarity, or does it slowly create confusion?

Families must also understand that spiritual deception often prospers in atmospheres where discomfort is ignored. If a child feels uneasy around someone, but the adults are too impressed to take that uneasiness seriously, deception has already gained an advantage. If a parent's spirit is unsettled but they push aside the concern because the person seems respectable, deception has room to operate. If boundaries are repeatedly tested but excused because the individual is well-liked, useful, or admired, deception is no longer merely outside the gate—it is being negotiated with inside it.

This is why parents must remain spiritually alive. A dull spirit is easier to deceive. A prayerless home is easier to infiltrate. A family that no longer tests atmospheres, weighs patterns, or listens to holy uneasiness becomes increasingly vulnerable to what arrives wrapped in brightness but carries corruption underneath. Spiritual discernment is not superstition. It is disciplined attentiveness before God. It is the refusal to call everything safe simply because it is socially affirmed.

It is the willingness to let Scripture, prayer, wisdom, and sober observation work together until truth becomes clearer.

The family that does not take spiritual deception seriously may become vulnerable not because danger was absent, but because danger was disguised. That disguise may take the form of a pleasant voice, a serving posture, a respected role, a familiar face, or a spiritual tone. But disguise does not make darkness holy. Presentation does not make a soul trustworthy. The parent who understands this will be far less likely to surrender the wall simply because what stands outside it appears acceptable.

Spiritual deception must therefore be confronted with more than emotion. It must be met with prayer, biblical clarity, accountability, visible boundaries, and a willingness to question what others too quickly affirm. Parents must teach their children that not everything that glitters is light, not every open door should remain open, and not every trusted face should be given unquestioned access.

Because some of the most dangerous things do not first appear dangerous.
They appear welcome.
They appear useful.
They appear safe.
And that is why the watchman must remain awake.

A spiritually discerning parent does not merely ask whether something looks good. They ask whether it is true, whether it is clean, whether it is accountable, and whether it remains healthy under examination.

That kind of watchfulness does not produce fear. It produces protection.

And in a world where darkness often arrives disguised, that protection is not optional. It is sacred.

❖ SPIRITUAL WARNING ❖

A Warning Against Spiritual Negligence

The Strategy of Familiarity / Over-Trust and Lack of Verification

Excessive trust often silences red flags. When discomfort arises, parents may hesitate to confront because "we know them." When behavioral shifts appear, they may dismiss them because "they would never." When a child expresses unease, it may be minimized because "they've always been good to us." This is how danger survives in environments that feel safe on the surface. It is not always protected by secrecy alone; it is often protected by familiarity. The more normal a person feels within the family, the more difficult some adults find it to imagine that person needing closer scrutiny. But goodness displayed publicly does not eliminate private danger. Public comfort does not prove inner purity. A trusted presence can still become a harmful presence if access expands while discernment grows quiet.

Familiarity is one of the enemy's most effective strategies because it gradually lowers defenses. It does not usually demand trust all at once. It earns comfort over time. Repetition creates emotional ease, and emotional ease can become spiritual carelessness. The more often people are around someone, the less likely they are to question them. A face becomes familiar. A voice becomes common. A pattern becomes routine. And what becomes routine is often left unexamined. This is how access deepens without scrutiny. This is how warning signs become easier to excuse. This is how instincts become easier to silence. Adults begin telling themselves that the relationship is too established to question, and in that very assumption, the wall of protection begins to weaken.

Parents must not allow history to replace discernment. Long-term presence does not remove the need for vigilance. Shared meals do not remove the need for boundaries. Church attendance does not remove the need for accountability. Family connection does not remove the need for questions. Familiarity does not cancel caution. A person should never become so normal in the life of the household that wise observation is treated as unnecessary. The longer someone remains around the child, the more their patterns should be known, not the less. Repeated proximity should not produce sleeping watchmen; it should produce clearer discernment.

The danger of over-trust lies in the absence of verification. It is not enough to assume safety because someone is known. It is not enough to rely on intuition without oversight. It is not enough to say, "I have a good feeling about them," while refusing to examine what kind of access is being created. Trust must be accompanied by boundaries.

Access must be accompanied by accountability. Any trust that requires the removal of wise oversight has already become unhealthy. Children should never be placed beneath the weight of an adult's confidence if that confidence has not remained accountable to structure, visibility, and prudence.

Healthy trust is built through transparency, accountability, and structure. It does not remove boundaries—it respects them. It does not resist parental awareness—it welcomes it. It does not require private exceptions to function. A wise parent understands that discernment protects trust from becoming naivety.

Trust is healthiest where nothing meaningful needs to be hidden. It is strongest where supervision is not resented, questions are not offensive, and access remains within visible, appropriate limits. In a well-guarded environment, trust is never asked to do the work that only vigilance was meant to do.

Over-trust assumes safety. Discernment verifies it.

That difference is not small. One assumes. The other examines. One relaxes because things feel fine. The other remains awake enough to know that what feels fine should still be weighed. A prudent parent does not operate in paranoia but in awareness. They observe interactions. They evaluate patterns. They limit unnecessary isolation between adults and children. They create environments where access is structured, not assumed. They do not hand children into situations simply because it would be easier to do so. They remember that convenience is never a worthy substitute for protection.

Open communication with children strengthens this protective framework. Parents must teach their children that no adult's authority overrides their right to safety. No secret involving touching is acceptable. Discomfort is reason enough to speak up. Familiarity does not cancel caution. These truths are powerful because they help remove the false guilt children often feel when discomfort arises around someone the family trusts. A child should know that they are not wrong for speaking up about unease. They are not disloyal for naming what feels wrong. They are not required to ignore the internal alarm simply because the adult involved is known, admired, or connected to the family.

When children are empowered to voice unease without fear of dismissal, protection increases significantly. But this requires parents to create a culture where the child's discomfort is taken seriously, even when it complicates adult assumptions. A child may not be able to explain everything clearly, but their unease still matters. Their changed behavior still matters. Their hesitation still matters. Wise parents do not demand polished evidence before allowing concern to influence the way access is managed. They know that children often sense misalignment before they can articulate it.

Trust is earned.
Access is regulated.
Vigilance is maintained.

That is the order of a protected home.

Parents must reject the cultural pressure to appear relaxed or overly agreeable. There is often subtle pressure to make everyone feel welcome, included, and affirmed—even at the expense of asking necessary questions. But a child's safety must never be sacrificed to preserve the appearance of social ease. It is better to be cautious and wrong than careless and regretful. Better to ask the uncomfortable question than to sit later with the agony of knowing you silenced your own discernment to keep the moment pleasant.

The perils of excessive trust are real. Many tragedies began not with obvious warning signs, but with unguarded familiarity. Protection weakens the moment trust replaces oversight.

A family does not need to fear every person to become wise. But it must become serious enough to understand that no person, no relationship, no title, and no history should ever be allowed to operate beyond healthy verification. A child's safety should never depend solely on someone else's character—it must rest on the discernment of the one God appointed to guard them.

Trust wisely.
Question respectfully.
Verify consistently.

Because over-trust is not faith.
Over-trust is vulnerability.

Guard carefully.
Trust cautiously.
Remain watchful.

For innocence cannot afford blind confidence.

❖ SPIRITUAL WARNING ❖

A Warning Against Spiritual Negligence

There are consequences for what we ignore. Not every failure begins with rebellion. Some begin with an assumption. Some begin with comfort. Some begin with the quiet decision to believe that vigilance is unnecessary because everything appears calm, familiar, or manageable. But Heaven does not overlook negligence disguised as innocence. God is not deceived by the outward calm that often surrounds inward carelessness. He sees when warning signs were softened to avoid conflict. He sees that when boundaries were relaxed, to preserve relationships. He sees that adults protect comfort more fiercely than they protect children.

When responsibility is entrusted, accountability is established. And when guardians grow passive, vulnerability expands. Spiritual negligence does not always look dramatic—it often looks calm. It looks like routine. It looks like "everything seems fine." It looks like a household continuing its normal rhythm while small compromises quietly gather strength. Yet danger does not require chaos to advance. It only requires opportunity.

There are gates in every home. Gates of influence. Gates of access. Gates of conversation. Gates of exposure. And every gate demands a watchman. If the watchman becomes distracted, infiltration becomes easy. Children suffer not only because evil exists, but because vigilance weakens. That is not a comfortable truth. But it is a necessary one. Evil has always sought opportunity. It often finds that opportunity not where people are openly rebellious, but where they have grown spiritually tired, emotionally hesitant, and too comfortable to stay alert.

God does not measure love by intention alone. He measures stewardship by diligence. It is not enough to feel protective. Protection must be practiced. It must be enforced. It must be maintained even when it is inconvenient.

Parents cannot claim guardianship while refusing the labor it requires. If warning signs are softened to avoid awkwardness, if discomfort is dismissed to preserve relationships, if boundaries are relaxed to maintain appearances, a door is opened. And some doors, once opened, cannot be closed without damage.

Spiritual apathy is a silent accomplice to harm. It whispers, "Don't overreact." It reasons, "It's probably nothing." It persuades, "You don't want to make this bigger than it is." But what if it is bigger than you realize? What if what you are calling small is the beginning of something that grows because no one interrupted it? What if what you are excusing today becomes the very thing you later weep over because your discernment was quieter than your desire to stay comfortable?

The soul must be shaken because complacency has become common. Many would rather protect their reputation than confront reality. Many would rather delay action than disrupt comfort. But delay multiplies damage. If you are entrusted with a child, you are entrusted with something sacred. That trust is not light. It is not casual. It carries divine expectation. You cannot afford spiritual sleep. You cannot afford emotional hesitation. You cannot afford selective discernment that only sees what is convenient to see.

If something shifts, pay attention. If something unsettles your spirit, investigate. If something in your child changes, lean in immediately. The cost of vigilance is temporary discomfort. The cost of negligence may echo for generations. Stand alert. Guard intentionally. Refuse to normalize what should be confronted.

Because Heaven is not only watching what enters your home—Heaven is watching how you guard it. And faithfulness requires watchfulness.

CHAPTER FIVE
HIDDEN PERILS WITHIN THE HOME
Invisible Influences and Digital Exposure

Danger is not always loud. It does not always break windows or force doors open. Some of the most destructive influences enter quietly, invisibly, and repeatedly—until their presence becomes normalized. Harm does not always arrive through obvious confrontation. Often it seeps in gradually, settling into the rhythms of daily life until its influence becomes familiar enough to escape notice.

Many parents focus on physical security: locked doors, alarm systems, safe neighborhoods, and carefully chosen environments. These are important safeguards. Yet while the front door remains secured, invisible gateways may remain wide open. The modern home is saturated with digital access, emotional atmospheres, and unseen influences that shape a child's mind long before behavior reveals the damage. Protection today must extend beyond physical safety into the unseen spaces where thoughts are formed, identities are influenced, and values are quietly cultivated.

Parents must understand this clearly: screen access is access to influence.

Digital exposure is one of the most underestimated dangers in the modern household because it often appears harmless at first. A phone may seem like a convenience. A tablet may appear educational. A computer may seem necessary for learning. A gaming system may seem recreational. But every device is also a gate, and every gate must be guarded. These tools do more than deliver information—they deliver environments. Within those environments, voices, images, conversations, and ideas can shape a child's thinking far more deeply than many parents realize.

When children are allowed to move through digital spaces without oversight, they are not simply exploring information—they are being shaped by whatever reaches them first and most often. Exposure forms familiarity. Familiarity forms tolerance. Tolerance forms acceptance. And acceptance eventually begins to shape desire, language, values, and behavior. What begins as curiosity can gradually become normalization. What once appeared uncomfortable can slowly begin to feel ordinary.

Digital access is never neutral. Every image carries influence. Every repeated message leaves an impression. What enters the mind repeatedly begins to shape the perception of reality. A child's understanding of relationships, identity, morality, sexuality, success, and self-worth can be influenced by voices that operate entirely outside the home. These voices may not share the family's values. They may not respect innocence. They may not honor truth.

What is seen privately often grows publicly. What is normalized in hidden spaces eventually influences visible conduct. Words heard repeatedly become language. Images viewed frequently become imagination. Conversations encountered online begin to shape expectations about the world. A child's behavior rarely changes suddenly; it changes gradually as the mind becomes accustomed to what once felt foreign.

This is why digital exposure requires intentional oversight. The danger is not simply that harmful content exists—it is that it can be encountered repeatedly without interruption. Repetition carries power. What a child sees once may disturb them. What they see repeatedly may begin to desensitize them. And once desensitization occurs, discernment weakens.

The digital world also removes many of the natural barriers that once protected children. In previous generations, exposure required physical proximity. Now it requires only a connection and a screen. Predatory individuals, manipulative communities, explicit content, distorted ideologies, and emotional pressures can all reach a child without crossing the threshold of the home. A child may be physically safe in their bedroom while being spiritually, emotionally, and psychologically exposed to influences that undermine their development.

Parents must therefore reject the assumption that digital freedom equals harmless exploration. Unrestricted access does not produce maturity—it often accelerates confusion. A child's developing mind is not prepared to process everything the digital world can present. What adults may recognize as inappropriate or manipulative may appear attractive or normal to a child who has not yet developed the discernment to filter what they encounter.

This does not mean technology must be feared. But it must be governed. Tools that are not supervised can quickly become teachers that parents never intended to invite into the home. Algorithms designed to maximize engagement often push content that is provocative, emotional, or extreme because such material captures attention. A child may begin searching for something innocent and gradually be exposed to increasingly distorted material simply because the digital system is designed to hold their attention as long as possible.

Parents must remain present in their children's digital lives. Awareness of what children watch, who they communicate with, what platforms they use, and how much time they spend online is not excessive—it is responsible stewardship. Healthy oversight communicates to children that their safety matters more than unlimited independence.

The goal is not to create fear but to cultivate wisdom. Children must learn that digital spaces are real environments with real consequences. They must understand that not every voice online is trustworthy, not every image is harmless, and not every community they encounter has their well-being in mind.

A guarded home, therefore, pays attention to what enters through screens just as carefully as it pays attention to who enters through doors. Conversations about digital influence must be open and ongoing. Parents must help children develop discernment so that they can recognize manipulation, resist harmful messaging, and understand why boundaries exist.

The unseen world of digital influence is powerful precisely because it often operates quietly. Yet quiet influence can shape a life just as profoundly as visible experiences. The mind of a child is fertile ground. Whatever is planted repeatedly will eventually begin to grow.

For this reason, the watchman of the home must stand guard not only at the door, but also at the screen.

Because what enters the eyes eventually reaches the heart.
And what reaches the heart eventually shapes the life.

Digital access is never neutral. What enters repeatedly leaves an imprint. What is seen privately often grows publicly. What is normalized in hidden spaces eventually influences visible conduct.

MEDIA INFLUENCE

First Corinthians 15:33 (KJV) warns with clarity: "Be not deceived: evil communications corrupt good manners." This is not limited to spoken conversation. Communication includes music, images, narratives, digital exchanges, humor, commentary, and cultural messaging. Whatever repeatedly speaks into a child's heart will eventually influence character. A child is not formed only by direct instruction from parents, teachers, or pastors. They are also shaped by the voices they hear most often, the images they see most often, and the stories they absorb most deeply. The media speaks, even when no one in the room is talking. It teaches, even when it presents itself as amusement. It disciples, even when it calls itself entertainment.

Corruption rarely begins with obvious rebellion. It begins with exposure.

That is what makes media influence so serious. It often arrives without resistance because it does not demand immediate agreement. It only asks for repeated attention. It does not need a child to embrace everything at once. It only needs enough access to become familiar. And once something becomes familiar, it becomes easier to tolerate. Once it is tolerated, it becomes easier to excuse. Once it is excused, it becomes easier to imitate. This is how influence moves from the screen into the conscience, and from the conscience into behavior.

Music filled with explicit content reshapes language and desensitizes conscience. Media that glorifies immorality subtly normalizes what Scripture calls destructive. Entertainment that trivializes sexual behavior rewires understanding of intimacy and respect. Violent video games and graphic films can dull sensitivity to aggression, making conflict appear entertaining rather than harmful. Content that celebrates rebellion, mocks purity, glamorizes revenge, elevates vanity, or turns shameful things into punchlines is not harmless simply because it is packaged skillfully. It is shaping appetite. It is training reflexes. It is forming emotional and moral expectations.

Repeated exposure forms perception.
Perception shapes belief.
Belief influences behavior.

This progression is often quiet. A child may not immediately begin acting out everything they see. That is not how formation usually works. First, the imagination is affected. Then the emotional response begins to shift. Things that once felt troubling no longer feel severe. Things that once felt inappropriate begin to seem normal. Humor changes. Taste changes. Language changes. Tolerance deepens. By the time outward behavior becomes visible, inward categories may already have been reshaped.

Media is not merely background noise. It is instruction disguised as entertainment. It teaches children what to laugh at, what to admire, what to desire, and what to excuse. It teaches what kind of beauty is worth pursuing, what kind of relationships are worth wanting, what kind of speech is acceptable, what kind of authority deserves mockery, and what kind of behavior should be celebrated. It can make darkness appear normal, and holiness appear strange. It can make discipline feel oppressive, and impulsiveness feel authentic. It can make moral restraint look weak and moral compromise look sophisticated. It can weaken moral reflexes before a child has the discernment to recognize what is happening.

This is one of the most dangerous aspects of media influence: it often shapes a child before the child realizes it is being shaped. They are not merely consuming content. Content is also consuming space in their imagination, emotional responses, standards, and expectations. The stories children live around begin to tell them what life is supposed to look like. If those stories repeatedly glorify dysfunction, sensuality, cynicism, mockery, and emotional chaos, then those things begin to feel less foreign and more familiar. Familiarity is powerful because what feels familiar often no longer feels dangerous.

Parents must therefore understand that the media is not neutral simply because it is common. Widespread acceptance is not proof of moral harmlessness.

Something can be culturally normal and spiritually destructive at the same time. Something can be celebrated publicly and still erode a child's discernment privately. Popularity does not sanctify content. Visibility does not make it wise. Cultural repetition does not make it safe.

This is why parents cannot afford to be passive about what fills the home's atmosphere. Content is not harmless simply because it is popular. Influence is not safe simply because it is common. Parents must evaluate media not by cultural acceptance, but by moral consequence. They must ask deeper questions than Is everyone watching this? Or is this trending? Or will my child feel left out without it? The better questions are: What is this teaching? What does this normalize? What does this celebrate? What kind of appetite does this create? What kind of conscience does this weaken?

A wise parent knows that what enters the home repeatedly becomes part of the home's atmosphere. Media choices influence more than leisure. They shape tone. They affect emotional climate. They affect language. They affect how children imagine adulthood, relationships, authority, success, and even themselves. A steady flow of noisy, sensual, aggressive, mocking, or morally careless content can quietly condition the household. Even if no one is openly discussing the influence, it is still doing its work.

This is especially important because many parents focus mainly on explicit content while overlooking formative tone. Yet tone matters deeply. A show may avoid obvious vulgarity and still glorify disrespect. A song may not contain graphic language and still stir sensuality or bitterness. A film may be artistically impressive and still normalize manipulation, revenge, moral confusion, or emotional instability. Parents must learn to evaluate not just what content to avoid, but what it promotes. Not just what it says openly, but what it trains subtly.

Children also tend to absorb media differently from adults. What an adult might interpret critically, a child may receive with an impressionable mind. What a mature person may recognize as satire, a child may absorb as permission. What an adult may know is exaggerated; a child may begin to view it as desirable. This is why parental discernment must stay ahead of the child's exposure.

The child is not yet equipped to filter everything well. That is why the watchman at the wall must remain awake.

This does not mean the home must become joyless, fearful, or suspicious of every creative expression. It means parents must be intentional. They must curate, not drift. They must guide, not surrender. They must help children understand why certain things weaken rather than strengthen, distort rather than clarify, and entertain in ways that cost more than they appear to. Discernment in media is not about legalism. It is about formation. It is about asking whether what fills the home helps the child love what is true, honorable, pure, and wise—or quietly trains them to tolerate what is dark, careless, corrupt, or degrading.

Parents who remain passive in this area often discover too late that the home was being discipled by forces they never deliberately invited. Language changed. Attitudes changed. Desires changed. Emotional sensitivity changed. Respect changed. And by the time the shift became obvious, the shaping had already been happening for some time. That is why media stewardship must begin before the damage becomes visible.

So guard what speaks often.
Examine what plays repeatedly.
Question: What becomes normal?
Filter what fills the atmosphere.

Because the media is never only entertainment.
It is formation.
And whatever repeatedly forms the child will eventually reveal itself in how that child thinks, desires, speaks, and lives.

UNMONITORED DEVICES

Predators and Digital Targeting

How Technology Becomes a Hunting Tool

The digital world has not only changed how children learn, communicate, and socialize—it has also changed how predators hunt. Devices designed for convenience, entertainment, and connection can become powerful tools in the hands of those intent on harm. For a predator, the internet is not merely a network of information; it is a map of opportunity. It allows them to observe, identify, approach, manipulate, and isolate potential victims with a level of access that previous generations could not imagine.

Predators do not move randomly. They study patterns. They observe environments. They search for openings. Technology enables them to do this quietly and at scale. Through social media platforms, gaming networks, messaging applications, and comment threads, predators can identify children who are active online, emotionally expressive, unsupervised, or seeking attention. A profile picture, a username, a posted location, a school name in a bio, a shared photograph in a familiar place—these small pieces of information can become fragments of a larger puzzle. When assembled, those fragments reveal routines, interests, friendships, emotional vulnerabilities, and daily habits.

This is how identification begins.

Once a potential target is identified, predators often move into observation. They watch how the child communicates online. They read posts. They observe the child's emotional tone—loneliness, frustration, curiosity, rebellion, insecurity. They look for signals that the child may be searching for validation, encouragement, or friendship. These signals do not make the child weak; they reveal the normal emotional needs of growing young people. But predators exploit those needs intentionally. They look for children who appear isolated, misunderstood, or eager for approval because such children may respond more quickly to attention.

Technology allows this observation to occur silently.

The predator does not need to stand on a street corner or follow a child physically. Instead, they can watch from a distance through screens, gathering information while remaining invisible. They learn what the child likes, what games they play, what music they listen to, what communities they participate in, and what emotional responses they display. This information allows the predator to tailor their approach so that it appears natural rather than suspicious.

After observation comes approach.

Predators rarely begin with obvious wrongdoing. They begin with friendliness. A comment on a post. A message in a game. A compliment about a shared interest. A casual conversation that appears harmless. They may present themselves as someone close in age, someone with similar hobbies, or someone who understands the child's frustrations. The goal at this stage is not control—it is comfort. If the predator can become a familiar voice, the next stages become easier.

This is how manipulation begins.

Gradually, the conversation deepens. The predator offers encouragement, sympathy, attention, and flattery. They may listen patiently to the child's struggles. They may present themselves as a safe confidant. The child begins to feel seen, understood, or valued. Emotional connection forms before suspicion ever appears. This stage is often called "grooming," but in practice, it is simply manipulation disguised as friendship.

During this phase, predators often attempt to create separation.

They may encourage private messaging. They may suggest moving conversations away from public spaces to private chats, encrypted apps, or platforms where messages disappear. They may tell the child that others would not understand their friendship. They may suggest keeping the conversation secret to protect the relationship. This secrecy is not accidental—it is strategic. Once the child feels responsible for protecting the conversation, the predator gains leverage.

Technology allows predators to escalate slowly.

A conversation that begins about hobbies can shift toward personal questions. Personal questions can become emotionally dependent. Emotional dependence can become requests for photos, video chats, or private interactions. Some predators begin introducing sexual language gradually. Others attempt to create guilt or obligation. Still others may threaten exposure if the child resists or tries to withdraw. What began as a friendly interaction can quickly become psychological captivity.

This is where stalking and pursuit intensify.

Predators may gather additional information about the child's life—such as school schedules, locations, family structure, or extracurricular activities. Through location tagging, photographs, or shared environments, they may identify places the child frequently visits. In extreme cases, online contact can lead to attempts at physical meetings. What began as invisible digital contact becomes a real-world threat.

The terrifying reality is that a child may not recognize the danger until the trap has already begun to close.

Children are not trained investigators. They do not naturally assume that a friendly person online may be deceiving them. They often assume honesty because they themselves are honest. They assume kindness because they are taught to value kindness. Predators exploit this innocence.

Technology, therefore, becomes a tool of pursuit.

It allows predators to:

Identify potential victims through profiles, posts, and shared content.

Observe routines, interests, emotional states, and vulnerabilities.

Approach through friendly interaction and shared interests.

Manipulate through emotional attention and false trust.

Isolate through private messaging and secrecy.

Control through guilt, pressure, or threats.

This entire process can unfold without a parent hearing a sound.

A child may appear to be gaming, chatting with friends, or scrolling through social media while the predator is quietly advancing through stages of grooming and manipulation. The physical home may feel safe while the digital door remains open to someone outside the family's awareness.

Parents must understand that predators rely on three conditions to succeed:

Access

Privacy

Silence

If a child has unrestricted access to devices, privacy in their digital life, and no safe path to speak openly about uncomfortable interactions, the predator's work becomes far easier.

This is why digital awareness must become a core part of household protection.

Children must be taught that not everyone online is who they claim to be. They must understand that kindness can be imitated and trust can be exploited. They must know that any adult or stranger requesting secrecy, personal photos, private conversations, or emotional dependence is crossing a dangerous line.

Parents must also remain actively involved in their children's digital lives. Devices should not become private territories beyond parental awareness. Open conversations, shared spaces for screen use, parental controls, and regular discussions about online experiences create an environment where manipulation is harder to conceal.

Most importantly, children must know that they can speak without fear.

If a child believes they will be punished or blamed for encountering something uncomfortable online, they may remain silent. Silence is the predator's greatest protection. But when a child knows they will be heard, protected, and supported, they are far more likely to reveal troubling interactions before they escalate.

Predators depend on darkness, secrecy, and isolation.

The antidote is light, awareness, and communication.

Parents must therefore remain watchful not only at the physical door of the home, but also at the digital gates that shape their children's world. The tools of technology are powerful. In a child's hands, they can educate and connect. In the hands of a predator, they can become instruments of stalking and manipulation.

The difference between those outcomes often rests on one question:

Is the watchman awake?

Guard the gates.
Guard the conversations.
Guard the access.

Because the modern battlefield for a child's safety is not only outside the home—it is often inside the screen.

PEER INFLUENCE

Invisible dangers do not come only through screens. They also arrive through companionship. Peer influence is one of the strongest shaping forces in a child's development because children and teenagers often absorb the habits, tone, attitudes, emotional patterns, and moral posture of those around them. Long before a parent notices the full change in behavior, influence may already be at work through repeated exposure. A child may begin speaking differently, reacting differently, valuing different things, or tolerating what once troubled them simply because the voices nearest to them have made those things feel ordinary.

Not every friendship is harmless simply because it is youthful. Not every influence is safe simply because it is common. Some peers introduce rebellion. Some normalize disrespect. Some encourage secrecy. Some make corruption seem adventurous rather than destructive. Some weaken a child's conscience by repeated exposure to attitudes and behaviors that would once have felt troubling. Some friendships sharpen character, and others slowly dissolve restraint. There are peer groups that strengthen courage, honesty, and reverence, and there are peer groups that reward risk, mock conviction, and make compromise feel like maturity.

A child who is consistently surrounded by compromise begins to adapt to it. What once felt uncomfortable can begin to feel normal if the surrounding voices repeat it often enough. This is one of the great dangers of peer influence: it rarely changes a child all at once. It often works by gradual adjustment. The child laughs at what they once would have questioned. They become quieter about what they know is right. They begin to hide what they are doing because they know it would not survive parental light. They become more defensive, more secretive, or more dismissive of correction. None of this may seem dramatic at first, but repeated accommodation to unhealthy influence reshapes the inner world.

This is why parents must pay attention not only to where their children go, but to who is shaping them. Friendships are not minor matters. Peer groups can reinforce truth or erode it. They can strengthen identity or confuse it. They can encourage courage or reward recklessness. Some relationships do not openly invite a child into obvious wrongdoing; instead, they quietly pressure them to fit in, stay silent, minimize discomfort, or loosen convictions to remain accepted. The danger is not only direct temptation. The danger is also the subtle pressure to become someone else to belong.

Wise parents do not mock their children's relationships, but they do examine them. They ask, "Who influences my child's language?" Who affects my child's emotional tone? Who shapes my child's values? Who makes secrecy feel acceptable? Who makes compromise appear harmless? Who leaves my child more grounded, and who leaves them more agitated, more defensive, more ashamed, more impulsive, or more confused? These are necessary questions because peer influence often manifests in fruit. A parent may not hear every conversation, but they can often observe what those relationships are producing in the child.

Peer pressure must also be understood as more than being dared to do something reckless. Sometimes it is emotional. Sometimes it is social. Sometimes it comes through exclusion, mockery, manipulation, or the fear of being left out. A child may silence their convictions to remain accepted. They may join what they inwardly know is wrong because rejection feels more terrifying than compromise. They may keep quiet about bullying, inappropriate behavior, dangerous challenges, sexual pressure, drug exposure, or emotional abuse because they fear losing belonging. This is why parents must not underestimate the emotional force of peer approval, for many children and teenagers, belonging feels urgent. If that longing is not shepherded carefully, it can become a doorway through which destructive influence enters.

Some children have taken their own lives under the crushing weight of peer pressure, humiliation, rejection, bullying, blackmail, online shaming, or chronic emotional torment from those their age. This reality must be faced with sobriety. Not all peer influence leads to visible acting out; some of it leads inward—toward despair, self-hatred, isolation, anxiety, self-harm, and silence. A child under peer pressure may become withdrawn, emotionally flat, unusually agitated, secretive, fearful of school or social settings, overly attached to a device, or deeply reactive to messages and notifications. Parents must stay diligent to recognize the signs. They must not dismiss profound emotional change as "just adolescence" without looking more closely. Sometimes the child is not merely moody. Sometimes they are carrying a social burden heavier than they know how to name.

This is why the home must become a place where children can talk honestly about friendship, pressure, belonging, conflict, and fear without being ridiculed or rushed. If the child only hears correction but never feels understood, they may hide the very relationships that need the most examination. Parents must build enough trust that the child can say, "I don't feel right around them," or "They keep pressuring me," or "I'm afraid of what they'll do if I say no," or "I don't know how to get out of this friendship," and know they will be met with wisdom rather than shame.

Parents should also teach children how to recognize unhealthy relational patterns early. A friend who demands secrecy, punishes honesty, pressures disobedience, mocks convictions, manipulates with guilt, thrives on drama, or isolates a child from healthy voices is not a harmless friend simply because they are young. Youth does not make corruption safe.

Immaturity may explain some behavior, but it does not remove its influence. A child should learn that friendship is not proven by intensity, but by fruit. A true friend does not make righteousness harder, honesty riskier, or safety feel embarrassing.

Peer influence must be watched carefully because children often become what they repeatedly accommodate. What they excuse long enough, they may eventually imitate. What they tolerate often enough, they may begin to defend. The longer they stay around, the more they may slowly become comfortable with it, even when it is shaping them in the wrong direction.

So parents must remain awake.

Watch the changes.

Study the fruit.

Listen to the silences.

Notice who your child becomes after repeated contact with certain people.

Companions can strengthen a child or quietly bend them. And a wise parent understands that guarding a child's future includes guarding the influences that are teaching them who to become.

SECRET ENVIRONMENTS

When children navigate digital spaces without oversight, they are vulnerable to predatory manipulation, grooming, hate speech, misinformation, ideological confusion, and emotional exploitation. The danger is not merely exposure—it is influence without guidance. A child may encounter something harmful and not know it is harmful. They may hear something false and not yet have the discernment to challenge it. They may be drawn into a conversation that feels flattering, exciting, understanding, or emotionally validating without realizing that it is slowly disarming them. This is what makes hidden environments so serious: they do not merely show a child something. They begin shaping the child in the absence of protective interpretation.

Secret environments are breeding grounds for hidden danger. Secrecy removes visibility. It weakens accountability. It creates space for manipulation to grow unnoticed. Harm develops most easily in places where observation is absent, and disclosure feels unsafe. Darkness does not need a large opening if it has privacy, time, and silence. It thrives where no one is looking closely, where no one is asking follow-up questions, and where the child has learned that telling the truth may create more pain than hiding it.

Some secret environments are digital. Some are relational. Some are emotional. Some exist in bedrooms behind closed doors, in private group chats, in hidden online accounts, in isolated conversations, or in atmospheres where a child has learned not to speak. A device can become a secret room. A friendship can become a secret room. An unspoken fear can become a secret room. A child may be outwardly present in the family while inwardly living in a hidden environment of shame, pressure, confusion, fantasy, or fear that no adult around them has yet recognized. That hidden world is dangerous not only because of what may be happening there, but because of how long it may remain untouched if silence continues.

Secret environments are especially powerful because they often become alternate worlds of formation. In them, children may be taught values that the home never intended to teach. They may be exposed to ideas that undermine their identity, messages that distort love, voices that reward secrecy, and communities that encourage emotional dependence on people their parents do not know. In such spaces, a child may learn to split their life in two: one version visible to parents, teachers, or church, and another version carried privately through hidden messages, hidden media, hidden thoughts, hidden habits, or hidden relationships. That division weakens integrity. It teaches concealment. It trains the child to live in compartments rather than in truth.

Conversation is critical. Children must feel safe discussing what they encounter without fear of immediate condemnation. When parents create open dialogue, they reduce secrecy. When secrecy diminishes, vulnerability decreases. This is why strong protection is not built only through restrictions. It is also built through relational safety. A child needs a home where they can say, "I saw something I didn't understand," or "Someone said something that made me uncomfortable," or "I've been talking to someone online," or "I feel pressure I don't know how to explain," and know that the adult hearing them will respond with steadiness, wisdom, and protection rather than panic, mockery, or crushing shame.

Children who fear shame often hide what should be exposed. Children who fear anger often silence what should be discussed. Children who believe they will not be heard often retreat deeper into secrecy. This is one of the enemy's most effective strategies: not merely to expose the child to harm, but to convince the child that remaining silent is safer than bringing the matter into the light. A child who believes they will be blamed may hide exploitation. A child who believes they will lose privileges may hide exposure. A child who believes the parent will overreact emotionally may protect the adult from the truth and carry the burden alone. This is why the emotional tone of the home matters so much. The home must be a place where truth can survive.

Parents must therefore become students of hidden patterns. Is the child suddenly guarding their device? Are they pulling away emotionally while insisting that nothing is wrong? Are they unusually anxious when messages arrive? Do they become defensive when simple questions are asked? Have they developed unusual fear around certain topics, people, or conversations? Are they overly relieved when privacy is granted and overly agitated when it is interrupted? These things do not automatically prove danger, but they are the kinds of signals that wise parents do not dismiss casually. Hidden environments often reveal themselves through subtle shifts before they are ever named directly.

The problem is not privacy in all its forms. Children do need age-appropriate dignity, personal space, and emotional respect. But secrecy is different from healthy privacy. Privacy protects dignity. Secrecy protects hidden influence. Privacy can exist within trust. Secrecy often grows where trust has weakened, fear has increased, or another voice has gained more power in the child's inner world than the parent realizes. Parents must learn to discern the difference. A child closing a door to change clothes is a form of privacy. A child constructing an entire hidden world of relationships, content, and emotional life that no trusted adult can safely enter is something else entirely.

This is why the home must become a place where light is normal, honesty is protected, and difficult conversations are not punished. Light means things can be named. It means questions can be asked. It means discomfort can be brought into words. It means a child is not forced to carry secret pressure because the adults around them are too uncomfortable to receive the difficult truth.

Honesty must not become dangerous in the very place where safety is supposed to live. A child should not have to choose between telling the truth and preserving their emotional survival.

Parents must also remember that secret environments often grow strongest where routine has replaced attentiveness. A child may sit in the same room every day while spiritually, emotionally, or digitally disappearing into hidden spaces. Familiarity with routine can lead adults to assume that, because the child is physically near, all is well. But physical nearness is not the same as relational visibility.

A child can be under the same roof and still be profoundly alone in their experience. That is why watchfulness must go beyond location. It must include presence, conversation, discernment, and willingness to ask what lies beneath the surface.

Invisible dangers flourish in neglect. They retreat in vigilance. Hidden things gain strength when parents stop watching the atmosphere, stop listening for shifts in tone, stop asking the deeper questions, or grow too tired to investigate what feels misaligned. But hidden things lose some of their power when the home is filled with truth, when access points are guarded, when secrecy is challenged, and when children know they can speak without being crushed.

So expose what secrecy protects.
Interrupt what hidden environments are shaping.
Build a home where light is not feared.
Build a home where truth has somewhere to go.
Build a home where the child does not have to suffer alone in silence.

Because secret environments do not stay empty.
They are always being filled by something.
And whatever fills them long enough will begin shaping the child from the inside out.

THE IMPACT OF A SPIRITUAL ATMOSPHERE IN THE HOME

Invisible dangers do not exist only outside the home. Some of the most shaping influences live within the atmosphere of the house itself. Constant conflict, careless language, unresolved anger, emotional inconsistency, spiritual coldness, and chronic tension can cultivate instability long before anyone names it. Children absorb tension. They internalize tone. They read the emotional climate of a room faster than many adults realize. Even when they cannot explain what feels wrong, they often live beneath its weight. Atmosphere shapes emotional security as powerfully as direct instruction, and in some cases more powerfully, because children often learn from what is repeatedly felt before they fully understand what is repeatedly taught.

A home may appear peaceful externally while internal influences quietly erode clarity. Doors may be locked. Alarm systems may be activated. Neighborhoods may be quiet. Schedules may be orderly. Yet if the spiritual climate within those walls is neglected, unseen influences can still take root. A family can be physically protected and spiritually exposed. A house can look stable while the emotional and moral atmosphere inside it is weakening the very people it is meant to shelter. True safety is not merely structural—it is spiritual.

Joshua 24:15 (KJV) declares with unwavering resolve, "As for me and my house, we will serve the LORD." This was not a casual statement. It was a declaration of atmosphere. It was a commitment that what governed the household would not be culture, convenience, or compromise—but conviction. Joshua was not merely talking about private belief. He was establishing what kind of spirit would rule the home environment. Every house serves something. Every household is governed by something. If it is not intentionally governed by truth, prayer, reverence, integrity, and spiritual sobriety, then something else will shape its climate by default.

Every home carries a spiritual temperature. That temperature is set by what is practiced consistently. What is repeated becomes normal. What is tolerated becomes part of the climate.

What is honored becomes formative. When prayer is frequent, it establishes a covering. When Scripture is spoken, it establishes truth. When worship is expressed, it establishes reverence. When forgiveness is modeled, it establishes healing. When repentance is real, it establishes humility. When consistency is present, it establishes stability. In this way, the atmosphere of a home is not built by what parents claim to value alone, but by what they actually practice with regularity.

A spiritually intentional home does not eliminate challenges, but it strengthens discernment. Children reared in such an atmosphere develop sensitivity to right and wrong. They learn to recognize discomfort in unhealthy situations.

They become aware of spiritual tension before it escalates into visible harm. They may not always have full language for what they sense, but they begin to know when something does not agree with the truth they have been taught and the peace they have experienced at home. That inner sensitivity is a form of protection. It is one of the reasons spiritual atmosphere matters so much. It trains the child not only to behave differently, but to perceive differently.

Atmosphere shapes perception.

If a home is filled with chaos, anger, sarcasm, emotional instability, manipulation, harshness, or spiritual inconsistency, children internalize insecurity. They may become anxious without understanding why. They may grow reactive, guarded, or confused because instability has become their emotional norm. If spiritual practices are absent or inconsistent, children grow without a reference point for moral clarity. They may hear isolated truths from time to time, but the atmosphere itself will teach them something else. They may begin to believe that prayer is ceremonial rather than necessary, that truth is optional rather than stabilizing, or that emotional disorder is simply part of life. But when a home is grounded in prayer, integrity, and biblical truth, children gain internal stability.

They begin to understand what peace feels like, what safety sounds like, and what clarity looks like when it governs ordinary life.

They learn that peace is normal. They learn that boundaries are loving. They learn that truth is protective. They learn that confession is safe. They learn that accountability is a strength. These are not small lessons. They shape how a child interprets relationships, authority, correction, and personal responsibility. A child who grows up in a home where truth is spoken with love, repentance is practiced without shame, and boundaries are enforced with steadiness learns that safety and holiness belong together. That child is less likely to interpret all boundaries as rejection or all correction as hostility, because they have lived in an atmosphere where love and structure worked together.

A spiritually fortified home cultivates emotional resilience. When conflict arises, it is handled with integrity rather than intimidation. When mistakes occur, correction is balanced with compassion. When fear surfaces, it is met with reassurance rather than dismissal. When questions arise, they are not crushed under shame. In such an environment, children learn that hard moments do not have to destroy safety. They learn that even when something is wrong, there is still a path back to truth, repair, and stability. This is one of the great gifts of a healthy spiritual atmosphere: it teaches children how to remain emotionally grounded even when life becomes difficult.

Children who grow up in a spiritually grounded environment are more likely to speak when something feels wrong. They recognize when a situation contradicts what they have been taught.

They understand that secrecy about inappropriate behavior is unacceptable. They feel safer bringing discomfort to light because they have already learned that truth is welcome in the home. A spiritually healthy atmosphere weakens the enemy's use of secrecy because the child has been trained to believe that light is not dangerous. Silence loses some of its power where honesty has been protected repeatedly.

Atmosphere determines response.

In a home saturated with spiritual awareness, danger is not ignored—it is confronted. Prayer is not an afterthought—it is foundational.

Conversations about faith are not occasional—they are integrated into daily life. God is not treated as a distant concept brought up only in crisis. His truth becomes part of the way the household interprets life, conflict, temptation, fear, correction, and relationships. This makes the home stronger, not because trouble never appears, but because the family is less likely to be spiritually unprepared when it does.

This does not require perfection. It requires consistency. Parents do not need to create an artificial atmosphere of flawless performance. In fact, pretending to be perfect often damages a home more than honest weakness handled well. What children need is not polished spirituality, but practiced truth. They need parents who pray consistently, repent sincerely, correct lovingly, and keep returning the home to its spiritual center. A child can live through imperfect moments without losing security if the overall atmosphere remains grounded in truth, humility, and reverence. But constant inconsistency teaches instability, even when the parents intend well.

Parents set the tone. Their habits shape the environment. Their emotional discipline influences stability. Their spiritual practices create either openness or vulnerability. A parent who lives in unchecked bitterness, constant agitation, careless speech, or spiritual neglect is not only affecting themselves; they are helping shape the climate the child breathes every day. On the other hand, a parent who guards their own heart, watches their words, remains prayerful, and handles conflict with integrity is strengthening the environment around the child in ways that may not always be visible but are deeply formative.

A spiritually secure home includes regular prayer over children and over the household. It includes Scripture discussed in practical, applicable ways. It includes honest conversations about moral challenges. It includes grace extended alongside correction. It includes clear standards upheld consistently. It includes emotional steadiness, a willingness to repent, and the refusal to let darkness settle comfortably in the atmosphere. These things do not make a family perfect. They make it guarded.

When children grow up in such a climate, they develop discernment early. They learn to recognize manipulative behavior. They sense when something violates their conscience. They understand that they are valued and protected. They become more resistant to voices that try to normalize what is unhealthy because their inner reference point has already been shaped by something stronger. They do not simply know rules. They know the feel of righteousness. They know what peace sounds like. They know what spiritual clarity feels like when it fills a home.

The spiritual atmosphere of a home is not decorative—it is formative. It shapes identity. It influences decision-making. It strengthens resistance to harmful influence. It prepares children for environments beyond the home. Eventually, every child steps into settings the parent cannot fully control—schools, friendships, workplaces, college campuses, relationships, digital spaces, and broader culture. The question is not whether they will face outside influence. They will. The deeper question is what atmosphere trained them before they got there. What spiritual climate taught them how to interpret the world? What environment helped shape their instincts, their conscience, and their response to pressure?

A home governed by spiritual conviction becomes a sanctuary where darkness struggles to gain a foothold. Not because problems never arise—but because light is consistently present. Darkness does not thrive easily where truth is lived, prayer is practiced, and spiritual dullness is resisted. A home may still face grief, tension, and challenge. Still, if its atmosphere is governed by conviction rather than compromise, those challenges need not define the family's spiritual direction.

The question every parent must ask is simple: What governs the atmosphere of my home? Is it distraction or devotion? Is it a reaction or a reflection? Is it chaos or clarity? Is it performance or sincerity? Is it emotional volatility or guarded peace? Is God truly welcomed as the governing presence of the household, or merely referenced when trouble becomes obvious? These questions matter because the atmosphere is never accidental for long. If it is not guarded intentionally, it will be shaped by whatever is strongest, loudest, most repeated, or most tolerated.

The impact of spiritual atmosphere cannot be overstated. It builds confident children who are grounded in truth. It fosters open communication. It nurtures courage. It reinforces identity.

It teaches children how to carry themselves under pressure, how to respond when something feels wrong, and how to recognize the difference between what is spiritually clean and what is spiritually corrosive.

Ultimately, the spiritual temperature within a home shapes how children interpret the world—and how they respond when challenges arise. If their atmosphere has taught them to be confused, they may interpret danger poorly.

If it has taught them peace, truth, accountability, and spiritual attentiveness, they are more likely to recognize what does not belong and bring it into the light before it deepens.

Establish the atmosphere intentionally.
Guard it consistently.
Strengthen it daily.

Because the spirit that governs your home will help guide your child's future.

❖ SPIRITUAL ❖

A Holy Interruption to a Careless Generation

✦

This is not a gentle reminder. This is a holy interruption. There are seasons when God whispers, and there are seasons when He warns. We are living in a warning season. The times are too perilous for soft hearing, and the pressures surrounding innocence are too aggressive for passive parenting. Something holy must interrupt the comfort that has made many guardians too relaxed, too distracted, and too willing to call obvious danger normal life.

Innocence is under pressure. Boundaries are dissolving. What once shocked society now entertains it. What once alarmed parents now barely unsettles them. Exposure has become normal. Vigilance has become optional. But Heaven has not adjusted its standard. God has not revised holiness to match culture. He has not lowered the value of innocence because a generation has grown numb. He has not become casual about what wounds a child simply because the world has learned how to package corruption attractively.

The greatest danger to a child is not merely an external predator—it is a spiritually inattentive environment. When guardians grow distracted, infiltration becomes effortless. When discernment is dulled, deception appears harmless. When watchfulness weakens, access expands. Evil does not need a formal invitation. It only needs open gates, tired watchmen, softened boundaries, delayed responses, and adults who prefer comfort over confrontation. That is why some of the most serious damage occurs not where people hated children, but where adults loved them sentimentally while failing to guard them soberly.

You cannot guard what you refuse to examine. You cannot confront what you refuse to acknowledge. You cannot protect what you are too uncomfortable to question. Many guardians want safety without scrutiny, peace without vigilance, and protection without the burden of hard decisions. But no home remains safe merely because the adults desire it. Safety is built through attention. It is preserved through boundaries.

It is strengthened by prayer, truth, courage, and a willingness to disturb what others would rather leave undisturbed.

There are children suffering not because love was absent, but because alertness was not at the forefront. Not because care was nonexistent—but because confrontation was avoided. Comfort was chosen over courage. Peace was preserved at the expense of protection. That is the tragedy of spiritual carelessness: it often appears kind yet remains ineffective. It may sound loving, yet they refuse to act. It may pray in public while avoiding the private responsibility to watch, question, and intervene. But affection without vigilance is incomplete guardianship. Concern without action is an open gate in softer language.

Let this truth shake you: silence has consequences. Ignored warning signs multiply. Dismissed behavioral changes deepen. Unchallenged boundaries collapse. And when collapse happens, regret cannot reverse it. Regret can grieve what negligence permitted, but it cannot go back and rebuild what watchfulness should have preserved. That is why delayed obedience is so dangerous in matters of protection. Some decisions cannot wait for the comfort of certainty. Some actions must be taken while warning signs are still unfolding, while the child is still signaling, and while the atmosphere is still shifting.

God does not entrust children casually. He assigns them. That assignment carries spiritual weight. It demands awareness. It demands discipline. It demands the courage to disrupt what feels awkward. To be placed over a child's life is not merely to receive a blessing; it is to receive a burden of stewardship. That stewardship is not fulfilled by good intentions alone. It requires alertness strong enough to observe, discernment clear enough to interpret, and courage steady enough to act before hidden things become visible damage.

You are not called to paranoia. You are called to vigilance. You are not called to suspicion without reason. You are called to discernment without hesitation. There is a difference. Paranoia imagines danger everywhere and loses clarity. Vigilance stays awake and keeps clarity. Suspicion accuses recklessly.

Discernment investigates wisely. But do not let the fear of seeming extreme push you into the opposite error of spiritual sleep. Some people have become so determined not to look fearful that they no longer look faithful. They would rather appear relaxed than remain responsible. They would rather be thought pleasant than be found watchful.

If something feels misaligned, investigate it. If your spirit is unsettled, pray and act. If your child shifts in ways that cannot be explained, lean closer—not further away. Do not let discomfort talk you out of duty. Do not let reputation silence what discernment is trying to say. Do not let familiarity blind you to what should still be questioned. Do not let convenience weaken the very response that may be needed most. The cost of vigilance is temporary discomfort. The cost of negligence may mark a lifetime.

There is a cost for spiritual carelessness. Not every tragedy begins with violence. Some begin with a gradual compromise. Some begin with a delayed response. Some begin with the quiet assumption that vigilance can wait until tomorrow. But tomorrow does not always give warnings twice. This is one of the cruelest realities of neglected watchfulness: some signals come early as mercy, but if they are ignored long enough, the next stage is no longer warning—it is consequence.

We live in a time where distraction is abundant, and discernment is scarce, where convenience is chosen over confrontation, and where familiarity is mistaken for safety, where discomfort is avoided even when instinct signals danger.

This is not an age that rewards passive guardianship. The greatest deception is not that evil exists. The greatest deception is that it can be managed casually. Evil does not require permission to approach—only opportunity to remain unchecked. It moves through assumptions. It settles into tolerated patterns. It grows where adults keep telling themselves they will address it later.

When red flags appear and are dismissed, when spiritual intuition stirs and is ignored, when a child's behavior shifts and is rationalized away, a door begins to open. And some doors, once opened, leave scars that never fully disappear.

That is why parents must learn to honor warnings before they are forced to mourn consequences. The small shift matters. The altered tone matters. The unusual fear matters. The secrecy matters. The unsettled spirit matters. The watchman does not wait until the enemy enters the city before sounding the alarm.

You cannot pray for protection while neglecting vigilance. You cannot ask God to guard what you refuse to watch. You cannot claim stewardship while tolerating compromise. Prayer without obedience becomes a contradiction. Concern without follow-through becomes weakness. Faith does not remove the need for watchfulness—it deepens it. The spiritually awake parent understands that God's protection and parental vigilance are not competing realities. They are meant to work together. Prayer should sharpen the eye of the watchman, not replace it.

This warning is not condemnation—it is awakening. The watchman who assumes safety eventually faces a crisis. The guardian who delays action eventually faces regret. There are moments when comfort must be sacrificed for courage, when relationships must be questioned, when access must be restricted, when silence must be broken. Because hesitation multiplies harm. The soul must be shaken because complacency has become comfortable. Many are more concerned about being perceived as extreme than being found faithful. Many would rather avoid conflict than prevent trauma. But what will perception matter if innocence is fractured? What will social harmony matter if a child carries hidden wounds?

So stand alert. Stand accountable. Stand unafraid to confront what threatens what God has entrusted to you. Stand when others would rather sit. Speak when others would rather soften. Watch when others would rather assume. Pray when others would rather rationalize. Move when others would rather wait. Heaven is not impressed by good intentions. Heaven responds to faithful stewardship. Heaven is not measuring how comfortable you were. Heaven is measuring how faithfully you stood.

This is the holy interruption.
This is the warning to the careless generation.
This is the summons to the wall.

Stand up.
Stand awake.
Stand sober.
Stand with conviction.

Because Heaven is watching not only what enters your home, but how you guard what has been placed under your covering, and faithfulness requires watchfulness.

CHAPTER SIX
IDENTIFYING SIGNS OF ABUSE
Physical and Behavioral Indicators

Recognizing abuse requires more than awareness—it requires courage. It requires the willingness to confront what we hope is not true. Ephesians 5:11 (KJV) commands, "And have no fellowship with the unfruitful works of darkness, but rather reprove them." Darkness thrives where denial lives. Evil gains room to operate wherever adults prefer comfort over truth, appearances over discernment, or delay over intervention. A parent who refuses to see what is changing in a child does not preserve peace; that refusal may unintentionally provide cover for harm to continue.

Children rarely announce abuse in clear language. Fear, confusion, manipulation, shame, or threats often silence them. Many children do not possess the vocabulary to describe what has happened. Some do not fully understand what they have experienced. Others may know something is wrong but be too frightened to say it plainly. Still others may have been coached, intimidated, or emotionally trapped into silence. This is why parents cannot depend solely on direct disclosure. They must become students of behavior, interpreters of silence, and guardians of subtle change.

Discernment is not suspicion without reason. It is spiritual attentiveness informed by love. It does not create fear in order to feel responsible. It pays attention because the child matters too much to be misread. A discerning parent learns that behavior often reveals what words conceal. A child's conduct may become the language of distress long before the mouth can form a direct explanation. What adults call mood, attitude, clinginess, rebellion, or emotional sensitivity may, in some cases, be the outward expression of something hidden and painful.

A child who once laughed freely but now withdraws into silence is speaking. A child plagued by nightmares, sudden aggression, unexplained anxiety, or heightened clinginess is communicating distress. A child who becomes fearful of certain places, hesitant around a particular individual, unusually startled by touch, emotionally flat, secretive, or chronically uneasy may also be signaling that something is wrong. These changes are not always rebellion—they are often coping mechanisms. Children under distress may become louder or quieter, more aggressive or more passive, more dependent or more withdrawn. The form may vary, but the message may be the same: something has shifted, and that shift demands attention.

Behavioral indicators often reveal themselves through patterns rather than isolated moments. One difficult day may mean very little. But repeated changes, especially when connected to specific environments, people, or routines, should never be ignored. A child who consistently resists going somewhere, becomes visibly distressed before or after certain visits, or changes emotionally after contact with specific individuals should not be dismissed lightly. The issue is not whether every change confirms abuse. The issue is whether adults are willing to take significant changes seriously enough to investigate before greater harm occurs.

Pay attention to statements such as:
"I don't want to go there."
"They told me not to tell."
"I don't like how they look at me."

Such phrases are not casual remarks. They are warning flares. They may come out suddenly, indirectly, or in fragments, but fragments still matter. A child does not need to deliver a polished report in order to be believed. In many cases, the first disclosure is partial, hesitant, or emotionally tangled. A child may test the waters with a small statement before revealing something larger. If the adult brushes past that first warning, the child may decide silence is safer than honesty.

Parents must also understand that behavioral indicators can appear in ways that do not immediately seem connected to abuse. A child may begin to have trouble sleeping, lose interest in activities they once enjoyed, become unusually angry, regress emotionally, avoid eye contact, struggle in school, begin lying more often, or show sudden changes in appetite or personal habits. A teenager may become detached, hyper-defensive, emotionally numb, self-isolating, or deeply anxious without knowing how to explain why. Some children become compliant to an unhealthy degree. Others become disruptive. Both can be signs that something inside the child is under pressure.

There are also moments when children reveal discomfort through body-based responses rather than direct statements. They may freeze around certain people. They may become unusually tense when a subject is raised. They may react to touch with fear or discomfort. They may panic at the thought of being left alone in certain settings. These reactions should never be mocked, minimized, or overridden simply because adults find them inconvenient or confusing. A child's body often reacts to danger before the child can explain it in words.

This is why the parent must learn to ask not only, What is my child doing? But also, what might this behavior be trying to communicate? The deeper question is often more important than the surface one. A child who is suddenly "difficult" may not need harsher control first; they may need understanding, safety, and careful investigation.

A child who is avoiding someone may not be disrespectful; they may be alarmed. A child who seems emotionally unstable may not be manipulative; they may be carrying fear they do not know how to process.

Parents must therefore resist two dangerous errors. The first is over-spiritualizing everything without practical discernment. The second is over-naturalizing everything and dismissing serious warning signs as phases, personality, or stress. Wisdom lives in the middle. It observes, listens, prays, and acts responsibly. It does not accuse recklessly, but it also does not delay carelessly. It understands that when a child changes suddenly or repeatedly, the most faithful response is not denial but attentiveness.

Psalm 34:17 (KJV) declares, "The righteous cry, and the LORD heareth, and delivereth them out of all their troubles." God hears the cry—but He often responds through attentive parents. Heaven is not deaf to the silent pain of children. The question is whether the adults entrusted with them are listening as carefully as Heaven. The child may cry through fear, through silence, through resistance, through aggression, through sleep disturbance, through emotional collapse, or through a half-finished sentence spoken at the right moment. Whatever form the cry takes, it must be heard.

To hear it requires more than parental affection. It requires parental sobriety. It requires the courage to let a child's change interrupt routine. It requires the humility to admit that something may be happening beyond what is immediately visible. It requires enough love to investigate, enough patience to listen, and enough strength to protect without apology.

Behavioral indicators are not inconveniences to manage away. They are signals to interpret wisely. They may be the first evidence that a child's world has been disturbed. And if adults are willing to notice, listen, and respond, what is hidden may be brought into the light before the wound grows deeper.

So watch closely.
Listen carefully.
Take changes seriously.
Do not force a child's distress into categories that make adults more comfortable.
Let the behavior speak.
Let the warning be heard.

Because sometimes the child's first cry for help is not spoken in plain words at all—it is written in behavior, and the faithful parent learns how to read it.

DAY CARE, BABYSITTERS, AND THE JUDGMENT OF STEWARDSHIP

There are moments in parenting where responsibility becomes sharply visible—not in theory, but in daily decisions. One of those moments occurs every time a parent or guardian places their child into the care of another individual. Whether it is a daycare facility, a babysitter, a relative, or a trusted acquaintance, what may appear routine on the surface is, in reality, a transfer of temporary access to a life that does not belong to you—it belongs to God.

This must be understood with soberness: access is not ownership, and trust is not immunity from accountability.

Every time a child is placed in another environment, the parent's responsibility does not decrease—it intensifies. Because while the child may be physically present in another location, the spiritual and moral accountability remains anchored to the one whom God entrusted that child to in the first place.

Psalm 127:3 (KJV) declares, "Lo, children are an heritage of the Lord: and the fruit of the womb is his reward."
If children belong first to God, then every decision concerning their care is being observed by Him.

This means no handoff is casual.
No assumption is harmless.
No oversight is insignificant.

When a parent drops a child off, they are not simply completing a task—they are making a decision that heaven takes record of.

THE DISCIPLINE OF DAILY EXAMINATION

A faithful parent does not operate on autopilot. They operate with awareness.

When a child is picked up—whether from daycare, a babysitter, or any environment outside the direct covering of the parent—there must be more than routine movement. There must be intentional examination.

Not paranoia.
Not fear.
But disciplined vigilance.

- Observe the child before you absorb the environment's report.
- Look closely:
- Has the child's demeanor changed?
- Is there unusual quietness, withdrawal, or hesitation?
- Is their body language guarded or tense?
- Are they avoiding eye contact or clinging in a way that is not normal?
- Is there a resistance to speaking or an eagerness to leave?

These are not small details.
These are signals.

Children often speak before they speak.
They reveal before they explain.
They show before they tell.

And the parent who ignores these signals is not lacking love—they are lacking attentiveness.

THE BODY TELLS WHAT THE MOUTH CANNOT

For children who cannot yet articulate clearly—infants, toddlers, or those who are emotionally overwhelmed—the body becomes the language.

This requires another level of responsibility.

There must be a consistent, respectful, and careful physical awareness:

- Observe for unexplained marks, bruises, or swelling
- Be attentive during bathing, changing, or routine care
- Notice reactions to touch, especially sudden discomfort or fear
- Pay attention to areas a child may guard or resist having examined

These actions are not excessive—they are protective.

Neglect in this area is dangerous because some harm leaves evidence before it leaves explanation.

And if that evidence is ignored, dismissed, or never sought, the opportunity for early intervention is lost.

THE DANGER OF ASSUMED TRUST

One of the most dangerous statements a parent can make is:
"I know them—they would never do that."

That statement has silenced more warnings than most realize.

Because history has already proven:

- Harm has occurred in familiar homes
- Abuse has come through trusted relationships
- Danger has worn the face of respectability

Trust must never replace discernment.

Even Scripture warns in Jeremiah 17:9 (KJV), "The heart is deceitful above all things, and desperately wicked: who can know it?"

This does not mean live in suspicion of everyone—but it does mean this:

Never allow comfort to cancel responsibility.

You are not being paranoid when you observe.
You are not overreacting when you ask questions.
You are not offending when you verify.
You are fulfilling your assignment.

THE ACCOUNTABILITY BEFORE GOD

This is where the matter becomes deeply spiritual.

A parent will not stand before God and answer for what they intended.
They will answer for what they permitted, ignored, overlooked, or failed to investigate.

Ezekiel 33:6 (KJV) gives a sobering warning: "But if the watchman see the sword come, and blow not the trumpet… his blood will I require at the watchman's hand."

If a watchman is held accountable for what they failed to warn about, how much more a parent for what they failed to guard?

God sees:

- When signs were present but dismissed
- When discomfort was noticed but ignored
- When questions should have been asked but were avoided
- When vigilance was replaced with convenience

This is not written to condemn the attentive parent.
This is written to awaken the passive one.

Because neglect is not always loud.
Sometimes it is quiet, consistent, and dangerously comfortable.

THE CONSEQUENCE OF NEGLECT

When vigilance is absent, two things happen:

1. The child becomes vulnerable
2. The environment becomes unchecked

And when those two meet, harm finds opportunity.

The consequence of neglect is not always immediate—but it is always impactful.

A missed sign today can become:

- A deeper wound tomorrow
- A silence that grows stronger
- A behavior that becomes harder to interpret
- A pain that takes years to uncover

And the most painful reality is this:

Many parents did not intend harm—
they simply did not pay attention soon enough.

FINAL CONVICTION

You are not just dropping off a child.
You are entrusting access to a life God placed in your hands.

You are not just picking up a child.
You are being given an opportunity to discern what may have happened in your absence.

So do not rush.
Do not assume.
Do not ignore.

Look closely.
Listen carefully.
Ask wisely.
Act courageously.

Because your child may not always say, "Something is wrong."

But their life may already be trying to tell you.

And heaven is watching to see if you are listening.

PARENT DAILY INSPECTION CHECKLIST

✦

Faithful Stewardship Requires Intentional Observation

This is not routine. This is responsibility.
This is not fear. This is discernment.
This is not optional. This is stewardship before God.

1. IMMEDIATE OBSERVATION (UPON PICK-UP)

☐ Observe facial expression before speaking
☐ Note energy level (normal / withdrawn / overly quiet)
☐ Watch body posture (relaxed/tense/guarded)
☐ Look for hesitation, fear, or urgency to leave
☐ Pay attention to eye contact (normal / avoiding / fearful)

2. VERBAL + EMOTIONAL CHECK-IN

☐ Ask simple, non-threatening questions:

- "How was your time?"
- "Did anything make you uncomfortable?"
- "Is there anything you want to tell me?"

☐ Listen without interrupting
☐ Watch for delayed responses or forced answers
☐ Note tone changes (fear, confusion, silence)
☐ Do not dismiss "small" statements

3. BEHAVIORAL SHIFT ANALYSIS

☐ Compare current behavior to normal baseline
☐ Sudden quietness or withdrawal
☐ Unusual clinginess or fear
☐ Irritability or emotional instability
☐ Resistance to returning to the same place/person
☐ New habits (silence, secrecy, avoidance)

4. PHYSICAL AWARENESS (DAILY EXAMINATION)

☐ Check for visible bruises, marks, or swelling
☐ Observe walking or sitting discomfort
☐ Note reactions to touch (flinching, fear, tension)
☐ During bathing/changing: Check arms, legs, back, and private areas
☐ Look for repeated complaints of pain without explanation

5. PATTERN DISCERNMENT

☐ Has this behavior happened before?
☐ Is there a repeated change after specific visits?
☐ Is the same person/place connected to discomfort?
☐ Are signs increasing, decreasing, or staying consistent?

6. ENVIRONMENTAL ACCOUNTABILITY

☐ Do I know exactly where my child was?
☐ Do I know who had access to my child?
☐ Was supervision clearly defined?
☐ Were there moments of isolation or unsupervised access?
☐ Am I relying on an assumption instead of verification?

7. SPIRITUAL DISCERNMENT CHECK

☐ Pray over what you observed
☐ Do not ignore internal conviction
☐ Do not override discernment with comfort
☐ If something feels "off," investigate further

⚠ DECLARATION ⚠

I will not ignore what I see.
I will not dismiss what I feel.

I will not silence what my child is revealing.
I will guard what God has entrusted to me.

⚠ WARNING SIGNS: DO NOT IGNORE ⚠

"Behavior is often the First Language of Distress."

——————— ✦ ———————

EMOTIONAL / BEHAVIORAL SIGNS

- Sudden withdrawal or unusual silence
- Fear of a specific person or place
- Clinginess beyond normal behavior
- Sudden aggression or emotional outbursts
- Regression (bedwetting, baby-like behavior)
- Avoidance of eye contact
- Isolation or secrecy

PHYSICAL SIGNS

- Unexplained bruises, marks, or swelling
- Pain when sitting, walking, or being touched
- Frequent complaints of discomfort
- Sensitivity in private areas
- Sudden fear during routine care (bathing, dressing)

COMMUNICATION SIGNALS

- Hesitation to speak
- Inconsistent or confusing explanations
- Sudden silence when certain topics arise
- Statements that seem small but feel significant

ENVIRONMENTAL RED FLAGS

- Resistance to returning to a specific place
- Over-attachment or fear toward a specific individual
- Lack of clarity about supervision
- Unexplained time gaps or access

WHEN YOU SEE THESE SIGNS:

- Do NOT dismiss
- Do NOT delay
- Do NOT assume

Investigate. Ask. Observe. Act.

SPIRITUAL REMINDER

"The prudent man foreseeth the evil, and hideth himself..."—Proverbs 22:3 (KJV)

Discernment is not suspicion.
It is protection in action.

EMOTIONAL INDICATORS

Emotional indicators are often the hidden tremors beneath visible behavior. Recognizing these signs can help parents feel responsible and vigilant, understanding that profound internal disruption may be present even without physical evidence. Fear, confusion, shame, intimidation, and emotional overload often surface in the inner world before they ever reveal themselves outwardly in obvious ways. This is why parents must not measure safety only by what they can see with the natural eye. Some of the earliest signs of harm appear in the emotional rhythm of the child long before any visible proof emerges.

A child's emotional world is delicate. When something unsafe enters that world, it does not always produce immediate disclosure. Often it produces a fracture. Some children become unusually fearful. Others become emotionally numb. Some begin to startle easily, cry without explanation, or appear constantly on edge. Others grow distant, guarded, or detached, as though they are attempting to retreat inward to survive what they cannot process outwardly. What looks like an overreaction may actually be overwhelm. What appears to be emotional coldness may actually be self-protection. What seems like an attitude may, in truth, be an inward strain that the child does not know how to carry.

An abused child may show anxiety in ordinary routines. They may dread certain visits, shrink when a certain person enters the room, or become visibly tense when specific subjects are mentioned. They may seem unusually watchful, as though their bodies have learned to stay prepared for discomfort even when no one else sees the threat. They may have trouble relaxing, trouble sleeping, trouble trusting, or trouble receiving normal affection without unease. Emotional distress does not always appear dramatic.

Sometimes it shows up as heaviness, irritability, withdrawal, or a sadness a child cannot explain. Sometimes the child cannot say, "I am afraid," but they live as though fear has settled into their nervous system.

Parents must also understand that emotional disruption often affects the child's sense of self. A child under hidden distress may begin to feel confused about their own worth, ashamed without knowing why, guilty over things they did not cause, or emotionally divided between what they feel and what they believe they are allowed to say. They may become people-pleasing in unhealthy ways, terrified of upsetting adults, or desperate to avoid any conflict that could bring more pressure upon them. Others may become emotionally volatile, moving quickly from tears to anger, from silence to outburst, because their inner world no longer feels stable enough to regulate itself well.

Some children carry distress in quiet ways that are easy for adults to overlook. They may stop initiating conversation. They may lose delight in things that once brought joy.

They may become unusually apologetic, unusually hesitant, or unusually eager to disappear into themselves. They may begin to fear being alone, or fear being with certain people, or fear being asked questions they do not know how to answer. In some cases, they may become emotionally flat—not because they are unaffected, but because shutting down feels safer than feeling everything they cannot control.

These emotional disruptions should not be dismissed as mere moodiness, attitude, or passing sensitivity. A child's emotional instability may be the soul's way of signaling that something unsafe has entered their world. Adults often misread emotional cues because they look only for dramatic evidence. But children do not always tremble loudly. Sometimes they ache quietly. Sometimes their distress is not explosive—it is lingering. It is the child who no longer rests the same, laughs the same, responds the same, or feels emotionally free in spaces where they once seemed secure.

Parents must pay attention to what changes in the child's emotional rhythm. That phrase matters because every child has a rhythm. Wise parents learn it. They know what peace looks like in their child, what joy looks like, what ordinary sensitivity looks like, what normal hesitation looks like, what their child's healthy personality sounds and feels like. Without that attentiveness, adults may miss when fear begins to replace ease, when dread begins to replace joy, or when emotional strain begins to rewrite the child's normal pattern. A child who no longer feels safe may not be able to articulate why, but their spirit often reveals what their mouth cannot yet say.

Emotional indicators may also intensify during particular times, settings, or relationships. The child may seem calm until a visit is mentioned, a name is spoken, a message appears, or a certain routine returns. They may suddenly become tearful, irritable, resistant, or withdrawn without an obvious reason to the adults in the room. This is why context matters. Parents should not only notice the emotion itself; they should notice what surrounds it. What happened before the shift? Who was present? What subject was raised? What environment preceded the change? Patterns often tell the truth before words do.

There is also a spiritual dimension to emotional indicators that parents must not ignore. A child's spirit can register danger before the child's mind can interpret it clearly. They may not yet know how to name manipulation, violation, intimidation, or unhealthy presence, but they feel its weight. Spiritually attentive parents can sense these subtle signals, fostering a deeper trust in their intuitive connection with the child.

The emotional disturbance becomes an alarm. It is not always precise, but it is significant. Parents who remain spiritually attentive will often recognize that something in the child's emotional life is signaling misalignment long before an explanation becomes plain, helping them feel more confident and connected in their caregiving.

This does not mean every emotional struggle points to abuse. Look for persistent, intense, or sudden changes like extreme anxiety or withdrawal that don't improve over time. Parents must not be careless with emotional change, especially when behaviors like prolonged sadness or fear seem disproportionate. The answer is not panic; it is attention. Not accusation; it is careful discernment. Not dismissal; it is a compassionate investigation. A wise parent does not punish emotional distress for being inconvenient. They slow down, observe, ask, pray, and create space for truth to come forward safely.

The child's emotions are not a nuisance to manage away. They are part of the language of the inner life. They tell us when something is unresolved, when something feels unsafe, when something is weighing heavily on the soul. If adults only respond to behavior while ignoring emotional distress, they may address the surface while leaving the wound untouched. But when emotional indicators are taken seriously, the parent becomes better equipped to protect what is being threatened before the damage deepens, encouraging a compassionate approach.

So listen to the tears.
Notice the tension.
Study the withdrawal.
Pay attention to the fear.
Respect the sadness that has no easy explanation.
Do not mock the heaviness.
Do not rush the child past what their soul is trying to reveal.

Because sometimes the first sign that something unsafe has entered a child's world is not found in what the body shows or what the mouth says, but in what the emotions can no longer hide.

PHYSICAL INDICATORS

Babies' and Toddlers'

Unrecognizable Language is not being heard.

✦

Physical signs of abuse must never be ignored, dismissed, or rationalized away. The body often reveals what the mouth cannot explain. Especially in children who are too young, too frightened, too confused, or too intimidated to speak clearly, the body may become the first witness. This is why parents must learn to take physical irregularities seriously. Not every sign confirms abuse, but every serious sign deserves attention. A wise parent does not explain away what should be examined. They understand that physical indicators are not inconveniences to be minimized; they are signals that may point to pain, violation, fear, or trauma already at work.

In infants, distress may manifest through violent crying when private areas are touched during diaper changes. Redness, swelling, unexplained bruising, bloodstains in diapers or undergarments—these are not minor irregularities. They are signals. An infant who suddenly stiffens, trembles, or resists being held by a specific individual is communicating discomfort. Babies cannot fabricate fear. Their bodies speak for them. They do not have a language sophisticated enough to construct false alarms. If an infant repeatedly reacts with unusual distress during care to certain touch or in the presence of a particular person, that reaction must not be treated casually. Their body may be telling the truth before anyone else in the room is prepared to hear it.

Parents must also pay attention to patterns of inappropriate physical positioning. Any adult who consistently places a child in direct contact with their genital area under the guise of affection, play, cuddling, or routine closeness must be confronted immediately. Boundaries are not optional—they are protective barriers. Safe adults do not need to cross physical boundaries to show affection. When physical contact consistently feels invasive, poorly placed, or difficult to explain, the parent must not surrender their discernment just because the person involved is familiar, respected, or socially trusted.

In toddlers and young children, physical or behavioral changes, such as difficulty sitting or walking, or regression to earlier behaviors, such as bedwetting or thumb-sucking, can be normal during growth. However, discernment is needed to identify when these are signs of distress. The key is not merely that a behavior appears, but when it appears, how suddenly it appears, and what else surrounds it. A child who suddenly begins complaining of pain, resisting diaper changes, guarding their body, or becoming unusually fearful during dressing, bathing, or toileting may be revealing distress connected to something deeper than ordinary discomfort.

As children mature into adolescence, signs can become more concealed. A teenager who suddenly wears excessively baggy or layered clothing may be attempting to hide physical marks or shield themselves from unwanted attention. Avoidance of bathing, extreme modesty beyond normal boundaries, or fear surrounding physical exposure may signal deeper harm. Some teenagers begin trying to disappear inside clothing not because of fashion alone, but because their relationship to their own body has become burdened by shame, fear, or a desire not to be seen. Others may avoid sports, medical exams, family activities, or situations that require changing clothes because the body has become a site of anxiety rather than safety.

Physical signs do not always scream—they often whisper.

Parents must listen.

There may also be uncomfortable but telling signs—unusual odors, abnormal redness, heightened anxiety during bathing or dressing, or panic when certain names are mentioned. These are not coincidences. They are indicators. The child who suddenly resists routine hygiene, infants and toddlers, becomes alarmed when undergarments are changed, or panics when a specific person is expected, may be communicating, through reaction, what they cannot yet explain through speech. A wise parent understands that physical indicators and emotional indicators often travel together. The body and nervous system often reveal what the child is still trying to survive in silence.

Parents must also pay attention to repeated injuries that do not fit the explanation given. Bruises in unusual locations, marks that recur, injuries that appear without a clear account, or physical discomfort that seems to cluster around certain times, people, or visits should never be treated with lazy assumptions. Children are active, and accidents do happen. But discernment asks whether the injury makes sense, whether the explanation is consistent, whether the pattern is repeating, and whether the child's emotional response matches what would normally be expected. It is not paranoia to notice an inconsistency. It is stewardship.

Another important reality is that physical indicators may not always be dramatic enough to force attention. Sometimes parents are waiting for catastrophic evidence while the child's body has already been offering quieter signs. Slight changes in posture. Guarding private areas. Flinching during routine care. New pain without a clear cause. Altered gait. Sudden discomfort sitting still. Avoidance of touch that was once normal. These things can be easy to miss in a busy home, but they matter. Not every child will bleed visibly. Not every injury will be obvious. Some signs are subtle, but that does not mean they are insignificant.

Parents must also resist the temptation to let embarrassment silence investigation. Because some physical signs involve private areas, bodily functions, or awkward conversations, adults may feel tempted to avoid the subject, delay the doctor visit, or reassure themselves too quickly. But embarrassment is a terrible guardian. A child's safety must outweigh adult discomfort. If something seems wrong, it must be examined. If the child shows pain, panic, or repeated physical irregularities, the matter must be pursued seriously. Silence has never healed an abused body. Delay has never protected a violated child.

Physical indicators should also be documented and evaluated carefully when they arise. Parents should pay attention to timing, frequency, location, and associated emotional or behavioral changes. A single sign may require observation; a cluster of signs demands stronger action.

The point is not to create panic, but to refuse passivity.

The body should not be ignored simply because the truth it may reveal feels painful to face. Children need adults who are willing to endure discomfort to protect them well.

At the deepest level, physical indicators remind us that abuse is not abstract. It touches real bodies. It produces real pain. It leaves real traces. Sometimes those traces are obvious. Sometimes they are faint. Sometimes they are dismissed by adults who do not want to imagine the possibility of harm. But a faithful parent must be willing to see what is there, not merely what they wish were true. Love requires that kind of honesty. Protection requires that kind of courage.

So notice the body.
Notice the pain.
Notice the stiffness, the flinching, the guarding, the change in posture, the repeated soreness, the fear around routine care.

Do not wave away what should be examined.
Do not let familiarity explain away what the body is trying to reveal.
Do not let discomfort keep you from investigating.

Because when a child cannot yet fully speak, the body may still be telling the story. And a wise parent learns how to listen before the whisper becomes a wound carried far too long.

SUDDEN PERSONALITY CHANGES

One of the clearest warning signs that something deeper may be wrong is a sudden personality change. Children do not usually change dramatically without reason. Their personalities may mature over time, their moods may shift with growth, and their interests may evolve as they develop. Still, a marked and abrupt alteration in who they seem to be often signals internal disruption. When a child's emotional posture changes quickly and significantly, wise parents must not rush to explain it away. A sudden shift in disposition may be the outward evidence of something hidden pressing inwardly on the child's mind, emotions, body, or sense of safety.

A once open child may become secretive. A once affectionate child may become avoidant. A once confident child may become fearful, withdrawn, angry, or confused. Sudden shifts in disposition should not be explained away too quickly, especially when no clear and healthy cause is present. Parents must learn the difference between ordinary developmental change and distress-driven alteration. Growth may change expression gradually. Harm often changes it abruptly. A child may still look like themselves physically while no longer feeling like themselves emotionally. That dissonance matters.

When innocence has been disturbed, the child's outward way of relating to the world may begin to change with it. This is because personality, especially in childhood, is not merely a fixed trait; it is also shaped by felt safety. A child who feels secure often moves through life with greater openness, ease, and trust. But when fear enters, when confusion settles in, when shame begins to weigh on the soul, the child's relational posture may shift to survive what they do not know how to explain. They may stop moving through life from trust and start moving through life from defense.

Some children become unusually aggressive because they do not know how to process what they are carrying. Anger can become a shield for fear. Irritability can become the outlet for silent distress. A child who feels overpowered inwardly may begin pushing outwardly because they have lost the internal steadiness they once had. Others become excessively compliant because fear has taught them to be silent. They stop resisting. They stop protesting.

They become overly eager to please because inwardly they are trying to avoid conflict, attention, or any reaction that might expose the turmoil they are carrying. A compliant child is not always a peaceful child. Sometimes they are frightened.

Some become detached and emotionally unreachable, while others become intensely reactive to touch, noise, correction, or routine interaction. A child who once laughed easily may begin living under a heaviness they cannot shake. A child who once made eye contact freely may begin avoiding it. A child who once ran toward trusted adults may begin pulling back from closeness. A teenager who once engaged in conversation may become inaccessible, guarded, and distant. These shifts may be quiet, but they are not small. They can indicate that something in the child's internal world has become unstable.

Parents must also pay attention to contradictions within the personality change. A child may appear normal in one setting and entirely different in another. They may seem cheerful around some people and visibly distressed around others. They may laugh publicly but collapse privately. They may become unusually mature in one moment and emotionally fragmented in the next. These contradictions are often clues that the child is trying to manage something they do not yet know how to carry out honestly. A child in distress may learn to perform the role of normalcy for survival while inwardly falling apart.

Sudden personality changes also affect how a child experiences correction, affection, routine, and relationships. A previously resilient child may now crumble at the slightest correction. A previously relaxed child may become tense in response to ordinary touch. A previously social child may isolate. A previously curious child may become flat, indifferent, or emotionally shut down. A previously trusting child may begin asking unusual questions about safety, secrets, or whether they are in trouble. These shifts should not be mocked. They should not be treated as an inconvenience.

They are not random disruptions to family life. They may be indicators that the child's inner sense of security has been wounded.

There is also a danger in labeling a changed child too quickly. Once adults call the child moody, rebellious, dramatic, difficult, disrespectful, hormonal, or attention-seeking, they may stop listening to what the change is actually saying. Labels can become a substitute for discernment. They give adults a category that feels manageable while hiding the deeper issue from serious examination. But a wise parent refuses to reduce a changed child to a convenient explanation. They understand that personality shifts often carry meaning, and that meaning must be investigated, not mocked.

These changes are not to be minimized. They are not to be labeled carelessly. They are to be examined with prayer, wisdom, and urgency.

Prayer matters because discernment is needed. Wisdom matters because not every change means the same thing. Urgency matters because delays can deepen harm. Parents do not need to panic, but they do need to pay attention. They should ask: When did this begin? What changed around the time this change appeared? Is there a person, place, device, conversation, or experience connected to the shift? Is my child becoming someone different because they are growing, or because they are carrying something unsafe?

A child rarely becomes inwardly unsettled for no reason. The reason may not always be abuse, but the change still deserves careful attention. The child's soul may be reacting to fear, bullying, secrecy, predatory pressure, digital exposure, shame, manipulation, or emotional injury. Or they may be overwhelmed by something else entirely that still requires serious care. The point is that a sudden personality change is rarely an invitation to dismiss the child. It is an invitation to draw near.

Parents must therefore remain close enough to know the child's normal emotional rhythm. Without that closeness, the shift may be missed until it becomes far more severe. But where parents are attentive, they can often recognize the difference between ordinary growth and hidden distress. They can sense when the child is no longer simply changing, but unraveling. And once that is sensed, the faithful response is not irritation. It is an inquiry. Not distance. Nearness. Not an accusation. Careful listening. Not delay. Wise action.

A child whose personality shifts suddenly may be signaling that something has disturbed the inner world from which that personality once flowed. That is why adults must not merely ask, Why is my child acting differently? They must also ask, What happened to the peace, trust, and safety from which my child used to live? That question often leads deeper than mere behavior management ever can.

So do not laugh at the change.
Do not punish the signal before you have understood the pain.
Do not settle for easy labels when the child's soul may be struggling to speak.

Look closely.
Pray carefully.
Listen deeply.
Respond quickly.

Because a sudden personality change is often more than a phase, sometimes it is the soul's alarm that something hidden has entered the child's world, and the faithful parent must be wise enough to hear it.

REGRESSION SIGNALS

Regression signals are especially important because they often reveal distress in children who cannot verbalize trauma directly. When a child does not have the words to explain what has frightened, confused, or overwhelmed them, the body and behavior may begin speaking in another language. One of those languages is regression. It is the child's movement back toward earlier patterns of behavior, not because they are simply being immature, but because something in their inner world has become too heavy to carry in the present.

A child who had progressed in maturity may suddenly begin reverting to earlier behaviors. Bedwetting may return. Thumb-sucking may reappear. Separation anxiety may intensify. Speech patterns may become more childish. Sleep disturbances may increase.

Clinginess may become excessive. A child who has grown more independent may suddenly seem much younger in how they respond, speak, attach, cry, or seek comfort. These changes often puzzle adults because they appear to move in the opposite direction of healthy development. But regression is not meaningless. It is often a signal.

While some forms of regression can occur naturally during seasons of stress or transition, repeated or unusual regression must not be dismissed without examination. Children may regress temporarily during a move, a loss, a family disruption, illness, or other major changes. But wise parents do not stop at general explanations when the pattern becomes intense, prolonged, or connected to other warning signs. Sometimes the child is not moving backward developmentally—they are signaling that something harmful has overwhelmed their sense of safety. What looks like childish behavior may actually be a frightened nervous system reaching for the last place it remembers feeling protected.

Regression is often the mind and body reaching backward for comfort because the present has become too heavy to process. A child may return to earlier self-soothing behaviors because they do not yet know how to carry what has entered their world. If fear, shame, confusion, intimidation, or hidden harm has unsettled them deeply, the body may retreat into older patterns in an attempt to survive the emotional burden. This is why regression should never be handled carelessly. It may look inconvenient, but it is often deeply revealing.

Parents must pay close attention not only to the regression itself, but to its timing, intensity, and surrounding context. When did it begin? What changed around that time? Is the child regressing after being around a particular person, in a certain environment, or after engaging with certain digital spaces or stressful situations? Is the regression isolated, or is it accompanied by fear, silence, irritability, sleep disruption, emotional withdrawal, or physical discomfort? These questions matter because regression often does not stand alone. It may come as part of a larger pattern of distress that the child cannot yet explain plainly.

Some children regress in ways that adults are tempted to shame them for. They may become unusually clingy, cry more easily, resist independence, or repeatedly need reassurance. Others may lose emotional regulation and respond with outbursts, helplessness, or behaviors they had seemingly outgrown. But what the child needs in these moments is not mockery, irritation, or embarrassment from the adults around them. They need careful attention. They need safety restored. They need wise parents who understand that regression may be the soul's cry for help, not the child's attempt to make life difficult.

This is especially true because regression often signals that the child's internal world has been shaken. Something has disrupted their felt sense of stability. Something has made the present feel less safe than it once did. So the child reaches backward toward old comforts, old behaviors, and older ways of seeking security. Adults must see beyond the behavior and ask what pain, pressure, or fear may be beneath it. A child wetting the bed again may not simply need correction. A child who suddenly cannot tolerate separation may not simply need firmness. A child who uses younger speech or becomes excessively dependent may not simply be acting out. They may be telling the truth, the only way their overwhelmed system knows how.

Regression can also be spiritually significant in what it reveals. It reminds parents that trauma not only affects memory or mood; it affects safety, trust, and emotional function. A child who no longer feels secure may begin acting out of fear rather than the maturity they once displayed. In this sense, regression is not always the loss of progress. Sometimes it is the evidence that the child's sense of protection has been pierced. If that wound is not understood, adults may punish the symptom while missing the deeper injury.

Parents must therefore not treat these signs as inconveniences. There may be evidence that the child's internal world has been shaken. And when the inner world is shaken, the answer is not careless frustration. The answer is discernment, prayer, observation, and compassionate investigation. A wise parent will not merely ask, How do I stop this behavior? A wise parent will ask, What has happened that made my child feel the need to return to this behavior? That question opens the door to deeper understanding and more faithful protection.

Regression signals matter because children often move backward externally when something has become unbearable internally. The behavior may seem smaller than open disclosure, but it should not be treated as less serious.

In many cases, regression is one of the earliest, clearest signs that the child's sense of safety has been disrupted in a way they cannot yet articulate.

So notice the return of old behaviors.
Notice the increased dependence.
Notice the sleep change, the childish speech, the bedwetting, the clinginess, the fear of separation.

Do not shame it.
Do not dismiss it.
Do not explain it away too quickly.

Look deeper.
Ask carefully.
Pray earnestly.
Respond wisely.

Because sometimes what appears to be backward movement is actually a signal that the child has been overwhelmed, and the faithful parent must be discerning enough to recognize that the child is not merely regressing—they may be crying for safety.

PROTECTIVE STRATEGIES FOR PARENTS

Protection must be proactive, not reactive. A wise parent does not wait for visible damage before taking serious steps to guard a child. By the time danger becomes obvious, innocence may already have been wounded, trust may already have been shaken, and confusion may already have taken root. Scripture gives no honor to careless delay. Proverbs 22:3 (KJV) teaches, "A prudent man foreseeth the evil, and hideth himself: but the simple pass on, and are punished." Prudence anticipates danger. It does not wait for absolute proof before establishing wise boundaries. It understands that prevention is one of the highest forms of protection.

First Peter 5:8 (KJV) commands, "Be sober, be vigilant; because your adversary the devil, as a roaring lion, walketh about, seeking whom he may devour." Vigilance is not paranoia—it is wisdom under threat. It is the sober recognition that innocence must be guarded intentionally because the world does not guard it automatically. A vigilant parent is not living in fear. They are living in awareness. They understand that what is precious requires protection, what is vulnerable requires covering, and what has been entrusted by God must not be left to chance.

Parents must know who has access to their children. That knowledge must go deeper than names and familiarity. It must include the kind of access, the frequency of access, the setting of access, and the accountability surrounding access. A parent should know which environments their children enter, which adults maintain consistent proximity to, and which digital platforms influence their lives. These are not excessive concerns. They are basic responsibilities of faithful guardianship. A child cannot evaluate every motive, interpret every atmosphere, or recognize every subtle danger. That is why parents must remain sufficiently involved to know what is shaping their child and who is allowed near them.

Protection also requires direct teaching. Children must be taught bodily autonomy from an early age. They must understand that private areas are private. They must know that their body is not public property for adult comfort, affection, or entitlement. They must be taught that no secret involving touching is to be kept—ever. Secrets that produce fear are not secrets; they are warning signs. A child should know, in simple and clear language, that they can say no to inappropriate touch, that discomfort matters, and that telling the truth about an unsafe interaction will never make them the guilty one.

Parents must also normalize these conversations instead of waiting until a crisis forces them. Children need regular, age-appropriate instruction on safety, boundaries, honesty, privacy, and the difference between healthy affection and inappropriate behavior. They should know that if someone says, "Don't tell your parents," that statement itself is a warning.

They should know that no adult's position, age, title, or relationship to the family removes the child's right to safety. Teaching these truths does not create fear in a child. It gives language to discernment and builds confidence against manipulation.

Sleepovers should never be automatic privileges. They should be rare and carefully vetted. Parents must know the home, the adults, the structure, the sleeping arrangements, the device access, and the overall atmosphere. Even then, caution remains wise. Many parents have become too casual with environments they did not examine deeply enough. Unannounced visits demonstrate attentiveness. So do follow-up questions, visible involvement, and the refusal to surrender oversight simply because a setting seems socially normal. Parents must be comfortable being labeled "overprotective" if that label prevents harm. It is far better to be thought strict than to become regretful because comfort was chosen over caution.

Digital protection is equally essential. Devices must be monitored. Apps must be approved. Passwords must remain accessible to parents. Late-night unsupervised internet use invites exposure to manipulation, grooming, pornography, distorted identity formation, and private worlds of secrecy that can shape a child long before parents see the fruit. A wise parent does not hand a child unrestricted digital access and call it trust.

They understand that digital spaces are environments, and every environment requires watchfulness. Screens may look quiet, but they can still carry predators, corruption, emotional pressure, and hidden influences directly into the child's inner world.

A protective strategy also requires a clear household structure. Doors should not always be closed without reason. Adults should not be given private, unquestioned time with children. Private messaging with children should not bypass parental visibility. Routines should make room for accountability rather than secrecy. A protected home is not one where everyone feels unrestricted; it is one where wisdom governs access. Structure is not the enemy of love. Structure is one way love guards what is vulnerable.

Open communication builds protective armor. When children trust that they will be believed—not blamed—they speak sooner. That may be one of the strongest protections a parent can give. A child who feels safe to speak is far less likely to carry fear alone in silence while harm deepens. But this kind of trust must be built intentionally.

The home must be a place where hard truths can be brought into the light without immediate humiliation, explosive anger, or careless dismissal. Children must know that their voice matters, their discomfort matters, and their concerns will not be brushed aside simply because the adult involved is known or respected.

Protective strategies also include paying attention to changes. Parents should not only manage schedules; they should study patterns. If a child changes around a certain person, after a certain environment, or following certain online interactions, that change matters. If a child becomes quieter, more guarded, more fearful, more secretive, more emotionally unstable, or more resistant to certain settings, the parent must take that seriously. Protection is not only about rules in advance; it is also about real-time observation. A vigilant parent notices what has shifted and follows the change rather than ignoring it.

Parents must also guard against their own hesitation. Many dangers grow because adults delay. They do not want to offend anyone. They do not want to seem suspicious.

They do not want to disrupt family peace, ministry comfort, or social expectations. But a child's safety must take precedence over an adult's discomfort. If something feels wrong, investigate. If access seems excessive, restrict it. If secrecy appears, expose it if the child is signaling unease, lean in. Protection weakens when parents become more loyal to appearances than to discernment.

A strong protective strategy is never built on a single principle. It is built on prayer, attentiveness, boundaries, teaching, communication, digital oversight, emotional presence, and the willingness to act before certainty becomes undeniable. It is built by parents who understand that innocence is too sacred to be guarded casually. They do not wait for a crisis to begin caring deeply. They care deeply enough to prepare.

So know who is near your child.
Know what is shaping your child.
Teach what your child must understand.

Guard the digital gate.
Guard the physical gate.
Guard the emotional gate.
Guard the atmosphere of the home.

Stay close enough to notice change.
Stay wise enough to respond early.
Stay courageous enough to be misunderstood if necessary.

Because protection is not a mood.
It is a practiced stewardship.
And the parent who guards proactively often prevents the very harm others only recognize after it is too late.

RESPONDING IN AN EMERGENCY

When warning signs appear, hesitation can compound harm. There are moments in parenting when delay is not caution—it is danger. If abuse is suspected, the first responsibility is not to protect the comfort of adults, preserve a family image, or wait until the situation feels less disruptive. The first responsibility is to protect the child. Emergencies demand clarity. They demand courage. They demand immediate response rooted in truth rather than emotion, fear, or denial.

Psalm 46:1 (KJV) assures, "God is our refuge and strength, a very present help in trouble." Divine help does not eliminate responsibility—it strengthens decisive action. God's presence is not an excuse for passivity. It is a strength for obedience. In a moment of crisis, parents must not confuse prayer with postponement. Prayer should steady the heart, sharpen discernment, and move the adult toward protective action. A praying parent must also become an acting parent.

If abuse is suspected, immediate safety must come first. Remove the child from the environment. Do not keep the child near the suspected person or place simply because the situation feels complicated, embarrassing, or difficult to explain. Safety cannot wait for everyone else to understand. Safety cannot be negotiated around adult feelings. A child who may have been harmed should not be required to remain exposed while adults deliberate, debate, or attempt to preserve appearances. The first movement of protection is separation from possible danger.

Medical evaluation should be sought promptly when appropriate. This is not only about treatment; it is also about proper examination. A child may have internal injury, physical pain, or evidence that needs professional attention, even when the signs are not fully visible to an untrained eye.

Parents must resist the temptation to minimize what might be "nothing serious" when a child's body or emotional state indicates otherwise. Prompt care communicates to the child that what happened matters, that their pain matters, and that adults are taking their safety seriously.

Documentation is also important. Photograph injuries if appropriate. Preserve clothing or materials that may serve as evidence. Write down the child's words exactly as spoken. Details matter, especially in the early stage when memory is fresh, and confusion can cloud what adults later try to reconstruct. Parents should avoid reshaping the child's words to make them sound more polished or more convincing. The power of the child's statement often lies in its honesty, not its sophistication.

Record what was said, how it was said, when it was said, and what circumstances surrounded the disclosure or the signs that raised concern.

This is where many adults make damaging mistakes. They begin asking too many leading questions, pressuring the child for details beyond what the child can give, or emotionally overwhelming the child with their own panic. In an emergency, the child does not need an adult collapsing into chaos. The child needs calm strength. Ask only what is necessary to understand immediate safety needs, and let trained professionals handle deeper forensic inquiry where needed. The parents' role is to protect, support, and preserve truth, not to turn the child into the manager of the adult's emotional response.

Proverbs 31:8 (KJV) commands, "Open thy mouth for the dumb in the cause of all such as are appointed to destruction." Children cannot always advocate for themselves. Parents must become their voice. That means speaking when the child is afraid, acting when the child is confused, and standing firm when others want to soften, excuse, or suppress the seriousness of what has occurred. A child should never have to carry the burden of convincing adults to care. The parent must not wait for a perfect presentation of pain before taking the matter seriously.

Never prioritize family reputation over a child's safety. Never delay action to preserve social comfort. This is where some of the deepest betrayals occur. Adults fear the consequences of exposure, the disruption of relationships, the shame of public discovery, or the fallout within family, church, or community structures. But a child's body, mind, and soul must never be sacrificed to keep adult systems looking intact. What good is a preserved reputation if a child is left to carry hidden trauma because the truth was inconvenient? What good is social peace if it was purchased at the cost of silence?

Time magnifies trauma. Swift response minimizes damage and accelerates healing. That does not mean every wound is quickly resolved, but it does mean early action reduces the length of exposure, communicates protection, and interrupts the child's sense of abandonment. A child who sees adults respond decisively learns something crucial: I matter. I am believed. I am not alone. What happened to me is not being ignored. That response becomes part of the child's healing. Not all pain can be prevented once harm has occurred, but much deeper pain can be added if the adults respond with denial, delay, or divided loyalty.

Intervention may be uncomfortable—but inaction is devastating.

Parents must also understand that emergency response is not only practical; it is spiritual. In a moment of abuse suspicion, two battles are often happening at once. One is the visible need to act decisively. The other is the invisible pressure to stay quiet, stay confused, and stay emotionally entangled in excuses.

The enemy often works in those moments through fear: fear of being wrong, fear of overreacting, fear of exposing someone respected, fear of family fracture, fear of social consequence. But holy courage must rise higher than fear. The child needs an adult willing to choose truth over comfort and protection over hesitation.

Responding in an emergency also means guarding the child after the initial action. The child may need reassurance, emotional steadiness, clear support, and careful protection from repeated questioning, shame, or exposure to adults who may minimize what happened. The emergency is not over simply because the first action was taken. Parents must continue to provide presence, clarity, and safety as the child processes what has happened. The home must become a refuge, not another place of confusion.

There are moments in family life when the watchman must move from warning to intervention. This is one of them. The faithful parent does not freeze in the face of possible harm. They do not surrender to fear. They act with sobriety, courage, and urgency.

They protect first. They seek help quickly. They preserve what matters. They become the child's advocate when the child cannot yet stand fully in that role alone.

So if warning signs appear, do not hesitate.
Protect the child.
Get help.
Preserve evidence.
Record truth.
Speak up.
Stand firm.

Because emergencies reveal whether the watchman is merely concerned—or truly faithful.

A CONCLUDING CONVICTION FOR CHAPTER SIX

Identifying signs of abuse is not optional knowledge—it is sacred preparedness. It is not information reserved only for specialists, investigators, counselors, or those who have already encountered tragedy firsthand. It is part of the holy responsibility of every parent, guardian, and caregiver entrusted with a child's life. Innocence is too precious to be guarded casually. A child's safety must never depend on whether the adult responsible happens to recognize danger by accident. Wisdom must be cultivated. Discernment must be sharpened. Awareness must be embraced before crisis demands it.

Parents who ignore behavioral shifts risk enabling harm. Guardians who dismiss physical signs risk prolonging trauma. Communities that silence discomfort create environments where predators operate quietly. Abuse rarely thrives in the open light; it grows where warning signs are minimized, where hesitation replaces action, and where adults convince themselves that what they are seeing is probably nothing. But neglecting the signs does not make the danger disappear. It only grants it more time to deepen.

This truth must be spoken with conviction: children are being abused all over the world. This is not a distant problem confined to isolated places or rare circumstances. It exists in cities and suburbs, in schools and neighborhoods, in families, in institutions, and even in environments that outwardly appear respectable and trustworthy. It happens behind closed doors, inside digital spaces, within familiar relationships, and sometimes within the very circles that claim to protect children. Because of this reality, vigilance is not an exaggeration—it is a moral necessity.

I cannot emphasize strongly enough the importance of every responsible adult doing their job. When God entrusts a child to a parent, guardian, teacher, or leader, that responsibility is not symbolic. It is real. It carries weight. It requires action. Protection is not accomplished by affection alone. It requires attentiveness, discipline, courage, and the willingness to intervene when something is not right.

Too many children suffer because someone who should have been watching decided not to see. Too many wounds deepen because the adult who should have spoken decided to stay silent. That must not continue.

Protection demands courage. Discernment demands prayer. Action demands conviction. Love that refuses courage becomes too weak to guard effectively. Concern without prayer becomes too dull to discern clearly. Awareness without action becomes too passive to protect at all. The faithful guardian must be willing to see what is painful, ask what is uncomfortable, and confront what others would rather leave hidden. This is not harshness—it is responsible stewardship.

Your child's safety is not a casual responsibility—it is a divine mandate. Children are sacred trusts placed under the watch of adults who are called to guard them faithfully. Their innocence is not a light matter. Their safety is not negotiable. Their signals—whether behavioral, emotional, or physical—must never be brushed aside simply because acknowledging them may be inconvenient. When a child signals distress, the adult's duty is not to rationalize it away but to investigate with seriousness.

Remain vigilant. Remain attentive. Remain unafraid to confront what threatens innocence. Do not allow routine to dull your awareness. Do not allow familiarity to weaken your discernment. Do not allow the fear of being misunderstood to silence your responsibility. It is better to ask the difficult question than to live with the devastating knowledge that silence allowed harm to continue.

The cost of awareness is discomfort. The cost of negligence is immeasurable.

Discomfort may require awkward conversations, closer examination, firmer boundaries, professional evaluation, or decisive action that disrupts relationships and appearances. But negligence can leave a child carrying wounds that follow them for years—wounds that shape their trust, their identity, their relationships, and their sense of safety in the world. No social peace, no family reputation, and no momentary convenience is worth that cost.

So let this chapter close with sober resolve. Learn the signs. Study the changes. Listen carefully when a child speaks and even more carefully when they struggle to speak. Pay attention to the body, the emotions, and the behavior. Do not dismiss what deserves examination. Do not call everything a phase when some things are warnings.

Children everywhere depend on adults who are willing to remain awake.

Because sacred preparedness is not fear—it is faithful love with open eyes. And the parent or guardian who takes their responsibility seriously may recognize the signal early enough to interrupt harm and protect what Heaven has placed under their care.

❖ SPIRITUAL WARNING ❖

A Solemn Warning To The Watchmen

There is a silence that Heaven does not ignore. There is a quietness that is not peace, but negligence. There is a stillness that is not safety, but surrender. When innocence is violated, and guardians look away, when warning signs flicker and are dismissed as an inconvenience, when discernment is dulled by familiarity and spiritual fatigue, God does not remain indifferent. He records. He weighs. He judges. What men excuse, Heaven examines. What families bury, Heaven uncovers. What leaders minimize, Heaven remembers.

This is not merely about protection. It is about accountability unto God.

Children are not casual additions to a household. They are not loose responsibilities handed to adults without expectation. They are divine entrustments. They are souls placed under human care by the hand of God. That means every parent, guardian, caregiver, and leader who has been given influence over a child stands under a holy obligation. You are not only responsible to society. You are responsible before the Judge of all the earth. You will not answer merely for what you intended. You will answer for what you guarded, what you ignored, what you tolerated, what you investigated, what you excused, and what you refused to confront.

We live in an hour where evil does not always break down doors—it is often permitted in through comfort, over-trust, spiritual laziness, and the refusal to disturb what feels familiar. It smiles. It serves. It helps. It attends gatherings. It speaks respectfully. It wears the language of normalcy. It hides behind reputation, history, personality, and position. And while adults debate appearances, children endure realities. While watchmen reassure themselves, the vulnerable bear the cost of their hesitation.

The greatest tragedy is not only that predators exist. The greater tragedy is that some watchmen no longer watch. Some have become emotionally dull, spiritually sleepy, and too comfortable to stand at their post with holy seriousness. Some would rather preserve a family image than protect a child's body. Some would rather protect a ministry name than confront what is hidden in its shadows. Some would rather keep relationships intact than ask the question that might expose corruption. But Heaven does not call that wisdom. Heaven calls that failure of stewardship.

Scripture makes it unmistakably clear that the harm of a child is not a minor matter before God. It is an assault against something sacred. Children are not ornamental blessings to decorate the family story. They are divine trusts. To neglect their protection is not a harmless oversight. It is not a light error. It is not something softened by phrases like "I meant well" or "I didn't want to believe it." To be placed in authority over a child and fail to guard them with seriousness is to mishandle something Heaven values deeply.

When behavioral changes are brushed aside, when physical indicators are minimized, when emotional distress is mocked as drama, when secrecy is left unchallenged, when discomfort is silenced for the sake of convenience, a door is opened. And doors opened through negligence rarely close without damage. Many wounds did not deepen because there were no signs. They deepened because signs were seen and then explained away. They deepened because an adult chose the comfort of disbelief over the burden of action. They deepened because somebody on the wall saw movement and said nothing.

The Lord sees what happens in hidden rooms. He hears what is whispered in secrecy. He knows when fear is carried alone. He sees the child whose body tenses but whose mouth cannot explain. He sees the teenager who grows withdrawn but cannot yet name the reason. He sees the sleepless nights, the shame, the confusion, the altered behavior, the trembling spirit, the silent panic. And He also sees the adults who were positioned to guard but chose instead to assume. He sees the parent who felt the nudge and suppressed it.

He sees the guardian who noticed the shift and delayed the question. He sees the leader who protects the image at the expense of innocence. He sees the watchman who slept through peace and awoke only when the damage could no longer be hidden.

Spiritual apathy is not harmless. It is fertile ground for destruction. It is not a personality flaw. It is not a minor weakness. It is a dangerous condition for a guardian. It whispers, “You’re overthinking.” It says, “It’s probably nothing.” It reasons, “Don’t make this bigger than it is.” It comforts the conscience while weakening the wall. It lets adults feel merciful while children remain exposed. But apathy has never protected a child. Delay has never healed one. Passive concern has never stopped a hidden predator.

Parents, guardians, leaders—this is not a suggestion. It is a summons before God. Do not confuse denial with peace. Do not confuse trust with wisdom. Do not confuse silence with safety. Silence can be the camouflage of negligence. Denial can be the language of cowardice. Trust without verification can be the open gate through which harm enters. If God gave you the assignment to guard, then He also gave you the responsibility to stay awake.

There will come a day when excuses will not stand. There will be no refuge in “I didn’t know,” if discernment was available but unused. There will be no shelter in “I didn’t want to accuse anyone,” if avoidance leaves a child exposed. There will be no safety in “I was trying to keep peace,” if that peace was built on the silence of a suffering child. There will be no reward for protecting appearances while innocence was left unguarded. When comfort is chosen over courage, Heaven sees it for what it is: avoidance under a religious mask.

Heaven requires watchfulness. Not sentiment alone. Not protective language alone. Not an occasional concern alone. Watchfulness. The kind that listens when behavior changes. The kind that notices when the atmosphere shifts. The kind that pays attention when a child withdraws, trembles, regresses, resists, or grows strangely quiet. The kind that asks again when the first answer does not settle the spirit. The kind that adults would rather misunderstand than fail a child before God.

If something shifts—investigate. If something feels unsettled—pray and act. If a child withdraws—lean closer, not further away. If boundaries are tested—reinforce them immediately. If access feels too comfortable—reexamine it. If your spirit is troubled, do not anesthetize discernment with excuses. There are moments when a parent must move with holy urgency, because delay is not neutrality. Delay can become a partnership with harm.

The cost of vigilance is effort. The cost of negligence is irreversible. Effort may exhaust you. It may inconvenience your schedule. It may expose relationships. It may strain family structures. It may force hard conversations and unwelcome truths. But irreversible damage costs far more. No awkward confrontation compares to a child carrying years of trauma because an adult would not act in time. No social embarrassment compares to a hidden violation. No preserved reputation is worth a wounded soul.

Let conviction replace complacency. Let courage overpower convenience. Let protection become relentless. Let every watchman remember that children are being abused all over this world, and Heaven is not asking whether you felt concerned—it is asking whether you did your job. A child should never have to pay the price for an adult's laziness, passivity, fear of conflict, or refusal to see. If a child has been placed under your guardianship by God, then your responsibilities extend beyond superficial aspects. It is sacred. It is binding. It is answerable to Him.

Because when God entrusts you with a child, He does not ask for passive care. He requires active guardianship. He requires eyes that stay open, ears that stay attentive, a conscience that stays tender, and a will that stays obedient. He requires parents who will stand between innocence and intrusion. He requires watchmen who fear Him more than they fear being misunderstood.

He requires guardians who know that children belong first to Him, and that stewardship over them is a holy charge.

Stand alert.
Stand firm.
Stand accountable.
Stand as one who knows that God is watching the wall.

Because Heaven is not only watching what enters your home—Heaven is watching who was standing guard when it entered.

God is not merely looking at the danger; He is looking at the steward. He is not only examining the influence that crossed the threshold; He is examining the level of discernment, obedience, and vigilance in the one He trusted to guard the gate. What God placed in your hands was never casual. Your children are not casual. Your home is not casual. Your assignment is not casual. Your authority is not casual. When God entrusts you with something precious, He also requires you to protect it with spiritual seriousness.

There is a difference between being present in the house and being watchful over the house. There is a difference between loving your children and guarding their souls. There is a difference between assuming everything is fine and discerning what is trying to gain access. The enemy does not always enter with noise; sometimes he enters through comfort, familiarity, over-trust, silence, distraction, and the people we never thought to question.

And on that day, when every hidden thing is brought before God, excuses will not stand where obedience was required. Good intentions will not replace faithful inspection. Busyness will not justify blindness. Trust will not excuse negligence. Love will not erase the responsibility to watch. God will not ask only what happened—He will ask what we guarded, what we allowed, what we ignored, and what we failed to confront.

Because when Heaven reviews the record, faithfulness—not explanations—will answer before God.

CHAPTER SEVEN

UNDERSTANDING GROOMING AND PREDATOR TACTICS

How Manipulation Gains Access

✦

Psychological Grooming

Every parent must grasp a sobering reality: predators are not impulsive opportunists—they are patient strategists. Their behavior is rarely spontaneous. It is deliberate. Calculated. Observed. Rehearsed. They do not move without intention. They study environments. They analyze family dynamics. They assess access points. They watch for emotional gaps, busy schedules, inattentive guardians, exhausted parents, distracted leadership, and children who appear isolated, eager for affirmation, emotionally hungry, or unsure of their own worth. They are not simply looking for a child. They are looking for weakness in the structure around the child.

Second Corinthians 2:11 (KJV) warns, "Lest Satan should get an advantage of us: for we are not ignorant of his devices." The principle is clear—ignorance creates advantage. Awareness disrupts it. Just as spiritual deception operates through strategy, so too does predatory behavior. Parents who refuse to learn patterns leave themselves vulnerable to manipulation. Evil often advances where people insist on remaining naïve. The unwillingness to understand how predators think does not protect a child. It protects the predator.

Predators invest time in building credibility before attempting harm. They often begin by gaining the trust of adults rather than targeting the child immediately. They volunteer. They assist. They appear dependable. They offer help during busy seasons. They position themselves as safe and trustworthy. They become useful enough that questioning them feels awkward. They become familiar enough that boundaries start to loosen. They become present enough that their access begins to feel normal rather than noteworthy. Access is not demanded—it is earned slowly.

This is grooming.

Grooming is the gradual process of normalizing inappropriate closeness. It often begins with excessive attention, special privileges, gifts, private conversations, unusual favoritism, emotional flattery, or subtle efforts to become indispensable. The predator may isolate the child quietly—creating opportunities for one-on-one interaction while minimizing suspicion. They may frame their closeness as mentorship, support, compassion, or special understanding. They may speak as though they are uniquely able to comfort, guide, or "really see" the child. But what appears caring on the surface may be calculated beneath it.

The sick-mindedness of a predator is not only in what they want to do. It is in how they think. They think in terms of access, leverage, secrecy, and control. They look at a child's loneliness and see an opening. They look at a parent's stress and see an opportunity. They look at a family's trust and see something to exploit. They do not honor vulnerability—they hunt it. They do not respond to innocence with protection—they respond to it with appetite. They do not see a child as sacred. They see a child as reachable, shapeable, manipulable, and, if possible, silenced.

That corruption runs deep. A predator often studies reactions the way a hunter studies movement. They watch what makes the child smile, what makes them open up, what makes the parent relax, what kind of attention the household welcomes, what emotional needs are unmet, what routines leave children alone, what adults are easiest to persuade, and what environments are least supervised. They may remember tiny details about the child—not out of wholesome care, but because information helps build control. They may notice favorite activities, fears, insecurities, and longings, then use those details to create emotional access. What appears attentive may actually be predatory calculation.

They may test boundaries incrementally, beginning with harmless-seeming gestures to measure reaction. A slightly too-personal comment. An unnecessary touch. An extra message. A private joke. A gift not mentioned to the parent. A request for secrecy dressed as trust. A moment alone was created under an innocent pretense.

A conversation that becomes emotionally intimate too quickly. If the boundary is not challenged, it advances. The predator reads silence as opportunity. A lack of correction becomes permission in their minds.

Matthew 7:15 (KJV) provides a powerful image: "Beware of false prophets, which come to you in sheep's clothing, but inwardly they are ravening wolves." The wolf does not announce its hunger. It disguises itself within the flock. It studies the shepherd's patterns. It waits for distraction. This is the psychology of predation. A wolf does not hate the sheep because of something the sheep did. It desires the sheep because it is vulnerable. That is the twisted nature of this evil. The predator's mind is not moved by empathy. It is moved by appetite and advantage.

Predators often identify specific vulnerabilities: children who crave affirmation or attention, children with low self-worth, children under emotional strain, children who fear conflict, homes lacking consistent oversight, families under stress or distraction, and situations where isolation is easy. They exploit emotional needs. They may use praise to create attachment, sympathy to create emotional dependence, and secrecy to create control. They may introduce inappropriate content gradually to desensitize the child. They may make the child feel chosen, special, mature, or deeply understood. This is not affection. It is manipulation. It is a sick mind turning normal human longings—belonging, comfort, validation—into tools for exploitation.

A predator's mind often works through layers. First, they want access. Then they want trust. Then they want secrecy. Then they want control. They may not rush because speed draws attention. They prefer slow corruption. They prefer to normalize wrong things before making them more direct. They may intentionally blur categories so the child struggles to distinguish kindness from violation, support from control, or closeness from danger. They may want the child confused, because confusion weakens resistance. A confused child is easier to silence. A guilty child is easier to trap. A child who fears not being believed is easier to keep hidden.

Some predators are especially sick in the way they seek emotional ownership. They may subtly compete with the parent for the child's loyalty. They may present themselves as the one who "really understands." They may encourage the child to share things privately that should be brought into the light. They may make the child feel that the relationship is unique, rare, or too special for others to understand. In their mind, the child is not a life to protect but a bond to possess. That possessiveness is part of the sickness. It is a corrupt attachment mixed with selfish appetite and an utter disregard for the soul of the child.

They may also manipulate the adults. They may appear humble, sacrificial, patient, and spiritually articulate. They may know exactly how to sound safe in front of parents while behaving differently in more hidden settings. They may count on adults being too polite, too grateful, too impressed, or too conflict-averse to confront what feels slightly off. This is why grooming is not only aimed at the child. It is aimed at the whole environment. The predator wants the adults softened, the child attached, and the structure weakened.

Parents must understand that grooming is not a harmless stage before danger. It is already in danger. It is the early architecture of abuse. It is the process by which a predator conditions the child, conditions the family, and conditions the environment to tolerate what should have been interrupted early. Once that process is underway, every ignored sign strengthens the predator's confidence.

Predatory behavior thrives where ignorance exists. It retreats where awareness stands firm. The more clearly parents understand these sick-minded tactics, the less easily they will be deceived by charm, service, emotional intelligence, or over-familiarity. A wise parent does not merely ask, Is this person nice? They ask, Why are they seeking this kind of access? Why are they trying to become this close? Why is secrecy appearing? Why is this child changing around them? Why does this relationship require privacy to survive?

Parents must not be embarrassed to think soberly. This is not being cynical. This is being responsible. A child's safety is too sacred to be guarded by wishful thinking.

The watchman who understands how the wolf thinks is far more prepared to keep the wolf from the flock.

So keep the content of this truth intact in your spirit: predators often move slowly, think strategically, exploit emotional need, study weakness, manipulate trust, and seek secrecy before overt harm. Their methods are sick because their motives are corrupt. Their patience is not kindness. Their attention is not innocent. Their interest is not harmless.

Learn the pattern.
Watch the access.
Challenge the secrecy.
Interrupt the overinvestment.
Protect the child before confusion deepens.

Because a predator's mind is bent toward exploitation, but an awakened parent can make that strategy far harder to advance.

GRADUAL ACCESS STRATEGY

Predators do not rush recklessly—they advance strategically. They understand that access is rarely granted all at once. It is usually developed through familiarity, usefulness, repeated exposure, and the quiet weakening of adult vigilance. They are patient because patience protects their intentions. They know that what is introduced gradually is often questioned less. What would alarm a family if attempted suddenly may be tolerated if it is built slowly over time. This is why the danger often does not begin with an obvious violation. It begins with a process.

They often begin by earning the household's confidence. They may volunteer eagerly, present themselves as spiritually mature, socially respected, emotionally intelligent, or exceptionally kind. They may offer help during busy seasons. They may align themselves with positions that grant credibility—mentor, coach, clergy, teacher, volunteer, counselor, family friend. They understand that parents lower their guard more quickly around people who appear stable, sacrificial, and familiar. In many cases, the predator does not first pursue the child. He first pursues the trust of the adults who control the child's environment.

Access is their objective.
Reputation is their shield.

That is why gradual access is so dangerous. It does not look like an immediate threat. It looks like involvement. It looks like service. It looks like generosity. It looks like reliability. But beneath that surface may be a deeper agenda: to become so normal in the life of the family that access no longer feels risky and accountability no longer feels necessary. Once a person is treated as safe by habit, adults often stop watching them with sober eyes. And that is exactly the atmosphere a predator wants to create.

The gradual access strategy depends upon patience. A predator does not always seek immediate privacy with the child. Instead, they first become familiar, useful, and trusted. They may show up repeatedly, offer practical help, speak respectfully, remember details about the family, and become emotionally comfortable within the household. They may intentionally appear non-threatening, even humble.

They may not ask for too much at the outset because they understand that small permissions lead to larger ones later. Once parental caution has softened, the space for deeper access widens.

That widening often happens quietly. First, it is an extra conversation. Then it is special attention. Then it is helping with transportation, staying late, private encouragement, direct messaging, one-on-one outings, or unusual emotional closeness.

A family may barely notice how much room has been created because each step felt only slightly larger than the last. This is how access grows—not always through force, but through accepted familiarity. The predator counts on the fact that adults are more likely to challenge a sudden request than a slowly normalized pattern.

This is why discernment must override comfort.

Parents must study patterns just as predators study access. They must observe who seeks excessive alone time with their child. They must question adults who ignore boundaries or attempt to bypass parental oversight. They must pay attention to behavior that feels overly invested in gaining the child's loyalty, affection, admiration, secrecy, or emotional dependence. They must notice when an adult's desire to play a role in the child's inner world becomes excessive. Wise parents do not wait until the behavior becomes obviously dangerous to begin paying attention. They recognize that by then, the strategy may already be well underway.

One of the darker elements of gradual access is that predators often want to become psychologically "necessary" before they become physically inappropriate. They may work to position themselves as the person the child enjoys most, confides in most, or feels most seen by outside the home. They may subtly compete with parental influence without making that competition obvious. They may present themselves as uniquely understanding, especially if the child feels lonely, misunderstood, insecure, or emotionally hungry. That is not innocent over-involvement. It may be the architecture of manipulation.

Parents must also recognize how gradual access can be built through adult weakness. A tired parent may welcome help without examining the cost of the access it creates. An overwhelmed household may become grateful for someone reliable without pausing to ask why that person always seems eager to be near the child. A family in stress may relax its boundaries because support feels needed. Predators know this. They study when the household is stretched. They know that fatigue weakens scrutiny and gratitude can silence discernment. That is why usefulness must never be allowed to outrun accountability.

Knowledge does not create paranoia—it creates preparedness. A parent who understands these tactics is not becoming fearful of everyone. They are becoming harder to manipulate. They are learning to distinguish healthy involvement from strategic positioning. They are learning that not every generous action is innocent, not every repeated presence is harmless, and not every respected role should be granted unquestioned access. Awareness steadies the watchman. It gives language to discomfort and structure to wise response.

Understanding tactics allows parents to disrupt strategy early. If grooming behaviors are identified and confronted immediately, progression is halted. If secrecy is exposed early, manipulation weakens. If inappropriate closeness is named while it still appears "small," it often prevents something much larger from developing later. This is why early confrontation matters. The predator depends on adults delaying action until the pattern becomes unmistakable. But a faithful parent understands that subtle danger often needs to be interrupted while it is still subtle.

When parents are informed, they recognize grooming early. They detect isolation patterns quickly. They respond to boundary violations decisively. They strengthen oversight consistently. They do not hand over access because someone is admired. They do not surrender caution because someone is useful. They do not confuse a polished image with proven integrity. They remain awake enough to ask, Why is this person always positioning themselves near my child? Why do they seem to want a deeper bond than their role requires? Why does this relationship keep moving toward privacy? Why is transparency becoming less welcome?

Ignorance grants an advantage.
Awareness removes it.

That is why the gradual access strategy must be taken seriously. It is not accidental behavior. It is intentional progression. It is the slow construction of familiarity so that later boundaries feel harder to enforce. It is the use of time, reputation, usefulness, and repeated presence to lower the household's defenses. It is the long game of a corrupt mind seeking room to operate.

So do not study only the obvious threat.
Study the pattern of access.
Study the progression.
Study who keeps moving closer and why.
Study who seems to need private space in order to maintain the relationship.
Study what is becoming normal and whether it should have been challenged earlier.

Because predators often do not begin by asking for everything.
They begin by asking for enough to return.
And if no one interrupts the strategy, what begins as comfort may become access, and what becomes access may become harm.

ISOLATION TACTICS

Isolation is essential to the predator's strategy. Harm is easiest to develop when visibility is removed, and accountability is reduced. Predators understand that if a child remains deeply connected to open parental communication, consistent oversight, and emotionally safe relationships at home, their strategy weakens. So they work to gradually separate the child from the protective presence. They do not always begin by removing the child physically. Often, they begin by creating emotional distance between the child and the people appointed to guard them. They know that a child who still tells everything, still trusts parental instincts, and still feels secure enough to disclose discomfort is much harder to manipulate.

Isolation does not always begin dramatically. It may begin with seemingly harmless one-on-one opportunities. Extra help. Special rides. Private talks. Exclusive outings. Personal mentorship. Emotional check-ins that slowly shift from public to private. At first, these moments may appear generous, attentive, or even beneficial. But when one adult repeatedly seeks unnecessary privacy with a child, especially outside normal boundaries and beyond parental visibility, wise parents must stop admiring the gesture long enough to examine the pattern. What begins as attention can become separation. What begins as access can become control.

This is why isolation must be recognized for what it often is: not innocent closeness, but strategic positioning. Predators know that if they can make the child feel singled out, chosen, favored, or especially understood, they can begin loosening the child's instinct to keep parents fully informed.

They may offer what feels like comfort, protection, affirmation, or a special interest, but beneath the surface, they are often trying to build a private channel of influence. They want a relationship that the parents do not fully see, do not fully govern, and may not fully understand. That privacy becomes the soil in which deeper manipulation grows.

Predators may position themselves as the "safe" adult. They may subtly undermine parental authority. They may make the child feel uniquely understood. They may encourage private communication under the guise of support. Their aim is to become emotionally central while reducing the child's instinct to remain open with parents. They may listen closely when the child feels hurt, correct when the child feels lonely, or affirm when the child feels unseen—not out of righteous care, but because emotional access creates leverage. If the child begins to believe, This person understands me better than my parents, then the predator has already begun moving into dangerous territory.

This emotional isolation can be even more damaging than physical isolation because it shifts loyalty. The child may begin to protect the relationship rather than question it. They may become reluctant to tell parents certain things because they do not want to "betray" the one who has made them feel special. They may begin filtering what they say at home because another voice has become too influential. This is one of the sickest parts of predatory strategy: they do not merely seek access to the child's time. They seek access to the child's trust, inner world, and relational allegiance.

They do not begin with overt harm. They begin with subtle boundary testing. A private joke that leaves the parent outside. An extra message no one else sees. A one-on-one conversation that lasts longer than necessary. A repeated effort to be the one who comforts, counsels, transports, guides, or "checks in" on the child. Each of these may appear small in isolation. But taken together, they may reveal a pattern of intentional separation. The predator wants the child to get used to exclusivity. Once that exclusivity feels normal, the next boundary becomes easier to cross.

Isolation also works by reducing the child's sense that parents will understand. A predator may plant subtle thoughts such as, They won't get it, They'll overreact, This is just between us, or You can talk to me because I'm safe. They may never openly attack the parent at first. Instead, they gently weaken the child's confidence in bringing things home. This is especially dangerous because the child may not feel forced into secrecy. They may feel persuaded into it. That persuasion is part of the trap.

Parents must therefore evaluate behavior patterns, not personalities. A pleasant personality can hide a dangerous pattern. A helpful role can hide a manipulative goal. The right questions must be asked: Does this adult seek excessive alone time with my child? Do they resist transparency? Do they bypass parental involvement? Do they create secrecy? Do they overinvest emotionally beyond appropriate boundaries? Do they keep trying to build a bond that grows more private, more exclusive, and more difficult for parents to observe clearly? These questions are not cynical. They are responsible.

Wise parents must also pay attention to the child's side of the pattern. Does the child become strangely protective of this adult? Defensive when simple questions are asked? Secretive about messages, outings, or conversations? Unusually emotionally attached? Quiet after time spent with them? Fearful of displeasing them?

These can all be indicators that the relationship is no longer functioning within healthy boundaries. Again, the issue is not merely whether the adult seems kind. The issue is whether the relationship is creating secrecy, dependency, and distance from the child's primary protection.

If targeting behaviors are noticed, increase oversight. If family grooming patterns appear, limit access. If isolation increases, interrupt it immediately. Parents must not wait until the pattern becomes blatant before responding. Early interruption matters. More visibility. Less privacy. Stronger boundaries. Clear questions. Restricted contact where necessary. The goal is not to be dramatic. The goal is to prevent the strategy from maturing into something more destructive.

Isolation tactics also operate digitally. Private messages, late-night chats, gaming conversations, disappearing content, and secret accounts can all become isolation chambers that draw a child away from healthy visibility and into a hidden bond. Parents must not imagine isolation only as a child being physically alone. A child can be isolated while sitting in the family room if the real conversation is happening on a device that no adult is watching. Emotional separation can happen through a screen just as powerfully as it can happen on a car ride, in a back room, or during an exclusive outing.

The great protection against isolation is a strong parental connection. A child who feels deeply safe with parents, heard without ridicule, and protected without hesitation is much harder to separate. Open communication weakens predatory secrecy. Visible boundaries weaken private access. Consistent oversight weakens hidden progression. Emotional closeness in the home makes counterfeit closeness easier to detect.

So parents must not merely ask whether someone is around the child. They must ask whether someone is trying to get between the child and their rightful covering. That is the deeper issue. Not all closeness is harmless. Not all attention is nurturing. Not all mentorship is pure. Some "support" is really strategic separation.

Watch who keeps moving the relationship into privacy.
Watch who wants exclusivity.
Watch who becomes too emotionally central.
Watch who seems to need the child alone in order to feel effective.

Because what begins as one-on-one attention may become emotional capture. And if isolation is not interrupted early, the child may slowly be pulled away from the very voices most capable of protecting them.

SECRECY MANIPULATION

Once access and trust are established, secrecy becomes one of the predator's strongest tools. At that stage, the predator no longer relies only on proximity or attention. They begin to work on the child's silence. They understand that as long as the child remains free to tell the truth, their control is fragile. But if they can bind the child to secrecy, they can create a private world where manipulation grows with less interruption. That is why secrecy is not a side tactic. It is central to the strategy. A predator does not merely want hidden behavior; he wants a hidden system of fear, confusion, and private loyalty strong enough to keep the child from reaching the very people God appointed to protect them.

They often use statements such as, "This is our secret," "No one will believe you," "You'll get in trouble too," or "I'm the only one who understands you." These are not casual phrases. They are instruments of control. They are crafted to confuse the child's conscience, weaken the child's confidence, and place the weight of silence on the one who should have been protected. Fear becomes their leverage. Shame becomes their tool. Silence becomes their shield. The predator wants the child to feel responsible for guarding what should have been exposed. That reversal is part of the corruption. The guilty party works to make the innocent feel burdened with protecting the lie. It is a deeply twisted exchange: the child carries the pressure, while the offender seeks the freedom.

Secrecy manipulation is dangerous because it makes the child feel trapped between fear and confusion. The child may not fully understand what is happening, but they begin to sense that disclosure will cost them something. They may fear punishment. They may fear not being believed. They may fear hurting their family. They may fear creating chaos, anger, embarrassment, or rejection. The predator exploits that fear. He creates the illusion that silence is safety, when in truth, silence only protects the offender. Silence may feel like survival to the child, but it becomes shelter for the abuser.

That is why a child can look outwardly compliant while inwardly carrying tremendous terror. Secrecy does not remove the burden. It only hides where the burden is being carried.

Predators often know exactly where to press. If the child is tenderhearted, they may use guilt. If the child fears discipline, they may use threats. If the child longs for connection, they may use false loyalty. If the child feels unseen, they may use exclusivity. They may imply that the relationship is special, that outsiders would not understand, that parents will overreact, or that speaking up will "ruin everything." They may speak in ways that make the child feel chosen one moment and threatened the next. This instability is not accidental. It is part of the trap. The child becomes emotionally disoriented, never fully secure, yet too afraid to break the silence.

The sick-mindedness in this is profound: the predator does not merely want access to the child's body or emotions; he wants to colonize the child's inner world so that fear begins doing his work for him.

This is why secrecy must be understood as a psychological cage. The child may feel bound by invisible chains—fear of consequences, fear of disbelief, fear of being blamed, fear of losing love, fear of being seen differently. Even if the child hates what is happening, they may remain silent because the predator has made silence feel safer than truth. A child can be deeply uncomfortable, spiritually disturbed, emotionally overwhelmed, and physically afraid while still protecting the secret because manipulation has convinced them that speech is more dangerous than concealment.

This is one of the cruelest effects of secrecy: it causes the child to participate in their own silence, not because they are guilty, but because they have been psychologically cornered.

Parents must also understand that secrecy does not always begin with something obviously abusive. It may start with small private exchanges, special messages, hidden gifts, exclusive jokes, or "don't tell your parents yet" moments that condition the child to keep certain interactions private. This is how the line is blurred. The child gets trained to think private loyalty is normal, that adult requests for secrecy can be harmless, or that boundaries around disclosure are part of being mature or trustworthy. But once secrecy becomes normal, danger becomes harder to expose.

A child who has been taught to keep "small" secrets for an adult may be far more vulnerable when the secret grows darker, because the pattern of concealment has already been established.

This conditioning matters because secrecy usually escalates by stages. First, the child is asked to hide something that seems insignificant. Then something personal. Then something uncomfortable. Then something frightening. By then, the child may already feel too entangled to know how to step out. The predator counts on this progression. He knows that children are easier to trap gradually than suddenly. That is why adults must not dismiss secrecy simply because its earliest forms appear small. What is being built beneath those small moments may be a framework for much deeper control.

This is why children must be educated about tactics in age-appropriate ways. They should understand that anyone who asks for secrecy regarding touching is wrong. They should know that no adult's authority supersedes their right to safety. They should be encouraged to report discomfort without fear. They should be taught the difference between healthy privacy and dangerous secrecy. Privacy protects dignity. Secrecy protects hidden wrongdoing.

A child should know that a birthday surprise is different from a secret that creates fear, confusion, pressure, or discomfort. They should know that if someone says, "Don't tell," that statement itself is a reason to tell. These lessons are not too strong for children. They are part of wise protection.

Parents must teach repeatedly that speaking up brings protection, not punishment. This truth cannot be mentioned once and assumed to be settled. It must be woven into the life of the home until the child believes it deeply. The child must know that if something makes me uncomfortable, I can tell. If someone says not to tell, I still can tell. If I am afraid, I can tell. If I made a mistake, I can still tell. If I feel confused, I can still tell. Children need this repeated assurance because predators work hard to convince them of the opposite. The family must therefore become stronger in truth than the predator is in deception.

The home should also be a place where truth isn't punished with emotional violence. If a child expects explosive anger, ridicule, panic, or blame when they share something difficult, they might hide what needs to be revealed. But when the child sees that honesty is met with calmness, protection, and genuine care, the power of manipulation weakens. A parent's response can either reinforce secrecy or help break it. That's why parents must not only teach children to speak up; they also need to be safe enough to listen. A child shouldn't have to weigh whether telling the truth will bring more danger at home than the dangers that already exist outside.

Transparency protects. Secrecy enables.

That contrast must remain sharp. Transparency keeps relationships visible. It keeps access accountable. It keeps children connected to protection. Secrecy hides patterns, removes scrutiny, and creates private rooms where corruption can grow undisturbed. Predators know this. That is why they work so hard to create private language, private bonds, and private fear. They understand that once secrecy is in place, the child begins carrying the burden alone. And when a child is carrying the burden alone, the predator has gained one of his greatest advantages.

A wise parent, therefore, treats the secrecy around a child seriously. Not every private moment is dangerous, but repeated secrecy, especially secrecy that excludes rightful guardians, must never be normalized. Parents should ask: Why does this relationship require hidden communication? Why does this adult need private emotional space with my child? Why does my child suddenly seem guarded about this person, this message, this gift, this conversation? Why does this interaction keep moving away from visibility? These questions are not overreactions. They are the work of a watchman refusing to let silence become a hiding place for harm.

Secrecy manipulation must be interrupted early. Bring things into the light. Ask the second question. Slow down the relationship. Increase visibility. Reinforce the child's right to speak. Make it clear that no adult's status, kindness, title, or connection to the family ever outranks the child's safety. Let the child know that truth will be handled with care, courage, and protection. Let the predator know, by the culture of the home itself, that secrecy will not survive easily there.

So teach it plainly.
Repeat it often.
Model it faithfully.
Protect it fiercely.

Because when a child learns that silence is not safety and that truth leads to protection, one of the predator's strongest weapons begins to lose its power.

EMOTIONAL CONTROL

Predators do not rely on force alone. They rely on manipulation. Force may appear later, but manipulation is often the earlier weapon because it is quieter, slower, and easier to hide. It does not always bruise the body first. It works on the emotions, the trust, the conscience, and the inner world of the child. It seeks to shape how the child feels, how the child interprets attention, how the child carries fear, and how the child responds to pressure. This is why emotional control is one of the most dangerous parts of predatory behavior. It invades the child from the inside.

Predators understand that children are naturally trusting. They know that children seek approval, affection, affirmation, and a sense of belonging. They recognize that a child's innocence, curiosity, tenderness, and limited life experience can be exploited if left unguarded. They know that a child often wants to please adults, especially adults who appear kind, interested, protective, or impressed by them. What should have been met with holy care becomes, in the hands of a predator, something to manipulate for personal control.

Manipulation begins with emotional targeting.

A predator studies a child's emotional landscape. They observe who feels lonely. Who craves attention. Who longs for validation. Who seems hesitant to speak up. Who fears punishment. Who wants badly to be liked. Who is eager to please adults. Who feels unseen at home or uncertain of their own value. These emotional openings become entry points. The predator does not need the child to be rebellious in order to exploit them. Sometimes the very child who is gentle, helpful, polite, eager, and emotionally hungry is the one they find easiest to shape.

Often, manipulation begins gently. It may start with gifts—small tokens that create a sense of obligation. It may include excessive compliments designed to elevate the predator's importance in the child's mind. "You're special." "You're more mature than the others." "I understand you better than anyone." "You can tell me things you can't tell other people." These statements are not random—they are strategic.

They are trying to make the child feel uniquely seen, uniquely valued, and uniquely attached. What appears to be an affirmation may actually be emotional bait.

Affection becomes attachment.
Attachment becomes influence.
Influence becomes control.

This progression is deadly because it often does not feel dangerous at first. The child may simply feel chosen. Noticed. Understood. Appreciated. But that emotional bond becomes the bridge over which manipulation travels. Once the child begins to care deeply about what this person thinks, wants, or feels, the predator has gained leverage. They can then shape the child's choices through approval and disappointment, praise and withdrawal, comfort and pressure. The goal is to become emotionally central enough that the child begins organizing their responses around preserving the relationship.

Fear is another tool. If the child hesitates or questions, intimidation may surface. Threats of punishment. Warnings about consequences. Statements such as, "You'll get in trouble too," or "No one will believe you." These tactics are designed to isolate and silence. They make the child feel that telling the truth will create greater harm than keeping the lie. This is emotional control at its ugliest: the predator tries to convince the child that exposure is more dangerous than abuse, that silence is more protective than honesty, and that the very people who should help cannot be trusted to do so.

Guilt compounds the manipulation. A predator may imply emotional fragility: "If you tell, you'll ruin my life." "You'll make everyone upset." "I'll get in trouble because of you." "You don't want to hurt me, do you?" The child, lacking emotional maturity to process these claims, may internalize responsibility for the predator's well-being. This is deeply twisted. The one causing harm tries to make the harmed child feel responsible for protecting the offender from consequences. That is not merely deception. It is emotional cruelty.

Shame becomes the barrier.
Confusion becomes the prison.
Silence becomes the shield for the offender.

Children who do not fully understand predatory behavior often feel complicit. They may believe they participated willingly. They may question their own perception. They may feel dirty, guilty, disoriented, or responsible for what happened because the predator has blurred every line between coercion and consent, affection and exploitation, secrecy and loyalty. This emotional turmoil deepens the sense of isolation and makes disclosure difficult. The child may wonder, Was it my fault? Did I do something wrong? Why didn't I stop it? Why did I go along? These thoughts are common in manipulated children, and they must be answered with truth, not blame.

Mark 10:14 (KJV) records Jesus saying, "Suffer the little children to come unto me, and forbid them not." Christ's posture toward children was protective, welcoming, and affirming. He did not exploit their openness. He honored it. He did not isolate them into secrecy. He drew them into safety and truth. Predators, in direct opposition to this model, isolate rather than include. They separate rather than safeguard. They manipulate rather than nurture. They exploit trust rather than protecting it. The contrast is clear. Christ draws children toward safety and truth. Predators pull children into secrecy and distortion.

Parents must also understand that emotional control does not always look dramatic. Sometimes it looks like a child becoming overly loyal to a particular adult. Sometimes it looks like the child is feeling responsible for someone else's emotions. Sometimes it looks like unusual defensiveness when a simple question is asked about a relationship. Sometimes it looks like secrecy, anxiety, unexplained guilt, or fear of upsetting a specific person. A child under emotional manipulation may begin protecting the predator emotionally long before they can describe what is happening clearly. They may fear disappointing them, angering them, exposing them, or "betraying" them. That is not a healthy attachment. That is evidence that control may already be operating.

Parents must therefore actively dismantle manipulation by building strong emotional foundations at home. Children who feel secure in parental love are less susceptible to external emotional traps. When affirmation is consistent within the home, they are less vulnerable to flattery from outsiders. When open communication is normal, secrecy struggles to survive. When a child knows that their voice matters, that their discomfort matters, and that they do not have to earn love by pleasing adults, manipulation loses some of its power. Proactive engagement is protection.

Parents should regularly reinforce these truths:
You will never be punished for telling the truth.
No adult should ask you to keep secrets about touching.
If someone makes you uncomfortable, you can tell me immediately.
Your safety matters more than anyone's feelings.

These conversations should not occur only once. They must be repeated with clarity and calmness. Children do not merely need information; they need repetition strong enough to outlast the lies a predator may try to place in their minds. Confidence in communication dismantles the power of shame. The more clearly a child hears the truth at home, the harder it is for manipulation to define reality for them elsewhere.

Parents must also become emotionally safe enough to receive the hard truth. If a child expects to be blamed, shamed, panicked over, or emotionally overwhelmed when they disclose something, they may remain silent. But when the child knows, I will be heard. I will be believed. I will be protected, then emotional control begins to weaken. A predator depends on the child feeling more afraid of disclosure than of secrecy. The parent must work to reverse that equation.

Manipulation thrives in ignorance.
It weakens under awareness.

When children understand tactics, they are less easily deceived. When parents understand patterns, they are less easily distracted. Predators depend on emotional control. Parents must build emotional strength. Illuminate the darkness with truth. Replace secrecy with openness. Counter manipulation with clarity. Teach children that real care does not pressure them into silence, real love does not make them feel trapped, and real authority does not demand unsafe loyalty.

Because when a child knows they are heard, believed, and protected, manipulation loses its strongest weapon. And the earlier deception is exposed, the less damage it can inflict.

THE COMPLEX NATURE OF PREDATORS

One of the most dangerous misconceptions about predators is the belief that they are easily recognizable. Many imagine them as visibly suspicious, socially awkward, unstable, or openly aggressive. In the public imagination, danger often wears an obvious face. But the reality is far more unsettling. Predators often survive precisely because they do not appear threatening. They survive because they appear normal, responsible, compassionate, and trustworthy. Their greatest disguise is not darkness—it is respectability.

Predators are often complex, adaptive, and socially intelligent. They understand perception. They study behavior. They observe how communities think and how families build trust. They learn how to present themselves in ways that disarm suspicion. They recognize that people tend to relax around those who seem helpful, generous, spiritually articulate, or socially admired. Because of this, they rarely survive by appearing threatening—they survive by appearing trustworthy. Their strength lies in their ability to blend into environments that assume goodness.

Psalm 55:21 (KJV) exposes this contradiction with piercing clarity: "The words of his mouth were smoother than butter, but war was in his heart." This verse captures the essence of a deceptive personality. Smooth speech. Warm tone. Gentle demeanor. A cooperative spirit. Yet beneath that exterior may exist calculation and intent. The outward expression and inward motive are not always the same. Scripture warns repeatedly that deception often travels through appearances that feel safe.

A predator's personality is often constructed, not accidental. They learn which qualities create confidence in others and intentionally emphasize those traits. They may appear charming, compassionate, attentive, and generous. They may show interest in the well-being of families. They may remember birthdays, celebrate achievements, and offer encouragement during difficult seasons. They may volunteer eagerly and position themselves where they appear indispensable. These behaviors, in isolation, may appear admirable.

Yet for a predator, such traits can function as social armor—protective camouflage that shields their true motives from scrutiny.

Positions that grant proximity to children are often attractive to individuals seeking opportunity. Roles such as clergy, pastor, deacon, church member, coach, mentor, teacher, youth leader, counselor, or volunteer carry built-in credibility. Society often assumes that those who hold respected roles must also possess strong moral character. Parents lower their guard because authority is assumed to equal safety. But authority does not guarantee integrity. Titles do not sanctify the heart. Public service does not eliminate private corruption.

This is part of what makes predatory behavior so complex. The predator may appear deeply committed to the community. They may appear devoted to helping others. They may be the one who shows up early, stay late, and offer assistance when others are tired. They may be articulate in spiritual language, fluent in moral values, and familiar with the expectations of their environment. Yet beneath that image may exist a completely different intention. Their involvement becomes a strategy for access rather than an expression of genuine service.

The complexity of predatory personality lies in its ability to adapt. Some predators are outgoing and charismatic. They easily build rapport and command attention in social settings. Others are quiet and observant, learning the rhythms of the environment before gradually inserting themselves. Some present themselves as deeply spiritual and articulate in religious conversation. Others appear humble and reserved, gaining trust through apparent modesty. They read the room. They study emotional dynamics. They adjust their demeanor to match expectations.

This adaptability makes detection difficult. There is no single personality profile that immediately exposes a predator. They may be admired by some and trusted by many. They may be described as helpful, dependable, or supportive. They may develop close relationships with families and become a familiar presence within the child's environment. Because their behavior often appears beneficial, questioning them can feel uncomfortable or even unfair. That discomfort is exactly what many predators rely upon.

Predators often cultivate a nurturing image. They may be the encouraging coach who praises a child's potential. The patient teacher who gives extra attention to a struggling student. The understanding mentor who listens carefully to personal struggles. The generous volunteer who provides special privileges or opportunities. These roles allow them to appear compassionate while simultaneously creating proximity to the child.

The persona is crafted intentionally.

A pleasant demeanor does not equal a pure motive. A warm personality does not eliminate hidden intention. Engagement does not guarantee safety. Parents must resist the instinct to equate likability with righteousness. A person can be admired publicly and still be morally compromised privately. The ability to present kindness does not prove the presence of integrity.

Many predators exploit relational gaps. They identify children who crave affirmation, those experiencing family stress, or those seeking belonging and identity. They recognize when a child feels overlooked, insecure, or emotionally vulnerable. Into those emotional spaces they step, offering attention that feels validating and supportive.

What begins as encouragement can gradually deepen into dependence. What begins as mentorship can evolve into manipulation.

This is why predators often attempt to become emotionally central in a child's life. They may position themselves as the "safe" adult who listens without judgment. They may subtly undermine parental authority by implying that parents do not understand the child's feelings or struggles. They may introduce private communication under the guise of emotional support or guidance. Over time, the relationship may shift away from open oversight toward greater privacy.

They do not begin with overt harm. They begin with subtle boundary testing. Small exceptions. Private moments. Emotional influence. Gradual normalization of closeness that moves further from parental visibility. Each step is small enough to appear harmless, but together they create a path toward deeper access.

Discernment, therefore, requires observation beyond surface interaction. It is possible for someone to be spiritually articulate yet morally compromised. It is possible for someone to be community-respected yet privately manipulative. It is possible for someone to appear sacrificial yet operate strategically. Character is not measured only by public reputation. It is revealed through patterns of behavior, respect for boundaries, and willingness to remain transparent.

Parents must anchor their trust in verification, not impression.

This does not mean living in a state of paranoia. It means living in awareness. Healthy communities function with accountability. Healthy environments encourage visibility. Healthy relationships respect boundaries without resistance. When adults welcome transparency and oversight, they demonstrate integrity. When they resist accountability or appear uncomfortable with healthy boundaries, that resistance deserves attention.

Discernment grows when parents watch patterns rather than personalities. Study how someone behaves when oversight is present. Observe whether they respect parental involvement or attempt to bypass it. Notice whether their closeness with a child remains appropriate or gradually becomes exclusive. These patterns reveal far more about a person's intentions than charm or friendliness alone.

Study patterns.
Observe behavior.
Maintain boundaries.
Refuse blind confidence.

Because deception does not rely on ugliness, it often relies on attractiveness. It depends on appearing admirable, helpful, and trustworthy long enough that guardians stop watching carefully. And a predator's greatest protection is often not cleverness—it is a guardian who judges character by personality alone rather than by patterns of conduct.

THE THREE STAGES OF GROOMING

Grooming is not random behavior. It is a process. It is intentional. It unfolds in stages, often so gradually that it escapes immediate detection. Understanding these stages is critical because prevention begins with recognition. Many adults look for sudden danger, but grooming often advances through slow familiarity, strategic patience, and carefully managed trust. It is not chaos in the beginning. It is an order with a hidden agenda. It is not always alarming at first glance. It is often persuasive, relational, and disarming.

Predators do not rush recklessly—they advance strategically. Grooming is designed to gain access, establish trust, and create silence. It is patient. It is rehearsed. It is manipulative by design. Psalm 10:8–9 (KJV) paints a sobering image: "He sitteth in the lurking places of the villages… his eyes are privily set against the poor… He lieth in wait secretly as a lion in his den: he lieth in wait to catch the poor." The imagery is deliberate—waiting, watching, calculating. Grooming operates in that same hidden patience. It studies before it acts. It measures before it moves. It learns where resistance is weak, where vigilance is low, and where the child can be reached with the least interruption.

The First Stage is Targeting the Child. This stage involves selection. Predators observe before they approach. They identify children who appear vulnerable—those who are shy, overly compliant, emotionally isolated, eager for affirmation, uncertain of themselves, fearful of conflict, or hungry for attention. They often focus on children who seem to crave validation or who lack consistent parental engagement. They look for emotional openings. Targeting is rarely accidental. It is a deliberate reading of a child's emotional accessibility. They are not drawn to strength—they are drawn to perceived reachability.

A predator may frequent environments where children gather, such as schools, churches, sports leagues, neighborhood settings, online gaming spaces, or community programs. They may observe which child lingers alone, which one seems disconnected, which one responds quickly to praise, and which one appears emotionally eager for someone to notice them. They study patterns. They watch how the child responds to encouragement, how closely the child is supervised, and whether the child appears likely to keep things to themselves. What adults might see as casual observation may actually be a calculated assessment.

Once the child is identified, the predator begins building rapport. This may appear harmless at first—extra compliments, small gifts, special privileges, increased attention, repeated praise, unusual personal interest, or emotional attentiveness that feels flattering. The child may feel seen, valued, and understood. That emotional hook is intentional. The predator is not merely being kind.

They are testing whether affirmation can become attachment. And this matters because affirmation becomes attachment, and attachment becomes influence. The child may begin to feel special in a way that blinds them to the danger beneath the attention.

This is why parents must recognize that sudden or excessive adult attention toward their child should be evaluated carefully. Healthy adults respect boundaries and encourage parental involvement. They do not need emotional exclusivity with a child in order to show care. They do not push themselves into unusually personal significance. Predators, however, often attempt to create special access under the cover of kindness. They want the child to feel uniquely chosen because emotional specialness is one of the easiest bridges into deeper control.

The Second Stage is Grooming the Family. The strategy now expands beyond the child to the household. Predators understand that parental trust is the gatekeeper. Before they deepen access to the child, they cultivate credibility with the family. They may present themselves as exceptionally helpful, dependable, spiritually committed, emotionally mature, or unusually available. They volunteer eagerly. They offer support during busy times. They remember details. They show concern. They make themselves appear indispensable. This is calculated positioning.

By ingratiating themselves with the family, they lower suspicion. The more they are trusted, the less their proximity is questioned.

Parents may feel grateful for their assistance, unaware that trust is being engineered. This stage creates a false sense of security. The predator becomes the one who "has always been there," "is so good with children," "is such a blessing," or "would never do anything like that." The more normal their presence becomes, the less carefully it is examined. That is why this stage is so dangerous. It does not merely build access to the child. It protects the predator through the adults' confidence.

A predator may align themselves with respected roles—mentor, coach, clergy, teacher, volunteer, counselor, family friend—because authority reduces scrutiny. They understand that reputation can shield access. Adults are often more hesitant to question someone admired by others, respected in the community, or trusted in spiritual or educational settings. But a title does not cleanse intent. Public service does not prove private purity. Wise parents must evaluate patterns, not personality. Excessive eagerness for unsupervised time, subtle bypassing of parental presence, encouraging private communication, offering exclusive experiences, becoming too emotionally central, or repeatedly creating situations of privacy—these are warning indicators.

Parents must learn to watch for engineered closeness. Does this adult seem to need private time with my child? Do they keep trying to make themselves emotionally important? Do they insert themselves into moments that should remain under parental visibility? Do they build a bond that feels increasingly special, increasingly private, or increasingly difficult to interrupt? These questions matter because by the time the family feels fully comfortable, the predator may already have built more room than wisdom should have allowed.

The Third Stage is Secrecy and Control. This is the most dangerous stage because the strategy shifts from access to containment. Once access and trust are established, the predator gradually introduces secrecy. It may begin subtly—"This is just between us." It may escalate into manipulation—"You'll get in trouble too." It may include threats—"No one will believe you." It may involve guilt—"If you tell, you'll ruin everything." Fear becomes control. Shame becomes containment. Silence becomes protection for the predator.

At this point, the child is often confused and emotionally entangled. They may feel responsible for the relationship. They may feel guilty, disoriented, ashamed, frightened, or uncertain whether what is happening is even allowed to be named. The predator may normalize inappropriate behavior incrementally, testing boundaries step by step. What first felt odd becomes more familiar. What felt uncomfortable becomes harder to challenge because the child has already been drawn into emotional loyalty, secrecy, and fear of consequences. This gradual progression desensitizes the child. That is one of the darkest features of grooming: it attempts to train the child not only to endure the wrong, but to lose clarity about the wrong.

Grooming is deception disguised as care. It is manipulation disguised as mentorship. It is exploitation hidden beneath apparent kindness. It often borrows the language of help, guidance, support, patience, and affection. But its true aim is never the child's good. Its aim is access without interruption, closeness without accountability, and silence without exposure. That is why understanding these stages matters so deeply. Parents cannot afford to judge only by surface appearance. They must learn to see progression.

The Three Stages reveal one undeniable truth: grooming depends on patience and silence. It depends on adults not noticing the early pattern. It depends on families confusing helpfulness with holiness. It depends on the child becoming attached before the adults become alert. It depends on secrecy deepening before truth is welcomed. But awareness disrupts patience. Communication destroys silence. Boundaries block access.

If targeting behaviors are noticed, increase oversight. If family grooming patterns appear, limit access. If secrecy emerges, confront immediately and decisively. Do not wait for the process to become obvious to everyone. Early interruption matters. The earlier grooming is exposed, the less room it has to mature. The earlier the secrecy is broken, the less leverage fear has. The earlier access is regulated, the safer the child remains.

Grooming thrives in ignorance.
It collapses under exposure.

Recognize the stages.
Study the patterns.
Trust discernment.
Act early.

Because prevention always costs less than recovery, the parent who understands the process is far better prepared to stop the strategy before the child bears the full weight of its damage.

❖ SPIRITUAL WARNINGS ❖

Warnings to the Watchmen

There is a danger more threatening than visible evil—it is unseen deception. Not every wolf growls. Not every threat looks threatening. Not every danger announces itself before it strikes. Some dangers move softly, patiently, and respectfully until they are so woven into the atmosphere of life that people no longer recognize them as danger at all. That is what makes hidden evil so dangerous: it often travels beneath ordinary routines, familiar relationships, and socially acceptable appearances.

We are living in a time when access is easy, oversight is inconsistent, and discernment is often dulled by familiarity. The enemy of protection is not always hostility—it is assumption. Assumption that proximity equals safety. Assumption that reputation equals integrity. Assumption that nothing has happened simply because nothing has yet been discovered. But what is hidden is not harmless. Hidden danger does not become innocent because it has not yet been exposed. Silence does not make corruption absent. It only makes it harder to interrupt.

Spiritual negligence often begins with comfort. It begins with the subtle thought: "It could never happen here." It begins when vigilance relaxes because everything appears normal. Yet many tragedies were preceded by normal appearances. Many children have been wounded in environments adults considered safe, among people adults considered trustworthy, beneath structures adults considered sound. The issue is not whether danger announced itself clearly. The issue is whether the watchman remained awake when things still looked ordinary.

Let this truth shake you: predators do not rely on force alone. They rely on access. They rely on secrecy. They rely on hesitation. They rely on guardians who hesitate to confront what feels uncomfortable. When intuition stirs, and you silence it, when patterns emerge, and you dismiss them, when boundaries blur, and you excuse them, you create opportunity. This is not paranoia—it is responsibility.

The child does not yet know what you know. The child may not understand grooming, emotional manipulation, secrecy, flattery, or hidden intention. But you are called to see what they cannot. You are appointed to detect what they cannot articulate.

If discernment whispers, do not ignore it. If discomfort lingers, do not rationalize it. If something feels misaligned, do not delay action. Delay strengthens deception. Time often favors the hidden thing when adults keep postponing the moment of truthful confrontation. Heaven does not measure how polite you were in confrontation. Heaven measures how faithful you were in protection. There are moments when peace must be disturbed to preserve safety. There are relationships that must be questioned. There are doors that must be closed firmly and without apology. Better to endure temporary awkwardness than permanent regret.

The soul must be shaken because indifference has become common. Too many rely on hope instead of vigilance. Too many assume safety rather than establish it. Too many trust without verifying. But innocence is not preserved by optimism. It is preserved by watchfulness. You have been positioned at the gate of your household. You have the authority to regulate access. You have the responsibility to guard what cannot guard itself. Stand alert. Stand unwavering. Stand courageous. Because once damage is done, explanations cannot undo it. Remain vigilant. Remain prayerful. Remain unyielding. The watchman who sees early prevents what others only mourn later.

❖ A WARNING ABOUT DECEPTION ❖

Not every danger looks dangerous. Some threats smile. Some threats serve. Some threats pray publicly and manipulate privately. The most unsettling reality is this: evil does not always introduce itself through hostility. It often introduces itself through familiarity. It borrows the appearance of goodness, the language of care, the reputation of service, and the posture of trustworthiness. That is why deception is so dangerous—it does not arrive asking to be feared. It arrives asking to be welcomed.

We have been conditioned to fear what looks frightening. Yet many of the most devastating harms have come from what looked harmless—charm, respectability, and reputation. Through people who knew how to be admired. Through people who knew how to appear spiritually clean, emotionally safe, socially useful, and publicly trustworthy. This is why discernment must go deeper than personality. Smooth words can conceal violent intent. Warm gestures can disguise a calculated strategy. Public faith can mask private corruption. If you rely only on appearance, you will miss what operates beneath it.

Spiritual deception thrives where discernment is shallow. Many guardians have lowered their watch because someone appeared sincere. Many parents have ignored discomfort because someone was well-known. Many communities have protected the image more fiercely than they have protected innocence. But image does not equal integrity. Position does not equal purity. Public admiration does not prove private righteousness. History has repeatedly shown that a title does not prevent corruption. In some cases, it gives corruption easier access.

The soul must be shaken because assumption has replaced vigilance. We assume safety because of the position. We assume goodness because of charisma. We assume purity because of religious involvement. Yet these assumptions have often become the very shield behind which harm continued. You cannot afford to evaluate character by charm. You cannot afford to measure safety by likability. You cannot afford to dismiss warning signs because someone is respected.

If something feels inconsistent, investigate it. If behavior patterns feel excessive, question them. If access appears inappropriate, restrict it. Better to confront awkwardness than to carry regret. Spiritual negligence does not begin with hatred. It begins with comfort. It begins when you silence the inner alarm because you do not want to disrupt relationships. It begins when you choose reputation over responsibility. But responsibility is sacred. When God entrusts you with a child, He entrusts you with vigilance—not partial awareness, not seasonal oversight, but consistent, unwavering watchfulness.

You are not called to suspicion without cause. You are called to discernment without delay. If deception hides beneath the surface of personality, uncover it. If manipulation hides beneath kindness, confront it. If boundaries are tested subtly, reinforce them firmly. The cost of vigilance is temporary discomfort. The cost of misplaced trust can be irreversible. Stand firm. Remain alert. Refuse to be impressed by the presentation. Because the most dangerous deception is the one you never questioned. And once innocence is compromised, explanations will never be enough.

❖ A WARNING ABOUT SILENCE ❖

There is a silence that protects peace. And there is a silence that protects predators. You must know the difference. Silence is not automatically noble. Silence is not automatically wise. Silence can sometimes preserve dignity, but silence can also preserve danger. The question is not whether things are quiet. The question is what that quiet is protecting.

We live in a generation that avoids discomfort at all costs. Questions are softened. Confrontation is delayed. Concerns are dismissed to keep relationships intact. But when protection bows to politeness, vulnerability expands. Silence is not neutral. Every time a warning sign is ignored to avoid tension, a door opens. Every time intuition stirs and is suppressed, access widens. Every time a child's behavioral shift is minimized, opportunity grows.

The soul must be shaken because delay has consequences. Predators do not depend on speed—they depend on secrecy. They do not require chaos—they require quiet. They do not thrive in exposure—they thrive in hesitation. If something feels misaligned and you say nothing, if boundaries blur and you do nothing, if access increases and you question nothing, you are not preserving harmony. You are enabling risk. This is not about suspicion—it is about stewardship. God does not entrust children casually. He assigns guardians deliberately. That assignment demands courage. It demands vigilance. It demands the willingness to disturb comfort to preserve innocence.

You cannot protect what you refuse to confront. You cannot guard what you refuse to question. You cannot claim vigilance while practicing avoidance. Some of the deepest wounds carried by children were not caused only by predators—they were deepened by delayed action. By adults who sensed something but hesitated. By guardians who feared awkward conversations more than hidden harm. Let this settle heavily: temporary discomfort is a small price to pay for permanent protection.

Heaven does not measure how agreeable you were. Heaven measures how faithful you stood. If secrecy appears, expose it. If isolation increases, interrupt it. If manipulation surfaces, confront it immediately. Better to ask hard questions early than to regret silence later. You are positioned at the gate of your household. You have the authority to restrict access. You have the responsibility to guard what cannot guard itself. Do not let politeness weaken you. Do not let familiarity blind you. Do not let silence betray you. Stand alert. Stand courageous. Stand unyielding. Because once innocence is compromised, no explanation will ever feel sufficient.

❖ A WARNING ❖

To Those Who Think It Could Never Happen

There is a dangerous phrase that has silenced too many alarms. "It could never occur in this place." Those words have preceded more regret than rebellion ever has. They have softened vigilance, muted discernment, and lulled guardians into spiritual sleep. They sound harmless. They feel reassuring. But they are often the first crack in the wall of protection. They make adults trust the appearance of safety more than the practice of safety. They make people treat possibility as impossibility simply because they would rather not face what could be true.

Evil does not require permission to exist. It requires an opportunity to advance. And opportunity is born when confidence replaces caution. The greatest threat to a household is not always visible chaos—it is invisible complacency. It is the slow easing of boundaries. The gradual surrender of oversight. The subtle preference for comfort over confrontation. When something feels off and you dismiss it, when patterns repeat and you rationalize them, when your spirit is unsettled and you silence it, you are not protecting peace. You are postponing prevention.

Spiritual negligence does not begin with hatred. It begins with hesitation. It begins when you fear being wrong more than you fear being late. It begins when you protect relationships more fiercely than you protect innocence. Let this truth press heavily upon your conscience: you will answer for how you guarded what God entrusted to you. Not how polite you were. Not how respected you appeared. Not how well others thought of you. But how faithfully you watched.

Children do not have the awareness to identify every threat. They rely on your discernment. They depend on your courage. They trust that your watchfulness will not waver because something feels awkward. If something disturbs your spirit, investigate immediately. If something alters your child's demeanor, lean closer. If something tests boundaries, reinforce them without apology.

Better to confront early than to regret later. Better to ask difficult questions than to live with irreversible answers.

This is not paranoia—it is stewardship. The watchman who assumes safety often awakens to crisis. The guardian who delays action often carries the weight of preventable harm. Do not allow familiarity to blind you. Do not allow reputation to silence you. Do not allow comfort to weaken you. Stand firm. Stand alert. Stand accountable. Because once innocence is fractured, no explanation will restore it completely. Heaven is not impressed by good intentions. Heaven honors faithful vigilance. Remain watchful. Remain courageous. Remain unyielding. For the wall you guard today protects the future you may never see.

PART III

PROTECTION

BUILDING PROTECTION

What Parents Must Actively Do

CHAPTER EIGHT
HOW TO TALK TO CHILDREN ABOUT SAFETY
Creating Open Dialogue and Trust

✦

Age-Appropriate Conversations

Many parents hesitate to speak openly about safety because they fear introducing anxiety into their child's world. They worry that discussing danger will rob their children of innocence, make them fearful, or burden them with concerns they are too young to carry. Yet silence does not preserve innocence—it leaves it unprotected. A child who has never been taught how to recognize danger is not safer because they are unaware. They are simply more vulnerable to what they have not been prepared to identify.

Unspoken risks do not disappear.
They simply remain unaddressed.

A child who is uninformed is not fearless—they are exposed. Education does not create fear; it creates readiness. When approached properly, safety conversations do not frighten children—they empower them. Knowledge equips the mind, strengthens awareness, and prepares a child to recognize when something does not align with what they have been taught. A child who understands safety is not burdened with unnecessary fear; they are strengthened with necessary wisdom. There is a difference.

Psalm 34:11 (KJV) declares, "Come, ye children, hearken unto me: I will teach you the fear of the LORD." This verse reflects a posture of instruction rather than intimidation. Teaching involves guidance, clarity, patience, and wisdom. The fear of the Lord is not terror—it is awareness rooted in understanding. It is a taught sensitivity to what is true, right, holy, and dangerous. In the same way, teaching children about safety is not about instilling panic.

It is about cultivating discernment. It is about helping them recognize that some things are safe, some are unsafe, and wisdom helps us tell the difference.

Safety conversations must begin early and continue consistently. They are not one-time speeches to be delivered awkwardly and then avoided forever. They are ongoing layers of instruction that deepen as the child matures. Parents should introduce concepts gradually, using age-appropriate language and relatable scenarios.

Young children can learn simple principles such as not speaking to strangers without permission, looking both ways before crossing the street, staying close to trusted adults in public, and identifying safe adults in emergencies. These early lessons establish the habit of awareness. They teach the child that paying attention is part of living wisely.

As children mature, conversations should expand. Parents must address emotional boundaries, peer pressure, manipulation, digital safety, private body boundaries, and the difference between kindness and secrecy. Each stage of development requires a deeper understanding. A conversation appropriate for a five-year-old will not be sufficient for a teenager navigating social media, messaging platforms, private online communication, dating pressure, emotional manipulation, and complex social dynamics. Children grow, and the dangers around them grow more sophisticated as well. Therefore, parental instruction must grow in clarity, depth, and specificity.

Clarity reduces confusion.

Many children remain vulnerable not because they are unwilling to listen, but because the adults around them speak too vaguely. General warnings like "Be careful" or "Stay safe" may sound responsible, but they often leave the child without a practical understanding. Children need more than warnings; they need language. They need to know which situations require caution, which words are red flags, which requests should be refused, and which discomfort should be reported immediately. If the child does not know how danger may appear, they may not recognize it when it comes dressed in familiarity, kindness, or emotional pressure.

This is why age-appropriate conversation does not mean watered-down truth. It means truthful instruction suited to the child's capacity. A young child may need simple and direct language: "Your body belongs to you." "Private parts are private."

If someone touches you in a way that makes you uncomfortable, tell me right away. If anyone says, "Don't tell," that is a reason to tell. An older child or teenager may need more developed language about manipulation, pressure, digital communication, emotional grooming, shame, and secrecy. The core truth remains the same, but the vocabulary matures with the child.

Parents must also understand that children learn best when safety is discussed calmly, clearly, and repeatedly—not only in a crisis. If safety conversations happen only after something alarming appears, the child may associate the topic with panic rather than wisdom. But when the topic is part of normal family life, the child learns that safety is not a strange subject. It is part of how the household lives. They begin to understand that asking questions is allowed, discomfort can be named, and truth does not need to hide.

Tone matters greatly in these conversations. If a parent speaks with alarm, confusion, embarrassment, or visible discomfort, the child may absorb that discomfort and conclude that some truths are too difficult to bring forward. But when a parent speaks with steadiness, clarity, and confidence, the child learns that these topics can be handled honestly and safely. The goal is not to frighten the child into suspicion of everyone. The goal is to equip the child with enough awareness that, when something feels wrong, they know they are allowed to recognize it and speak up.

Children should also be taught that unsafe situations do not always look obviously dangerous. Some dangers are loud. Others are subtle. Some appear through strangers. Others appear through people who seem friendly, familiar, or respected. Age-appropriate conversation must therefore prepare children for both obvious and hidden forms of concern. A child should know that discomfort matters even when the person involved is kind, admired, or known to the family.

This kind of teaching is essential because many children assume that if others trust an adult, that adult must always be safe. Parents must gently correct that assumption without teaching paranoia. They must teach discernment.

Safety instruction should also include the right to speak. A child must know not only what danger may look like, but what they are supposed to do when they encounter it. They need repeated assurance that if something happens, if something feels strange, if someone says something confusing, if someone shows them something inappropriate, if someone asks them to keep something secret, they can come to their parent without fear. It is not enough to teach children how to identify danger if they have not also been taught how to bring danger into the light.

As children grow older, parents must prepare them for the emotional complexity of unsafe situations. Teenagers, especially, may encounter situations that do not seem like obvious threats at first. Attention may feel flattering. Pressure may be disguised as affection. Secrecy may be framed as loyalty. Online communication may feel exciting before it becomes manipulative. Peer influence may make wrong things seem normal. A parent's role is to prepare the child in advance so that, when these things arise, the child does not have to interpret them without guidance. They already have a framework of truth.

This is why repeated conversation matters so deeply. A child will not remember every lesson perfectly from one talk. They need repetition. They need examples. They need room to ask questions. They need to hear the same truth expressed in different ways over time until it becomes part of how they think. Repetition builds reflex. Reflex matters in moments of pressure. A child who has repeatedly heard "You can tell me anything" is more likely to reach for the truth when fear tries to silence them. A child who has repeatedly heard "No one should ask you to keep secrets about touching" is more likely to recognize that such a request is wrong. A child who has repeatedly heard "Your safety matters more than anyone's feelings" is more likely to resist emotional manipulation.

Parents must not wait until the child seems "old enough" to begin. Safety instruction starts small and grows steadily. The child who learns early that wisdom belongs in everyday life is far better prepared when more serious situations arise later. In this way, age-appropriate conversation becomes not merely information, but formation. It shapes how the child interprets the world.

It teaches them that awareness is part of love, that safety is worth discussing, and that wisdom is not fear—it is protection.

When children clearly understand safety principles, they are better prepared to recognize situations that require caution. The goal is not to burden them with fear, but to equip them with wisdom that strengthens their ability to navigate the world safely. A child who has been taught with patience, clarity, and consistency is far less likely to be caught entirely off guard by manipulation, secrecy, or inappropriate pressure.

So begin early.
Speak clearly.
Teach patiently.
Repeat consistently.
Make room for questions.
Welcome honesty.
Let wisdom grow with the child.

Because age-appropriate conversations do more than inform, they help build a child who can recognize what is safe, name what is not, and seek help before confusion becomes harm.

TEACHING BODY BOUNDARIES

One of the most important aspects of safety education is teaching children clear and healthy body boundaries. This is not a minor conversation. It is foundational. A child who does not understand bodily boundaries may struggle to recognize when those boundaries are being crossed. But a child who has been taught clearly, calmly, and consistently is far better prepared to identify inappropriate behavior, resist unsafe pressure, and speak when something feels wrong. Body-boundary instruction is not shame-based teaching. It is protective training.

Parents should use correct anatomical terms for body parts. This removes ambiguity and normalizes healthy conversation about the body. When children are familiar with proper language, they are better able to communicate concerns if something inappropriate occurs. Vague language can create confusion. Confusion weakens clarity. But clear language gives the child precision. It also removes the false sense that some parts of the body are too unspeakable to name. If a child feels they cannot speak plainly, they may remain silent when plain speech is most needed.

Children should be taught that certain areas of the body are private and should not be touched by others except in clearly defined circumstances, such as parental care, age-appropriate hygiene assistance, or medical examinations conducted properly and with parental knowledge. They need simple, repeated instruction that helps them understand not only what is private, but why privacy matters. Their bodies are not public property. It is not open to someone else's curiosity, authority, or desire. A child should know that privacy around the body is not secrecy—it is dignity.

Make this truth unmistakable: no one should ever ask you to keep a secret about touching. If anyone says, "Don't tell your parents," that is a warning sign. Children must hear this enough times for it to become fixed in their thinking. A child may forget many details under pressure, but repeated truth can stay with them when confusion begins.

They should know that a request for secrecy around touch is never normal, never acceptable, and never something they are required to protect.

Children must also understand that they have the right to say no when something makes them uncomfortable. Respecting their voice strengthens their confidence in their own instincts. When children believe their feelings matter, they are more likely to speak when something does not feel right. This is crucial because many children are taught to obey adults quickly but are not equally taught how to respond when an adult behaves inappropriately. They need language that allows them to resist unsafe behavior without feeling disobedient. They should know that saying no to inappropriate touch is not rebellion. It is wisdom.

Parents must reinforce that affection is never an obligation. Children should not feel pressured to hug, sit with, kiss, or engage physically with anyone who makes them uncomfortable. Too many children are taught to override their discomfort to appear polite, respectful, or agreeable. But forced affection can confuse a child's internal alarm. If adults repeatedly require physical closeness from people the child feels uneasy around, the child may begin to believe that discomfort must be ignored for the sake of manners. That lesson is dangerous. Courtesy should never outrank safety.

When adults honor a child's boundaries, the child learns that their body is worthy of respect. That lesson reaches deeper than a single interaction. It teaches the child that their "no" has meaning. It teaches them that unease should not be mocked. It teaches them that their instincts are not foolish. If a child says they do not want to sit on someone's lap, hug a relative, be tickled, or engage in physical play, wise adults do not shame that response. They listen to it. They respect it. Even when the situation appears harmless, honoring appropriate bodily boundaries helps the child learn that they are not required to surrender personal comfort just because another person expects access.

Teaching body boundaries must also include the difference between safe touch, unwanted touch, and confusing touch. Safe touch helps, protects, or cares appropriately. Unwanted touch is uncomfortable and should be discussed.

The child may not immediately understand

confusing touch, but it still leaves them uneasy, ashamed, or unsettled. Children need to know that if touch confuses them, they can still tell. They do not need to have perfect language or certainty before bringing it to a trusted adult. Confusion itself is enough reason to speak.

Parents should not wait for a crisis to begin these conversations. Body-boundary teaching works best when it becomes part of the child's normal understanding of life. It should be calm, clear, age-appropriate, and repeated over time. A child should hear not only the rules but also the reassurance: "Your body matters." "Your voice matters—your safety matters." "You can always tell me the truth." Repetition builds confidence. Confidence helps break fear. And fear, when left unchallenged, is often what keeps children silent.

Another important part of teaching body boundaries is helping children understand that adults do not have unlimited rights over them simply because they are older. Children are often taught to respect adults, and that is right. But respect must never be confused with submission to inappropriate behavior. A child can respect an adult and still report that adult's wrongdoing. A child can obey authority in general and still resist unsafe touch in particular. They need to know that no title—family member, teacher, pastor, coach, babysitter, leader, or friend—removes their right to safety.

Parents must also examine whether their own household models a healthy respect for bodily boundaries. Do adults listen when a child pulls away? Do they avoid mocking discomfort? Do they stop physical play when the child says stop? Do they refrain from forcing affection for the sake of appearances? Children learn from what they live. If boundaries are honored in the home, they are more likely to expect boundaries elsewhere. If boundaries are routinely ignored, they may become confused about what is normal.

Healthy boundaries build safety. But more than that, healthy boundaries help build identity. They teach the child that they are not powerless. They teach them that dignity is theirs. They teach them that they are not responsible for managing adult disappointment when protecting their own safety. These are not small lessons. They shape how a child understands consent, trust, personal value, and the right to speak.

So teach it clearly.
Repeat it gently.
Model it consistently.
Honor their voice.
Protect their dignity.
Refuse to let politeness train them to ignore discomfort.

A child who understands body boundaries is better prepared to recognize violations, resist manipulation, and seek help before silence becomes suffering.

TEACHING VERBAL DISCLOSURE

Safety education must also teach children how to communicate when something feels wrong. It is not enough for a child to recognize discomfort if they do not know how to put that discomfort into words, how to bring it to a trusted adult, or how to believe that speaking will lead to protection rather than punishment. Many children remain silent not because they have nothing to say, but because fear has already begun to shape their responses. Some fear getting in trouble. Some fear not being believed. Some fear making adults angry. Some fear they somehow caused what happened. Others feel confused and do not know whether what they experienced is serious enough to mention. This is why parents must teach verbal disclosure intentionally, clearly, and repeatedly.

Parents must dismantle that fear early. A child should not have to guess whether honesty is safe in the home. They should know it. They should hear it often enough that it settles deeply into their thinking: You will never be in trouble for telling the truth. That assurance is not a small statement. It is a shield. It removes one of the greatest weapons predators use against children—the fear that speaking up will cost them more than staying silent. Even if a child made a mistake, went somewhere they were told not to go, answered a message they should not have, or kept something hidden for too long, telling the truth must still be met with protection rather than condemnation. Correction may come later, where needed, but first, there must be safety. The child must learn that truth opens the door to help, not humiliation.

Many children stay silent because they assume adults will focus first on their disobedience rather than on their danger. They may think, If I say this, I'll get punished. Or, If I admit what happened, they'll ask why I didn't stop it. Or, If I tell them I answered that message, went in that room, or kept that secret, they'll be angry with me. These fears are powerful. That is why wise parents must deliberately teach the opposite. The child must know that when something unsafe has happened, the truth will be received with seriousness, care, and protection.

If that culture is built early, secrecy loses some of its power before it ever has a chance to take root.

Teaching verbal disclosure also means giving children actual language. Many children feel distress but do not know how to begin. They may need simple phrases they can remember and use, such as That made me uncomfortable. I need to tell you something. Someone told me not to tell. I didn't know what to do. Something happened, and I'm scared. These kinds of statements give the child a doorway into truth. Parents should not assume that children naturally know how to report danger. Speech under pressure often becomes difficult. Fear can make language collapse. So if children are taught what they can say, they are better equipped to speak when the moment comes.

Role-playing scenarios can help children practice responses without fear. This is not about creating panic. It is about creating readiness. Parents may ask: What would you do if someone asked you to keep a secret from me? How would you feel if someone made you uncomfortable? Who could you tell if something didn't feel right? What would you do if someone showed you something on a phone or screen that made you feel uneasy? What would you say if someone tried to touch you in a way that was not right? These exercises create mental rehearsal. When a situation arises in real life, the child is not starting from nothing. They already have language, pattern, and permission.

This kind of rehearsal matters because fear often shuts down clear thinking in the moment. A child who has never imagined what to say may freeze. But a child who has practiced simple responses is more likely to remember that they can speak, leave, tell, refuse, or ask for help. Rehearsal builds confidence. Confidence does not guarantee ease, but it weakens helplessness. The child begins to understand that they are not expected to carry confusion silently. They are allowed to name what feels wrong.

Colossians 4:6 (KJV) reminds us, "Let your speech be always with grace, seasoned with salt." Conversations about safety must be firm yet compassionate. Children must feel safe speaking honestly without fear of anger, ridicule, or judgment. The tone of the parent matters. If safety conversations are filled with panic, harshness, or embarrassment, children may conclude that these topics are too volatile to bring up easily. But if parents speak with clarity, steadiness, and grace, children learn that truth can be handled safely. They begin to understand that even hard things can be brought into the light.

Parents must also teach children that they do not need perfect certainty before they speak. A child may think, Maybe I misunderstood. Maybe it was nothing. Maybe I'm making too much of it. Maybe they didn't mean it that way. Predators often rely on that uncertainty. But children should be taught that if something feels confusing, uncomfortable, pressuring, shameful, or strange, that alone is enough reason to tell. They do not need to resolve the situation before reporting it. They only need to speak. The adult's responsibility is to help examine, discern, and protect.

Another critical part of teaching verbal disclosure is helping children understand that telling is not betrayal when safety is at stake. Many children are manipulated into thinking that speaking up is disloyal, mean, or destructive. They may fear that they are "getting someone in trouble." Parents must correct this lie firmly. Telling the truth about unsafe behavior is not cruelty. It is courage. Protecting oneself is not selfishness. It is wisdom. A child must know that the wrongdoer is responsible for the wrongdoing, not the child who speaks it into the light.

Parents should also make sure children know multiple safe people they can tell if needed. While parents should be the primary refuge whenever possible, children should also know other trustworthy adults approved by the family—perhaps a grandparent, pastor, teacher, counselor, or another safe authority figure—so that if fear or confusion arises in a different setting, they still know there is a path to help. Verbal disclosure becomes stronger when the child understands not only that they can speak, but also to whom they can speak.

When children understand boundaries, they gain confidence. When they feel heard, they speak sooner. When they trust their parents' response, secrecy weakens. Communication becomes preventative protection. It interrupts isolation. It exposes manipulation. It shortens the distance between discomfort and help.

And that distance matters greatly, because the longer a child remains silent, the more time fear has to grow, and deception has to settle.

Parents must therefore do more than say, “You can tell me anything.” They must prove it by how they respond to smaller truths. Do they listen without mocking? Do they stay calm when a child admits fear or confusion? Do they take discomfort seriously? Do they thank the child for telling the truth? These everyday responses build the foundation for larger disclosures later. A child often learns whether it is safe to speak about major things by how the adults respond to smaller ones.

So teach disclosure clearly.
Practice it often.
Make honesty safe.

Give children words.
Give them permission.
Give them confidence that truth will be met with protection.

Because when a child knows how to speak, knows they will be heard, and knows that telling the truth will not make them the problem, one of the strongest chains of silence begins to break.

HOW PREDATORS MANIPULATE PARENTS

Predators do not only groom children—they groom parents. Before gaining deeper access to a child, they often work to disarm the guardian. They understand a critical reality: if they can secure the parent's trust, soften the parent's caution, or make the parent feel emotionally comfortable, the path to the child becomes easier. Many adults imagine manipulation begins with the child alone, but often the first target is the one standing at the gate. The predator knows that if the watchman can be relaxed, impressed, distracted, indebted, or emotionally persuaded, the wall becomes weaker without ever appearing broken.

Proverbs 26:24 (KJV) warns, "He that hateth dissembleth with his lips, and layeth up deceit within him." This is the language of hidden motive. It speaks of a person whose mouth presents one thing while the heart conceals another. That is what makes parental manipulation so dangerous. The predator does not come announcing appetite. He comes offering assistance. He does not begin by appearing harmful. He begins by appearing useful. His words may sound supportive, respectful, spiritual, and sincere, while inwardly he is calculating how to gain trust, reduce scrutiny, and position himself closer to what he wants.

Predators may present themselves as helpful, dependable, emotionally mature, or spiritually articulate. They volunteer during busy seasons. They offer assistance. They present themselves as allies within the family's life. They may notice when the household is under stress, when the parent is tired, when schedules are heavy, or when support feels welcome. And then they step in—not necessarily because they are moved by selfless love, but because usefulness can become a bridge to access. A parent who feels helped may begin to feel grateful. A grateful parent may relax. And a relaxed parent may stop examining what should still be watched carefully.

But generosity can be a strategy.

This is one of the most uncomfortable truths for many parents to accept. We want to believe that kindness always proves goodness, that support always comes from pure motives, and that helpful people should be rewarded with trust. Yet predatory manipulation often thrives on exactly that assumption. The person may show up consistently, offer practical help, remember details, speak warmly, and appear deeply invested in the family's well-being. But apparent service can sometimes be the outer garment of hidden intention. Help is not always given because the helper is safe. Sometimes it is given because the helper understands that gratitude lowers defenses.

Some manipulate through flattery, praising a parent's character, affirming their parenting style, and speaking as though they deeply admire the family's values. They may complement how well the children are being reared, how strong the home feels, and how admirable the parents' dedication appears. This kind of flattery is not always innocent. It can be designed to create emotional ease. A parent who feels seen, affirmed, or respected may become less guarded around the one speaking those affirmations. Flattery makes people feel safe too quickly. It creates warmth without verification. And warmth, if left unguarded, can become the atmosphere in which caution quietly fades.

Others appeal to sympathy. They may present themselves as lonely, overworked, misunderstood, emotionally burdened, or in need of connection. They may subtly invite the parent to see them as someone deserving special trust because of what they have "been through." This can create an emotional pressure to be extra kind, extra flexible, or extra accommodating. But pity is a poor foundation for child safety. A parent must never allow compassion for an adult's circumstances to become an open door to the child. The child is not therapy. The child is not a repayment. The child is not comfort for a wounded adult. Yet access to a child is never a repayment for assistance. Access is not a courtesy. It is a privilege.

That truth must remain firm. No one earns unsupervised closeness to a child simply because they have helped the family, shown generosity, offered transportation, provided support, or spoken kindly.

Practical assistance may be appreciated, but it does not suspend the need for boundaries. Emotional warmth does not remove the need for verification. A family must never start thinking, They've done so much for us, as though that means access should now be granted without structure. A child's safety is not a gift to be exchanged for adult helpfulness.

Predators may also manipulate parents by making boundaries feel rude. They may create subtle tension around accountability. They may act disappointed when certain limits are upheld. They may imply that a cautious parent is overreacting, mistrustful, extreme, or unfair. They may not argue directly with the parent, but their demeanor may pressure the parent emotionally to relax. This is one reason boundaries matter so much: healthy adults respect them. Unsafe adults often try to make them feel awkward.

Healthy adults welcome accountability. If someone resists transparency or becomes uncomfortable with reasonable boundaries, that response reveals more than words ever could. A safe adult does not need secrecy to function. A safe adult does not need exclusive emotional space with a child in order to be supportive. A safe adult does not resent parental visibility. In fact, transparency protects everyone involved.

So when an adult begins pushing back against clear oversight, becomes irritated by ordinary questions, or acts as though accountability is an insult, that reaction must be taken seriously.

Parents must remain courteous but cautious, kind yet unwavering in their responsibility to protect their child. Courtesy without caution can become vulnerability. Kindness without firmness can become exposure. It is possible to be gracious without surrendering discernment. It is possible to be respectful without handing over unnecessary access. It is possible to appreciate someone's help while still keeping clear walls around the child.

Parents must also understand that manipulation of the parent is often aimed at creating permission before creating privacy. If the predator can become a trusted presence in the family's life, the next requests feel smaller. A ride does not seem like much. A private conversation feels understandable. A little extra time seems harmless.

A special outing sounds generous. A direct message feels innocent. But these small permissions, once multiplied, can create a pattern of access that would have looked deeply concerning had it been proposed all at once.

This is how the process works: not through one outrageous request, but through many tolerated ones.

The wise parent, therefore, watches not only what a person says, but what kind of access their behavior is quietly building. Is this person always trying to become more central? Do they seem unusually eager to help, specifically when it brings them near the child? Do they keep offering things that create private or special time? Do they seem to enjoy the parents' trust more than they respect the parents' boundaries? These are not cynical questions. They are stewardship questions. They help reveal whether the person's involvement is truly healthy or whether it is gradually pressing toward something more dangerous.

Parents must anchor their judgment in patterns, not feelings alone. A person may feel pleasant and still be unsafe. A person may sound spiritual and still be deceptive. A person may appear supportive and still be strategic. That is why a guardian cannot afford to be governed merely by gratitude, sympathy, admiration, or surface comfort. The child must remain more important than the adult's impression. The parents' first responsibility is not to preserve another adult's feelings. It is to guard what God has entrusted into their care.

So be kind, but do not be naïve.
Be gracious, but do not be easily disarmed.
Be appreciative, but do not confuse false help with holiness.
Be warm, but stay watchful.

Because predators often know that the fastest way to a child is through the trust of the adults who should have been guarding the door.

THE SPIRITUAL NATURE OF PROTECTION

Protection is not only practical—it is spiritual. It is not limited to rules, routines, supervision, locked doors, restricted access, or guarded devices, though all of those matter deeply. Protection also involves the unseen atmosphere in which a child is being shaped. It involves the condition of the home, the discernment of the parent, the prayer covering over the family, and the spiritual alertness that recognizes when something is not right even before all the evidence is visible. A child can be physically near safety and still be spiritually vulnerable if the environment around them is neglected in the unseen realm.

Ephesians 6:12 (KJV) declares, "For we wrestle not against flesh and blood, but against principalities, against powers… against spiritual wickedness in high places." This passage reveals that the battle for innocence has both visible and invisible dimensions. Predatory behavior does not merely damage physically—it often distorts trust, identity, emotional security, self-worth, and even a child's perception of authority, love, and safety. The harm may begin in the natural, but its effects often reach deeply into the spiritual and emotional life. That is why parents must not view protection only as a matter of external management. The struggle is deeper than behavior alone. It touches atmosphere, influence, discernment, and spiritual resistance.

Parents must cultivate both awareness and spiritual sensitivity. Awareness helps them recognize patterns, behaviors, environments, and relationships that require caution. Spiritual sensitivity helps them discern what may be misaligned even before everything can be explained clearly in natural terms. There are times when the spirit of a watchful parent senses disturbance before the mind has fully organized the facts. That stirring should not be treated lightly. It should be carried into prayer, examined with wisdom, and followed with sober attentiveness. Spiritual sensitivity is not superstition. It is the fruit of a life that stays close enough to God to recognize when peace has been disturbed by something that should not be ignored.

Prayer strengthens protection. It does not replace responsibility, but it deepens it. A praying parent is not excused from action; they are strengthened for it. Prayer quiets distraction, sharpens discernment, and keeps the heart of the guardian from becoming dull, careless, or spiritually sleepy. When parents pray over their children by name, over their minds, their friendships, their influences, their environments, and their futures, they are not engaging in empty religious routine. They are laying spiritual covering over lives that are too precious to be left unguarded. Prayer also helps parents resist panic. It steadies the inner life so they can respond with wisdom rather than chaos when something troubling appears.

Scripture sharpens discernment. The Word of God does more than comfort; it clarifies. It teaches the difference between what is holy and what is unclean, what is wise and what is deceptive, what is nurturing and what is manipulative. Parents who live in Scripture are often harder to deceive because their categories are being formed by truth rather than by culture, appearances, or emotional convenience. The Word teaches them not to confuse charm with character, familiarity with safety, or religious language with righteousness. A home where Scripture is spoken, discussed, and lived out develops a moral clarity that helps both parents and children recognize when something does not belong.

Spiritual attentiveness exposes subtle danger. Not every threat enters loudly. Some things arrive quietly—through repeated exposure, through gradual emotional shifts, through tolerated compromise, through subtle secrecy, through relationships that seem harmless on the surface, through atmospheres that feel increasingly unsettled, though no one has yet named the cause. A spiritually attentive parent does not live in paranoia, but they do remain alert. They are not easily lulled by appearances. They understand that what is hidden may still be active, and that what is spiritually corrosive may first appear emotionally or relationally attractive before its damage is fully seen.

A home grounded in truth and prayer becomes an environment where manipulation struggles to take root. That does not mean trouble will never attempt to enter. It means the ground is less welcoming to deception. In a spiritually guarded home, prayer is not occasional decoration, but regular practice.

Truth is not distant theology but daily language. Repentance is not humiliating but normal. Forgiveness is not weakness but strength. Boundaries are not treated as oppression but as wisdom. In that kind of atmosphere, children are more likely to recognize when something feels wrong, more likely to believe that honesty is safe, and more likely to bring hidden discomfort into the light before it grows.

When children feel spiritually and emotionally secure, secrecy loses some of its influence. That security matters greatly. A child who knows they are covered in prayer, loved with steadiness, and welcomed in truth is less easily controlled by fear, flattery, secrecy, or emotional manipulation. They may still face pressure, but the inner ground beneath them is stronger. They have reference points. They know what peace feels like. They know what safety sounds like. They know what honest love looks like. That inner clarity becomes part of their protection.

Parents must therefore understand that spiritual protection is not abstract. It is built through daily choices. It is built when prayer is practiced instead of postponed. It is built when the Word is opened rather than neglected. It is built when the home's atmosphere is guarded from bitterness, chaos, sarcasm, impurity, and spiritual drift. It is built when parents watch their own hearts, their own habits, and their own sensitivity to the Spirit of God. A dull parent will struggle to guard a child sharply. A distracted parent will often miss what a prayerful parent is quicker to notice.

The spiritual nature of protection also means that parents must refuse the false separation between practical wisdom and spiritual vigilance. These are not opposing realities. They belong together. A parent can pray fiercely and still set firm rules. A parent can trust God deeply and still verify access carefully. A parent can speak Scripture boldly and still monitor devices, restrict unsupervised contact, ask hard questions, and confront secrecy immediately. Spiritual protection is not passivity dressed in religious language. It is faith working through obedience, discernment, and steadfast guardianship.

So let prayer remain active.
Let Scripture remain near.

Let the home remain guarded.
Let the spirit of the watchman remain awake.
Let truth govern what enters, what lingers, and what is allowed to shape the child.

Because the battle for innocence is not only around the child.
It is also over the atmosphere surrounding the child.
And a home rooted in truth, prayer, and spiritual attentiveness becomes far less hospitable to the subtle work of darkness.

SOMETHING TO ALWAYS REMEMBER

You cannot protect your home from what you refuse to understand. That truth is simple, but it is weighty. Many dangers do not gain strength because they are unstoppable; they gain strength because they are misunderstood, underestimated, or avoided. Ignorance does not create safety—it creates exposure. What a parent refuses to learn, the child may one day be forced to endure. What the guardian calls "too uncomfortable to study" may become the very thing that enters through an unguarded door. Refusing to understand predatory tactics does not preserve peace. It only weakens preparation.

Understanding predatory behavior does not produce fear; it produces readiness. Awareness strengthens discernment. Knowledge exposes manipulation before it gains momentum. When parents understand how grooming works, how secrecy develops, how access is cultivated, how predators study weakness, and how emotional control is built gradually, they become far more difficult to deceive. They are less likely to be impressed by the wrong things, less likely to dismiss subtle warning signs, and less likely to confuse charm with integrity. Knowledge does not make a parent suspicious of everyone. It makes them wiser about what deserves attention.

Safety is not accidental. It is not the product of luck, wishful thinking, or blind trust. It is constructed through education. It is reinforced through boundaries. It is strengthened through spiritual alertness. It is maintained through communication, observation, correction, and courage. Safe homes do not happen merely because parents love their children. They happen because that love takes form in discipline, attentiveness, instruction, and watchfulness. Affection without awareness is incomplete. Concern without preparation is weak. Love must learn how to guard.

Parents must also remember that danger often grows where adults keep hoping things will remain harmless on their own. But what is left unexamined can become normalized. What is normalized can become tolerated. What is tolerated can become entrenched.

This is why education matters so deeply. An informed parent knows what questions to ask, what patterns to watch, what access to regulate, what signals to take seriously, and when to act without delay. Preparedness does not eliminate every threat, but it greatly reduces preventable harm.

Prepared parents reduce preventable harm. That statement should remain fixed in the mind. Many tragedies cannot be undone, but some can be interrupted, exposed, or prevented when adults are sober enough to recognize what is happening early. Preparation changes response time. Preparation sharpens the eye of the watchman. Preparation keeps a parent from being emotionally paralyzed when subtle danger first appears. It builds the kind of steadiness that knows how to respond with both wisdom and conviction.

So never despise the work of learning.
Never call awareness unnecessary.
Never treat discernment as optional.
Never assume that because danger is unpleasant to study, it is less necessary to understand.

Learn what protects.
Teach what prepares.
Guard what God has entrusted.
Stay awake in spirit, clear in mind, and steady in courage.

Because the home is safest not when parents know everything, but when they refuse to remain ignorant about the things that threaten what they love.

❖ SPIRITUAL WARNING ❖

A Warning Against Delay

There is a moment when hesitation becomes dangerous. There is a point at which waiting is no longer wisdom, but exposure. Many people imagine delay as harmless because it feels calm, measured, and reasonable. But in matters of protection, delay can become the silent ally of harm. What should have been examined early is often allowed to deepen because someone wanted more certainty, less discomfort, or a more convenient time to act. Yet danger does not always wait for the adult to feel emotionally ready. Harm often grows while someone is still deciding whether the signal was serious enough to confront.

Delay is dangerous because it gives hidden things time. Time for manipulation to deepen. Time for secrecy to solidify. Time for fear to settle into the child's heart. Time for the predator to strengthen control. Time for the child to begin to believe that no one is coming, no one notices, and no one will intervene. What adults call waiting to be sure can sometimes become the very space in which damage multiplies. The wound is rarely helped by delay. It is often deepened by it.

When something unsettles your spirit, do not silence it. A discerning disturbance should not be smothered under politeness, rationalization, or emotional convenience. When boundaries blur, reinforce them immediately. When secrecy appears, confront it directly. When a child changes in a way that does not sit right in your spirit, do not explain it away simply because you would rather not face what might be true. Some of the deepest regrets in guardianship are not rooted in what adults never saw, but in what they sensed and postponed.

Better to be wrong in caution than late in response. Better to ask the question and discover there was no threat than to remain silent and realize too late that your silence gave danger room to grow. Better to disturb comfort than repair trauma. Better to tighten access, increase oversight, and reexamine a situation than to carry the lifelong burden of knowing you hesitated while a child suffered under your watch. Temporary awkwardness is a far lighter burden than permanent regret.

Heaven does not reward hesitation. Heaven honors vigilance. God does not commend the watchman for how comfortable he kept the atmosphere while danger approached. He honors the one who stayed awake, who moved when warning came, who responded before the breach became obvious to everyone else. A faithful guardian does not wait for the situation to become undeniable before acting responsibly. They understand that prevention is often strongest when it moves early, while the pattern is still forming and before harm has fully matured.

Delay often disguises itself in noble language. "I don't want to overreact." "I need more proof." "I don't want to accuse anyone unfairly." "Maybe it's nothing." These thoughts may sound measured, but when used to silence warranted concern, they become dangerous. They can give an adult permission to postpone what should be addressed now. And while the adult is trying not to seem extreme, the child may be carrying confusion, fear, shame, or hidden danger alone. This is why spiritual and parental responsibility must rise above the desire to appear calm. Protection is not preserved by image. It is preserved by action.

Stand firm. Act quickly. Remain alert. Do not let the fear of discomfort delay what discernment is urging you to examine. Do not let another person's reputation outweigh a child's safety. Do not let routine make you slow. Do not let familiarity make you passive. The moment something shifts, wisdom should move closer, not further away. The moment secrecy appears, light should follow. The moment the spirit is troubled, prayer should lead to sober action.

Because prevention delayed is often prevention denied. What might have been interrupted early can become far harder to undo later. And once innocence has been wounded, no explanation about why you waited will ever feel weightier than the child's pain.

CHAPTER NINE

CREATING A NURTURING EMOTIONAL ENVIRONMENT

Breaking the Power of Secrecy

The Foundation of Emotional Safety

Physical safety alone is not enough. A child can live behind locked doors, sleep in a secure home, attend the right schools, and still feel emotionally unprotected. True protection includes the heart. It includes the unseen places where fear settles, where confusion forms, where shame hides, and where silence can quietly take root. A child may be physically near safety yet inwardly carry instability if the emotional climate of the home does not give them room to be honest, heard, and handled with care. This is why wise protection must go deeper than structure. It must reach into the child's emotional life.

Children require an emotionally secure space just as deeply as they require physical shelter. They must know that within the walls of their home, their voices are safe. They must be confident that their fears will not be mocked, their mistakes will not be weaponized, and their vulnerability will not be dismissed. A child should not have to measure whether honesty is emotionally dangerous before speaking. They should not have to wonder whether tears will be shamed, whether confusion will be ridiculed, or whether pain will be minimized because it is inconvenient for the adults in the room. Emotional safety means the child can bring their inner world into the light without fearing that the light itself will injure them.

Psalm 147:3 (KJV) reminds us, "He healeth the broken in heart, and bindeth up their wounds." God responds to emotional injury with compassion and restoration. He does not mock the brokenhearted. He does not shame the wounded for bleeding. He does not punish pain for appearing. Parents are called to mirror that divine pattern. When a child's heart is bruised—whether by disappointment, fear, embarrassment, confusion, rejection, betrayal, or trauma—the response must be healing rather than harshness. Correction has its place, but a bruised heart cannot be helped by unnecessary cruelty. What is wounded needs wise care, not careless force.

An emotionally secure home does not minimize feelings. It listens. It does not shame vulnerability. It protects it. It does not punish confession. It welcomes it. That does not mean every emotion governs the house or that every reaction is automatically righteous.

It means the child's inner world is taken seriously enough to be explored rather than instantly dismissed. A child may not always interpret things perfectly, but they still need space to say what they feel, what they fear, and what they do not understand. If the home becomes a place where emotions are always mocked, rushed, or silenced, the child may eventually learn to keep painful things hidden until they have already grown deep roots.

This matters because children often bring danger to light first through emotion, not explanation. A child may not say, "I am being manipulated," "I feel unsafe, or something happened to me." They may become quiet, fearful, reactive, withdrawn, defensive, clingy, unusually sad, or emotionally unstable. If the adults around them only know how to manage behavior without listening to the emotional signal beneath it, the deeper truth may remain hidden. Emotional safety gives those hidden signals somewhere to go. It creates room for truth to surface before the child has fully formed the language to present it cleanly.

When children are met with empathy and stability, they develop resilience. They learn that emotional pain can be processed safely. They understand that mistakes do not result in rejection. They discover that their identity is not defined by their failures, their fears, or their hardest moments. This is deeply protective. A child who knows that home is a place of restoration rather than humiliation is far more likely to bring forward what hurts, what confuses, and what threatens them. They do not have to choose between pain and belonging. They learn that they can carry both truth and safety in the same room.

Emotional safety also teaches children what healthy love feels like. That is critically important. A child who regularly experiences patient listening, truthful guidance, steady comfort, and respectful correction begins to recognize the difference between nurturing love and manipulative attention. They learn that real care does not rush them into secrecy, flatter them into silence, pressure them into pleasing, or punish them for telling the truth. That means emotional safety in the home becomes one of the strongest defenses against counterfeit forms of "care" offered by predators, manipulators, and emotionally unhealthy influences outside the home. This kind of environment becomes a powerful defense against predatory manipulation.

Predators often target emotional hunger. They look for children who feel unseen, unheard, unsteady, or unsure of their worth. They exploit loneliness, confusion, fear of rejection, and the longing for affirmation. But when the home is already giving the child healthy attention, stable affection, honest conversation, and meaningful reassurance, the predator's counterfeit attention loses some of its power. A child who is securely loved is not immune to pressure, but they are often harder to trap with flattery and emotional control because they already know what safe care feels like.

Parents must also understand that emotional safety is built through pattern, not slogans. It is not created by saying, "You can tell me anything," if the child has repeatedly learned that honesty brings anger, ridicule, dismissal, or emotional withdrawal. It is built when the parent listens even when tired, when they slow down enough to notice tone, tears, hesitations, and shifts, when they apologize for mishandling a moment. When they correct without humiliating, when they make it clear that truth is welcome, even when truth is uncomfortable, these repeated responses build the emotional architecture of the home.

An emotionally secure home also knows how to handle weakness without contempt. Some children cry easily. Some freeze. Some struggle to explain themselves. Some become emotional before they become clear. Some test whether it is safe to speak by revealing pieces rather than the whole story. Wise parents do not punish that process. They make room for it.

They understand that children often reveal pain in fragments before they can reveal it fully. If the fragment is rejected, the deeper truth may stay buried.

Parents who want to build emotional safety must also examine their own emotional patterns. A volatile parent can weaken safety even if they deeply love their child. A dismissive parent can train silence without meaning to. A sarcastic home can teach children that tenderness is dangerous. Emotional safety grows where adults practice self-control, humility, and attentiveness. Children absorb atmosphere. They learn not only from what is said to them but also from how the room feels when they enter it carrying something difficult.

The foundation of emotional safety is therefore not softness without truth. It is love with steadiness. It is truth without cruelty. It is correction without humiliation. It is listening without mockery. It is compassion without confusion. It is the creation of a home where the child knows: I can bring what hurts here. I can bring what scares me here. I can bring my questions here. I can bring my mistakes here. I may be corrected, but I will not be cast away. I will be heard. I will be helped. I will be protected.

That kind of home does more than comfort children. It strengthens them. It prepares them. It teaches them what safety, dignity, and trustworthy love actually feel like. And once a child knows that, the false versions offered by manipulative people become easier to question.

So guard the child's heart, not only their environment.
Protect their voice, not only their schedule.
Make room for tears, for questions, for fear, for confession, and for truth.
Let the home become a place where wounded things are not mocked, but mended.

Because the child who is emotionally safe at home is far more likely to speak before silence becomes bondage, and far more likely to recognize when something outside the home is trying to offer counterfeit safety instead of real protection.

BUILDING TRUST

Trust is not established through one conversation—it is built through consistent relational investment. It grows over time through repeated evidence that the child is safe, heard, protected, and taken seriously. A child does not build deep trust merely because a parent says, "You can tell me anything." Trust is formed when that statement is proven through how the parent listens, responds, follows up, and protects. It is built in ordinary moments long before a crisis ever appears. That is why trust must be cultivated intentionally, not assumed automatically simply because the child lives in the home.

Children must know that their parents are their ultimate protectors. Not occasionally. Not conditionally. But consistently. They need to hear and see that their parents will believe them, that they will act decisively, and that they will prioritize safety over convenience, over reputation, over social pressure, and over the comfort of other adults. A child must never be left wondering whether the truth will cost them their parent's support. They should know with settled confidence: If I speak, I will not stand alone. If I tell the truth, I will not be abandoned. If something is wrong, my parents will move toward me, not away from me.

When children trust that their voice produces protection rather than punishment, confidence grows. That confidence becomes part of their safety. It gives them courage to speak sooner, to ask questions sooner, to report discomfort sooner, and to resist secrecy more firmly. But this kind of trust does not happen by accident. A nurturing emotional environment is built intentionally. It is built through consistent, patient listening. Calm responses to difficult disclosures. Affirmation of a child's worth. Clear assurance of protection. Stability in discipline without humiliation. Regular affirmation of unconditional love. Each of these practices tells the child something essential: You are safe with me. Your voice matters here. You do not have to earn the right to be heard.

When parents react with anger to vulnerability, children retreat. When parents respond with ridicule, children conceal. When parents dismiss discomfort as exaggeration, children internalize fear.

When children are taught—whether directly or indirectly—that honesty will be met with shame, impatience, or emotional chaos, silence begins to look safer than truth. This is why the tone of the home matters so much. A parent may deeply love a child and still unintentionally weaken trust if every difficult conversation becomes a place of emotional volatility. Children do not open up deeply where they expect to be handled carelessly.

But when parents respond with steadiness and courage, children lean in. Steadiness matters because it reassures the child that truth does not make the parent collapse. Courage matters because it shows the child that difficult things will be faced rather than avoided. A parent who can receive hard information without mocking, panicking, or punishing creates a refuge where the child's inner world can come forward. This kind of response teaches the child that fear does not have the final word and that difficult truth can still be carried inside loving hands.

A strong emotional bond forms the foundation of safety. That bond is not a sentimental weakness. It is protective strength. Children who are securely attached to their parents are often harder to manipulate because the home already supplies what predators try to counterfeit—attention, affirmation, protection, and relational safety. When a child knows they are deeply seen and deeply valued at home, they are less likely to be easily drawn by unhealthy outside voices offering "special" attention. Secure attachment becomes protective armor.

That armor is strengthened when parents do not merely manage behavior, but remain present in the child's inner life. They ask how the child is doing, not just what the child is doing. They notice shifts in tone, changes in mood, and patterns in behavior. They create room for the child to speak without rushing, defending, or immediately correcting. They let the child know that their fears can be named, their confusion can be explored, and their discomfort can be brought into the light without being dismissed. This kind of relational presence is not a luxury in parenting—it is part of how safety is built.

My spouse and I have consistently emphasized to our daughters, through our shared commitment, the importance of their protection. From an early age, when they were in our care, and even now that they are grown up, we have made it clear that no individual's status or position diminishes our responsibility to ensure their safety and well-being. No personality or position outweighs their safety. We taught them that they could approach us about anything—no matter how uncomfortable or frightening—and that we would respond with strength and clarity if something threatened them. We instilled in them that we were not afraid of anyone or anything when it came to their protection and care; we would move mountains. Now back to the book: That posture creates confidence. It teaches children that fear does not have the final word. It reassures them that they are not alone in facing threats. It replaces isolation with solidarity. It tells the child, If danger comes near me, I do not face it by myself. My covering is provided by my parents.

By the Grace of God, this kind of parental unity is powerful. When children see that the adults responsible for them are steady, aligned, and serious about protection, it reduces confusion. It also weakens manipulation, because predators often look for division, inconsistency, or uncertainty in the home. But when the child knows, My parents are together in this. My safety is not negotiable. My voice will be taken seriously; that clarity becomes a wall against secrecy and emotional control.

Trust also grows when parents are faithful in small moments. If a child says, "That made me uncomfortable," and the parent listens, that matters. If a child reveals a fear and the parent does not laugh, that matters. If a child makes a mistake and the parent corrects without crushing dignity, that matters. Trust is built in these repeated moments of emotional honesty and safe response. Then, when a more serious matter arises, the child already has a history of knowing what the parent will do with the truth.

Secure attachment becomes protective armor. When children feel secure, they speak sooner. When they feel heard, they disclose earlier. When they feel protected, they resist manipulation more confidently.

They are less likely to believe the lie that they are alone, less likely to be trapped by secrecy, and less likely to assume that telling the truth will destroy their place in the family. Trust gives them a relational footing. It gives them the courage to step toward the light.

So build trust deliberately.
Listen slowly.
Respond steadily.
Protect fiercely.
Affirm consistently.

Let the child see, again and again, that your love is not fragile when truth gets difficult.

Because when trust is strong, the child does not have to choose between honesty and belonging. They learn that in a guarded home, both remain intact.

BREAKING THE POWER OF SECRECY

Predators thrive in silence. Their primary weapon is secrecy. They understand that hidden things grow fastest where a child feels afraid to speak, unsure how to speak, or unconvinced that speaking will help. That is why secrecy is never a small matter in the life of a child. It is often the protected atmosphere in which manipulation deepens, fear hardens, and harm continues longer than it should. A predator does not merely seek private access to a child; he seeks private control over the child's voice.

They often threaten children with consequences—harm, embarrassment, separation from family, punishment, disbelief, or the loss of someone they care about—if they dare to speak. Fear becomes the cage. Silence becomes the lock. The child may begin to believe that telling the truth will destroy everything, that speaking will make life worse, that honesty will bring blame instead of rescue. This is one of the cruelest parts of predatory control: the child who most needs help is manipulated into feeling that asking for help is the very thing they must avoid.

But silence cannot survive where communication is normal.

This is why the atmosphere of the home matters so deeply. When a home cultivates open dialogue, predators lose leverage. When children are taught from an early age that no topic is forbidden, no fear is too small, no question is shameful, and no concern will be dismissed, they are more likely to disclose early signs of danger. They learn that the home is not a place where difficult things are hidden to preserve appearances, but a place where truth can come forward and be handled with courage. In such an environment, silence begins to weaken because the child no longer feels emotionally trapped.

Emotional safety disrupts isolation. That is one of its greatest strengths. Secrecy works by making the child feel alone—alone in fear, alone in confusion, alone in responsibility, alone in what they know, and alone in what they are carrying. But children reared in environments of trust understand something essential: they are not alone. They know that if something frightening happens, their parents will stand beside them rather than turn against them. They know that difficult truth will not make them lose their place in the home. They know that confession is not a doorway into rejection, but a doorway into protection.

Breaking secrecy begins with repeated reassurance. A child should not have to guess how a parent will respond to a hard truth. They must hear clearly and often: You can tell me anything. You will never be in trouble for telling the truth. If something makes you uncomfortable, I want to know. If someone tells you not to tell me, that is exactly when you should tell me. Your safety matters more than anyone's feelings. These assurances are not sentimental phrases. They are protective declarations. They weaken the fear that predators rely upon to silence victims. The more clearly the truth is welcomed at home, the harder it becomes for fear to convince the child that secrecy is safer.

Parents must also understand that secrecy is broken not only by what they say, but by how they respond. If a child brings forward something difficult and is met with panic, blame, ridicule, harshness, or disbelief, that child may become more silent the next time, not less. But if the child is met with steadiness, protection, careful listening, and courageous follow-through, the grip of secrecy begins to crack. The child learns something powerful: When I tell the truth, I am not abandoned. I am helped. That lesson is deeply protective. It trains the child to bring darkness into the light before the darkness can settle too deeply.

It is also important to teach children the difference between privacy and secrecy. Privacy protects dignity. Secrecy protects wrongdoing. A child should know that some things are private in the healthy sense—like changing clothes, using the bathroom, or keeping personal thoughts until they are ready to share them. But secrecy becomes dangerous when it carries fear, pressure, shame, or instructions to hide something from the people who are meant to protect them. Children must be taught that secrets about touching, secrets that make them uncomfortable, secrets that make them feel afraid, and secrets that isolate them from parents are not safe secrets to keep. They are warning signs.

Parents break the power of secrecy by making honesty part of the home's culture. That means asking more than surface questions. It means creating regular room for children to talk. It means listening carefully when a child hesitates, changes tone, or circles around something difficult. It means not always requiring the child to speak perfectly or immediately. Sometimes children reveal the truth in fragments. Sometimes they test safety before they fully open. Wise parents do not despise that process. They make room for it. They understand that silence is often broken little by little before it breaks fully.

A guarded home also breaks secrecy by refusing to idolize comfort. Some families are so committed to keeping things pleasant that children learn early not to bring up anything disruptive. But that kind of comfort is dangerous. It trains children to bury what should be exposed. A truly safe home is not one where difficult truths never appear. It is one where difficult truths can be brought forward without being buried under fear. Truth may disturb the room, but it also protects the child. And the child matters more than the room.

Predators depend on children believing that silence is necessary. Parents must build an opposite conviction into the child's heart: truth is safe here. That conviction is built through repeated reassurance, calm responses, visible protection, and a home atmosphere where speaking up is treated as courage, not inconvenience. When children know they are heard, believed, and protected, secrecy loses its hiding place. It becomes harder for manipulation to survive where truth has been welcomed consistently.

When honesty is welcomed, secrecy loses its power.

So say it clearly.
Repeat it often.
Model it faithfully.
Protect every honest disclosure with seriousness and care.
Do not let fear become stronger than the child's confidence in your response.

Because the power of secrecy is broken when the child learns that the truth does not lead to abandonment—it leads to protection.

ENCOURAGING HONESTY

Honesty flourishes in environments where truth is safe. Children do not become consistently honest merely because they are told to tell the truth. They become honest when they learn, through repeated experience, that truth can be brought forward without destroying their sense of safety. If a child tells the truth and is met with explosive anger, emotional volatility, harsh ridicule, panic, or immediate dismissal, the lesson they learn may not be that truth matters. The lesson they learn may be that the truth is dangerous. And once that lesson settles into the heart, silence becomes easier than honesty.

Children must experience calm responses when they share uncomfortable information. If the reaction they receive is unpredictable, humiliating, or excessively intense, they may hesitate to speak again. Even a child who wants to be honest may begin measuring the cost of honesty if they fear the parent's emotional response more than they trust the parent's protection. That is why emotional steadiness in the parent is not a small matter. It is part of the architecture of safety. A calm response does not mean the issue is small. It means the parent is strong enough to handle the truth without making the child carry the weight of the adult's instability.

Encouraging honesty requires emotional discipline from parents. It requires listening before reacting. It requires patience when a child struggles to explain something confusing, embarrassing, or frightening. It requires a parent to slow down, ask carefully, and create space for the child's words to emerge without being rushed, interrupted, or overpowered. Children often do not tell the truth in polished language. They may hesitate, circle around the point, speak in fragments, or reveal only part of what happened first. A wise parent understands that truth sometimes arrives trembling. It must still be received.

It also requires separating the mistake from the child's identity. A child may tell the truth about something that includes their own poor decision, poor judgment, or disobedience. Perhaps they responded to a message, accepted a gift, went somewhere they were told not to, kept something hidden for too long, or failed to speak up earlier.

In those moments, the parent must be careful not to let correction crush honesty. The child must learn that a mistake does not make them the enemy, and that telling the truth about the mistake is still an act of courage. Correction may still be needed, but it must not cancel protection. If a child feels that every mistake becomes an identity label—bad, foolish, shameful, disappointing—then truth will become harder to speak.

Encouraging honesty means parents must also be watchful about sarcasm, mockery, and dismissive speech. Some children do not hide because they expect open anger. They hide because they expect to be laughed at, talked over, or treated as if their concern is foolish. A child who hears, "That's nothing," "You're overreacting," or "Why didn't you just say something?" may retreat into silence even if they had gathered real courage to speak. But when parents respond with seriousness, gratitude, and careful attention, the child learns that honesty is worth bringing forward—even when the truth is messy.

Honesty also grows where parents model it. Children learn not only from what they are told, but from what they observe. A home where adults hide, deflect, excuse, and avoid difficult truth trains children to do the same. But a home where parents admit when they are wrong, apologize sincerely, correct themselves, and live truthfully teaches children that honesty is not weakness. It is strength. It is not humiliation. It is integrity. This kind of modeling is powerful because it shows the child that truth is part of how healthy people live—not just a rule children are expected to follow while adults escape it.

When honesty is encouraged, children develop the confidence to speak early. And early disclosure is often the difference between prevention and prolonged harm. Many situations become far more damaging because the child stayed silent until fear, shame, or confusion had already deepened. But when a child has been taught and shown that truth is welcome, they are more likely to speak while the situation is still emerging, while warning signs are still fresh, and while intervention can happen before greater damage is done. In that sense, encouraging honesty is not merely a moral lesson. It is a protective strategy.

Encouraging honesty means teaching children that truth is always welcome—even when it is difficult. Even when it exposes something uncomfortable. Even when it reveals poor choices. Even when it interrupts family plans, social comfort, or the image of peace. Truth must be treated as more valuable than appearances. A child should know that honesty does not make them a burden. It does not make them disloyal. It does not make them the cause of the problem. It gives the family something sacred to work with: reality brought into the light.

Parents should also communicate gratitude when a child tells the truth. A simple response such as, "Thank you for telling me," can become deeply healing. It tells the child that honesty is seen, valued, and handled with care. That kind of response can lower shame, reduce fear, and strengthen the child's willingness to keep speaking. A child who feels honored for telling the truth is less likely to hide next time. A child who feels punished for it may go silent.

The home must therefore become a place where truth does not have to fight for permission to exist. It should not have to force its way through fear, shame, and emotional unpredictability. It should be welcomed. Protected. Taken seriously. This kind of environment does not remove the difficulty of the hard truth, but it changes what the child expects to happen when the truth arrives. And that expectation matters greatly.

So listen before reacting.
Stay calm enough to hear what is being said.
Separate the child from the mistake.
Correct without crushing.
Thank them for honesty.
Make truth a safe path, not a dangerous gamble.

Because when honesty is encouraged, children speak sooner, fear weakens, and the light reaches places where secrecy hoped would remain hidden.

THE HOME AS A SANCTUARY OF BOUNDARIES

A home without boundaries is not a sanctuary—it is an open field. And an open field may feel spacious, relaxed, and unrestricted, but it is also easier to enter, easier to cross, and easier to exploit. Sanctuary is not created by affection alone. It is built through order, wisdom, protection, and clearly established limits. A child does not feel safe simply because people in the house claim to love them. Safety is strengthened when that love has structure. Without boundaries, even sincere love can become careless. With boundaries, love becomes guarded, clear, and trustworthy.

Boundaries are not barriers against love; they are structures that protect it. They are not restrictions designed to suffocate growth; they are safeguards that preserve dignity, identity, and safety. They give shape to what is healthy and expose what does not belong. Boundaries tell the child, There are lines here because you matter. There are limits here because your peace is worth protecting. There are things we welcome and things we do not permit because safety is sacred in this home. That is not oppression. That is stewardship.

Ephesians 5:11 (KJV) instructs believers: "Have no fellowship with the unfruitful works of darkness, but rather reprove them." This principle applies directly to the home. What threatens safety must not be entertained. What undermines protection must not be tolerated. What blurs lines around dignity, privacy, truth, bodily respect, or moral clarity must not be welcomed simply because it arrives in a familiar form. A sanctuary is not maintained by wishing darkness would behave. It is maintained by refusing to give darkness room.

Children must be taught clearly that their body belongs to them, that they have the right to say no to unwanted touch, that no adult should ask them to keep secrets about touching, and that any request causing discomfort must be reported immediately. These truths must not be vague suggestions whispered occasionally. They must be taught with clarity, repeated with calmness, and reinforced through how the home actually operates. A child who knows these truths does not become fearful. They become more grounded. They begin to understand that discomfort matters, that personal dignity matters, and that their voice is not optional when something feels wrong.

Secrecy is the soil in which abuse grows. Boundaries disrupt secrecy. This is one of the great reasons boundaries matter so much. They interrupt the hidden progression of wrong things. They make it harder for unsafe people to create private worlds with children. They reduce confusion. They create a structure that exposes what would otherwise grow quietly.

When a household lives casually around privacy, touch, access, digital communication, and personal space, it often creates unnecessary room for manipulation. But when boundaries are clear, secrecy has less room to root itself.

Parents must also distinguish clearly between privacy and secrecy. Privacy safeguards a person's dignity. Secrecy shields misconduct. Children who understand this distinction are far less susceptible to manipulation. Privacy is healthy when it honors personhood and respect, such as dressing, bathing, using the restroom, or having age-appropriate personal space. But secrecy becomes dangerous when it hides discomfort, isolates the child from protection, or pressures them to conceal what should be brought into the light. A child must know that not everything hidden is evil, but anything hidden that creates fear, confusion, shame, or pressure should be spoken about immediately.

A sanctuary of boundaries also models respect. Parents must demonstrate healthy physical affection, appropriate speech, and consistent discipline. Children learn boundaries not only by being told, but by watching how adults treat one another and how the home responds to their own voice. When a child explicitly declines a hug and subsequently experiences mockery, pressure, or indifference from those around them, the underlying lesson imparted is not one of safety and comfort, but rather an instruction in acquiescence to feelings of discomfort. In instances where a child's hesitance is met with laughter or where their unease is dismissed as mere rudeness, the message conveyed becomes particularly hazardous: it suggests that the expectations and desires of others hold greater importance than the child's own internal instincts and warnings.

This creates an environment where the child's ability to recognize and assert their boundaries is undermined. In contrast, when parents and caregivers respond to a child's boundaries with respect and understanding, the child learns a fundamental lesson about the significance of personal boundaries. They come to understand that being treated with respect is not only normal but essential, and that expressions of love and affection should never come at the expense of one's sense of safety and comfort. This nurturing approach fosters a healthy understanding of boundaries and reinforces the child's ability to advocate for their own emotional and physical well-being.

Children learn boundaries by observing them. If adults model healthy restraint, respectful affection, and consistent regard for bodily dignity, children begin to recognize those patterns as right and normal. If adults model intrusion, sarcasm, forced affection, emotional manipulation, or careless handling of personal space, the child may begin to normalize what should not be accepted. The atmosphere of the home teaches even when no formal lesson is being given. That is why parents must watch not only what they instruct, but what they demonstrate.

Boundaries must also extend beyond physical contact. They include digital activity, friendships, online communication, and personal space. A sanctuary cannot be strong physically while remaining careless digitally. A child's device use, private messages, apps, social platforms, late-night access, and hidden accounts all fall within the realm of boundary stewardship. The same is true of friendships and social influences. Who has access to the child emotionally? Who communicates privately? Who is allowed repeated closeness without visibility? What becomes normal in the child's peer environment? Boundaries must reach those spaces as well, because danger does not only move through physical touch. It also moves through words, images, pressure, emotional dependency, secrecy, and access.

A sanctuary does not operate casually. It operates deliberately. That means the parent does not wait for a crisis before building structure. The watchman does not build the wall after the breach. Healthy homes think ahead. They ask what access points need guarding, what habits need tightening, what conversations need to happen, what digital practices must be monitored, and what family rhythms help keep truth near and secrecy weak. Deliberate homes are not rigid for the sake of control. They are careful for the sake of protection.

When boundaries are strong, confidence grows. Children begin to understand where the lines are, what is safe, what is not, and what they are allowed to say when something feels off. Boundaries help them trust their own discomfort instead of dismissing it. They help them interpret relationships more wisely. They make it easier for them to recognize when someone is asking for too much, pressing too close, or moving into spaces that should remain guarded. Strong boundaries do not merely restrict danger—they strengthen the child's inner clarity.

When boundaries are weak, vulnerability expands. Confusion enters more easily. Manipulation finds softer ground. Children may become unsure of what is acceptable, unsure whether their discomfort matters, unsure whether adults will back them if they speak, unsure whether privacy is dignity or concealment. Weak boundaries do not create freedom. They often create uncertainty. And uncertainty is one of the environments in which grooming and manipulation work most effectively.

Boundaries communicate love. They declare: You are valuable. Your body is sacred. Your voice matters. They tell the child that adults in this home will not surrender their safety to politeness, convenience, fear of conflict, or careless openness. They communicate that this household takes dignity seriously, that bodily respect is not optional, and that truth matters more than appearances. A child reared in that kind of environment begins to internalize those messages. They learn not only that they are protected, but that they are worth protecting.

A sanctuary of boundaries is therefore not cold or controlling. It is warm with wisdom. It is loving with structure. It is open to truth and closed to what threatens innocence. It is a place where adults understand that unrestricted access is not generosity, that blurred lines are not compassion, and that passive oversight is not trust. It is a home where safety is not hoped for—it is built.

So establish the lines clearly.
Honor the child's dignity.
Guard the digital doors.
Respect bodily boundaries.
Teach the difference between privacy and secrecy.
Let the child's voice matter.
Make the home deliberate, not casual.

Because a sanctuary is not simply where people live. It is where what is sacred is actively protected.

THE ONGOING COMMITMENT TO CONSISTENCY

Protection is not an event. It is a lifestyle. It is not something accomplished by one serious conversation, one emotional warning, one family meeting, one set of rules, or one moment of spiritual intensity. One conversation about safety is not enough. One warning about boundaries does not secure a future. One prayer over a child does not replace ongoing vigilance. Children are not protected by occasional seriousness surrounded by long stretches of inattention. Protection requires rhythm, repetition, and resolve. It must become part of the daily culture of the home.

First Corinthians 16:13 (KJV) commands, "Watch ye, stand fast in the faith, quit you like men, be strong." Watching is not a moment. It is a posture. It is a sustained condition of readiness. The watchman does not become alert only when the threat is already visible. He remains alert because part of his assignment is to notice what others might miss before it fully emerges. In the same way, parents cannot afford to think of vigilance as something reserved only for emergencies. The strongest protection is often built long before the crisis ever appears.

Consistency means showing up repeatedly—not only during a crisis but also in calm. It means checking in emotionally. Observing behavioral changes. Monitoring environments. Reinforcing boundaries. Maintaining spiritual covering through prayer. It means paying attention when nothing dramatic seems wrong, because some of the most important work of protection happens in ordinary days. A child should not experience a parent's watchfulness only when something has already gone bad. They should live inside the steady security of ongoing care.

Children thrive in predictable stability. When parents remain emotionally present and spiritually grounded, children feel secure. They learn what steadiness feels like. They learn that safety is not random, that parental presence is not fragile, and that truth can be brought forward consistently.

A child who knows the parent will still be listening tomorrow, still be asking next week, still be paying attention next month, and still be praying next season develops a deeper confidence than a child living under occasional bursts of concern and long periods of emotional absence.

Consistency builds confidence.

That confidence becomes part of the child's protection. It teaches them that their life matters enough to be watched carefully, not anxiously, but faithfully. It tells them that the adults responsible for them are not casually drifting through the assignment of guardianship. They are present. They are paying attention. They are staying engaged. They are not only reacting to what goes wrong; they are cultivating an environment that makes it easier to catch what is changing.

Inconsistent vigilance creates gaps. Gaps create opportunity. Opportunity invites risk. But consistent presence closes those gaps. A parent who checks in only occasionally may miss the early shift in emotion, tone, behavior, or relationships. A parent who reinforces boundaries only when it is convenient teaches the child that boundaries are flexible. A parent who prays fervently in crisis but lives spiritually distracted in ordinary life may weaken the atmosphere that should have been guarded all along. Children are shaped not only by the values parents proclaim, but by the patterns parents repeat.

Consistency also keeps parents from being fooled by false peace. Sometimes things look calm simply because no one is asking the deeper questions. Sometimes a child appears "fine" because the adults around them have stopped paying close enough attention to notice what has changed. But the consistent parent does not interpret calmness as proof that no watchfulness is needed. They understand that protection is strongest when it continues through ordinary seasons. The daily rhythm of attentiveness is what keeps small warnings from becoming large wounds.

Protection requires endurance. It is easier to have one conversation than a lifetime of them. It is easier to react once than to remain alert daily. It is easier to tighten up after something goes wrong than to stay disciplined before it does. But ease does not equal safety.

The call to guard a child is not fulfilled by what is easiest. It is fulfilled by what is faithful. Endurance matters because children grow, environments change, dangers evolve, and the forms of pressure they face do not remain static. What protects a child at five will not be enough by itself at fifteen. Consistency means the parent keeps growing in the work as the child grows in life.

This kind of endurance communicates something powerful to a child: You are worth my attention. You are worth my vigilance. You are worth my daily investment. Those truths do not only comfort a child; they strengthen them. They help shape a child who knows they are not an interruption to the parent's life, but a sacred responsibility within it. The repeated presence of a watchful parent becomes a kind of living reassurance: I am not being left to navigate danger alone.

Over time, this steady commitment becomes protective covering. It is built in repeated conversations, in calm listening, in follow-up questions, in guarded access, in watched patterns, in noticed changes, in enforced boundaries, in family prayer, in open dialogue, in emotional availability, and in spiritual attentiveness. These things, repeated faithfully, create more than routine. They create safety. They create a child who is more likely to speak early, resist pressure, recognize manipulation, and trust the parent enough to come forward when something feels wrong.

Consistency also protects against parental drift. Adults can become tired, distracted, overconfident, or numb to what once felt urgent. But the commitment to consistency resists that drift. It reminds the parent that vigilance is not seasonal. It is part of stewardship. Even when life gets busy, even when routines feel repetitive, even when nothing alarming appears on the surface, the parent stays engaged. Not with panic. With discipline. Not with suspicion toward everyone. With sober care. Not with emotional instability. With steady watchfulness.

A consistent home is not a perfect home. It is a deliberate home. A home where the parent keeps returning to what matters.

A home where truth is repeated, where prayer is practiced, where boundaries are upheld, where questions are welcomed, where emotional changes are noticed, and where the child does not have to guess whether protection is still active.

That kind of consistency becomes part of the child's internal stability. It helps them know what love looks like when it refuses to get lazy.

Safety is preserved not by intensity alone—but by endurance.

So stay present in calm seasons.
Keep checking in.
Keep listening.
Keep praying.
Keep watching the patterns.
Keep reinforcing the boundaries.
Keep making room for the truth.
Keep showing the child that your care is not occasional, but constant.

Because the long obedience of daily watchfulness often protects what dramatic reactions alone never can.

A Warning Against Complacency

There are dangers that approach with noise, and there are dangers that approach with comfort. The dangers that alarm us loudly are often easier to confront because they announce themselves. But some of the most devastating harm enters quietly—through distraction, through misplaced trust, through delayed action, through softened boundaries, through the assumption that because nothing obvious has happened, everything must be fine. Complacency is the silent accomplice of destruction. It rarely appears as cruelty. More often, it appears as relaxation, routine, and the dangerous belief that vigilance can afford to loosen its grip.

When vigilance fades, exposure increases. That is the law of an unguarded wall. What is not being watched carefully is more easily entered. What is not being examined soberly is more easily excused. What is repeatedly excused eventually becomes tolerated, and what is tolerated long enough can become a doorway through which harm quietly advances. Complacency does not need to hate children in order to fail them. It only needs to become passive. It only needs to decide that concern can wait, that awkward questions can be postponed, that troubling patterns are probably nothing, and that discomfort is too small to investigate seriously. Yet many injuries that changed lives forever began in those very moments of delay.

There are homes where love is present, but watchfulness is weak. There are parents who care deeply but have become tired, distracted, emotionally overextended, or too comfortable with appearances. There are guardians who no longer ask the second question, no longer notice the shift in atmosphere, no longer interrupt subtle access, and no longer treat early warning signs with the seriousness they deserve. But when the watchman becomes casual, the gate becomes easier to breach.

Complacency may look peaceful on the surface, but beneath that surface, it often grants room for confusion, secrecy, manipulation, and hidden influence to grow without resistance.

If something unsettles your spirit, pay attention. Do not treat spiritual discomfort as imagination simply because you cannot yet explain it perfectly. If your child's behavior shifts suddenly, investigate. Do not dismiss the change as moodiness, attitude, or a passing phase without looking more closely. If boundaries blur, address it immediately. Do not wait for the pattern to become undeniable before you become responsible. The longer danger remains unchallenged, the more deeply it can root itself in the child's emotions, trust, and sense of safety.

The cost of vigilance may be inconvenience. It may require difficult conversations, stricter boundaries, interrupted plans, more oversight, or the courage to be misunderstood by others. But the cost of negligence may echo for a lifetime. A child can carry the consequences of adult passivity far longer than the adult carried the discomfort of avoiding action. That is why complacency must be confronted ruthlessly. It is not harmless. It is not neutral. It is one of the enemy's quietest tools because it convinces good people to do too little for too long while danger studies the gaps.

Stand watch. Remain alert. Refuse to let routine dull your discernment. Refuse to let comfort lull your soul into sleep. Because when God entrusts you with a child, He expects you to guard that life with conviction. Not occasionally. Not emotionally. But faithfully, soberly, and with unwavering seriousness before Him.

❖ A WARNING ❖

To Those Who Guard the Gate

You are positioned at the gate of your household. That is not sentimental language. It is a spiritual and practical reality. You are the one entrusted to regulate access, to examine what enters, to discern what lingers, and to stand between innocence and intrusion. You have the authority to restrict access. You have the responsibility to guard what cannot guard itself. A child does not choose their watchman. God appoints one. That appointment is not decorative. It is sacred.

The gate is where permission is either granted or denied. It is where the parent decides what relationships will be welcomed, what behaviors will be tolerated, what influences will be allowed near the child, and what must be kept outside the walls. If the gate is weak, the home becomes vulnerable. If the gate is guarded, the child lives beneath stronger protection. This is why parental authority is not merely about discipline or household order. It is about stewardship. It is about whether the one assigned to protect is actually using that authority to preserve what Heaven has placed under their care.

You cannot claim love while avoiding vigilance. Love that refuses to watch carefully becomes vulnerable to deception. Love that avoids hard questions becomes easier to manipulate. A love that prefers comfort over courage can leave a child exposed while still insisting that its intentions were good. But good intentions do not guard a gate. Watchfulness does. Discernment does. Boundaries do. Follow-through does. A guarded household is not built merely because parents feel concern. It is built because they act on that concern before danger deepens.

You cannot pray for protection while ignoring warning signs. Prayer and vigilance are not rivals. They belong together. The same God who commands watchfulness also strengthens it. The same Spirit who stirs discernment expects that discernment to be honored, not silenced. When warning signs appear—behavioral shifts, inappropriate access, secrecy, discomfort, blurred boundaries, emotional entanglement, changes in atmosphere—the guardian cannot afford to look away and call that peace. Peace without truth is not peace. It is delay.

Heaven is not measuring how comfortable you were. Heaven is measuring how faithfully you watched. It is not asking whether others approved of your caution. It is not asking whether your boundaries made everyone feel at ease. It is asking whether you stood where you were assigned to stand. Whether you tightened what should have been tightened. Whether you confronted what should have been confronted. Whether you protected what could not protect itself.

Stand firm. Remain alert. Refuse to compromise. Do not surrender the gate to politeness, overconfidence, social pressure, flattery, reputation, or emotional fatigue. Do not let another adult's feelings become more important than a child's safety. Do not let familiarity make you careless. Do not let repeated exposure trick you into believing that what is common must be safe. Watchfulness is not optional. It is sacred. The gate you guard today may determine whether danger is interrupted early or allowed to advance in silence.

HOMEFRONT

The home is not merely a residence—it is the first line of defense. Before children encounter teachers, peers, media, social pressure, digital culture, or the broader moral confusion of the world, they encounter the atmosphere of their household. What is established there becomes their first reference point for safety, truth, authority, and belonging. The home teaches them what love feels like, what boundaries sound like, what honesty costs, what correction means, and whether discomfort can be brought into the light without punishment. For that reason, the home is never spiritually neutral. It is always shaping something.

If the home is weak, vulnerability increases. A weak home is not always one that lacks affection. Sometimes it is one that lacks structure, clarity, and watchfulness. It may have love but little oversight, warmth but weak boundaries, good intentions but poor discernment. In such a home, children may be fed and clothed while still being emotionally, spiritually, or relationally under-guarded. They may live in comfort while remaining exposed to subtle dangers the household has failed to take seriously. Weakness in the home does not guarantee harm, but it does make resilience harder and access easier.

If the home is guarded, resilience strengthens. A guarded home creates more than rules; it creates an atmosphere in which truth is welcome, boundaries are honored, prayer is active, and vigilance is normal. Children reared in such a home begin to develop inner steadiness. They learn that discomfort matters. They learn that safety is worth protecting.

They learn that manipulation is not the same as care, secrecy is not the same as privacy, and trusted adults do not need hidden access in order to love well. They become stronger not because the world is less dangerous, but because the home has prepared them better to recognize what does not belong.

Your home must function as a watchtower. A watchtower sees early. A watchtower responds quickly. A watchtower does not ignore what approaches. It does not shrug at movement near the wall. It does not confuse stillness with safety. It remains elevated in awareness, grounded in truth, and ready to act. That is what the home must become—a place where adults are paying close enough attention to notice what shifts, what enters, what lingers, and what begins to move in a direction that threatens the child's peace.

Strengthen the walls with prayer. Prayer establishes spiritual covering, sharpens discernment, and keeps the watchman awake. Reinforce the gates with boundaries. Boundaries regulate access, protect dignity, and make secrecy harder to hide. Secure the atmosphere with truth. Truth keeps manipulation from becoming normal, keeps children from feeling trapped in silence, and gives the household a moral clarity strong enough to resist the false comforts of deception. A home grounded in prayer, truth, and disciplined vigilance becomes harder ground for hidden darkness to cultivate.

Stand at your post with unwavering conviction. The homefront cannot be guarded casually. It must be guarded deliberately. The child should feel that the walls are not weak, that the gate is not careless, and that the watchman is not asleep. Safety is not secured by chance. It is secured by commitment. Not one intense moment of concern, but a sustained pattern of faithful guardianship. Not by hoping danger stays away, but by building a home strong enough to recognize and resist what approaches.

Because the safety of your children is not secured by chance.
It is secured by commitment.

CHAPTER TEN
ESTABLISHING CLEAR BOUNDARIES
Practical Safeguards for Parents and Leaders

The Need for Clear Boundaries

Clear boundaries are not optional safeguards reserved for extreme situations—they are necessary structures for everyday protection. A home, church, school, ministry, team, classroom, or community setting cannot remain safe simply by assuming goodwill. Safety does not sustain itself through optimism, reputation, or the hope that everyone means well. Safety must be established intentionally, communicated clearly, and enforced consistently. When structure is absent, confusion grows. And confusion is one of the most useful environments for manipulation, secrecy, and hidden harm.

Boundaries are not signs of distrust. They are signs of wisdom. They do not exist because every adult is dangerous. They exist because every child is valuable. They do not accuse everyone in advance; they protect what is too precious to be left exposed. The purpose of a boundary is not to create fear, but to remove opportunity. It is to eliminate unnecessary ambiguity, reduce secrecy, regulate access, and make manipulation harder to begin and far harder to conceal. A wise boundary says, This line exists because innocence matters here. It does not apologize for existing. It understands its purpose.

When boundaries are weak, access expands. When access expands, vulnerability increases. When vulnerability increases, protection weakens. That progression must be understood clearly, because many harmful situations do not begin with obvious evil. They begin with excessive openness, casual assumptions, blurred lines, private exceptions, and environments where people are allowed too much unexamined access simply because no one wanted to seem rigid. But what some call relaxed, others may exploit. What some call harmless flexibility may become a door through which confusion and danger enter unnoticed.

This is why clear boundaries must be established before discomfort ever arises. Parents and leaders must not wait until something feels wrong to decide what should have already been made plain. Structure is strongest when it is built in advance. Boundaries are most effective when they exist before they are tested. Once an uneasy situation appears, people are already emotionally involved, socially pressured, or tempted to interpret the moment through sympathy and discomfort rather than through principle. But when the boundary was already established, enforcement becomes clearer. The question is no longer "What should we do now?" The answer is already present in the structure.

Boundaries protect both the vulnerable and the trustworthy. They guard children from unnecessary exposure, and they also protect healthy adults from false ambiguity, misunderstood closeness, or avoidable situations that should never have been normalized. This is important because some people resist boundaries as though boundaries imply accusation. But healthy adults do not need unrestricted access in order to function with integrity. In fact, healthy adults often welcome clear expectations because they understand that visibility, accountability, and wisdom serve the good of everyone involved. Resistance to healthy boundaries often reveals more concern than the boundary itself ever does.

The absence of clear boundaries creates a dangerous environment where children must interpret too much on their own. They may have to decide whether an adult's behavior is normal, whether a private interaction is acceptable, whether a request should be questioned, or whether secrecy is expected. That burden should not rest on the child. Adults are responsible to create structures that make unsafe ambiguity less likely. Children are not supposed to build the guardrails around adult behavior. Guardians and leaders are.

Clear boundaries also reduce the power of social pressure. Without structure, people often rely on personal judgment in emotionally charged moments. They may think, "This person seems kind," "They've always been around," "I don't want to offend them," or "This is probably harmless." But boundaries help remove the fog created by personal impressions.

They provide objective lines that do not depend on mood, charisma, position, or popularity. They say, This is how we operate here, not because we are fearful, but because we are responsible.

Every environment that includes children must therefore be governed by more than assumptions. It must be governed by clarity. Who may be alone with a child? Under what circumstances? What kinds of communication are appropriate? What types of contact are off-limits? What reporting procedures exist when something feels wrong? What expectations guide leaders, volunteers, staff, teachers, or mentors? These things must not be left undefined. Undefined spaces become a breeding ground for misjudgment at best and exploitation at worst.

Boundaries are also deeply formative for children. When children grow up in environments where boundaries are visible, respected, and consistently upheld, they begin to understand something vital: safety is not accidental, and their dignity matters enough to be protected deliberately. They learn that adults should respect limits, that their discomfort matters, and that healthy care does not require secrecy, private privilege, or emotional pressure. Strong boundaries help children recognize what belongs and what does not. That recognition becomes part of their long-term protection.

The need for clear boundaries is therefore not merely practical. It is moral. It is spiritual. It is a statement of value. It says that children are not to be handled casually, that access is never to be assumed, and that safety is too sacred to be left to unspoken expectations. A boundary is not a wall against love; it is a wall around what love has been assigned to guard.

So let the lines be clear.
Let the expectations be known.
Let the structure be steady.
Let access be governed wisely.
Let no child live under the burden of adult ambiguity.

Because protection begins where confusion ends, and clear boundaries are one of the strongest ways a faithful guardian says, What has been entrusted to me will not be left exposed.

ACCESS CONTROL

Access control is one of the most practical and effective forms of protection because predators often depend on privacy, exclusivity, gradual familiarity, and unchallenged opportunity. They do not always begin with overt wrongdoing. They often begin with access—more time, more closeness, more private communication, more emotional significance, more unmonitored presence. That is why access must never be treated casually. The issue is not merely whether someone seems trustworthy. The issue is whether the structure around the child is wise enough to prevent unnecessary opportunity. A child should never be left protected only by assumptions about another adult's character. Protection must also be built into the environment itself.

Clear boundaries must be established and enforced consistently: no closed-door meetings between children and unrelated adults; no secret gifts or "special" exchanges without parental knowledge; no private messaging that bypasses parental oversight; no one-on-one excursions without explicit parental awareness and approval; no adult communication that excludes parental visibility. These rules are not distrust—they are structure. They do not accuse every adult of hidden evil. They acknowledge that children are too valuable to be left exposed to unnecessary risk. The purpose of access control is not to create suspicion around every interaction. It is to reduce the kinds of conditions under which manipulation grows quietly, and harm becomes easier to conceal.

Predators often rely on being treated as exceptions. They want to become the adult who is so trusted, so appreciated, so familiar, or so admired that ordinary boundaries no longer seem necessary around them. They want special permission, unusual flexibility, emotional centrality, and unexamined access. That is why access control matters so much. It interrupts the slow expansion of privilege. It prevents private channels from becoming normal. It removes many of the conditions predators use to test boundaries, build secrecy, and deepen influence without immediate detection.

When those pathways are blocked early, opportunity narrows. When adults know that interaction with children will remain visible, accountable, and regulated, unhealthy intentions lose room to operate. Hidden motives do not thrive as easily under bright structure. Private manipulation struggles where communication is visible. Emotional grooming becomes harder where parents remain present, questions remain normal, and access remains supervised. Access control does not eliminate every threat, but it greatly reduces the amount of quiet room in which a threat can mature unnoticed.

Healthy adults respect accountability. They do not resist reasonable boundaries. They do not push for secrecy. They do not attempt to isolate a child from parental involvement. They do not act offended because a parent wants visibility, clarity, or shared oversight. In truth, adults with clean motives often welcome good structure because they understand that boundaries protect everyone involved. They know that wisdom is not the enemy of care. It is one of its expressions. So when an adult begins pressing against healthy limits, repeatedly seeking privacy, bypassing parental knowledge, or trying to establish exclusive contact with a child, those efforts must not be dismissed as harmless personality quirks. Repeated resistance to visibility often reveals something that words alone will not.

An adult who genuinely values a child's well-being will not be threatened by transparency. They will welcome parental visibility. They will understand that boundaries protect everyone involved. But when someone consistently attempts to move outside those lines—seeking private conversations, hidden favors, special access, emotional exclusivity, or direct communication that weakens parental oversight—those efforts must not be ignored. The parent must not be emotionally pressured into relaxing standards simply to avoid appearing suspicious. A child's safety is more important than an adult's preference for comfort.

Access is not a casual privilege. It must be regulated carefully. It must be supervised intentionally. It must never be assumed safe simply because it feels familiar. Familiarity is not proof of purity. Repeated presence is not proof of integrity. Being liked by the family, admired in the community, or respected in a church, school, or team setting does not remove the need for structure. In fact, trusted settings often require even greater sobriety because people tend to lower their guard there the fastest. What is familiar is often questioned the least, and that is exactly why access must still be governed clearly.

Acts 20:29 (KJV) warns, "For I know this, that after my departing shall grievous wolves enter in among you, not sparing the flock." This passage underscores the necessity of vigilance even within familiar environments. Threats do not always emerge from obvious places. They may arise within trusted circles—schools, churches, sports leagues, mentorship programs, youth activities, volunteer settings, family friendships, and community spaces that appear stable on the surface. That is why access control is not excessive. It is biblical prudence. The flock is not protected merely because the people nearby look respectable. It is protected because the shepherd remains awake.

Parents and leaders must therefore move beyond vague concern and into a practical structure. They must ask: Who is allowed private access? Why? Under what conditions? Who communicates with children directly? What platforms are being used? What situations are creating exclusivity or emotional dependency? What patterns are quietly widening? These are not overreactions. They are stewardship questions. They help keep access from becoming emotional, social, or logistical chaos disguised as normal interaction.

Access control is also a way of teaching children something essential: not everyone gets unrestricted entry into your life. Not everyone gets your time, your trust, your attention, your personal space, or your private communication simply because they are older, respected, helpful, or admired. This lesson is deeply protective. It helps children understand that safety is not built on pleasing adults, but on wise limits. It teaches them that visibility is healthy, that boundaries are normal, and that adults who care well do not need secret channels in order to show concern.

The strongest access control systems are not reactive. They are established before tension appears. They are stated plainly, applied fairly, and upheld consistently. They do not shift based on charm, title, pressure, or social status. They create a culture where everyone understands the lines and no one is surprised when the lines are enforced.

This kind of consistency protects children because it removes confusion and makes it harder for unsafe adults to exploit special exceptions.

So keep the doors visible.
Keep the communication accountable.
Keep the access supervised.
Keep the boundaries clear.

Do not hand out privacy where wisdom requires structure.
Do not surrender oversight to convenience.
Do not let familiarity become a substitute for discernment.

Because access is often the first thing a predator studies, and wise guardians make sure it is also the first thing they guard.

SUPERVISION STRUCTURE

Boundaries must be supported by supervision. Rules without oversight become weak suggestions. Structure without follow-through becomes false security. A household, church, classroom, team, or ministry can speak strongly about protection and still remain vulnerable if no one is actually watching how those protections are being lived out. Children are not guarded by policies alone. They are guarded when those policies are embodied by adults who remain present, attentive, and unwilling to drift into careless assumption. Supervision is what gives boundaries weight. It is what turns stated values into lived protection.

Prevention requires proactive engagement. Parents must observe behavioral changes quickly. They must notice when a child becomes unusually secretive about an adult. They must question excessive attention. They must act decisively when boundaries are tested. Delay benefits the manipulator. Consistency protects the child. The longer troubling patterns go unexamined, the more room they have to become normal. What should have been interrupted early can become embedded when adults keep postponing the moment of honest scrutiny.

A supervision structure means adults remain aware of who is present, who is interacting with the child, under what circumstances, and with what level of transparency. It means children are not passed casually into the care of others without discernment. It means environments are not trusted simply because they are familiar. It means leaders and parents remain present enough to see patterns before those patterns become crises. Supervision is not merely being nearby physically. It is being mentally engaged, emotionally alert, and spiritually sober enough to register what is shifting beneath the surface.

Supervision is not overreaction. It is stewardship.

That truth must be established firmly, because many adults fear that strong supervision will make them appear controlling, suspicious, or extreme. But wise supervision does not emerge from panic. It emerges from responsibility. It is the sober understanding that children are too valuable to be left under casual oversight. It is a recognition that what is watched carefully is harder to manipulate quietly. It is not the child who should bear the burden of interpreting every relationship, every tone, every gesture, every shift in access, or every private dynamic. That burden belongs to the adults assigned to guard.

Supervision includes noticing who always wants to be alone with a child. It includes paying attention to adults who consistently create reasons for exclusive access. It includes questioning repeated "special attention" that seems to build loyalty, secrecy, or emotional dependence. It includes watching not only actions, but patterns. A single moment may not always reveal much, but repeated moments often tell the story. The adult who repeatedly volunteers for private time, repeatedly seeks emotional centrality, repeatedly offers unusual privileges, or repeatedly positions themselves between the child and ordinary visibility should not be ignored simply because each individual instance appears explainable.

A wise supervision structure also watches the child's side of the interaction. Does the child become tense when a certain person arrives? Defensive when simple questions are asked? Quiet after being alone with a particular adult? Overly attached in ways that seem emotionally unusual? Secretive about messages, gifts, conversations, or outings? These things matter. The goal is not to treat every irregularity as proof of harm, but to refuse the laziness that treats repeated patterns as meaningless. Supervision is strongest when adults are close enough to notice change and courageous enough to follow the change rather than dismiss it.

A strong supervision structure also communicates something powerful to both children and adults: this environment is guarded. That message matters. Children begin to feel the safety of visible protection. They sense that adults are paying attention, that access is not random, and that their lives are not being managed casually. At the same time, adults interacting with children receive a clear signal that this is not a loose environment where boundaries fade into the background. It is a guarded space. The lines are visible. The watchmen are awake. The patterns are being noticed.

Predatory strategies often rely on lax oversight. They flourish where adults are distracted, where accountability is inconsistent, and where behavior goes unexamined. They flourish where children are handed over without much thought, where unusual closeness is romanticized as kindness, where warning signs are softened by familiarity, and where no one wants to seem rude enough to ask why a pattern keeps repeating. But when a household or ministry maintains visible structure, quiet observation, and clear follow-through, strategy loses momentum. Predatory planning depends on gaps. Supervision reduces those gaps.

Structure discourages strategy.

That phrase carries tremendous weight. A visible adult presence. Open doors. Shared spaces. Clear communication. Check-ins before and after events. Follow-up questions. Limited unsupervised contact. Thoughtful awareness of who is creating emotional bonds and how. These are not oppressive measures. There are ways of closing the quiet spaces in which manipulation often prefers to grow. Structure does not accuse every person in advance. It simply refuses to make hidden access easy.

Supervision also requires adults to resist the seduction of routine. Familiarity can make people stop noticing. The same faces, same programs, same volunteers, same patterns, same trusted circles can slowly create a false sense that because something has always seemed normal, it must still be safe. But wise supervision never becomes lazy just because a setting is familiar. In fact, familiar environments sometimes require deeper attentiveness because they are the very places where people stop asking questions fastest. What has been repeated many times may still need to be examined if the pattern starts changing.

Grooming prevention also involves modeling strength. When parents enforce boundaries without apology, children learn that protection outweighs social pressure. When adults in the child's life see that oversight is firm and consistent, predatory strategies lose opportunity.

The child learns that no one gets automatic private access simply because they are liked, admired, useful, spiritual, or familiar. The surrounding adults learn that this family or ministry will not surrender the child to vague trust and emotional convenience. That clarity itself is protective.

A mature supervision structure also includes communication among responsible adults. Parents should not supervise in isolation from all other wise voices. Safe settings are strengthened when the adults involved know expectations clearly, share concerns soberly, and do not dismiss each other's observations carelessly. A teacher noticing something, a parent sensing a shift, a ministry leader observing a pattern, a coach detecting unusual closeness—these things should not be buried under politeness. They should be handled with seriousness. Supervision becomes stronger when adults are humble enough to compare notes and courageous enough to act when patterns align.

Most importantly, supervision must be consistent in both calm and crisis situations. Some adults become extremely alert after an incident but gradually drift back into looseness once the emotional urgency fades. That kind of inconsistency creates dangerous openings. Children are safest when supervision is not driven only by recent fear, but by ongoing conviction. The watchman's value is not proven only when danger is obvious. It is proven in the steady discipline of watching before danger becomes visible to everyone else.

So stay present.
Watch the patterns.
Follow the changes.

Notice who seeks privacy.
Notice who builds exclusivity.
Notice what keeps repeating.

Do not call it overreaction to guard what God has placed under your care.

Because supervision is not merely about seeing what is happening now. It is about seeing early enough to stop what others may only recognize once the damage has already begun.

HOUSEHOLD SAFETY RULES

Parents must educate their children clearly and calmly. Safety cannot remain an assumed value, quietly floating in the background of family life. It must be spoken, taught, repeated, and practiced until it becomes part of the way the household thinks. Children need more than vague encouragement to "be careful." They need clear language, repeated truth, and practical rules that help them recognize danger before danger gains momentum. A child should not have to guess what to do when something feels wrong. The home should have already made that path plain.

Children need to understand that the phrase "Don't tell your parents" is a major warning sign. That phrase should never be treated as small, playful, or harmless when it appears around matters of touch, private communication, gifts, access, outings, emotional dependence, or anything that causes discomfort. A child must be taught that any adult who discourages communication with parents is violating appropriate boundaries. Healthy adults do not need secrecy to care well for a child. Safe adults do not build relationships by teaching children to hide. The moment an adult begins trying to separate a child from parental visibility, that moment should be understood as dangerous ground.

Children must also be reassured repeatedly that telling the truth will never result in punishment for the act of telling. That reassurance matters because many children keep silent not only because of what someone threatened, but because of what they fear will happen at home if they speak. They may worry they will be blamed for not speaking sooner, judged for something they did not fully understand, or punished because they answered a message, accepted a gift, entered a room, or failed to say no quickly enough. Parents must dismantle that fear early. The child must know that protection comes before punishment, truth is welcomed, and honesty is never treated as betrayal.

These lessons must not be treated as one-time speeches. They must become part of the household culture. A family culture of safety is not built through one awkward conversation followed by silence. It is built through repeated instruction, calm reminders, open questions, healthy follow-up, and a home atmosphere where truth is easier to bring forward than secrecy is to maintain. Children need repeated clarity because the pressures they face are often repeated as well. What is taught once may be forgotten. What is taught often begins to become instinct.

Communication is one of the most powerful deterrents to grooming. When children feel heard and believed, secrecy loses power. When conversations about safety are normalized, manipulation weakens. Regular, open discussions about boundaries, discomfort, private communication, bodily safety, peer influence, and emotional pressure should be woven into everyday life—not reserved only for moments of visible crisis.

A child who knows that safety can be discussed naturally is more likely to speak when something subtle begins to feel wrong. A child reared in a home where difficult subjects are avoided may struggle to bring forward what feels awkward, confusing, or shameful.

Household safety rules should be simple enough for children to remember, yet clear enough to guide action. A child should know: I can always tell my parents the truth. No adult should ask me to keep secrets from my parents. My discomfort matters. My safety matters more than someone else's feelings. If something feels wrong, I must speak up immediately. These rules do more than transfer information. They create reflexes. They help children identify danger sooner, respond more confidently, and seek help without hesitation. In moments of pressure, clarity matters. A child who has heard these truths repeatedly is more likely to recognize that something is wrong before confusion fully settles in.

These rules also create a moral culture in the home. They teach the child that safety is not something negotiated around adult feelings. It is not secondary to politeness. It is not something that must wait until a situation becomes extreme. The child learns that discomfort is not trivial, that secrecy is not loyalty, that pressure is not kindness, and that safety outranks another person's desire for access. These lessons become part of how the child interprets relationships, authority, and their own right to speak.

The clearer the communication, the weaker the manipulation. Predators thrive where children are uncertain, where language is vague, where lines are blurry, and where the child is left to interpret too much alone. But when the rules of the home are direct, repeated, and embodied by the adults themselves, manipulation has a harder time gaining traction. A child who has been clearly taught is not immune to danger, but they are better equipped to recognize what does not belong. They are less likely to mistake secrecy for loyalty, pressure for affection, or uncomfortable attention for harmless care.

Prevention is not paranoia—it is preparedness. It is the deliberate construction of safeguards that reduce access, eliminate secrecy, and reinforce communication. That construction takes intention. It means parents do not merely hope children will know what to do. They teach them. It means they do not merely react once something goes wrong. They build wisdom into daily life before it does. It means household safety is treated as part of faithful parenting, not an occasional emergency response. Close the doors early. Address red flags immediately. Reinforce boundaries consistently. Normalize safety conversations regularly. These are not excessive measures. They are expressions of responsibility. They say, This house will not wait until confusion deepens to decide what matters. This family will not leave the child to navigate danger alone. This home will not surrender clarity to convenience.

Grooming depends on gradual progression. Prevention depends on immediate interruption. The earlier patterns are recognized, the less damage can occur. The stronger the boundaries, the fewer opportunities exist. The clearer the communication, the weaker the manipulation. Early action matters because many harms that later appear overwhelming first entered quietly. They grew because no one interrupted the pattern while it was still small enough to confront without ambiguity.

Prevention is not fear-driven—it is wisdom-driven. It is built by parents who understand that children deserve more than good intentions. They deserve a home where truth is practiced, safety is taught, and boundaries are visible. They deserve adults who do not grow embarrassed to speak plainly, too distracted to follow up, or too passive to regulate access. They deserve a household where protection is not assumed—it is enacted.

Guard proactively. Engage intentionally. Stand firmly. Let the rules of the household be more than words posted in memory. Let them become the daily language of a guarded home. Let children hear them, see them modeled, and feel their protection in the life of the family.

Because safety is not preserved by assumption—it is preserved by action.

❖ CLOSING CONVICTION ❖

Chapter Ten

Let this be said plainly, soberly, and without softening: failing to establish clear boundaries around children is not a minor parenting weakness. It is not a harmless oversight. It is not a small administrative gap that can be excused with, "I meant well." When God places a child under your care, He does not give you the option of casual guardianship. He gives you a charge. He gives you a post. He gives you a life to protect. And if you leave that life exposed through carelessness, fear of confrontation, emotional laziness, or refusal to establish structure, Heaven does not treat that lightly.

Establishing clear boundaries is not an act of suspicion—it is an act of love with structure. It is the refusal to leave innocence exposed in order to avoid awkwardness. It is the decision to value protection more than convenience, and clarity more than comfort. But when adults refuse to build those boundaries, what they are really saying—whether they realize it or not—is that the comfort of the environment matters more than the safety of the child. That is a dangerous message. That is a grievous exchange. And that exchange has cost too many children too much.

A household without boundaries may appear relaxed, easygoing, flexible, and socially comfortable, but it is not necessarily safe. In fact, what some call "laid back" is often just unguarded. What some call "trusting" is often just unexamined access. What some call "not wanting to offend anyone" is often the cowardice that lets danger breathe longer than it should. A household with boundaries may appear firm, but it is often deeply loving. Children do not suffer because too much wise structure was present. They suffer when access was too loose, oversight too weak, truth too delayed, and silence too tolerated.

This is the reality check: children are suffering all over this world while adults keep explaining away the very structures that could have reduced the opportunity for harm. Some children were not failed because nobody loved them. They were failed because the adults responsible for them refused to hold the line. They were failed because warning signs were ignored, access was handed out too freely, privacy was given where accountability was needed, and weak oversight was excused as normal. Love without structure is not enough. Concern without follow-through is not enough. Prayer without watchfulness is not enough. Good intentions without firm boundaries are not enough.

Boundaries protect what affection alone cannot. They guard privacy. They regulate access. They strengthen communication. They remove opportunities for manipulation to deepen unnoticed. They create environments where secrecy has less room to grow. They make it harder for predatory behavior to move quietly under the cover of familiarity. Without them, children are often left to bear the consequences of adult passivity. And no child should have to carry wounds because the watchman over them was too passive, too distracted, too intimidated, or too eager to keep peace with other adults.

Parents and leaders must not apologize for what protection requires. There are some doors that should remain closed. There are some forms of access that should remain restricted. There are some patterns that should be confronted immediately and without hesitation. There are some adults who should never be granted the privacy they seek. There are some lines that should never be crossed, blurred, or negotiated. And if enforcing those lines makes someone uncomfortable, then let them be uncomfortable. Better wounded pride in an adult than a wounded soul in a child.

This is where accountability before God must be faced honestly. The Lord does not merely watch the predator. He watches the watchman. He watches the parent. He watches the guardian. He watches the leader. He sees what was noticed and ignored. He sees what was sensed and silenced. He sees the moments when conviction stirred, and action was delayed. He sees when an adult chose social comfort over holy responsibility. And let no one deceive themselves: there will be no lasting refuge in excuses before God. Not "I didn't want to believe it." Not "I didn't want to accuse anyone." Not "I thought everything was fine." Not "I trusted them." If discernment was available and stewardship was neglected, accountability remains.

This is your wake-up call: innocence is too sacred for casual parenting. Children are too precious for lazy oversight. Boundaries are too necessary for adults to keep treating them like optional preferences. If you have been careless, wake up. If you have been too relaxed, wake up. If you have confused familiarity with safety, wake up. If you have let reputation silence your discernment, wake up. If you have ignored the shift in your child because you did not want to face what it might mean, wake up. This is not the hour for soft excuses. This is the hour for repentance, clarity, and holy resolve.

Because once innocence is violated, explanations lose their power. Once trust is fractured, regret does not restore what structure should have protected. Once harm is done, people may cry, apologize, and say they never meant for it to happen—but that does not erase the child's wound. This is why boundaries matter before the crisis, not after it. This is why visible structure matters before the damage, not only after exposure. This is why courage must move early, while people still think you are overreacting, because by the time everyone finally agrees something was wrong, the child may already have paid the price.

Safety must be built on more than good intentions. It must be built on a visible structure. On consistent supervision. On clear communication. On courage that does not bend under social pressure. On adults who fear God more than they fear awkwardness. On parents and leaders who understand that their assignment is sacred, and that sacred assignments must be guarded with seriousness.

So establish the boundaries. Hold the line. Stay watchful. Do not bend because someone is respected. Do not soften because someone is familiar. Do not relax because everyone else thinks you are too strict. Do not let the culture shame you out of protecting what God told you to guard.

Because the clearer the boundary, the stronger the protection. And the stronger the protection, the fewer openings evil has to exploit. And if God entrusted that child to you, then guarding that child is not optional.

It is your duty.
It is your stewardship.
It is your accountability before Heaven.

❖ SPIRITUAL WARNING ❖

A Warning Against Passive Protection

There is a dangerous illusion many guardians carry: I would know if something was wrong. That sentence has comforted more adults than it has protected children. It sounds confident, but often it is built on assumptions rather than vigilance. Harm does not always announce itself loudly. Manipulation does not always look threatening. Deception does not always feel sinister at first. Some of the deepest injuries enter quietly, behind normal routines, familiar faces, helpful gestures, spiritual language, and environments adults stopped examining because everything looked ordinary enough to trust.

The greatest vulnerability in a household is not always lack of love—it is passive protection. It is the kind of care that feels deeply but watches loosely. It is the kind of concern that speaks strongly in theory but acts slowly in reality. It is the kind of guardianship that assumes affection is enough while structure weakens, boundaries soften, oversight drifts, and warning signs are repeatedly explained away. You cannot guard what you casually monitor. You cannot defend what you inconsistently oversee. You cannot prevent what you refuse to confront. A child may be deeply loved and still dangerously under-protected if the watchman over them has become passive.

Spiritual negligence rarely begins with open rebellion. It begins with routine. It begins when vigilance becomes relaxed because nothing dramatic has occurred. It begins when prayer becomes symbolic rather than strategic. It begins when discernment is treated as optional rather than essential. It begins when adults slowly hand over access because people seem nice, familiar, useful, spiritual, or trusted by others. It begins when the parent stops asking deeper questions because life is busy, the atmosphere is comfortable, and no one wants to disturb what appears peaceful. But peace without watchfulness can be an illusion, and normal appearances have concealed many tragedies.

Darkness does not require chaos to advance. It requires access. It requires openings. It requires adults who are willing to call things harmless before they have truly been examined. When boundaries are loosened to avoid conflict, when secrecy is excused as privacy, when discomfort is dismissed to preserve relationships, an opening is formed. That opening may seem small, but small openings can still invite serious damage. Evil often moves through the door that adults were too tired, too trusting, too intimidated, or too passive to close in time.

This is not written to incite fear. It is written to awaken conviction. There is a difference. Fear paralyzes. Conviction mobilizes. Fear imagines danger everywhere. Conviction learns how danger actually works and stands ready to interrupt it. This warning is not a call to panic. It is a call to wakefulness. It is a call to throw off the spiritual sleep that has made too many guardians slow to move when they should have acted, slow to question when they should have investigated, slow to tighten boundaries when they should have held the line.

God does not entrust children casually. When a child is placed under your authority, it is not only a blessing—it is a sacred assignment. That assignment carries accountability. It carries expectation. It carries holy weight. The child is not merely under your roof. The child is under your stewardship before God. That means your role is not fulfilled by provision alone. It is not fulfilled by saying you care. It is not fulfilled by hoping things remain fine. It demands active guardianship. It demands attentiveness. It demands moral courage. It demands the willingness to act before certainty becomes proof and before hidden danger becomes visible damage.

Let this reality settle with force: children are suffering all over the world while adults keep assuming they would know. Children are being manipulated while guardians keep trusting appearances. Children are carrying confusion while adults keep protecting comfort. Children are learning silence while parents keep delaying hard questions. Some are suffering because the very adults who should have guarded them were too casual with access, too weak with boundaries, too distracted to notice change, or too emotionally compromised to confront what they sensed.

This is not a small matter before God. It is a grievous failure when those assigned to protect refuse to stand watch with seriousness.

If something unsettles you, investigate immediately. Do not silence the stirring because you lack full language for it. Do not train yourself to distrust discernment simply because you cannot yet prove what is wrong. If patterns feel inconsistent, address them directly. If access appears excessive, restrict it firmly. If your child changes, if secrecy increases, if someone keeps needing private space with your child, if the atmosphere around a relationship begins to feel guarded, strange, or emotionally heavy, move toward the issue. Do not wait for the pattern to mature. Do not wait for the child to collapse. Do not wait until everyone else can finally see what you were supposed to watch.

Better to confront early than to regret later. Better to enforce boundaries than to repair broken trust. Better to be thought cautious than to stand before God knowing you ignored what should have been examined. Better to disturb a relationship than bury a child under preventable pain. Adults often fear being wrong in confrontation, but the far greater fear should be being late in protection. Some things can be corrected if addressed early. Some things become lifelong wounds if delayed too long.

Heaven does not measure how calm your home appeared. Heaven measures how faithfully you guarded it. That truth must cut through every excuse. God is not deceived by a peaceful-looking atmosphere if the gate is unguarded. He is not persuaded by how respected the adults were, how polished the image seemed, or how socially comfortable everything looked from the outside. He sees whether the watchman was awake. He sees whether warning signs were honored or silenced. He sees whether the parent chose faithfulness over ease, courage over politeness, and truth over appearances.

The watchman who waits for visible danger often responds too late. The guardian who hesitates because of social pressure may carry lifelong regret. Comfort cannot outrank responsibility. No adult's feelings should matter more than a child's safety. No reputation should matter more than innocence. No title should matter more than truth. No relationship should be protected at the cost of the vulnerable.

If maintaining social peace requires you to ignore what may threaten a child, then that peace is corrupt and must be disturbed.

Let this settle deeply: your child's safety must matter more than someone else's feelings. You were not assigned to be agreeable. You were assigned to be vigilant. You were not called to keep everyone comfortable. You were called to guard what cannot guard itself. You were not placed at the gate to smile at every approach. You were placed there to regulate access, to discern what is wrong, and to stand between innocence and intrusion with holy seriousness.

This is your reality check.
Wake up if you have grown passive.
Wake up if you have confused love with leniency.
Wake up if you have called loose oversight "trust."
Wake up if you have been more afraid of offending adults than failing children.
Wake up if you have been praying without watching, feeling without acting, or sensing without confronting.

Passive protection is not protection at all. It is the appearance of concern without the substance of guardianship. And once innocence is compromised, no explanation will ever feel sufficient. Not I didn't want to overreact. Not I never thought it could happen. Not They seemed like good people. Not I trusted them. Not I was trying to keep peace. Those words will never carry the weight of a child's wound.

Stand alert.
Stand decisive.
Stand unwavering.
Stand as one who knows God is watching how you watch.

Because when Heaven places a child under your care, it is not asking whether you meant well.
It is asking whether you guarded well.

CHAPTER ELEVEN
DIGITAL VIGILANCE
Guarding the Modern Gate

✦

The Modern Gate of Influence

Digital vigilance has become one of the most urgent responsibilities of modern parenthood. Previous generations guarded front doors, windows, neighborhoods, and physical access points with watchful care. Those protections still matter. But today, many of the most powerful influences no longer knock at the front door. They enter through screens, notifications, streaming platforms, gaming systems, social media feeds, private messages, hidden apps, disappearing content, algorithm-driven suggestions, and constant digital access. The danger is no longer only what walks up the driveway. It is also what reaches the child silently, repeatedly, and persuasively through a device that may sit only inches from their hands, eyes, and mind.

The modern gate is no longer only physical.
It is digital.
It is emotional.
It is spiritual.

A child can be physically inside the home and still be exposed to influences that bypass parental awareness entirely. A locked door does not stop a corrupt message. A quiet bedroom does not guarantee safety. A device placed in a child's hand without oversight becomes an open gate to voices, images, agendas, manipulation, and confusion that may quietly shape the child long before the parent ever sees a visible change. In many homes, the child is under the roof but not fully under protection, because the digital gate has been left wider open than the front door ever would have been.

This is why digital vigilance cannot be treated as optional, excessive, or temporary. It is not a side issue for overprotective parents. It is part of faithful stewardship in an age where access is immediate, private, persuasive, and often addictive. The digital world is not neutral terrain.

It is a contested environment, filled with influences that do not all care about the child's soul. Some aim to entertain. Some aim to persuade. Some aim to exploit. Some aim to distort identity, normalize confusion, desensitize conscience, isolate the child emotionally, or slowly erode the boundaries that protect innocence.

The question is no longer, Who comes into my home? It is also, What enters my child through the screen? What voices are discipling them? What images are shaping their imagination? What patterns are influencing their desires, fears, insecurities, expectations, and identity? A gate left unguarded does not remain empty for long. If parents do not govern what enters digitally, something else will. And what governs a child repeatedly often begins to shape that child deeply.

Digital access carries a unique danger because it often feels harmless at first. A screen may appear quiet. A message may appear casual. A video may seem small. A platform may seem normal because "everyone uses it." But digital influence rarely remains small when it is repeated. What is seen repeatedly becomes familiar. What becomes familiar begins to feel normal. What feels normal begins to shape belief. And what shapes belief eventually shapes behavior. The child may not realize they are being formed by the digital environment, but formation is happening nonetheless.

This is where many parents need a reality check. Some are guarding the physical home while leaving the digital gate unguarded day and night. They would never let a stranger sit alone with their child in the bedroom, but they allow unmonitored devices to do exactly that through apps, messages, video calls, gaming chats, suggestive content, pornography, ideological manipulation, predatory contact, and algorithm-fed images that keep returning until the imagination is no longer innocent in the same way.

This is not a light matter. Many children are being shaped, seduced, misled, isolated, and spiritually dulled by what enters quietly through a screen, while adults assume the home is safe because the child has never left the house.

Digital influence is also relentless. It does not tire. It does not wait politely. It does not require a special occasion to reach the child. It can enter early in the morning, late at night, in moments of loneliness, boredom, insecurity, anger, or curiosity. It can meet the child in private emotional spaces and begin shaping them there. If the child feels unseen, digital voices will speak. If the child feels insecure, digital culture will offer a sense of identity. If the child feels curious, the digital world will answer—often long before the parent even knows the question existed. That is why digital vigilance is not only about restriction. It is about shepherding influence.

The spiritual dimension of this cannot be ignored. The screen is not merely a tool. It is a channel. And channels carry influence. Some influences strengthen wisdom, learning, creativity, and healthy connections. But some influence corrupts slowly. Some carry impurity, comparison, lust, despair, false identity, mockery of holiness, contempt for authority, and subtle emotional manipulation. Some digital spaces normalize what should grieve the conscience. Some train children to laugh at what should alarm them. Some invite them into private rooms of confusion before they are mature enough to understand what is being planted in their minds.

Parents must therefore stop thinking of digital vigilance as a minor technical issue and start seeing it as a frontline matter of discipleship and protection. The child is not only consuming content. The child is being catechized by whatever appears most often before their eyes and settles most deeply into their imagination. Screens teach. Feeds disciple. Algorithms preach. Notifications interrupt thought patterns and create cravings. Private messages build secret emotional worlds. Hidden apps create concealed access. Late-night scrolling often invites thoughts and images into the child's inner life that no wise parent would ever intentionally permit face-to-face in the living room.

This calls for holy seriousness. God will hold parents accountable not only for who they physically allowed near their children, but also for what they casually permitted to disciple their children in private. A parent cannot say, I was there in the house, if the child was being shaped by a corrupt influence behind a locked screen and no one cared enough to examine the gate. This is not said to produce panic. It is said to produce awakening. Too many adults are asleep at the digital wall.

Too many are handing children powerful tools without strong oversight, then acting surprised when secrecy, confusion, emotional volatility, addictive patterns, sexual corruption, or hidden relationships begin to surface. The surprise is often not because there were no warning signs. It is because the gate was treated casually.

Digital vigilance, therefore, requires more than device settings. It requires a mindset. It requires parents who understand that the modern gate must be watched with the same seriousness as doors, streets, and neighborhoods once were. It requires adults who ask not only what the child is doing online, but what the online world is doing to the child. It requires spiritual discernment, emotional presence, practical boundaries, and the courage to regulate access even when the culture mocks such caution as unnecessary.

Children are too valuable to be reared inside homes that are physically guarded and digitally neglected. A device in the wrong atmosphere, with the wrong level of secrecy, at the wrong stage of maturity, under the wrong level of oversight, can become a training ground for confusion, addiction, isolation, predatory contact, and spiritual erosion. That is why parents must not shrug at the modern gate. They must stand there.

Watch what enters.
Watch what repeats.
Watch what shapes imagination.
Watch what normalizes darkness.
Watch what whispers identity, desire, and worth into the child's mind.

Because a gate left unguarded does not remain empty for long, and in this generation, many of the voices shaping children are not standing outside the home asking permission to enter. They are already inside the screen, waiting for a parent careless enough to leave the gate open.

DEVICE OVERSIGHT

Device oversight is one of the clearest ways a parent guards the modern gate. Devices are useful tools, but they are also access points. A phone, tablet, laptop, gaming console, smart television, smartwatch, or internet-connected device is not merely technology—it is a channel of influence. It carries voices, values, images, invitations, ideologies, temptations, predators, pressures, and patterns into a child's inner world. A parent must stop thinking of devices as neutral objects that become dangerous only in extreme situations. They are modern gateways, and gateways must be guarded.

Parents must understand this plainly: a device without oversight becomes a door without a lock. It is access without structure. It is influence without filtering. It is exposure without accountability. And in many homes, devices are being placed in children's hands with more freedom than the front door, more privacy than the family car, and more unsupervised access than parents would ever allow in physical space. That is not wisdom. That is a dangerous contradiction.

Oversight is not distrust. It is protection. It is structured. It is wisdom. It is the adult who refuses to abandon their post simply because the threat is digital rather than physical. Children and teenagers do not yet possess the maturity, discernment, or emotional steadiness to manage every influence presented to them through digital devices. They may be curious without being cautious. They may be technologically skilled without being spiritually grounded. They may know how to navigate a platform while having no real understanding of the hidden dangers behind what appears entertaining, harmless, or popular. A child may know how to open an app long before they know how to discern a lie, resist grooming, identify manipulation, or process what repeated sexualized or violent content is doing to their imagination.

That is why device oversight must be intentional. Parents should know which devices their children use, when and where they use them, which apps are installed, who they communicate with, which platforms they frequent, and whether private or disappearing communication features are active. These are not excessive questions. They are baseline responsibilities in a digital age. A parent who does not know what is regularly entering the child's mind through a screen is not truly overseeing the gate. They may be physically nearby, but they are absent where influence is actually being formed.

Unrestricted late-night device usage invites secrecy. Private browsing without accountability invites hidden exposure. Locked screens that parents never examine create distance where oversight should exist. Devices in bedrooms behind closed doors increase vulnerability, not independence. What is called privacy in modern culture often becomes the cover under which addiction, isolation, predatory contact, pornography, self-harm content, identity confusion, emotional manipulation, and hidden relationships take root. Many children are being discipled in private by things their parents have never examined because adults have surrendered oversight in the name of convenience, peace, or fear of conflict.

Let this be a reality check: some parents are failing their children digitally while still imagining they are protecting them physically. They pay attention to seatbelts, schools, locked doors, and curfews, yet hand over devices that grant direct access to corruption, seduction, shame, and spiritual erosion. Then, when the child's heart changes, sleep patterns shift, secrecy deepens, emotional instability rises, or hidden content is discovered, adults act surprised. But surprise is often what happens when stewardship has been replaced by assumption. A child should not suffer because the modern gate was treated casually.

Digital privacy is often celebrated in culture, but parental stewardship requires visibility. A child's safety must matter more than the culture's demand for unrestricted personal access. The world may call it controlling. Heaven calls it guarding.

The world may tell parents they are violating trust by checking devices. But what kind of trust leaves a child undefended in a digital world engineered to capture attention, exploit curiosity, and normalize hidden access? Trust without oversight is not biblical wisdom. It is often passive protection wearing modern language.

Healthy oversight may include keeping devices in shared spaces, setting time limits, requiring password transparency, regularly reviewing apps, disabling private browsing where possible, restricting downloads without parental knowledge, and establishing device-free times and zones within the home. It may also include removing internet-enabled devices from bedrooms at night, disabling notifications during sleep hours, checking message settings, reviewing contact lists, examining gaming chat features, and having regular conversations about what the child sees, hears, feels, and hides. Structure is not punishment. It is protection. It is the parent refusing to let the child navigate an aggressive digital world without rails, covering, and accountability.

Parents must also understand that oversight is not only about catching wrongdoing. It is about shaping wisdom. It teaches children that access carries responsibility, that influence matters, that privacy is not always safe, and that freedom must be governed by maturity. A wise parent is not only trying to prevent disaster. They are training discernment. They are teaching the child how to live with technology without becoming mastered by it, deceived by it, or silently wounded through it.

Device oversight also requires parental honesty about their own stewardship. Some adults are too digitally distracted to notice what their children are becoming digitally dependent on. Some are so immersed in their own screens that they have little moral authority when trying to regulate the child's screen time. Some want peace more than engagement, so the device becomes a babysitter, pacifier, reward system, or escape hatch rather than a tool under clear limits. But a screen that keeps the child quiet is not necessarily helping the child. Sometimes it is merely making the child easier to ignore while harmful influences move in quietly.

This is where the warning from God must be heard clearly: if He entrusted a child to your care, then you are accountable for how you guard the gates of their life—including the digital ones. You will not stand innocent before Heaven because the danger was technological instead of physical. A digital doorway is still a doorway. A hidden message is still a hidden influence. A private feed is still a private voice shaping the soul. The Lord is not confused by modern tools. He still requires watchfulness from those assigned to guard. Parents cannot hide behind phrases like "I didn't know how it worked," "everyone else lets their kids have it," or "I didn't want to upset them." Those excuses may comfort the passive adult, but they will not heal the child harmed by neglected oversight.

Children may not always appreciate oversight in the moment. But parental faithfulness is not measured by a child's immediate approval. It is measured by consistent stewardship. A wise parent understands that discipline today may prevent devastation tomorrow. The child may roll their eyes at limits, protest the checks, resent the restrictions, or compare your standards to homes with weaker walls. But the calling of a parent is not to win a popularity contest. It is to stand at the gate. It is to be faithful when culture says to relax, when convenience says to ignore it, and when social pressure says to let it slide.

So know the devices.
Know the apps.
Know the hours.
Know the contacts.
Know the habits.
Know what enters through the screen.
Know what your child is carrying after they put the screen down.

Because a device without oversight is not a small risk, it is a modern opening. And if you leave that opening unguarded, do not call it trust. Call it what it is: exposure.

ONLINE PREDATORS

One of the gravest reasons digital vigilance is essential is the reality of online predators. Predators no longer need physical proximity to begin manipulation. They no longer need to stand near the school gate, linger in the neighborhood, or seek direct access through familiar community roles before contact begins. They can initiate contact through games, messaging apps, social media platforms, video chats, online communities, live streams, hidden accounts, and comment threads—all while appearing harmless, friendly, relatable, supportive, or even childlike. They can enter a child's life without ever setting foot inside the house, and that reality should shake every parent out of digital passivity.

This is what makes digital danger so deceptive. The predator may be miles away and still be emotionally present in the child's world every day. He may not look dangerous. He may not sound threatening. He may not begin with anything openly sexual, aggressive, or alarming. He may begin with attention. With humor. With shared interests. With flattery. With emotional availability. With the kind of listening that makes a lonely child feel noticed. He may study the child's posts, their tone, their interests, their insecurities, their boredom, their curiosity, their social isolation, their frustrations with home, and their need for affirmation. The digital world gives him access not only to the child's screen but also to the child's emotional landscape.

Predators often do not appear predatory at first. They appear attentive. Interested. Kind. Funny. Understanding. They may flatter a child, mirror their interests, listen to their frustrations, comment on their appearance, praise their maturity, or offer the kind of attention that feels validating to a lonely or curious heart. That is part of the danger. They do not begin by frightening the child. They begin by appealing to the child. They know that once emotional trust begins to form, the child may stop evaluating the interaction soberly. What feels like friendship to the child may actually be calculated access in the mind of the predator.

They study emotional openings. They look for loneliness. They look for curiosity. They look for secrecy. They look for children who feel unseen, misunderstood, angry, insecure, or eager for connection. They know how to spot children who post emotionally vulnerable content, who seek validation in public ways, who seem isolated socially, or who respond quickly to attention. They do not always need a rebellious child. Sometimes they prefer the sensitive child, the curious child, the trusting child, the child who wants to be polite, or the child who is desperate to feel special. Digital spaces make this easier because children often reveal far more about themselves online than they would ever say aloud in a living room.

And because digital communication creates distance from parental observation, those interactions can deepen quickly without immediate detection. A parent may see only a quiet child looking at a screen. But beneath that silence, a manipulative relationship may already be building. This is one of the greatest deceptions of digital danger: the room appears calm while the child's emotional safety is being steadily compromised. The child may be physically safe inside the house and still be under the influence of someone who is studying, flattering, pressuring, and grooming them in private.

Predatory behavior online often follows familiar patterns: initiating seemingly casual conversation, building emotional rapport, increasing private communication, asking personal questions, introducing secrecy, testing boundaries, and eventually shifting toward manipulation, exploitation, or grooming. At first, the contact may look insignificant. A comment. A joke. A direct message. A gaming chat. A response to a story. A "how are you?" Then it becomes more personal. More frequent. More private. The predator may begin asking about the child's feelings, friendships, conflicts at home, insecurities, or daily habits. He may try to find out when the child is alone, how closely the device is monitored, whether the parent checks messages, and how far secrecy can go without being interrupted.

The danger is not only explicit content or overt threats. The danger is relationship-building with hidden intent. That is the trap many adults still fail to recognize. They imagine danger only once the conversation becomes openly sexual or once the request becomes clearly inappropriate. But by then, the emotional groundwork may already be laid. The child may already trust the person, feel attached to the attention, and fear losing the relationship. The predator may already know what the child longs to hear, what the child fears, and what emotional pressure will work best.

A child may think, This person understands me.
A predator thinks, This child is becoming accessible.

That contrast must be understood clearly. The child interprets the attention through the lens of need. The predator interprets the interaction through the lens of opportunity. The child may feel chosen, noticed, and cared for. The predator may feel progress, leverage, and increasing control. That is why digital grooming is so dangerous. It often does not feel dangerous to the child in the early stages. It feels validating. It feels exciting. It feels private in a way that seems special rather than threatening—until the pressure shifts.

Parents must teach children clearly: not every online friend is who they claim to be; no one online has a right to private images; no one has a right to sexualized conversation; no one should ask them to hide communication from their parents; and any request for secrecy is a warning sign, not a compliment. These truths must be spoken plainly, repeated often, and backed by a home atmosphere where questions can be asked without shame. A child must know that strangers are not the only risk. Someone who feels emotionally familiar online can still be deeply unsafe. A profile picture can lie. A username can lie. A claimed age can lie. A kind tone can lie. A child needs to know that digital familiarity does not equal safety.

Children should also be taught that predators often use fear, guilt, and emotional manipulation once contact deepens. They may threaten exposure. They may say, "You'll get in trouble too." They may claim emotional attachment. They may say, "You're all I have," "Don't betray me," or "If you tell, you'll ruin everything."

They may pressure the child into sending photos, keeping secrets, staying online late, deleting messages, moving to another app, or proving loyalty. They may shift from kindness to intimidation quickly once they sense the child is hesitant. This is part of the sick-mindedness of online predation: the same person who pretended to care may become cruel the moment secrecy is threatened.

Some predators also weaponize shame. Once a child has shared something personal, answered an inappropriate message, sent an image, or participated in a conversation they regret, the predator may use that moment to deepen control. The child may feel trapped, thinking, I've already messed up. I can't tell now. I'll be blamed. My parents will be angry. Everyone will know. This is why parents must not only teach rules. They must build a relationship strong enough that the child believes truth can still be told after a mistake. Otherwise, shame becomes the predator's accomplice.

This is also where God's warning must fall heavily on adult hearts. Too many parents are underestimating this battlefield. Too many are treating devices like toys while predators treat them like hunting grounds. Too many have given children digital freedom far beyond their maturity and called it trust. Too many are allowing private accounts, disappearing messages, locked screens, late-night device access, and unmonitored platforms while assuming that "my child would never" or "I would know if something was wrong." That kind of passive thinking is not harmless. It is exposure. And if God entrusted that child to your care, you will answer for whether you guarded the digital gate with seriousness or left it open through laziness, distraction, fear of conflict, or technological ignorance.

This is your reality check: predators are actively searching where many parents are sleeping. They are moving through apps while their parents scroll their own screens. They are building rapport while guardians assume the child is just "online." They are studying children while adults are still debating whether oversight is too strict. But Heaven is not confused about this moment. God sees the modern gate. He sees what enters through the screen, what disciples the imagination, what manipulates the heart, and what adults have failed to regulate.

A parent cannot plead innocence because the danger was digital. Neglected oversight is still neglected oversight. Unwatched gates are still unwatched gates.

This is why ongoing conversation is essential. If children only receive rules without relational connection, they may hide digital mistakes out of fear. But when they know their parents will respond with truth, strength, and protection, they are more likely to disclose concerns before damage deepens. A child needs both structure and refuge. They need boundaries, but they also need a place to run when those boundaries are crossed, when confusion has already set in, or when shame tries to keep them silent.

Parents must become students of this battlefield. They must know the platforms, the risks, the hidden features, the disappearing tools, the private channels, the fake accounts, the emotional hooks, and the escalation patterns. Not because fear should rule the home, but because stewardship must. It is no longer enough to say, Be careful online.

Parents must know what "online" actually means in their child's life, which doors are open, which conversations are happening, and which patterns are forming.

So teach clearly.
Watch closely.
Check regularly.
Ask directly.
Stay involved.
Do not hand your child a modern gate and then walk away from the wall.

Because online predators do not need to enter the house physically to reach the child, they only need a screen, silence, and a parent passive enough to leave the gate unguarded.

SOCIAL MEDIA INFLUENCER PREDATOR

Social media does more than entertain. It shapes perception, identity, desire, attention span, self-worth, emotional regulation, and worldview. It does not merely show children and teenagers what others are doing; it silently teaches them what to admire, what to desire, what to envy, what to imitate, and what to normalize. It can influence a child or teenager long before the parent sees the fruit of that influence in language, behavior, mood, modesty, conviction, or moral sensitivity. By the time the outward change appears, the inward shaping may already have been happening for quite some time.

The influence of social media is constant because it is repetitive. What is seen repeatedly becomes familiar. What becomes familiar often begins to feel normal. What feels normal eventually begins to shape belief and behavior. This is why social media influence must not be underestimated. It is not merely a platform for content. It is an atmosphere of repetition. It trains through constant exposure. It conditions through pattern. It teaches not only through obvious messages, but through tone, humor, imagery, reward systems, and the emotional weight attached to visibility and approval.

Children and teenagers are often exposed to comparison culture, curated false identities, sexualized content, distorted beauty standards, rebellion framed as authenticity, disrespect framed as boldness, confusion framed as freedom, and visibility treated as value. Over time, this can quietly reshape identity. The child may begin to absorb the idea that to be seen is to matter, that to be desired is to be valuable, that to be envied is to be successful, that to be provocative is to be powerful, and that to be constantly noticed is to be worthy. These are not harmless messages. They are counterfeit measurements of human worth.

A child may begin measuring their value by reactions, likes, views, comments, shares, and digital affirmation. A teenager may feel pressure to perform, to appear desirable, to remain visible, or to imitate voices that are popular rather than righteous. Self-worth can become tied to digital approval. Insecurity can deepen while appearance seems confident. A child may look bold online while inwardly becoming fragile, dependent on applause, and unable to rest without the reassurance of attention. This is one of the quiet corruptions of social media: it teaches children to seek identity in being watched rather than in being grounded.

Social media also distorts time, focus, and emotional steadiness. It trains the mind to move quickly from image to image, outrage to outrage, trend to trend, comparison to comparison. The child may become accustomed to constant stimulation and lose the inner stillness needed for reflection, prayer, patience, and sober thought. This matters spiritually. A constantly flooded mind is often easier to distract, easier to agitate, and harder to settle before God. The child may not know why they feel restless, fragmented, or emotionally thin. Yet the repeated digital atmosphere may be quietly discipling them into instability.

Social media also amplifies emotional pressure. It increases exposure to cyberbullying, peer exclusion, subtle humiliation, unhealthy comparison, envy, constant overstimulation, and the feeling that everyone else is happier, prettier, more accepted, more exciting, and more visible. A child may appear outwardly fine while inwardly becoming anxious, discouraged, distracted, emotionally fragmented, and quietly burdened by the pressure to keep up. Some children are not merely scrolling; they are suffering while they scroll. They are watching other people's curated lives and concluding false things about their own worth, their own body, their own family, and their own future.

This is where parents need a reality check. Many are handing children direct access to social media and then acting surprised when self-worth becomes unstable, modesty begins to erode, attention spans weaken, emotional sensitivity rises, and spiritual conviction becomes thinner. But social media is not just "something kids use." It is one of the most aggressive shaping forces in the modern world. It reaches the eyes repeatedly, the imagination quietly, the emotions constantly, and the conscience gradually. If left unexamined, it can become a silent discipler in the child's life—teaching values the parents never intended to permit.

Parents must not assume that because content is common, it is harmless. What is normalized on social media is not automatically healthy. What is popular is not automatically safe. What is trending is not automatically true. Many destructive ideas become dangerous precisely because they are presented as ordinary, humorous, liberating, empowering, fashionable, or widely accepted. Repetition gives error the appearance of legitimacy. Popularity gives distortion the appearance of truth. But a lie repeated often enough is still a lie, even if millions applaud it.

Social media also creates a dangerous moral confusion by rewarding exhibition and punishing quietness. It teaches children that private growth is less valuable than public performance, that hidden character matters less than visible image, and that attention is a form of currency to be pursued at almost any cost. This can make humility appear weak, modesty appear outdated, reverence appear strange, and self-restraint appear unnecessary. But a child shaped by Scripture cannot be left undefended in an environment that rewards the very things holiness often resists.

Digital vigilance, therefore, requires more than blocking explicit material. It requires helping children interpret what they see. Parents must ask questions, initiate conversation, and teach discernment. They must help children understand that not everything visible is honest, not everything celebrated is righteous, and not everything admired is worthy of imitation. A child must learn not only how to avoid danger, but how to recognize distortion. They must learn to ask: What is this trying to make me want? What is this teaching me to admire? What does this say about my worth? Is this drawing me toward truth or away from it?

Parents must also be willing to confront the lie that unrestricted access to social media is necessary for belonging. Belonging purchased at the cost of innocence is too expensive. Visibility purchased at the cost of peace is too high a price. Digital participation without wise limits is not proof of healthy development. Sometimes it is simply adult surrender to cultural pressure. A child does not need unlimited access to everything the culture celebrates. A child needs wise protection from what the culture normalizes but cannot govern.

This is where accountability before God must be taken seriously. If He entrusted a child to your care, then you are responsible not only for feeding them, housing them, and loving them in sentiment, but also for guarding their influences and discipling their mind. You cannot leave a child under the constant preaching of social media and then act shocked when their values, identity, and emotional stability begin to shift. Heaven will not call that harmless modern life. Heaven will call the parents to account for what they allowed to shape the child unchecked. This is not written to condemn parents into panic. It is written to wake them up. Too many have mistaken digital commonness for moral safety.

A child must learn that identity is not built on views, worth is not measured in likes, filters do not define beauty, trends do not decide truth, and freedom is not the right to imitate every visible voice. Those lessons do not grow automatically. They must be taught. Reinforced. Modeled. Protected. A parent who fails to teach these things is leaving the child exposed to a system that is already teaching the opposite.

So do not merely ask what your child is posting.
Ask what social media is forming in them.
Do not merely ask whether the content is explicit.
Ask whether it is shaping appetite, insecurity, vanity, rebellion, or confusion.
Do not merely block the worst.
Interpret the rest.

Because social media influence is not light.
It is forming hearts, discipling imaginations, and reshaping identity in real time.
And if parents will not stand at this gate with sobriety and conviction, the digital crowd will gladly rear the child in their place.

SPIRITUAL WARFARE OVER THE HOME

Spiritual warfare is not symbolic language—it is a lived reality. It is not confined to dramatic manifestations, sensational stories, or rare moments of visible crisis. It operates quietly, consistently, and strategically in everyday environments. It moves through patterns, atmospheres, influences, appetites, distractions, and compromises. Every home exists within a spiritual atmosphere, and whether acknowledged or ignored, that atmosphere influences thought patterns, behaviors, emotions, reactions, desires, and decisions. A family may not often speak about spiritual warfare, yet still live in the middle of it every day.

Ephesians 6:12–13 (KJV) declares, "For we wrestle not against flesh and blood, but against principalities, against powers, against the rulers of the darkness of this world, against spiritual wickedness in high places. Wherefore take unto you the whole armour of God." This passage removes illusion. The battles confronting families are not merely social, cultural, educational, emotional, or psychological. There is a spiritual dimension that seeks to undermine peace, distort identity, weaken conviction, fracture unity, normalize compromise, and dull discernment until what should have been confronted is quietly tolerated. The visible problems are often fed by invisible neglect.

For parents, this truth elevates responsibility. Protecting a home is not only about locks, schedules, routines, education, and supervision. It requires spiritual guardianship. It requires awareness that unseen forces attempt to influence visible outcomes. A parent who ignores the spiritual dimension may spend years fighting symptoms while leaving the deeper roots unchallenged. They may try to manage behavior without examining the atmosphere, regulate their schedule without guarding their influence, or address emotional instability without confronting what is feeding it spiritually. But a home cannot remain truly guarded if its protectors only see what is natural while neglecting what is spiritual.

This is where many need a wakeup call. Some parents are guarding doors while leaving the atmosphere unguarded. They are monitoring attendance, meals, grades, and routines, yet failing to ask what is shaping the house's spiritual climate. They assume that because the family is functioning, the home must be fine. But a home can remain outwardly functional while inwardly becoming spiritually weakened. Peace can be replaced by tension, sensitivity by numbness, truth by confusion, vigilance by passivity, and holiness by quiet compromise—and all of it can happen slowly enough that no one notices the atmosphere changing until the fruit begins showing up in behavior, hunger, attitude, speech, and emotional fragility.

Digital exposure is not only technological. It is spiritual territory. What repeatedly enters a household's eyes and ears helps shape its atmosphere. What is consumed regularly does not remain external. It begins to influence perspective, hunger, sensitivity, resistance, and appetite. What the family watches, laughs at, excuses, listens to, scrolls through, normalizes, and permits into the imagination eventually begins to settle into the house itself. The issue is not only whether the content is entertaining. The issue is what the content is training the heart to tolerate. Entertainment choices must therefore be evaluated carefully. Media that glorify darkness, normalize occult themes, sexualize children, trivialize violence, mock purity, celebrate rebellion, or make perversion appear ordinary gradually desensitize the atmosphere.

What is repeatedly consumed eventually influences perception. It teaches the conscience what to shrug at. It teaches the imagination what to replay. It teaches the emotions what to crave. It teaches the mind what to normalize. A child who repeatedly consumes confusion will not remain spiritually clear. A home that repeatedly welcomes corruption through the screen should not be surprised when moral resistance begins to weaken. Spiritual warfare includes guarding what enters the eye gate and ear gate. That phrase must not be treated lightly. The eye gate and ear gate are not passive openings. They are entry points. They are pathways through which imagery, language, ideology, seduction, fear, impurity, comparison, and emotional pressure can travel inward.

Parents who neglect these gates while claiming to care about the soul of the home are failing to understand how warfare often works now. Darkness does not need to break down the front door if it is already being invited through the screen, the speaker, the algorithm, the playlist, the video, and the private feed.

A family that treats screens casually may eventually find its atmosphere altered quietly. Confusion may increase. Peace may weaken. Moral resistance may soften. The home may remain outwardly functional while, spiritually, becoming less guarded, less sensitive, and less anchored. Arguments may become more common. Impatience may increase. Respect may weaken. Modesty may erode. Prayer may become irregular. The Word may feel distant. Things that once grieved the conscience may barely register. This is how erosion often works—not through one dramatic collapse, but through repeated tolerated influence that keeps pressing the soul until holy sensitivity begins to dull.

The atmosphere is never neutral.

That truth needs to strike with force. Every home is being shaped by something. If truth is not actively governing the atmosphere, then other forces are. If prayer is not strengthening the walls, then spiritual drift is already weakening them. If Scripture is not clarifying the conscience, then the culture is gladly discipling the imagination in its place. If watchfulness is absent, then subtle compromise is rarely absent for long. Neutrality in the home is an illusion. What is not intentionally guarded will eventually be influenced by something stronger than passivity.

This is also where accountability before God becomes sobering. Parents cannot say they did not know warfare was happening simply because it did not look dramatic. They cannot stand before God and act as though the condition of the home was outside their responsibility while they repeatedly allowed confusion, sensuality, occult fascination, digital secrecy, corrupt humor, ungodly influence, and spiritual laziness to move through the house unchecked. If God entrusted you with a home, then He entrusted you with the responsibility to guard its spiritual climate. That includes what is played, what is watched, what is tolerated, what is repeated, what is celebrated, and what is allowed to remain unchallenged.

This is not merely about keeping bad things out. It is also about actively filling the home with what strengthens spiritual life. Prayer is not decoration; it is warfare. Scripture is not a ritual; it is atmosphere-setting truth. Worship is not background noise; it is a spiritual declaration. Repentance is not weakness; it is cleansing. Forgiveness is not sentiment; it is protection against bitterness gaining legal room to remain. Parents must not only oppose darkness. They must establish light. A spiritually guarded home is not one that merely says "no" to corruption. It is one that says "yes" to what strengthens discernment, peace, reverence, unity, purity, and holy attentiveness.

Children are deeply affected by the spiritual atmosphere of the home. They may not always have language for it, but they live inside it. They feel whether the home is governed by peace or chaos, truth or confusion, discipline or passivity, prayer or neglect, reverence or casual compromise. A child reared in a spiritually attentive home is often better able to recognize when something outside the home feels off, because there is already a healthier atmosphere within them to compare it against. But when the home itself becomes spiritually muddy, children lose that internal clarity. They become easier to shape by whatever is strongest around them.

This is why parents need a reality check and a wakeup call: you are not only rearing children. You are governing the atmosphere. You are not only managing behavior. You are standing in a war over minds, appetites, identity, and holiness. You are not only deciding what the family does. You are deciding what will be allowed to shape the household's moral and spiritual climate. That is a holy responsibility, and it cannot be handled casually without consequence.

So guard the eye gate.
Guard the ear gate.
Guard the atmosphere.
Guard the rhythms of the house.
Guard what the family repeatedly welcomes.
Guard what the children are learning to call normal.

Do not call it harmless because it is common.
Do not call it entertainment because it is popular.
Do not call it nothing because the damage is still subtle.

Because the home is not merely where your family lives.
It is where your family is being formed.
And if the atmosphere is left unguarded, the consequences will not stay invisible forever.

STRENGTHENING THE SPIRITUAL COVERING

If parents are going to engage effectively in spiritual warfare over the home, they must do more than admire biblical truth—they must wear it. The armor of God is not poetic language to decorate sermons. It is an instruction for survival. Too many households admire Scripture while living unarmed. Too many parents want peace without putting in the work that protects it. Too many speak about God's covering while leaving the home's spiritual atmosphere exposed through neglect, compromise, prayerlessness, and passive leadership. This must be said with force: a child cannot be safely covered by a parent who is spiritually careless. If the watchman is undisciplined, the wall becomes easier to breach.

The belt of truth anchors the home in clarity. Truth exposes deception and eliminates confusion. A household grounded in truth resists manipulation more effectively than one governed by emotion, assumption, image, or convenience. Truth says what is holy, what is dangerous, what is acceptable, and what must be confronted. Truth keeps a parent from calling darkness harmless merely because it is common. Truth keeps a household from drifting into moral softness. When truth is weak, confusion multiplies. When confusion multiplies, discernment weakens. And when discernment weakens, the enemy gains room to operate.

The breastplate of righteousness guards integrity. Parents must model moral consistency because compromise in leadership weakens spiritual authority. A parent cannot lead children into sobriety while living privately in contradiction. A home cannot be spiritually fortified if the adults assigned to guard it are feeding appetites that disorder the atmosphere. Hidden sin, tolerated compromise, corrupt entertainment, unrepented bitterness, sexual impurity, and careless speech do not remain "personal matters." They affect the spiritual weight of the home. Children may not always understand what is wrong, but they often live under what is spiritually unresolved. Righteousness is not perfection.

It is submitted living. It is a refusal to make peace with what God has called unclean.

The shoes of the gospel of peace establish stability. When the atmosphere of a home is marked by prayerful peace rather than chaos, children develop emotional resilience. Peace is not the absence of problems. It is the presence of order under God. It is the steadying influence of a household that does not live in panic, rage, confusion, or spiritual disorder. A home ruled by outbursts, sarcasm, tension, and instability becomes easier ground for fear and manipulation. But a home where peace is cultivated through prayer, truth, and disciplined presence gives children an inner reference point. They begin to know what a healthy spiritual atmosphere feels like, and that helps them recognize what is wrong outside the home.

The shield of faith extinguishes doubt and fear. Faith does not deny reality—it confronts it with confidence in God's authority. A parent walking in faith is not naïve about danger. They are strengthened to face it without surrendering to passivity or panic. Faith steadies the hand of the watchman. It says, I will not let fear make me silent. I will not let uncertainty make me lazy. I will not let cultural pressure weaken my responsibility. Faith is not sentimental optimism. It is spiritual resistance anchored in the character of God. It keeps parents from folding under intimidation and from treating unseen warfare like an optional category.

The helmet of salvation protects identity. Children must understand who they are in God so that external pressures do not redefine them. The world is aggressive in its efforts to assign identity through visibility, sexuality, popularity, confusion, performance, comparison, and digital affirmation. If children do not know who they are in God, the loudest outside voice often begins to shape them by default. Parents must therefore help children understand that they are not defined by likes, peer approval, online attention, emotional instability, false labels, or sinful invitation. Identity rooted in God becomes a defense against the countless voices trying to rename them.

The sword of the Spirit—the Word of God—is both defensive and offensive. Scripture spoken within a home shapes perspective, corrects thinking, fortifies conviction, and breaks the passive atmosphere in which confusion prefers to grow. The Word does not merely comfort. It confronts, exposes, orders, cleanses, and strengthens. A home that rarely hears Scripture will eventually be discipled by something else. If God's Word is not shaping the imagination, the culture will. If truth is not being spoken, error will not stay quiet for long. Parents who want spiritual covering over the home must become serious about bringing the Word into the daily life of the family—not as empty ritual, but as governing truth.

Spiritual warfare requires practice, not theory. Parents must engage in intentional, consistent prayer—covering each child by name. Prayer is not ritual; it is reinforcement. It builds a hedge of protection. It strengthens discernment. It invites divine wisdom into daily decisions. It teaches the home that help comes from God, not from human confidence alone. A praying parent is not doing a religious performance. They are standing in their role. They are resisting drift. They are refusing to let children walk through the world uncovered because the adult is too distracted to pray.

Fasting, when appropriate and led by conviction, sharpens spiritual sensitivity. It recalibrates priorities and deepens reliance on God's guidance. It is not about outward display or ritual deprivation. It is about focused surrender. It is about making room to hear more clearly, pray more intensely, and break the stubbornness of the flesh that often dulls the watchman. Some battles in the home are not only fought by tighter rules. They are also fought by deeper consecration. Parents who live spiritually cluttered, chronically distracted, and prayerlessly reactive will often miss what a more consecrated life would have exposed sooner.

Declaring Scripture audibly within the home reinforces spiritual atmosphere. Words shape environments. What is spoken repeatedly begins to set the tone, expectation, and moral climate. When truth is spoken consistently, confusion loses ground. When parents bless the home with Scripture, pray over rooms, speak life over children, rebuke fear, confront darkness, and fill the atmosphere with the Word, they are not engaging in superstition. They are refusing to leave the home's climate morally and spiritually unattended. A silent house is still being shaped. Better that it be shaped by truth than by unattended influence.

James 4:7 (KJV) provides a direct strategy: "Submit yourselves therefore to God. Resist the devil, and he will flee from you." Submission precedes resistance. Authority flows from alignment. When a family intentionally surrenders its patterns, attitudes, decisions, entertainment, conversations, and priorities to God's will, spiritual protection strengthens. But resistance must also be active. Evil does not retreat because the home has good intentions. It retreats where there is submitted resistance, clear spiritual authority, and adults who refuse to leave the gate unguarded.

Parents must renounce spiritual footholds within the home. Unforgiveness invites bitterness. Bitterness fractures unity. Unity weakened creates vulnerability. Resentment poisons the atmosphere. Hypocrisy weakens clarity. Secret compromise dulls discernment. Clearing resentment through repentance and reconciliation restores spiritual strength. Homes do not become strong merely by denouncing outside darkness while tolerating inside disorder. The covering is strengthened when what belongs to darkness is confronted inside the walls, not merely complained about outside them.

Ungodly covenants—unhealthy relational ties, destructive habits, generational patterns, tolerated immorality, occult fascination, sensual compromise, and repeated surrender to impurity—must be confronted and severed through prayer and intentional change. Silence does not dissolve strongholds; deliberate action does. Parents must stop expecting passivity to protect what only vigilance can preserve. Some things in a household must be repented of, removed, turned off, broken off, and refused. A spiritually guarded home is not one that merely hopes darkness stays weak. It is one that stops feeding what strengthens darkness.

Psalm 91 provides imagery of divine protection, describing angels encamping around those who trust in God. Parents should boldly pray for divine covering over their children—over their schools, friendships, digital interactions, emotional vulnerabilities, developing identity, future decisions, and unseen battles. But this must be understood clearly: bold prayer does not excuse passive parenting. Divine covering is not a substitute for stewardship. It is a strength for stewardship. God's protection is not permission for parental laziness. It is empowerment for parental faithfulness.

A spiritually fortified home is not fearful—it is grounded. It is not anxious—it is anchored. It is not reactive—it is prepared. But let there be a reality check here: many homes are not prepared because the adults are spiritually casual. Prayer is inconsistent. Scripture is occasional. Entertainment is unfiltered. Distractions are constant. Bitterness is tolerated. Devices are unguarded. Boundaries are weak. Then, when confusion, rebellion, fear, emotional instability, or digital corruption begins to surface in children, adults act surprised. But some surprises are simply the fruit of an unattended atmosphere. This is not written to condemn without hope. It is written to wake sleeping watchmen.

When prayer becomes routine, peace increases. When Scripture becomes central, confusion decreases. When submission becomes consistent, authority strengthens. Spiritual warfare over the home is not optional for parents who desire lasting protection. It is an ongoing assignment. Engage daily. Guard intentionally. Submit fully. Resist firmly. Because the atmosphere of your home will either be shaped by intentional faith or influenced by unattended forces.

Need more conviction? Then hear this plainly: God will hold parents accountable for how they guarded what He entrusted to them. Children are not accessories to adult life. They are souls under stewardship. And if the home remains spiritually weak because the adults assigned to guard it chose distraction, compromise, laziness, or religious shallowness over active covering, Heaven does not call that harmless. It calls it neglect. Too many want God's blessing over houses they have left spiritually unguarded. Too many want peace without prayer, clarity without truth, covering without consecration, and deliverance without discipline. But God is not mocked. What parents repeatedly leave open will eventually influence what children are exposed to.

This is your wakeup call. Strengthen the covering. Put on the armor. Clean the atmosphere. Confront the compromise. Guard the eye gate. Guard the ear gate. Guard the habits of the house. Guard the prayer life. Guard the Word. Guard the unity. Guard the child. Stop treating spiritual warfare like a sermon topic and start treating it like the daily reality of your assignment.

Choose to build a sanctuary. Choose to strengthen the covering. Choose to stand spiritually alert. For a home fortified in faith becomes a place where darkness struggles to advance—not because the battle is imaginary, but because the watchmen finally woke up.

CLOSING CONVICTION

Chapter Eleven

Digital vigilance is not merely about technology management. It is about guarding access in an age where influence moves fast, hides easily, and speaks constantly. It is about recognizing that the modern gate is open more often than many parents realize, and that what enters quietly can shape deeply. It is about understanding that a child does not have to leave the house to be influenced, groomed, confused, desensitized, seduced, pressured, or spiritually weakened. The world now enters through the screen with a speed, privacy, and persistence that previous generations never had to confront in this form. If parents do not take that seriously, they are not simply behind the times—they are leaving a gate unguarded.

A device may be small, but its influence can be enormous. A message may seem casual, but its intention may be calculated. A feed may appear entertaining, but its formation of the mind may be profound. A late-night scroll may seem insignificant, but repeated exposure can slowly reshape appetite, attention, conviction, modesty, emotional stability, identity, and moral reflex. This is how digital influence often works—not always through one dramatic moment, but through quiet repetition. What is seen often begins to feel normal. What feels normal begins to shape desire. What shapes desire begins to shape direction. By the time the fruit appears in the child's behavior, mood, secrecy, language, insecurity, or spiritual dullness, the shaping may already have been happening for a long time.

This is why parents must not drift into passive digital parenting. Screens must be watched. Platforms must be examined. Communication must remain open. Boundaries must stay firm. Oversight must be consistent. The modern gate cannot be left to self-government by a child who is still developing emotionally, spiritually, and morally. A child may know how to open apps, create accounts, delete history, use disappearing messages, and navigate hidden channels, yet still have no maturity to discern what is pure, what is manipulative, what is predatory, what is addictive, and what is quietly corroding the soul. Technological ability is not the same as spiritual readiness. Digital skill is not the same as moral wisdom.

But the deeper issue is still spiritual. A digitally careless household often becomes spiritually vulnerable. A spiritually grounded household becomes more discerning about digital influence. The practical and the spiritual cannot be separated. They strengthen each other. Parental oversight without prayer grows tired. Prayer without practical boundaries grows incomplete. Monitoring without discernment becomes mechanical. Discernment without action becomes ineffective. But together, they form stronger protection. The parent must watch the device and the atmosphere. They must regulate access and guard the spirit of the home. They must know the apps and know how to pray. They must ask hard questions and remain close enough to God to recognize when something is spiritually off before the evidence is fully visible.

This is where a reality check is needed. Too many parents have surrendered the digital gate and then acted shocked when the child's peace, modesty, sleep, attention, emotional health, or spiritual hunger began changing. Too many have called it normal because it was common. Too many have mistaken convenience for wisdom and silence for safety. Too many have handed children unrestricted access to devices, private feeds, closed screens, hidden messaging, and unmonitored content, then wondered why secrecy increased, why comparison deepened, why identity became unstable, and why discernment weakened. However, some of what parents refer to as "surprise" is simply the result of careless supervision. Children are being shaped every day by what repeatedly enters, and parents who refuse to govern that gate are not remaining neutral. They are leaving formation to whatever influence arrives first and stays longest.

This must also be heard as a warning before God. He will hold parents accountable for how they guarded the gates of influence around their children. This is not merely about whether you loved them emotionally or provided for them physically. It is also about whether you watched what was discipling them privately. It is about whether you allow digital voices to preach into their minds without question. It is about whether you let screens become secret rooms where confusion, lust, fear, comparison, false identity, predatory access, and spiritual erosion could work without challenge. The Lord is not confused by modern technology. He still requires ancient watchfulness. A digital gate is still a gate. A hidden message is still hidden access. A repeated feed still has a repeated influence. And a parent who leaves that unguarded through laziness, distraction, ignorance, or fear of conflict is still accountable for the negligence.

So let conviction rise where passivity once lived. Let the sleeping watchman wake up at the digital wall. Stop assuming the child is safe because they are quiet. Stop assuming they are fine because they are home. Stop assuming the screen is harmless because the culture calls it normal. Stop assuming your child can handle what you have not even taken the time to understand yourself. This is not the hour for casual parenting. This is the hour for sober stewardship. The world is constantly speaking to children. Predators are searching constantly. Algorithms are constantly shaping. Temptation is constantly reaching. Confusion is discipling constantly. If parents are not equally vigilant, then the child is being formed by voices that do not love them, fear God, or honor innocence.

Guard the device.
Guard the message.
Guard the atmosphere.
Guard the child.

Because the modern gate is open every day.
And whatever enters repeatedly
will try to shape what remains.

So do not be passive.
Do not be lazy.
Do not be intimidated by technology.
Do not call neglect trust.
Do not call silence safety.
Do not call unrestricted access freedom.

Stand at the gate.
Watch with prayer.
Watch with structure.
Watch with courage.
Watch like Heaven is watching how you guard what it entrusted to you.

Because it is.

❖ SPIRITUAL WARNING ❖

A Warning to the Sleeping Watchman

There is a difference between rest and neglect. Rest is temporary. Neglect is dangerous. A watchman who sleeps while the gate stands open may not intend harm, but intention does not stop intrusion. In the same way, a parent who becomes spiritually passive may not desire danger, yet passivity still creates opportunity. Children are not protected by what adults meant to do. They are protected by what adults actually guard. That distinction must be faced with trembling, because too many households are suffering under the consequences of intentions that never became vigilance.

Spiritual warfare does not pause because you are tired. Darkness does not retreat because you are busy. Temptation does not wait until you are prepared. The enemy does not respectfully postpone his movements until the family schedule slows down, until the parent is less distracted, or until the house becomes more prayerful. He watches the unguarded hour. He studies the weak point. He searches for the neglected gate. That is why spiritual passivity is so dangerous. It tells the watchman that nothing urgent is happening, even as erosion is already underway beneath the surface.

If prayer becomes occasional, covering weakens. If Scripture becomes secondary, discernment dulls. If vigilance becomes inconsistent, access widens. These are not dramatic truths meant only for extreme cases. They are ordinary laws of spiritual erosion. A home does not have to openly rebel against God to become spiritually vulnerable. It only has to drift. It only has to become distracted enough to stop guarding what matters. It only has to replace deliberate spiritual leadership with casual routine, religious language, and the false comfort of assuming everything is fine because no visible crisis has yet erupted.

The enemy does not need chaos to infiltrate a home. He needs a gradual compromise. He needs a distraction. He needs spiritual laziness disguised as normal life. He needs parents who are too exhausted to examine the atmosphere, too comfortable to confront what feels off, too routine-driven to sense when the house has lost its spiritual sharpness. He needs bitterness left unchecked, screens left unguarded, conversations left undiscerning, prayer left shallow, worship left absent, and repentance left delayed. He does not always storm the house. Often, he seeps through the cracks the watchman stopped noticing.

Many households do not fall in a single dramatic moment. They erode slowly. Through unchecked bitterness. Through tolerated compromise. Through ignored convictions. Through unfiltered entertainment. Through careless digital access. Through prayerlessness that still uses spiritual vocabulary. Through a home that appears functional on the outside, while becoming less guarded, less sensitive, less clean, and less anchored in truth on the inside. The house still stands. Meals are still eaten. Schedules still continue. But the atmosphere begins to change. Peace feels thinner. Discernment feels duller. Tension grows easier. Temptation feels closer. Holy sensitivity fades. And if no one inspects the wall, the family may keep living inside erosion while calling it normal.

Let this settle deeply: if you do not intentionally govern the spiritual climate of your home, something else will. The atmosphere is never neutral. It is always being shaped. When worship fades, noise increases. When truth weakens, confusion grows. When authority softens, resistance diminishes. When parents stop leading spiritually, other voices begin leading in their place. The child will still be discipled—either by the truth of God or by the repeated influences left unchallenged in the atmosphere. There is no empty space in the soul for long. Something will fill what the watchman failed to guard.

You were not called to casually inhabit your home. You were called to guard it spiritually. That means more than living there. It means governing the atmosphere. It means noticing what enters repeatedly, what attitudes remain unchecked, what conversations are shaping the tone, what media is training the imagination, what bitterness is poisoning the room, what secrecy is weakening trust, what distractions are crowding out prayer, and what subtle compromises are no longer being confronted because everyone has gotten used to them.

A spiritually guarded home does not happen by accident. It is built by parents who take the assignment seriously enough to examine the climate of the house before the consequences become visible in the children.

The enemy studies patterns. He watches weakness. He probes for openings. If he cannot enter through obvious doors, he will attempt subtle cracks—resentment left unresolved, media left unfiltered, relationships left unquestioned, fatigue left unguarded, devices left unmonitored, disciplines left abandoned, truth left unspoken. He knows that small compromises often feel too minor to confront. But small doors lead to larger breaches. Small tolerances become larger permissions. Small drifts become deeper disorders. And the family that keeps excusing the little things may eventually find itself wrestling something far larger than it should have allowed to grow.

Do not dismiss small compromises. That is one of the most dangerous habits of a sleeping watchman. The subtle things matter. The sarcastic tone that has become normal. The unresolved anger that lingers in the room. The repeated digital secrecy. The entertainment that keeps pushing the conscience lower. The prayer life that has thinned to almost nothing. The Word of God that has become decorative instead of directive. The child's emotional shift that no one has followed. The discomfort that no one has addressed. The atmosphere that no one has taken time to examine. These things matter because spiritual erosion is rarely loud in the beginning. It becomes loud later, after it has been fed quietly for too long.

A house may appear peaceful on the outside while spiritual pressure builds quietly within. That is why appearance is not enough. Order is not enough. Routine is not enough. Respectability is not enough. The watchman must inspect, not assume. If you sense tension, address it. If you sense compromise, correct it. If you sense distance from God's presence, return quickly. Do not let the home drift further because you do not want to disturb the routine. Delay strengthens intrusion. What is left unchallenged today often becomes harder to uproot tomorrow.

The watchman who assumes all is well without inspection invites surprise. The guardian who replaces prayer with routine risks losing spiritual edge. The parent who keeps postponing repentance, postponing hard conversations, postponing spiritual correction, postponing the restoration of discipline, and postponing honest examination of the house is not preserving peace. They are giving time to what should have been confronted earlier. This is where the wakeup call must sound clearly: God will hold parents accountable for the atmosphere they cultivated, the compromises they tolerated, the truths they neglected, and the children they left under weakened covering because they refused to take spiritual leadership seriously.

Stand up. Reinforce the gate. Strengthen the wall. Guard the atmosphere. This is not fear-driven urgency. It is an assignment-driven responsibility. Your home must not drift spiritually. It must be led intentionally. Pray deliberately. Correct quickly. Repent swiftly. Forgive completely. Resist firmly. Do not wait until the children are already emotionally unstable, morally confused, digitally entangled, spiritually cold, or relationally fractured before deciding the atmosphere needs to change. By then, damage may already be speaking through them.

Because once spiritual erosion becomes visible, damage has often been present for some time. The outburst may be recent, but the drift was older. The confusion may now be obvious, but the weakening began earlier. The secrecy may now be surfacing, but the atmosphere that allowed it was formed gradually. That is why the watchman must wake up before the evidence becomes undeniable to everyone else. The purpose of spiritual leadership is not merely to react to visible decline. It is to detect early and act faithfully.

Wake up, watchman. Strengthen your post. Reclaim your authority. Return to the wall. Return to prayer. Return to the Word. Return to repentance. Return to holy seriousness. Return to the work of governing what enters your home, what remains in your home, and what is shaping your children while you live under the same roof. Stop calling drift normal. Stop calling neglect busyness. Stop calling spiritual weakness a phase. Stop calling an unguarded atmosphere harmless.

For the atmosphere you cultivate today determines the protection your children live under tomorrow. And a guarded home is not merely safe—it is fortified. A fortified home is not perfect, but it is awake. Not flawless, but alert. Not untouched by battle, but intentionally covered. And in an hour where too many watchmen have grown passive, Heaven is still looking for guardians who understand that what God entrusted must be guarded with conviction, not merely visited with concern.

PART IV

HEALING

HEALING AND RESTORATION

For Children Already Wounded

CHAPTER TWELVE
EMOTIONAL HEALING FOR THE WOUNDED CHILD

Restoring the Heart After Harm

Abuse does not end when the incident stops. It echoes. It lages (memory and learning) in the mind, settles into the body, alters emotional reflexes, disturbs trust, and reshapes identity. What happened in a moment can continue to speak for months or years if healing is not taken seriously. Children who endure trauma often carry wounds that are invisible yet profoundly influential. Those wounds may surface in anxiety, anger, withdrawal, fear of authority, sudden outbursts, numbness, shame, self-blame, confusion, difficulty sleeping, difficulty trusting, difficulty concentrating, or difficulty forming healthy relationships. Some children become loud in their pain. Others become quiet. Some fight. Others disappear inwardly. But whether the wound speaks loudly or silently, it still needs to be healed.

This must be understood with conviction: when a child has been harmed, the responsibility of the adults does not end with stopping the threat. Protection must be followed by restoration. If guardians intervene only at the point of crisis and do not remain present in the healing process, the child may survive the event yet continue to live in its shadow. Too many wounded children have been rescued from the immediate danger only to be left carrying the emotional aftermath in isolation. That is not complete protection. A child does not only need to be removed from harm. A child needs help recovering from what harm has been done to them.

Healing must therefore be intentional. It will not happen merely because time passes. Time can soften some pain, but untreated wounds often do not simply fade. They settle deeper. They alter personality. They distort self-perception. They shape future relationships.

They influence how the child sees affection, authority, safety, and even God. That is why emotional healing must not be treated like a side issue after the "real problem" has passed. It is part of the real problem. A wounded heart is not a minor concern. It is a sacred responsibility.

The first and most critical step in emotional restoration is belief. When a child speaks—even hesitantly—about harm, their story must be taken seriously and with compassion. Doubt deepens damage. Dismissal compounds trauma. But belief begins restoration. When a child hears, I believe you, it dismantles isolation and interrupts shame. Those words do more than comfort; they begin to reestablish reality in a heart that has often been confused by fear, secrecy, manipulation, and self-doubt. Abuse often distorts the child's sense of what is real. Belief begins to restore that broken ground.

This is where many adults fail grievously. Some children are wounded first by the abuse and then wounded again by the response. They finally tell, and the adults closest to them hesitate, minimize, reinterpret, question tone instead of pain, or subtly defend the environment that failed them. In many instances, children find themselves in situations where they must muster incredible courage just to express their thoughts and feelings. Unfortunately, when they do find the bravery to speak up, they often face a disappointing reality: the very adults they have relied upon for support and understanding seem to prioritize their own interests over the child's well-being. These adults may be preoccupied with maintaining a certain image in their community, protecting their relationships with others, sidestepping any potential conflict, or insisting on absolute proof before acknowledging the child's distress. As a result, what should be a nurturing and empathetic response to a child's pain is overshadowed by the adults' concerns, leaving the child feeling unheard, invalidated, and isolated in their suffering. That kind of response can deepen the wound with terrifying force. It tells the child, You are alone even now. That must never be the message a wounded child receives in a home that claims to love them.

Children who have experienced abuse often internalize guilt. They may believe they caused it. They may think they should have stopped it. They may carry silent responsibility for something they never initiated. They may replay the moment and conclude that if they had said something sooner, moved differently, resisted more strongly, or understood the danger earlier, none of it would have happened. This is one of trauma's cruelest lies. It takes what was done to the child and tries to make the child feel responsible for it. Parents must speak this truth repeatedly and clearly: "It was not your fault." Those words are not optional—they are foundational. They must be spoken until shame begins to loosen its grip.

Psalm 147:3 (KJV) declares, "He healeth the broken in heart, and bindeth up their wounds." Healing is not theoretical. It is a promise rooted in the character of God. The brokenhearted are not forgotten. The wounded are not abandoned. Psalm 34:18 (KJV) reinforces this assurance: "The LORD is nigh unto them that are of a broken heart; and saveth such as be of a contrite spirit." Trauma often convinces children that they are alone, dirty, ruined, strange, or spiritually distant. Scripture declares the opposite. God draws near to pain. His presence is not distant in suffering—it is attentive. He is not repelled by wounds. He moves toward them.

Parents must model that nearness. A wounded child should not have to wonder whether their pain is too much, too inconvenient, too messy, too confusing, or too prolonged for the adults around them to bear. The child should not feel rushed because their healing makes others uncomfortable. They should not feel like a burden because their wounds did not close on someone else's preferred timeline. Emotional healing requires patience. Trauma recovery is not linear. Some days will show progress; others may reveal regression. A child may revisit memories unexpectedly. Triggers may arise without warning. A smell, a voice, a location, a phrase, a season, a sound, or an innocent circumstance may reopen fear with startling force. Parents must resist frustration and replace it with understanding.

Healing unfolds gradually. This must be received with seriousness. Adults who want quick emotional resolution may become irritated when the child is not "over it" fast enough. But healing is not a performance for adult comfort. It is a process through which the child slowly relearns safety, trust, emotional regulation, and identity after something has deeply violated them. Some days, the child may seem strong. On other days, they may feel small, frightened, angry, confused, or exhausted by memories they cannot control. This does not mean healing has failed. It means the heart is still recovering from a real injury.

Compassionate listening becomes a powerful instrument of restoration. This means listening without interrupting, correcting, or minimizing. It means allowing tears without rushing to fix them. It means validating emotions even when they are difficult to hear. It means making room for grief without demanding immediate closure. It means the parent does not become so uncomfortable with the child's pain that they shut the child down in order to calm themselves. A wounded child needs more than answers. They need presence. They need someone strong enough to sit with pain without turning away from it.

A stable, predictable environment also strengthens recovery. Consistency builds safety. When routines are reliable and parental presence is steady, the nervous system begins to relax. Safety is not only declared—it must be demonstrated. A child must experience it repeatedly. They must feel that the ground beneath them is no longer shifting. Trauma often leaves the child feeling that danger can come at any time and that trust is unstable. A predictable environment begins teaching the body and mind that not every day is a threat, not every room is unsafe, and not every relationship will wound them.

This is why healing cannot happen well in chaos. If the household remains emotionally explosive, spiritually careless, dismissive of boundaries, or casual with the child's triggers, restoration becomes harder. The environment matters. Children heal more effectively where adults are steady, where words are careful, where trust is rebuilt slowly, where they are not mocked for fear, and where the home has become visibly safer than the place where the harm occurred. Healing is helped by order, by gentleness, by repetition of truth, and by adults who do not keep reopening wounds through impatience or negligence.

Professional support is not a sign of failure; it is a sign of wisdom. God often works through experienced therapists, trauma-informed counselors, skilled advocates, and compassionate pastoral leaders. These individuals can provide tools that complement parental love. Trauma-informed counseling can help children process memories, reframe distorted beliefs, regulate emotions, and rebuild confidence. Wise intervention does not compete with faith; it often serves as one of the means through which God administers healing. Adults who refuse outside help merely because they want to appear strong or "spiritual enough" may unintentionally prolong what wise support could have helped address more fully.

Parents must avoid pressuring a child to "move on" prematurely. Statements such as "It's over now," "You need to let it go," "Don't think about it anymore," or "You have to be strong" may sound motivating to adults, but they can silence ongoing pain. Healing requires space. It requires validation. It requires time. The child does not need pressure to perform at a strength level. The child needs permission to heal honestly. Strength is not pretending nothing happened. Strength is moving through what happened without being abandoned in the process.

Walking alongside a wounded child means remaining present even when the journey feels long. It means refusing to disappear emotionally because the healing is slower than expected. It means saying with action and repetition: "You are safe." "You are loved." "You are believed." "You are not broken beyond repair." These truths must not be offered as slogans alone. They must be embodied. The child must feel them in the home, in the parents' responses, in the pace of healing, and in the steadfastness of the adults who remain.

Spiritual encouragement should be gentle and nurturing. Avoid spiritual clichés that place pressure on the child to appear instantly healed. Do not burden them with shallow answers when their hearts are carrying deep pain. Instead, offer truth rooted in compassion. Pray with them when they are ready. Read Scripture with tenderness. Remind them that God's presence is not dependent on emotional strength. A child does not have to sound strong to be loved by God. They do not have to hide pain to be spiritual. They do not have to force smiles to prove faith. God is not asking them to deny the wound.

He is drawing near to heal it.

Emotional healing also involves restoring identity. Trauma can distort how a child sees themselves. They may feel damaged, dirty, weak, different, less worthy, or permanently marked by what happened. Parents must actively rebuild identity through affirmation, support, truth, and consistent love. Reinforce their value. Reinforce their strength. Reinforce their future. Speak over them what trauma tried to silence. Remind them that what happened to them is not the sum of who they are. The wound may be part of their story, but it is not their name. Their pain is real, but it is not their identity. Their trauma is true, but it is not the total truth about them.

This restoration of identity must be persistent. A child who has been harmed may need truth spoken repeatedly because trauma often repeats its lies repeatedly. Parents must therefore keep placing truth where shame tries to live. "You are still valuable." "You are still worthy of love." "You are still seen by God." "You are still capable of joy." "You are still not alone." "You still have a future beyond this wound." These truths rebuild what trauma often tries to tear down from the inside.

Healing does not erase memory—but it can restore hope. This is an important distinction. The goal is not pretending the harm never happened. With patient support, intentional care, professional guidance, spiritual covering, and consistent truth, children can move from survival to strength. Their story does not have to end in brokenness. It can include restoration. It can include resilience. It can include a future in which the wound no longer has the final word.

But let there also be a warning for the adults: if you fail the child now in the healing, you deepen what was already done. If you grow impatient, dismiss pain, refuse wise help, prioritize your discomfort, or demand quick recovery so life feels easier again, you are not merely mishandling emotion—you are failing a sacred assignment before God. A wounded child is not an inconvenience to manage. They are a life to restore. Heaven watches how adults respond after the crisis, not only during it. God does not merely see whether you stopped the harm. He sees whether you stayed for the healing.

The wounded child is not defined by what happened to them. They are defined by who they are becoming. And with love, truth, wise care, spiritual steadiness, and faithful presence, healing becomes not only possible—but powerful. Not easy. Not quick. But powerful. Because what was wounded can still be restored, and what was shaken can still be strengthened when the child is not left to heal alone.

❖ SPIRITUAL WARNING ❖

A Warning About the Wounds You Cannot See

Not all damage bleeds. Some wounds sit quietly beneath smiles. Some scars hide behind obedience. Some trauma speaks through silence, avoidance, overachievement, sudden maturity, emotional numbness, sleeplessness, irritability, fear, or a strange calm that adults misread as recovery. And one of the most dangerous mistakes a guardian can make is assuming that what looks calm is healed. Outward quiet is not always inward peace. A child may stop talking about what happened and still be living under its weight every day. Silence is not always evidence of restoration. Sometimes, it is evidence that pain has gone underground.

Pain that is ignored does not disappear. It buries itself deeper. It reshapes identity quietly. "It whispers lies in the dark. It teaches the child to reinterpret themselves through the wound. It may say, I am damaged now. I am different now. I am hard to love now. I am unsafe forever. I am to blame. I should have stopped it. I should be over it. Something must be wrong with me." These lies do not always enter loudly. They settle slowly. They begin to influence how the child receives love, handles correction, interprets authority, trusts others, and even approaches God. What is untreated in the heart rarely stays still. It starts building a false identity around the wound.

If a wounded child is rushed past their pain, if their grief is minimized, if their fear is spiritualized instead of understood, you do not strengthen them—you silence them. If every tear is treated as a weakness, if every struggle is treated as a lack of faith, if every setback is met with impatience, the child learns a dangerous lesson: my pain is not safe here. That lesson does not produce maturity. It produces suppression. And suppressed pain does not become strength. It becomes buried pressure. It becomes inner fragmentation. It becomes a quiet wound that continues to shape reactions long after adults have decided the crisis is over.

Suppression eventually surfaces. It may appear in broken relationships, distorted self-worth, misplaced anger, chronic fear, emotional detachment, self-protection disguised as independence, mistrust of authority, confusion about love, fear of vulnerability, or even mistrust of God. A child who was never allowed to heal honestly may grow older while still carrying the original rupture in hidden ways. What adults once rushed past may later emerge in adolescence, adulthood, marriage, parenting, spiritual life, or private thoughts no one else sees. This must shake the conscience of every guardian: a child who survives trauma without proper healing may carry that wound into adulthood, and unhealed wounds often have generational consequences.

You cannot demand resilience without providing restoration. You cannot preach faith while ignoring fracture. You cannot call it moving on if healing has not taken place. Faith is not the denial of pain. Faith is the courage to bring pain into the light where God can heal it through truth, presence, wise care, and patient restoration. Too many children have been told to be strong when what they really needed was to be safe. Too many have been told to forgive before they were first allowed to grieve honestly. Too many have been told to stop crying when the wound was still speaking through every part of them. This is not spiritual strength. It is often adult discomfort forcing a child to hide what still needs healing.

God heals—but He often heals through intentional care, through patient listening, through wise counsel, through steady presence, through the kind of adults who refuse to leave the child alone with what was done to them. Healing is not less spiritual because it is slow. Healing is not less holy because it includes tears, questions, setbacks, counseling, emotional exhaustion, and repeated reassurance. God is not frightened by the child's broken places. He draws near to them. And adults who represent Him well must do the same. The wounded child does not need performance spirituality. They need truthful compassion.

If you dismiss emotional pain as weakness, if you grow impatient with slow recovery, if you assume time alone will repair what trauma broke, you risk compounding the injury. This is where many caregivers fail without realizing how deeply. They think the danger has passed because the event ended. They think the child should be improving faster. They think enough time has gone by. But trauma does not always follow the adult's preferred timeline. It returns in waves. It resurfaces in triggers. It often reappears when the child reaches a new developmental stage and understands something more clearly than before. A wise guardian prepares for that. An impatient guardian resents it. And resentment in the presence of a wounded child can deepen shame in devastating ways.

Healing requires vigilance just as protection does. You must guard against bitterness taking root. You must guard against shame shaping identity. You must guard against silence becoming normal. You must guard against the child deciding that their pain is too complicated for anyone else to bear. You must guard against false narratives settling in the heart. The enemy does not only want to wound the child. He wants to interpret the wound for the child. He wants to turn injury into identity, trauma into destiny, and suffering into a lifelong lens through which the child sees themselves and the world. That is why healing is spiritual warfare, too. The battle is not only against memory. It is against meaning.

A wounded child does not need pressure. They need presence. They need reassurance. They need safety reinforced repeatedly. They need to know that they are not too much, not too late, not too broken, not too inconvenient. They need adults who will remain steady even when healing is slow. They need homes where their tears are not a disruption to be silenced, but a signal to be tended. They need room to ask hard questions without being shamed. They need permission to say, I'm still hurting, without feeling like they have failed everyone's expectations.

Do not rush them. Do not shame them. Do not grow weary of the process. Weariness in the adult can translate into abandonment in the child. A child who senses that the people around them are tired of the healing process may begin to hide their struggle to avoid becoming a burden. That hidden struggle then becomes another layer of isolation. Guardians must therefore ask God not only for insight, but for endurance. Emotional restoration often requires long obedience. It requires staying present after the emotional intensity of the crisis has faded. It requires continuing to notice what the child is carrying even when others have moved on.

The enemy seeks not only to wound—but to redefine. To convince the child that they are damaged beyond repair. To distort how they see themselves and how they see God. To make them think they are permanently changed for the worse, permanently unsafe, permanently less worthy of joy, trust, purity, or love. That narrative must be interrupted immediately. Parents and guardians must consistently speak life. Affirm value intentionally. Create space for tears without embarrassment. Create space for questions without judgment. Speak against the lie that the wound gets the last word.

This is also where accountability before God must be faced honestly. If He entrusted a wounded child to your care and you chose irritation over patience, image over honesty, quick appearances over deep restoration, or religious phrases over real help, Heaven does not call that harmless. The Lord sees how adults respond after harm, not only during it. He sees whether the child was truly shepherded toward healing or merely managed until their pain became less inconvenient to others. Guardians will answer not only for whether they stopped the threat, but also for whether they stayed for the restoration.

Because untreated trauma does not fade—it festers. And a guardian who neglects emotional restoration may unknowingly allow the wound to shape destiny. That is not light language, but this is not a light matter. The child's future relationships, spiritual life, self-worth, emotional stability, and ability to trust may all be influenced by whether the wound was treated seriously or left to harden in silence. What is healed can become testimony. What is neglected can become bondage.

Stand firm in compassion. Stand patient in the process. Stand unwavering in support. Do not step back because healing takes time. Do not grow cold because progress is uneven. Do not assume quietness means wholeness. Keep showing up. Keep listening. Keep praying. Keep helping. Keep reminding the child that what happened to them is not the end of who they are.

For healing is not optional—it is essential.
And a child who is restored properly does not merely survive—
They rise.

CHAPTER THIRTEEN
TRAUMA AWARENESS AND RECOVERY

Understanding the Long Road of Restoration

Trauma recovery is not a quick return to normal. It is the long, careful work of rebuilding what harm disrupted. It is not only about helping a child feel better after a painful event. It is about restoring stability where fear took root, restoring trust where betrayal entered, restoring clarity where confusion settled, and restoring identity where trauma tried to leave behind a false name. That is why trauma awareness matters so deeply. If adults do not understand what trauma does, they may misread the child, mishandle the recovery, and deepen wounds they were supposed to help heal.

Isaiah 41:10 gives a steady promise in the middle of fear: "Fear thou not; for I am with thee… I will strengthen thee; yea, I will help thee; yea, I will uphold thee." This is not a shallow comfort for wounded people. It is a declaration that God does not abandon those who are trembling. Trauma often leaves a child feeling unsafe even after the danger has passed. It can make the body remember what the mind is trying to forget. It can make ordinary rooms feel uncertain, ordinary correction feel threatening, ordinary affection feel confusing, and ordinary silence feel heavy. But God's promise stands over the long road of restoration: I am with thee. That means the child is not left to walk the recovery alone, and the adults around that child must not abandon them in the process either.

What trauma disrupts, recovery must carefully rebuild. That rebuilding does not happen in a single breakthrough moment. It happens through repetition, stability, truth, and care. Trauma can affect sleep patterns, learning capacity, memory, concentration, emotional regulation, relationships, appetite, physical tension, startle responses, self-worth, and even the child's view of God, authority, and safety. It can make ordinary situations feel threatening. It can make healthy affection feel suspicious.

It can make corrections feel dangerous. It can make a child prepare for harm in moments when none is present. This is why trauma awareness matters: it helps caregivers interpret behavior through understanding rather than irritation, and through wisdom rather than judgment.

A traumatized child may not respond like other children. They may appear unusually reactive, emotionally flat, highly guarded, intensely clingy, unusually controlling, unusually compliant, or strangely detached. They may misread safe situations because their internal alarm system has been shaped by harm. What looks like an overreaction may actually be a survival response. What appears defiant may be fear. What seems distant may be self-protection. What feels like stubbornness may actually be a body and mind still trying to recover from a world that once became unsafe too quickly. A parent who does not understand trauma may keep correcting symptoms while missing pain. A parent who does understand trauma begins asking a better question: not only, What is this child doing? But also, What may this child be carrying?

This is the reality check many adults need: some wounded children are punished for the very responses that reveal they were hurt. They are called difficult when they are dysregulated. They are called "dramatic" when triggered. They are called “disrespectful” when they are terrified. They are called distant when they are protecting what has already been violated. That is a grievous mistake. It is possible to love a child and still wound them further if you keep demanding normal responses from a traumatized heart without first understanding what trauma has done. Adults must wake up to this. Healing requires more than authority. It requires informed compassion.

Recovery is not simply the absence of visible symptoms. It is the gradual return of internal stability. It is the slow rebuilding of trust. It is the reestablishing of safety in the body, in the mind, in relationships, and in the rhythms of daily life. It is the ability to breathe again without fear ruling every room. It is the restoration of a sense of self that trauma tried to fracture. It is the child slowly learning that not every hand harms, not every room traps, not every adult betrays, and not every moment of discomfort means danger is about to happen again.

Second Corinthians 5:17 declares, “Therefore if any man be in Christ, he is a new creature.” While trauma may be part of a child’s history, it does not define their destiny. Parents must speak life over their children, reminding them of their identity in Christ, their worth, and their future. With God, restoration is possible. But that restoration must not be treated as a magical denial. The truth that a child can become whole in Christ does not mean pain is instantly erased. It means pain does not get the final word. It means history is not destiny. It means trauma may explain some wounds, but it does not own the child’s future. It means the child is more than what happened to them, and God is greater than what tried to break them.

Recovery includes helping a child reestablish trust in safe adults. That takes time. It includes helping them name emotions that once felt overwhelming or confusing. It includes helping them understand that fear may visit without being allowed to rule. It includes teaching them that their body, emotions, thoughts, and voice matter. It includes creating rhythms of safety strong enough to challenge the internal chaos trauma created. Meals at predictable times, bedtime stability, calm conversations, repeated reassurances, honest answers, safe touch, careful listening, and adults who stay emotionally present—these things may seem small, but they are part of the holy architecture of healing.

Trauma awareness also requires the adults around the child to remain teachable. Parents, guardians, and ministry leaders must be willing to learn what trauma does to the mind, body, and emotional life of a child. They must resist simplistic interpretations. They must resist moralizing pain that needs understanding. They must resist the temptation to expect adult-level emotional processing from a wounded child. A child may not know why they are angry, why they cannot sleep, why they panic, why they go numb, why they lie about small things, why they suddenly cling, or why they shut down in ordinary moments. The adult must be mature enough not to turn that confusion into shame.

Recovery is patient work.
It is holy work.
It is repetitive work.

And it requires adults who understand that healing often looks like small victories before it ever looks like a dramatic transformation. A child who sleeps peacefully after months of fear is healing. A child who tells the truth after seasons of silence is healing. A child who asks for help instead of hiding is healing. A child who begins to laugh again without scanning the room is healing. A child who can sit through a conversation without shutting down is healing. A child who receives healthy affection without freezing is healing. A child who no longer carries all the blame in their own mind is healing. These moments matter. They may not look impressive to an impatient adult, but Heaven sees them as the deep work of restoration.

Do not despise slow restoration. God often rebuilds deeply before He rebuilds visibly. Adults often want the visible signs first—calm behavior, quick trust, emotional steadiness, easy smiles, and obvious progress. But deep healing often happens beneath the surface before it appears clearly in behavior. God is not always in a hurry the way adults are. He rebuilds foundations. He restores trust line by line. He heals the hidden places that no one else can see. The adults around the child must learn to honor that process rather than rush it.

Trauma awareness and recovery call the family not only to compassion, but to endurance. Healing may require revisiting grief, retraining responses, rebuilding trust, and restoring joy in stages. There may be setbacks. There may be days when progress seems invisible. There may be moments when the child appears to move backward emotionally after making significant gains. That does not mean recovery has failed. It means healing is still happening in layers. The family must not abandon the process because it is longer than expected. Some children have been deeply wounded over time; it should not shock us that healing also takes time.

This chapter also demands a warning to the adults: if you fail to understand trauma, you may start punishing what should have been shepherded. If you grow irritated with the child's slowness, dismiss their triggers, mock their fear, weaponize Scripture against their pain, or demand rapid recovery to make life easier for yourself, you are not just being insensitive—you are mishandling a sacred trust. God will hold adults accountable not only for how they protected children from harm, but for how they responded after harm came. It is not enough to say, I got them out. Heaven also asks, Did you help rebuild what was broken? Did you stay for the restoration? Did you handle their wound with truth and compassion?

A child's trauma may be real.
But so is their future.
Their pain may be deep.
But so is God's power to restore.

So stay with the process. Learn the patterns. Honor the slow victories. Speak life over the child. Build stability around them. Refuse to let shame define them. Refuse to let impatience rush them. Refuse to let trauma become the loudest voice in their story.

Because the long road is still a road toward life, and when adults walk it faithfully with a wounded child, recovery becomes more than survival—it becomes restoration with roots deep enough to hold.

❖ SPIRITUAL WARNING ❖

A Warning Against False Recovery

Not every smile means healing. Not every quiet season means peace. Not every return to routine means restoration. Sometimes a child appears "better" because they have learned how to hide pain more efficiently, how to stay quiet more consistently, and how to give adults the appearance of progress because they sense that the people around them are more comfortable with performance than with process. That is one of the most dangerous illusions in recovery: the belief that reduced visibility of pain automatically means the pain is gone. Often it does not. It has only gone deeper.

That is why trauma awareness is essential. A guardian who celebrates outward calm while ignoring inward fracture may mistake suppression for recovery. But suppressed pain does not become healed pain simply because it has become less visible. A child may stop crying and still be breaking internally. A child may go back to school, return to routines, answer questions politely, and still be carrying fear in silence. A child may appear strong simply because they have learned that visible pain makes adults nervous, impatient, or spiritually shallow in their responses. So they adapt. They quiet down. They manage themselves. They become easier to handle—but not necessarily more healed.

Beware of demanding performance when restoration is still in process. That warning must carry weight, because many adults unintentionally train children to fake recovery. The pressure may not always be spoken aloud, but children often feel it. They sense when the adults want life to feel normal again. They sense when tears are becoming inconvenient. They sense when their fear is making the room too heavy. They sense when people are more relieved by visible calm than concerned with invisible pain. So they begin to perform steadiness, which they do not yet possess. They may smile sooner than they are healed, comply sooner than they are restored, and stay silent longer than they should. That is not maturity. That is adaptation under pressure.

If a child feels pressured to appear strong before they feel safe enough to be honest, recovery is being interrupted. If they are taught to manage the appearance of healing more than the reality of it, the wound may change hiding places. It may move from tears into numbness, from fear into anger, from confusion into false control, from grief into emotional shutdown, from visible distress into invisible mistrust. This is why adults must stop measuring healing only by what makes the household feel calmer. A quieter child is not always a healed child. A more manageable child is not always a restored child. Sometimes the wound has only gone underground.

Do not be deceived by surface order. Some children become louder in pain. Others become quieter. Some break down openly. Others disappear inwardly. Some react strongly. Others become emotionally flat. Some cling. Others withdraw. Some speak often about what happened. Others never mention it again. But both kinds of children may still need deep healing. Adults who only respond to obvious pain may completely miss the child whose wound has learned to hide behind normalcy, obedience, humor, productivity, or emotional distance. And that hidden pain can remain active for years while everyone else assumes the child is fine because they no longer disrupt the room.

A child cannot be rushed into wholeness through adult impatience. They cannot be lectured into recovery or pressured into peace. Healing must be nurtured, not demanded. This is where many falter. They protect the child from the incident but not from the aftermath. They respond to the event but not to the echo. They remove the danger but do not help rebuild what the danger damaged. That is not full restoration. It is an interruption without guidance. It is an emergency response without long-term care. Too many children are left bearing the aftermath alone because adults believed solving the crisis meant the task was complete.

But God doesn't just remove what harms; He restores what has been damaged. He isn't only interested in stopping injury but also in healing the broken places left behind. If you are entrusted with a wounded child, you must commit not just to intervention but also to long-term restoration. This means staying present when healing is slow, listening when the child revisits the pain, and not growing impatient when progress is uneven. It also means refusing to call the child "dramatic," "stuck," or "too sensitive" just because the wound takes longer to heal than your comfort allows.

This is also where accountability before God becomes serious. Some adults think they have fulfilled their duty because they eventually believed the child, removed the obvious threat, or changed the environment. But Heaven looks beyond the intervention. Heaven judges whether the child was shepherded afterward. Heaven observes if pain was respected or hurried. Heaven sees whether the child was pressured to make everyone else feel better before the child genuinely began to heal. And Heaven does not regard that as harmless. When adults settle for just symptom relief because true restoration is too hard, they are still failing in stewardship. A wounded child is not a problem to be silenced. They are a life to be restored.

Do not settle for symptom relief. Seek real healing. Do not celebrate silence too soon. Look for restored trust, restored voice, restored peace, restored identity. Look for the child becoming safe enough to speak honestly, not just quiet enough to stop alarming others. Look for the return of grounded joy, not just the return of routine. Look for emotional openness, not merely behavioral compliance. Look for the child beginning to believe again that they are safe, worthy, heard, and not defined by what happened. Those are deeper signs of restoration than surface calm ever could be.

Because the wound you no longer see may still be shaping the life you are watching. It may still be teaching the child how to hide, how to mistrust, how to brace, how to detach, how to fear affection, how to fear exposure, and how to protect themselves through silence. And if adults are satisfied too early, they may leave the child trapped in a wound that simply learned how to wear cleaner clothes.

So let this be the wakeup call: do not call a child healed because the room feels easier. Do not call it restoration because the visible tears have stopped. Do not call it peace because the child no longer protests. Ask deeper questions. Stay longer in the process. Pay attention to what is missing beneath the calm. Refuse to let appearance replace discernment.

Because false recovery is one of the cruelest deceptions after trauma, it provides adults with relief but leaves children unhealed. And God will hold watchmen accountable not only for whether they stopped the harm but also for whether they stayed long enough to help heal any remaining damage.

CHAPTER FOURTEEN
RESTORING SAFETY AFTER BREACH

Rebuilding Trust and Stability

Once trust has been broken, safety can't be restored through words alone. It needs to be rebuilt with action, consistency, transparency, and time. A breach changes how a child perceives people, environments, authority, affection, and even routine activities. What once felt normal may now seem threatening. What once felt safe may now feel uncertain. A room may look the same, a schedule may be unchanged, familiar faces may still be there, but the child's internal world no longer perceives these things the same way. That is what a breach does. It damages more than just the moment; it alters the child's view of the world.

Restoring safety after a breach means rebuilding the world around the child in a way that is both believable and stable. That word matters: believable. A child who has been wounded does not automatically trust declarations of safety simply because adults speak them. They have already learned that danger can exist where safety was assumed. They have already learned that trusted spaces can fail, that familiar people can wound, and that adults do not always see what they should have seen. So safety must be rebuilt in a way that the child can experience repeatedly, not merely hear described. Words matter, but after a breach, actions speak louder.

It begins with one clear reality: the child must not be expected to feel safe again because adults say they are safe. Safety must be experienced repeatedly before it is trusted again. This is where many caregivers misunderstand restoration. They assume that once the danger has been removed, the healing is complete. But removal of danger is not the same as restoration of safety. A child may be physically protected and still internally unsettled. They may still scan rooms. They may still hesitate around affection. They may still fear secrecy, pressure, manipulation, or unexpected contact. Their body may still expect harm long after the threat is gone. Their heart may still remain alert even while the adults around them are eager to "move forward."

So safety must be rebuilt intentionally. That rebuilding includes restoring predictable routines, reinforcing boundaries, reducing unnecessary chaos, ensuring emotional access to trusted adults, and making the home environment feel consistent rather than unstable. A child recovering from breach needs repeated evidence that adults now see what they once missed, guard what they once failed to guard, and respond where they once may have delayed.

The child must begin to experience a new pattern: the adults are awake now, the wall is stronger now, the room is safer now, my voice matters now, and what hurt me before is no longer being ignored. Trust is repaired through consistency. Not intensity. Not speeches. Not promises alone. Consistency. A dramatic response in the first week means little if the months that follow are careless, distracted, emotionally unavailable, or spiritually passive. A child watches whether the adults have actually changed. They watch whether boundaries hold. They watch whether the home remains attentive after the emotional crisis fades. They watch whether the concern was temporary or whether protection has truly become part of the structure. A child often believes what adults repeat, not merely what adults announce.

This is where a reality check is necessary. Some adults want restored trust without paying the long-term cost of becoming trustworthy again. They want the child to calm down faster than they are willing to change the environment. They want the child to stop fearing while still leaving the same cracks in the wall. They want peace in the house more than they want the child genuinely rebuilt. That is not restoration. That is adult impatience trying to rush what only faithful consistency can repair. If the breach revealed weak oversight, loose boundaries, delayed response, emotional unavailability, or spiritual passivity, then those things must be corrected, not merely regretted. Regret without reform does not rebuild trust.

As children transition into their teenage years, the threats they face evolve significantly. The risk of encountering dangerous individuals often comes not just from strangers but from peers, romantic interests, social circles, and various online platforms where anonymity, emotional pressure, and hidden access embolden predators and manipulators. This shift in danger necessitates a more vigilant and mature approach from parents and guardians. Teenagers may not be as vulnerable as younger children, but they are still vulnerable. In some ways, the complexity increases because pressure begins to wear the clothing of desire, belonging, romance, autonomy, and social acceptance.

Proverbs 22:3 declares, "A prudent man foreseeth the evil, and hideth himself." This underscores the importance of foresight in protecting our youth. Parents play a crucial role in guiding their teens to develop the skills needed to identify warning signs in interpersonal relationships. They must teach them how unhealthy relationships work, how pressure hides behind attention, how control masquerades as care, and how secrecy often signals danger rather than depth. A teenager must be taught that not every intense bond is healthy, not every emotionally charged connection is safe, and not every person who "understands" them deserves private access to their inner world.

Parents need to have open dialogues with their teens about the characteristics of unhealthy relationships. Key red flags include controlling behavior, in which one person attempts to dictate another's actions, clothing, social interactions, digital access, schedule, or responses. Secrecy is another red flag, especially when communication becomes guarded, coded, hidden, or resistant to healthy adult oversight. Teens should also be made aware of pressure to conform—whether peer pressure to engage in risky behavior, emotional manipulation intended to elicit guilt or obedience, or romantic pressure disguised as love. Inappropriate requests that cross personal boundaries, degrade dignity, or make the teen uncomfortable must be named plainly and discussed without embarrassment. Teens do not need vague warnings; they need language clear enough to recognize danger before it takes root.

By equipping teens with the knowledge to recognize these signs, parents foster awareness and empowerment. But after a breach, this awareness is even more essential. The goal is not simply to return the child or teen to what existed before. The goal is to establish a wiser normal. A wiser normal means the child is not merely being comforted; they are being strengthened. It means they are taught how to recognize unsafe patterns earlier than before, how to say no with more confidence, how to question secrecy, how to identify pressure, and how to seek help without hesitation. It means the family does not pretend the breach taught nothing. It means the pain is not wasted, even though it should never have happened.

First Timothy 4:12 says, "Let no man despise thy youth; but be thou an example of the believers." This reminds us that youth is not weakness by definition. It is a season that can still carry dignity, discernment, strength, and conviction. Teenagers should be empowered with the skills to establish personal boundaries, confidently say no to pressures that do not align with truth, and recognize when they need support in uncomfortable situations. After a breach, this becomes especially important. The teen must not be left feeling that harm has permanently made them powerless. Restoration includes helping them learn that they can still live wisely, speak clearly, resist pressure, and walk with dignity.

Safeguarding children and teens after a breach requires a foundation of open and honest communication, mutual respect, and ongoing mentorship. By maintaining a dialogue that welcomes difficult questions, emotional honesty, and truthful reflection, parents create a safe space for expression. Consistent guidance helps children and teens navigate life's complexities while reinforcing their value and potential. A young person who has been harmed often needs more than just rules. They need wise adults who can walk alongside them, interpret what they are feeling, and help them understand what is healthy, what is manipulative, and what belongs nowhere near their future.

After a breach, mentorship becomes especially important. A child or teenager who has experienced violation often needs repeated relational proof that safe adults still exist, that healthy authority still exists, and that love can still operate without manipulation. Rebuilding trust means showing them that boundaries can be strong without being cruel, accountability can be firm without being threatening, and care can be consistent without hidden motives. They need to see safe strength in action. They need to know that not every authority figure dominates, not every correction humiliates, not every relationship demands secrecy, and not every form of closeness is unsafe.

Restoring safety also involves restoring agency. A child who has experienced a breach often feels powerless. Their choices may have been ignored. Their voice may have been silenced. Their discomfort may have been dismissed. Therefore, restoration must include helping them regain a sense of personal agency. This might mean inviting their voice, providing safe choices when appropriate, reinforcing their right to speak up, teaching them how to recognize and leave unsafe situations, and showing them that their discomfort shouldn't be buried to keep others comfortable. The goal isn't to create fear-driven independence but to foster wise, supported confidence.

A renewed environment says: You don't have to face this alone. You are allowed to speak, question, and refuse what jeopardizes your safety. You are no longer powerless. These messages not only comfort the wounded child but also reprogram the soul. They challenge the falsehood that the child's voice no longer matters or that their boundaries are only meant to be crossed. They help recover what was stolen by violation: confidence, clarity, and the right to feel safe.

This chapter also demands a warning to adults. If you fail to rebuild trust through action, you force the child to live with the consequences of your unfinished stewardship. If you remove the obvious danger but leave the child in chaos, inconsistency, emotional distance, spiritual neglect, or weak boundaries, then you have not fully restored safety. If you demand trust before you have become trustworthy through repeated faithful action, you are asking the child to carry a burden they were never meant to carry. And Heaven sees that. God does not only see whether a breach occurred. He sees how adults responded after it did. He sees whether they rebuilt the walls or merely talked about peace while leaving the weak points exposed.

Rebuilding trust and stability is not an easy task. It's layered, patient, and intentional. But it is possible. A breach may have fractured peace, but it doesn't have to define the future. With steady guidance, open communication, protective structures, emotional faithfulness, and spiritual covering, children and teens can relearn what safety feels like. They can carefully rebuild trust. They can honestly reclaim stability. They can grow stronger—not because what happened was small, but because healing is taken seriously. Not because the breach is denied, but because restoration is pursued with courage.

Restoring safety after a breach means more than recovering from damage. It means rebuilding life with greater clarity, stronger protection, and wiser discernment than before. It means the family learns, changes, strengthens, and refuses to leave the child under the same vulnerable conditions that allowed harm to enter. And that kind of restoration does not merely repair what was broken. It fortifies what remains.

❖ Spiritual Warning ❖

A Warning After the Breach

A breach changes more than circumstances. It changes the atmosphere. It changes trust. It changes the way a child looks at doors, voices, rooms, affection, authority, correction, privacy, and even silence. What once felt ordinary may now feel uncertain. What once felt harmless may now feel threatening. What once brought comfort may now awaken caution. That is why the aftermath must never be treated lightly. A child may be removed from danger and still remain deeply affected by what it taught their heart, body, and mind.

What was broken externally may have also damaged something internally. If adults only focus on removing the offender without rebuilding the child's world, the restoration remains incomplete. The danger might be gone from the room, but the wound can still be live in the child. The manipulator might be absent, but fear can still persist. The crisis may be over publicly, but confusion, vigilance, shame, and mistrust can continue privately. A child does not heal just because the situation has ended. Sometimes, the end of the event is only the start of a long process of healing.

Some guardians think the crisis ended when the exposure ended. It did not. The visible threat may be gone, but the internal alarm may still be ringing. The child may still be carrying fear into ordinary moments. They may still be flinching inwardly when no one else sees it. They may still be asking silent questions: "Am I safe now? Will they protect me this time? Will anyone listen sooner next time? Can I trust what adults say? Can I trust this house? Can I trust my own instincts?" Those questions are not answered by speeches. They are answered by repeated evidence. They are answered by what the adults do next.

These questions must be answered not only with words, but with consistent action. You must rebuild what the breach shattered. Rebuild trust. Rebuild safety. Rebuild structure. Rebuild voice. Rebuild stability. Rebuild the child's confidence that the adults around them are no longer asleep at the wall. Rebuild the environment so thoroughly and faithfully that the child no longer has to live under the same uncertainty that once left them exposed. Rebuilding is slow, but it is sacred. And parents or guardians who shrink back from that work because it is emotionally exhausting are failing the child a second time.

And do not grow impatient in the process. That warning must be heard with force. Some breaches do more than harm innocence. They tempt adults into a false sense of urgency—an eagerness to get past the event faster than the child can heal from it. Adults may want the tears to stop, the tension to lift, the routines to normalize, the house to feel easier again. But a child is not healed because the adults are tired of the aftermath. A child is not restored because everyone else wants life to move on. Healing cannot be rushed to satisfy adult discomfort.

Resist that temptation. The child's recovery is not an inconvenience to manage. It is a sacred stewardship to honor. Do not ask them to trust quickly. Do not ask them to feel normal on command. Do not ask them to return to ease while their inner world is still rebuilding. Do not call them dramatic because the wound still affects them. Do not call them ungrateful because they are not recovering according to your preferred pace. Do not use spiritual language to pressure them into looking healed before they actually are. That is not care. That is impatience dressed as leadership.

What has been breached must be restored carefully. Carefully means watchfully. Carefully means patiently. Carefully means truthfully. Carefully means the adults must remain emotionally available, spiritually awake, and practically consistent. The child must see that the walls are stronger now, that their voice is believed now, that secrecy is confronted now, that boundaries are firmer now, and that the adults who may once have missed something are no longer casual about what they have been assigned to guard. Restoration after breach is not sentimental. It is structural. It is spiritual. It is relational. It is daily.

Because if the breach is treated casually, fear may remain hidden beneath forced stability. And hidden fear, left unaddressed, can quietly shape a life. It can shape how the child attaches, how they receive love, how they respond to authority, how they interpret correction, how they handle touch, how they carry shame, how they expect danger, and how they see God. What adults rush past often does not disappear. It buries itself deeper. It waits. It resurfaces later in different forms. And then people wonder why the child grew older but never seemed fully free. Sometimes the answer is simple and devastating: the breach was addressed, but the aftermath was not faithfully shepherded.

This is also where accountability before God becomes sobering. Heaven is not only watching whether adults intervened in the crisis, but also observing what they do afterward. God sees whether the child was patiently healed or simply managed. He notices if the adults grow weary of the healing process and subtly pressure the child to return to normalcy. He also observes whether the home was truly rebuilt into a safer environment or if the family merely hopes that time will resolve what stewardship has neglected. The Lord treats the aftermath with gravity because He understands how deeply it influences a child's future.

Stand present after the breach. Stand patient after the breach. Stand protective after the breach. Do not disappear once the visible emergency passes. Do not retreat emotionally because the harder work now lacks public urgency. Do not hand the child back to routine and call that restoration. Keep showing up. Keep listening. Keep reinforcing safety. Keep rebuilding trust through action. Keep guarding what fear is still trying to occupy. Keep refusing the lie that time alone will repair what faithful love has not yet helped restore.

Because restoration does not happen automatically, it happens when faithful adults decide that the aftermath matters as much as the emergency. It happens when the child is not left alone to carry what the breach awakened. It happens when the adults say, through their actions, What happened to you matters. What it did inside you matters. And we will not stop at removing the threat. We will stay until what was shaken is strengthened again.

That is the warning after the breach: do not stop too soon. Do not relax because the crisis is no longer visible. Do not assume the child is fine because the room is quieter. Do not choose your comfort over their full restoration. What was broken needs more than rescue. It needs rebuilding. And God will hold watchmen accountable not only for whether they responded when the wall was breached, but for whether they stayed long enough to help restore what the breach damaged.

THE FINAL CHARGE

CHAPTER FIFTEEN
SPIRITUAL ACCOUNTABILITY

The Responsibility of Watchmen

Parenting is a lifelong calling, but it is more than commitment—it is accountability before God. As children grow and change, wise guardianship must also grow and change. Toddlers require one kind of protection. Teenagers require another. Young adults require still another. But while methods may shift with age and season, the calling itself does not. The mission remains the same: to nurture, guide, protect, correct, discern, and stand faithfully over the life God has placed in your hands. Parenting is not a sentimental role to be carried by emotion alone. It is a sacred trust, and every adult entrusted with a child will answer before God for how that trust was handled.

Children communicate in many ways—through words, tone, silence, behavior, resistance, fear, withdrawal, agitation, curiosity, and sudden change. A wise parent does not merely hear what a child says; they learn to discern what a child is revealing. This responsibility goes far beyond observation. It requires spiritual attentiveness, emotional presence, and practical vigilance. It requires adults who understand that children do not always possess the words to explain what they feel, what they fear, or what has shifted around them. A child may detect danger long before they can describe it. They may communicate distress through a change in mood, sleep, tone, behavior, or appetite before they ever speak it plainly. That is why a watchman is necessary. The child may feel what is wrong, but the guardian must be sober enough to recognize what the child cannot yet name.

With the unwavering truth of God's Word as their foundation, parents must seek direction through the Holy Spirit, whose promptings illuminate what is hidden and sharpen what is true. Each day they must cultivate vigilance, remaining alert to subtle threats—harmful influences, emotional turmoil, spiritual confusion, predatory access, digital corruption, false teaching, relational manipulation, and internal wounds that may not be visible at first glance. This kind of parenting is not accidental. It is deliberate. It requires prayer, self-discipline, moral clarity, courage, and the refusal to drift into lazy assumption. A child's future should never be surrendered to whatever influence is nearest, loudest, most popular, or most persistent.

The role of a watchman is not passive. It never has been. A watchman does not merely stand in place and hope danger never comes. A watchman observes. A watchman discerns. A watchman warns. A watchman acts. In Scripture, the watchman was accountable not only for what he saw, but for what he did after he saw it. If he recognized danger and failed to sound the alarm, he was not innocent simply because he did not cause the threat. His guilt was in neglecting the responsibility of response. That truth is severe, and it should be. Because many adults want innocence without vigilance, peace without prayer, safety without structure, and children without the burden of true guardianship. But Heaven does not reward passive love. Heaven honors faithful stewardship.

That truth carries enormous weight for every parent, guardian, and leader entrusted with children. To watch is not merely to be present. To watch is to be attentive. To watch is to refuse spiritual laziness. To watch is to recognize that what is entrusted to you must be guarded with intention. Presence alone is not protection. A parent can be in the room yet absent in discernment. A guardian can claim deep love and still be dangerously passive. A leader can speak about the importance of children while failing to regulate the access, atmosphere, influences, and vulnerabilities surrounding them. This is where the reality check must come: many children have suffered not because no adult was nearby, but because the adults nearby were not truly watching.

Children do not choose their guardians. God allows them to be placed in the care of adults who must answer for how that care was carried out. That is why parental responsibility cannot be reduced to provision alone. It is not enough to feed a child if you do not also guard them. It is not enough to love a child emotionally if you refuse to confront what threatens them. It is not enough to pray over a child while ignoring what discernment has already detected. It is not enough to say, I would do anything for my child, while leaving the gates of access, secrecy, influence, atmosphere, and accountability weakly defended.

Love that does not guard is incomplete. Concern that does not act is insufficient. Protection that exists only in words is fragile.

A true watchman does not separate affection from accountability. Love that refuses vigilance is incomplete. Concern that refuses action is insufficient. Protection that exists only in speech is weak. The responsibility of watchmen is to stand at the gate of the home, the heart, the mind, the atmosphere, and the future of the child under their care. It is worth noticing what others dismiss. It is to ask what others avoid. It is to confront what others excuse. It is to remain awake when comfort tempts sleep. It is to strengthen weak places before the breach. It is to regulate access before familiarity becomes danger. It is to build a structure before a crisis exposes what should have already been in place. It is to understand that safety is not preserved by hope alone, but by active, faithful, God-conscious guardianship.

This assignment is holy. It is weighty. It is not symbolic. It is real. And every generation must decide whether it will rise to that responsibility or neglect it. This is where the warning from God must be heard clearly: Heaven does not only see what was done to children. Heaven also sees what the adults assigned to guard them left undone. It sees the parent who sensed something and silenced it. It sees the guardian who noticed the change and called it nothing. It observes a leader who places greater emphasis on maintaining their public image rather than prioritizing the well-being and innocence of the individuals they are supposed to protect.

This leader seems more concerned with how others perceive them than with the ethical implications of their decisions or the impact those decisions have on the vulnerable. It sees the household where boundaries were weak, the atmosphere was unguarded, the devices were unmonitored, the access was too loose, the warnings were minimized, and the child was left more exposed than the adults were willing to admit. And God does not call that small. He calls it stewardship mismanaged.

There is a dangerous illusion many adults carry: I love my child, so that should be enough. But love without vigilance has failed many children. Sentiment without structure has failed many children.

Spiritual language without practical obedience has failed many children. Some adults have confused affection with guardianship and emotion with stewardship. But Scripture does not honor that confusion. The watchman is not judged by how deeply he felt concern while he slept through the breach. He is judged by whether he stood awake at the wall. Intention does not erase neglect. Desire does not excuse passivity. Tears after the damage do not carry the same weight as faithfulness before it.

Let this chapter, therefore, function as a wake-up call. If you have grown passive, wake up. If you have mistaken routine for safety, wake up. If you have trusted appearances more than patterns, wake up. If you have allowed social pressure to weaken your boundaries, wake up. If you have been more afraid of offending adults than failing children, wake up. If you have been giving children provision without protection, wake up. If you have been praying without watching, sensing without acting, or claiming concern while avoiding confrontation, wake up. The time for casual guardianship has passed. Children are being shaped, targeted, manipulated, wounded, and spiritually pressured in ways that require stronger watchmen than sentiment alone can produce.

The responsibility of watchmen also includes personal accountability. Before guarding the house, the watchman must examine himself. A spiritually dull parent cannot guard a child closely the way the word of God has for them to do it, if they are not obeying God's word. A leader who tolerates compromise in private weakens authority in public. A guardian ruled by distraction, bitterness, lust, fear of man, emotional inconsistency, or unaddressed wounds becomes easier prey for deception. Watchfulness begins in the inner life. Parents must repent quickly, pray seriously, walk honestly, and refuse to normalize their own drift. It is dangerous to want children protected while the adults themselves are spiritually asleep. A sleepy watchman cannot keep a strong wall.

This is why spiritual accountability is not only about what parents do around children. It is also about what they allow within themselves. What habits are weakening discernment? What fears are silencing necessary confrontation? What compromises are dulling conviction? What distractions are stealing attentiveness? What unresolved wounds are making them inconsistent? These questions matter because children live under the covering of adult stewardship. If the adult becomes careless inwardly, that carelessness often appears outwardly in the quality of the protection they provide.

The responsibility of watchmen is also generational. What one generation refuses to guard carefully, the next generation may suffer from deeply. Neglect has ripple effects. Silence echoes. Weak boundaries teach future weakness. Unguarded homes often rear children who struggle to recognize what safety even looks like. But faithfulness also multiplies. A guarded home teaches clarity. A praying household teaches spiritual sensitivity. A boundary-conscious family teaches dignity. A watchful parent strengthens not only the present child but often the child's future home, future discernment, future relationships, and future children as well. What is guarded today shapes what becomes possible tomorrow.

So let this settle upon the conscience with force: parenting is not merely about rearing functional adults. It is about standing before God as one who understands the sacredness of the life entrusted to them. It is about answering not only, Did I love them? But also, Did I guard them? Did I listen? Did I respond? Did I act when the warning came? Did I build what should have been built? Did I confront what should have been confronted? Did I remain awake at my post? Those are watchman questions. And every guardian who claims to love a child must one day face them honestly.

Stand at the gate of the home.
Stand at the gate of the mind.
Stand at the gate of the atmosphere.
Stand at the gate of access, affection, influence, and truth.
Stand when others grow passive.
Stand when comfort tempts compromise.
Stand when culture mocks vigilance.
Stand when discernment says act.

Because this assignment is real.
It is holy.
It is weighty.
And God is watching how the watchmen watch.

STEWARDSHIP BEFORE GOD

The responsibility of watchmen is ultimately rooted in stewardship before God. Children are not possessions. They are not extensions of the adult ego. They are not ornaments to decorate a family image, props to maintain a reputation, or temporary assignments to be handled casually until adulthood arrives. They are lives entrusted by God into human hands for a season of shaping, guarding, guiding, correcting, covering, and preparing. That truth should humble every parent and shake every careless guardian. A child is not "mine" in the absolute sense. A child is a trust from Heaven. And every trust from Heaven comes with accountability.

That means every parent lives under divine accountability. Stewardship before God means recognizing that authority is borrowed, not owned. Parents do not stand as sovereign over the souls of their children. They stand as stewards who will one day answer for how they handled what Heaven placed within their reach. That is where this matter becomes deeply sobering. Parenting is not merely a private family matter. It is a sacred assignment under the eye of God. The decisions made in the home are not hidden from Him. The atmosphere of the home is not hidden from Him. The failures of the home are not hidden from Him. The way a child was listened to, dismissed, protected, exposed, corrected, ignored, believed, or silenced is all fully visible before the Lord.

God sees not only the visible failures but the hidden ones. He sees not only acts of direct harm, but acts of neglect. He sees when a child's discomfort was dismissed because an adult did not want to deal with it. He sees when warning signs were minimized because facing them would have been inconvenient. He sees when convenience outranked courage. He sees when adults protected image more fiercely than innocence. He sees when social comfort, ministry appearance, family pride, or adult relationships were preserved at the expense of a child's safety. He sees what was ignored in private long before it ever became visible in public. And God is not casual about stewardship.

This is the reality check many adults need: it is possible to commit no direct act of abuse and still stand guilty of grave failure before God because you neglected what you were assigned to guard. It is possible to say, I love my child, and still have left that child vulnerable through laziness, inconsistency, weak boundaries, loose access, prayerlessness, digital carelessness, emotional dismissal, or delayed action.

It is possible to weep after damage is done and still have to face the truth that the wall should have been stronger before the breach. This is why stewardship cannot be reduced to affection. Love that does not guard is incomplete. Concern that does not act is insufficient. Good intentions do not erase neglected responsibility.

The stewardship of children includes guarding their bodies, protecting their emotions, strengthening their identities, instructing their conscience, cultivating their spiritual sensitivity, and building an environment where truth, safety, and accountability can live together. That is a broad and holy work. It means more than providing food, shelter, clothing, and education. It means paying attention to atmosphere, access, influence, speech, boundaries, emotional climate, and spiritual health. It means understanding that a child is being formed every day by what the home allows, what the home ignores, what the home celebrates, and what the home corrects. Parents are not only managing a household. They are shaping a soul-bearing environment.

Parents must understand that every unchecked atmosphere teaches something. Every tolerated compromise creates something. Every careless pattern reproduces something. Stewardship is not only about what we intentionally say—it is also about what our homes consistently communicate. A child is always learning. They are learning from what adults excuse, what adults avoid, how adults respond under pressure, whether adults tell the truth, whether adults notice danger, whether adults protect quickly, whether adults honor discomfort, and whether adults live the values they preach. The home is always discipling, even when no formal lesson is being taught.

A household may declare values verbally while undermining them practically. But children learn through repeated experience. They watch what is permitted. They notice what is ignored.

They remember what was tolerated. They feel the difference between a house that speaks about God and a house that is actually governed by reverence, truth, vigilance, and holy order. Stewardship before God, therefore, requires integrity between what is taught and what is lived. It is not enough to speak about safety while leaving access unregulated. It is not enough to pray publicly while living carelessly. It is not enough to quote Scripture while dismissing discernment. It is not enough to claim the child is precious while continually leaving that child under weak protection.

This is why parenting must remain prayerful, disciplined, and humble. No parent will carry this responsibility perfectly. But perfection is not the standard God demands. Faithfulness is. A faithful steward remains teachable. A faithful steward stays alert. A faithful steward repents when wrong, adjusts when corrected, and refuses to defend failure when truth has exposed it. A faithful steward does not hide behind excuses, ego, or self-justification. They do not say, "That's just how I am," when the truth reveals weakness in their watch. They do not say, "I meant well," as though that erases what negligence produced. They let God correct them. They let truth humble them. They let conviction move them to change.

The call is not to flawless parenting. The call is to accountable parenting. The call is to intentional stewardship under the eye of God. That means adults must stop treating parental authority as casual power and start treating it as a sacred responsibility. They must stop measuring themselves only by whether they provided materially and start asking whether they guarded spiritually, emotionally, relationally, and practically. They must stop using love as a blanket excuse for weak vigilance. They must stop assuming that because they did not mean harm, they bear no responsibility for the harm that came through what they failed to watch.

And that stewardship must never be treated as light. This is where the wakeup call must sound: if God entrusted you with a child, then your negligence is not small. Your passivity is not small.

Your refusal to listen is not small. Your fear of confrontation is not small. Your digital carelessness is not small. Your tolerance of unhealthy access is not small. Your dismissal of warning signs is not small. These things are not minor parenting oversights in the courts of Heaven. They are stewardship issues. And God deals seriously with stewardship.

Too many adults want the blessing of children without the burden of watchfulness. Too many want the title of parent without the cost of disciplined guardianship. Too many want to be seen as loving while resisting the firmness, structure, correction, and holy seriousness that real protection requires. But children are too sacred for casual parenting. Their innocence is too holy for adults to keep drifting through stewardship half-awake. God did not place children in our care so we could merely enjoy them. He placed them in our care so we could guard them, guide them, and answer faithfully for them.

So let this settle with weight: one day, every steward will answer. Not only for what they gave the child, but for what they allowed near the child. Not only for what they taught, but for what they tolerated. Not only for how deeply they felt love, but for how faithfully they practiced protection. Those are hard questions, but they are holy questions. And any adult entrusted with a child should live in a way that is preparing to answer them honestly before God.

So stay humble.
Stay teachable.
Stay prayerful.
Stay watchful.

Repent quickly.
Adjust when truth exposes weakness.
Do not defend what God is trying to correct.

Because stewardship before God is not a light thing.
It is a sacred charge.
And the child placed under your care is not merely passing through your house.
That child is passing through your hands on the way to destiny.

GENERATIONAL CONSEQUENCES

What parents permit, protect, ignore, excuse, confront, or establish rarely ends with one generation. Homes are never shaping only the present moment. They are training patterns, building instincts, forming expectations, and establishing emotional and spiritual templates that children often carry far beyond childhood. There are generational consequences to both vigilance and neglect. What adults call small today may become normal tomorrow. What is tolerated in one generation may become repeated in the next. What is guarded faithfully today may become inherited wisdom tomorrow.

When children grow up in homes where truth is clear, love is strong, boundaries are consistent, repentance is practiced, and safety is taken seriously, they carry those patterns into the future. They are more likely to build homes marked by wisdom rather than confusion, discernment rather than passivity, courage rather than avoidance, and prayer rather than drift. What was modeled becomes a template. What was reinforced becomes instinct. What was honored becomes culture. A child who was taught that discomfort matters, that secrecy is dangerous, that truth is welcome, that safety is sacred, and that God's presence governs the home does not simply benefit in the moment. That child often carries those convictions into marriage, into ministry, into parenting, into leadership, and into the shaping of yet another generation.

In this way, righteousness multiplies. Vigilance multiplies. Wise protection multiplies. Emotional honesty multiplies. A child who experienced healthy boundaries often grows into an adult who can recognize unhealthy access more quickly. A child who was believed when they spoke often grows into an adult who knows how to listen well when someone else is trembling with truth. A child who was guarded faithfully often grows into an adult who does not treat guardianship casually. What was planted in one generation often becomes fruit in the next. That is one of the mercies of God—that faithfulness does not end where it begins.

But the opposite is also true. When neglect is normalized, it echoes. When silence is rewarded, it repeats. When manipulation is overlooked, it teaches future tolerance for confusion and harm. When children are reared in homes where boundaries are weak, warnings are minimized, pain is dismissed, and image is protected more fiercely than innocence, those children often carry invisible distortions into adulthood unless those patterns are confronted and broken. They may struggle to recognize what is unsafe because what was unsafe once felt familiar. They may normalize secrecy because secrecy lived in the walls. They may doubt their own discernment because adults taught them to override discomfort for the sake of keeping peace.

Unhealed wounds do not always stay contained in the generation that first carried them. They often spill forward. They may influence future marriages, future parenting, future ministry, future relationships, and future responses to crisis. A child who was not protected may later overcompensate in fear, or else drift into passivity because no one ever modeled holy vigilance. A child whose voice was dismissed may become an adult who struggles to speak, struggles to trust, or struggles to listen when others speak. A child reared in chaos may unconsciously recreate instability. A child formed in secrecy may find openness frightening. That is why generational consequence is so serious: neglected patterns do not usually die quietly. They travel unless they are interrupted.

This is why a reality check is necessary. A guardian may think they are dealing only with the present, only with one decision, one compromise, one moment of weakness, one tolerated pattern, one avoided confrontation, one excused warning sign. But what is ignored in the present may shape the future far beyond what they imagine. A single avoided conversation, a single silence where truth should have been spoken, a single pattern of tolerated compromise, a single season of passive protection may widen into years of emotional, spiritual, and relational fallout if left unchallenged. Too many adults think only in terms of immediate convenience. God sees generational ripple. He sees what today's neglect will cost tomorrow's children.

This is where the warning from God must be felt with holy seriousness. Parents and guardians are not only being observed for how they handled the moment in front of them. They are being weighed for what their stewardship is setting in motion beyond them. Heaven does not see parenting as a private experiment with limited consequences. Heaven sees lineages, atmospheres, inheritance, and patterns. God sees whether truth is being planted or whether confusion is being permitted. He sees whether courage is being modeled or whether avoidance is being normalized. He sees whether repentance is breaking cycles or whether pride is preserving them. And He does not call that light.

Yet this truth is not only a warning. It is also hope. Because what has been passed down destructively can also be interrupted intentionally. Generational cycles are not invincible. They can be broken through repentance, truth, vigilance, healing, humility, and obedience. A parent who chooses to confront what was previously excused becomes a turning point. A family that chooses to rebuild boundaries where they were once absent becomes a new pattern. A guardian who stops protecting appearances and starts protecting innocence becomes a break in the line of neglect. A watchman who awakens can protect not only the current child, but children not yet born.

That is one of the most powerful realities in this work: faithfulness in one generation can become shelter for another. A mother or father who says, "It stops with me," is not making a small declaration. They are standing in spiritual opposition to what has been repeating quietly for years. They are saying that silence will not be inherited, that passivity will not be normalized, that unguarded homes will not continue, that emotionally wounded children will not simply be expected to survive without restoration, and that what was once overlooked will now be confronted with truth. That kind of decision has far-reaching power.

This is why accountability matters so deeply. You are never guarding only the moment in front of you. You are often guarding the generations behind it. The child who learns truth today may teach it tomorrow. The child who experiences safety today may build it tomorrow. The child who is believed today may become the protector of someone else tomorrow.

The child who sees boundaries honored today may establish them firmly in a future home. The child who is helped to heal today may one day become the safe presence someone else desperately needed. Faithfulness reproduces too.

Generational consequences are real. So let righteousness be the thing that multiplies. Let wisdom be what echoes. Let vigilance be what is inherited. Let healing be what gets passed down. Let courage become the new family pattern. Let truth become the atmosphere children grow up breathing. Let repentance become stronger than pride. Let spiritual seriousness become stronger than family habit. Let the next generation receive something cleaner, safer, wiser, and more God-governed than what came before.

Because what is established in one generation often becomes the atmosphere of the next. And what you tolerate today may become someone else's battle tomorrow—but what you confront faithfully today may become someone else's protection tomorrow.

❖ THE FINAL WORD ❖

A Final Charge and a Solemn Warning

The final word of this book is not fear. It is a responsibility. It is not panic. It is preparedness. It is not suspicion toward everything. It is discernment toward anything that threatens what God has entrusted. This book has not called parents, guardians, pastors, teachers, or leaders into paranoia. It has called them into awakening. It has called them to holy seriousness. It has called them to understand that innocence is too sacred to be guarded casually, and children are too valuable to be left under weak walls, drifting atmospheres, delayed responses, and half-awake watchmen.

The call throughout these pages has been clear: innocence must be guarded, children must be heard, boundaries must be established, secrecy must be broken, healing must be taken seriously, and parents must remain spiritually and practically awake. This is not a burden given to crush the parent. It is a charge given to awaken them. It is Heaven's reminder that love is not proven only through affection, emotion, provision, or sacrifice. Love is also proven through vigilance, structure, courage, truth, and the refusal to let danger move unchallenged through the gates of a child's life.

Children deserve more than affection without awareness. They deserve protection with conviction. They deserve homes where safety is not assumed but built. They deserve adults who do not shrink from discomfort when truth requires courage. They deserve watchmen who remain awake when culture grows careless, when access grows easier, when manipulation grows subtler, and when darkness learns to wear a polite face. They deserve adults who do not merely say, I love you, but who prove that love by what they regulate, what they confront, what they refuse, what they listen for, and what they guard.

If this book has made anything unmistakable, it is this: protection is not automatic. It is intentional. Healing is not accidental. It is cultivated. Discernment is not optional. It is necessary. A home must not merely look peaceful. It must be guarded. A child must not merely be told they are loved. They must also experience the structure, vigilance, and courage that prove that love protects. A parent must not merely hope for safety. They must labor for it in prayer, wisdom, consistency, humility, truth, and watchfulness. Safety is too sacred to be left to assumption.

This final word is therefore a summons. Stand at the gate. Guard the atmosphere. Listen closely. Respond quickly. Pray deliberately. Correct courageously. Love steadfastly. Lead faithfully. Because what you guard today may shape lives far beyond what you will ever fully see. A child under your watch is not merely passing through a season of dependence. That child is being formed. That child is learning what safety feels like, what truth sounds like, what discernment does, what healthy authority looks like, and whether the adults closest to them will rise when danger nears. What you build now may become their future standard. What you fail to build may become their future struggle.

And when the day comes to answer before God for the stewardship of those entrusted to you, may it be said that you did not sleep through your assignment. May it be said that you watched. May it be said that you stood. May it be said that you guarded what Heaven placed under your care. May it be said that when warning stirred, you did not suppress it; when truth confronted you, you did not resist it; when boundaries needed strengthening, you did not weaken them to preserve comfort; and when the child needed covering, you did not leave the gate unattended.

❊ A SOLEMN WARNING ❊

This is the final warning—not because the danger is ending, but because the responsibility must now be undeniable. There will always be pressure to relax. There will always be voices that call vigilance excessive, caution unnecessary, boundaries extreme, and discernment judgmental. There will always be temptation to preserve comfort, reputation, convenience, ministry image, social ease, and adult relationships at the expense of difficult action. But none of those things are worth the cost of neglected protection. A child's safety is too sacred for casual oversight. Innocence is too precious for half-hearted guardianship.

Let this settle with full weight: if you are entrusted with a child, you are entrusted with a watchman's post. You do not have the luxury of permanent passivity. You do not have the freedom to remain spiritually asleep. You do not have the right to let awkwardness silence discernment. You do not have permission to call delay wisdom when truth is demanding action. You do not get to hide behind good intentions while the wall is weak, the atmosphere is unguarded, the devices are unmonitored, the access is too loose, the warning signs are minimized, and the child is left more exposed than your words of love would ever admit.

Heaven is watching how you watch. God is not measuring how well appearances were kept. He is not measuring how socially agreeable you remained. He is not measuring how much discomfort you avoided. He is measuring faithfulness. He is measuring whether you listened when something shifted, whether you acted when something was wrong, whether you strengthened the gate when the wall showed weakness, whether you chose truth over convenience, and whether you treated the child under your care as the sacred trust they truly were. If warning signs surface and you excuse them, faithfulness is compromised. If your spirit is stirred and you suppress it, faithfulness is weakened. If access becomes inappropriate and you still remain silent, faithfulness is endangered. If the child's pain becomes inconvenient and you rush them into silence instead of healing, faithfulness is wounded.

This warning is not written to condemn the tenderhearted parent who is trying, learning, repenting, and growing. It is written to confront the dangerous illusion that parenting can remain shallow while the culture grows darker, the access grows wider, the digital gates remain open, the predators grow subtler, and the children grow more exposed. That illusion must die. The fantasy that affection alone is enough must die. The excuse that busyness weak oversight must die. The lie that familiarity guarantees safety must die. The habit of protecting appearances more fiercely than innocence must die. The tendency to defend sleep when the watchman should have awakened must die.

You were called to more than maintenance. You were called to guardianship. You were called to stewardship. You were called to spiritual accountability. You were called to stand between innocence and intrusion, between confusion and truth, between manipulation and safety, between fear and faithful protection. That calling is not light. It is not decorative. It is not symbolic. It is a post, and that post carries holy consequences.

So remain awake. Remain humble. Remain teachable. Remain discerning. Remain unwavering. And if you have failed before, then repent quickly, rise again, and strengthen what remains. A sleeping watchman must not defend his sleep. He must wake up. A careless guardian must not protect his ego. He must repent. A parent who sees weakness in the wall must not explain it away. They must rebuild it. The mercy of God is real, but so is His demand for faithful stewardship. Repentance is not merely sorrow. It is correction. It is waking up and doing differently what truth has now exposed.

This is the final charge: do not grow comfortable. Do not grow careless. Do not grow spiritually dull. Do not grow emotionally passive. Do not surrender the gate. Do not hand the child over to culture, secrecy, compromise, or unchecked influence and then call it trust. Do not let the modern world disciple your child while you remain casual at the wall.

Do not call neglect grace. Do not call passivity peace. Do not call weak boundaries love.

Stand.
Watch.
Pray.
Guard.
Listen.
Act.
Repent.
Strengthen the wall.
Answer the call fully.

Because children are listening. Children are depending. Children are being shaped. And generations may stand stronger or weaker because of how faithfully you carried your post. What you tolerate may echo. What you guard may multiply. What you build may outlive you. What you neglect may wound farther than you imagined. And when Heaven weighs your stewardship, may it not find a watchman who loved in words but slept in practice. May it find one who understood the hour, heard the warning, and stood faithfully at the gate.

❋ CLOSING DECLARATION ❋

There comes a moment when warning is no longer suggestion—it is mercy. This is that moment. We have entered an hour where innocence is not merely something to be cherished; it is something that is actively contested. Childhood is no longer being shaped slowly and safely by family, faith, and careful formation alone. Minds are being approached before they are matured. Hearts are being influenced before they are stable. Desires are being stirred before discernment is strong enough to govern them. Access now moves faster than wisdom, influence travels faster than instruction, and many doors are being opened digitally, emotionally, socially, and spiritually without serious examination. What once required physical nearness now requires only access. What once had to knock at the front door can now enter through a screen, a message, a voice, a relationship, an atmosphere, or an unguarded permission. And too often, permission is granted without prayer, without scrutiny, and without the kind of holy caution that stewardship demands.

Many assume safety because catastrophe has not yet announced itself. But visible damage is rarely the beginning of danger—it is the exposure of what was quietly developing. Corruption is patient. Compromise is strategic. Darkness does not rush; it studies. It watches habits. It reads atmospheres. It notes fatigue. It looks for adults who love deeply but watch loosely. It looks for homes where values are spoken but not enforced, where discomfort is felt but not followed, where warnings are sensed but not acted on. The absence of a visible crisis does not equal the presence of security. Just because nothing has erupted does not mean nothing is evolving beneath the surface. Silence is not safety. Calm is not confirmation. Sometimes the room is quiet because the threat has learned how to hide.

The greatest tragedies do not begin with explosions; they begin with exemptions. A boundary is relaxed. A question is avoided. A discomfort is dismissed. A warning is rationalized. A behavior is explained away. A private pattern is excused because confronting it would be inconvenient, awkward, or socially costly. Small compromises are seeds, and seeds do not look threatening when first planted. Yet given time, what was tolerated in subtlety grows into something that demands emergency. What felt insignificant becomes influential. What seemed harmless becomes habitual. What looked manageable becomes devastating. The crisis adults later call sudden was often not sudden at all. It was slow, tolerated, and insufficiently confronted.

Overlooked discomfort is often Heaven's early alarm system. That hesitation you felt, that pause in your spirit, that unsettled stirring that would not rest—those things should not be dismissed as paranoia simply because they disrupt comfort. When action is required but delayed, vulnerability expands. Delay gives access. Silence gives permission. Avoidance gives opportunity. That is why this is not the hour for passive guardianship. This is the hour for spiritual alertness. Pray before you permit. Discern before you delegate. Investigate before you ignore. Because what is protected intentionally is preserved. But what is assumed safe without vigilance eventually proves otherwise.

Innocence is sacred. Guard it like it is irreplaceable—because it is. Once fractured, it does not return in the same untouched form. Healing is possible, restoration is real, and God is merciful, but that does not make innocence replaceable. Complacency is not harmless. It is an opening. And too many adults have confused relaxed oversight with healthy trust. Too many have called passivity peace. Too many have treated casual access as normal, while danger moved quietly through the very spaces that should have been guarded with holy seriousness.

You cannot afford to sleep spiritually in a generation that is awake to weakness. The enemy does not move randomly. He observes, analyzes, studies patterns, and waits for openings. He watches rhythms. He learns emotional fatigue. He studies where the family has grown soft, where the wall is weakest, where the gate is least examined, where the atmosphere is spiritually dull, and where discernment has been repeatedly silenced in favor of convenience. Spiritual sleep is not merely inactivity; it is the dulling of discernment. It is when prayer becomes routine instead of revelation, when conviction grows quiet, when urgency weakens, and when caution is replaced with comfort. A watchman does not lose the wall in one night. He loses it moment by moment through tolerated neglect.

If your spirit senses movement, do not silence it. God does not stir you without reason. You cannot afford emotional avoidance when the Holy Spirit unsettles you. Discomfort is often divine communication. When something refuses to rest in your spirit, that agitation is not always anxiety—it may be instruction. Avoidance postpones confrontation, but it never prevents consequences. What you refuse to face today may mature into what you cannot control tomorrow. Courage in the spirit realm requires you to lean into what feels inconvenient, to ask the hard questions, to examine what others would rather ignore, and to refuse the false peace that comes from pretending what is wrong could not possibly be near.

You cannot afford to dismiss behavioral shifts simply because addressing them may disrupt familiarity. Patterns change before outcomes collapse. Subtle withdrawal, secretive movements, altered tones, emotional heaviness, compromised convictions, fear around certain people, changes in digital behavior, sudden guardedness, strange loyalty, or unexplained agitation—these are not always random fluctuations. They are often indicators. Discernment requires attention. Love requires intervention. Leadership requires vigilance. To notice and say nothing is not kindness—it is negligence. When something changes, investigate with wisdom. When something feels hidden, bring it to light with grace. Spiritual maturity does not look like staying agreeable while danger grows stronger. It looks like staying alert when the atmosphere is shifting.

Stay awake. Guard your heart. Test what you see. Confront what you sense. The cost of ignoring discernment is always greater than the discomfort of addressing it. **What are you saying, Preacher?** I'm glad you asked. I am saying this: stay awake—not casually alert, but spiritually disciplined. Refuse to drift into comfort when vigilance is required. A drowsy spirit cannot recognize a subtle threat.

What you fail to watch, you eventually surrender. Wakefulness is not fear; it is stewardship. Guard your heart with intention, because it is the gateway to perception, conviction, and decision. If it becomes compromised, everything downstream follows. Protect what shapes your thoughts. Protect what influences your emotions. Protect what feeds your spirit. What enters consistently will eventually rule internally.

Test what you see. Not everything that appears harmless is holy. Not everything that feels good is safe. Not everything popular is pure. Not everything familiar is trustworthy. Weigh motives. Examine patterns. Measure fruit. Discernment is not suspicion—it is spiritual intelligence rightly applied. If something cannot withstand examination, it does not deserve access. Confront what you sense. When your spirit hesitates, do not silence it. When peace withdraws, investigate why. Courage is not loud aggression; it is quiet obedience to what God is revealing. Addressing an issue may feel uncomfortable, but avoiding it compounds the damage. Silence today becomes sorrow tomorrow. Delay today becomes a consequence later. What you refuse to face will not disappear—it will develop.

Let this truth settle heavily upon your heart: when God entrusts you with a child, He does not assign you comfort—He assigns you responsibility. That responsibility requires vigilance when others relax. It requires courage when others hesitate. It requires confrontation when others prefer quiet. It requires you to value truth above social ease and safety above image. You will not be measured by how agreeable you were. You will be measured by how faithful you stood. If warning signs appear and you delay, if access feels excessive and you ignore it, if your spirit stirs and you silence it, you are not maintaining harmony—you are postponing prevention. And prevention delayed often becomes regret sustained.

The soul must be shaken because too many rely on hope instead of oversight. Too many assume safety rather than establish it. Too many protect reputations while innocence remains exposed. Too many say they would do anything for their children while refusing the vigilance, structure, discipline, confrontation, and prayer that real protection requires. There is no neutral ground in guardianship. You are either watching—or you are vulnerable. You are either confronting—or you are permitting. You are either guarding—or you are assuming.

This is not paranoia. It is stewardship. It is the sober recognition that if God placed a life under your care, then your role is not symbolic. It is accountable.

If something shifts, lean in immediately. If something unsettles you, investigate thoroughly. If something threatens your household, address it decisively. Better to endure temporary discomfort than permanent damage. Better to ask difficult questions than live with irreversible answers. Better to be misunderstood for vigilance than remembered for negligence. Stand at your post. Guard your gate. Refuse to surrender vigilance to convenience. Refuse to let culture mock you out of holy seriousness. Refuse to let emotional fatigue become your excuse for spiritual neglect. Refuse to let repeated exposure make you blind to what should still be confronted.

Because Heaven is not only aware of the threats outside your home—Heaven is aware of how faithfully you guarded what was inside it. God sees not only the predator, but the parent. Not only the danger, but the diligence. Not only what was done, but what was left undone. And once innocence is compromised, no explanation will ever feel sufficient. Not I was tired. Not I did not want to offend anyone. Not I assumed everything was fine. Not I trusted them. Not I never thought it could happen here. Those explanations may comfort an adult conscience for a moment, but they do not erase a child's wound.

Remain alert. Remain courageous. Remain unyielding. The watchman who stands firm saves more than peace—he preserves destiny. What you guard today may shape generations you will never meet. What you protect now may become someone else's future wisdom. What you refuse to ignore may become the reason a child still has clarity, dignity, trust, and hope later in life. So do not sleep through your assignment. Do not abandon your post. Do not treat this charge lightly.

This is the closing declaration: wake up, watchman. Stand where God placed you. Guard what Heaven entrusted. Protect with conviction. Listen with sobriety. Pray with urgency. Act with courage. And let it be said before God that when innocence was under threat, you did not turn away, grow passive, or choose ease over faithfulness—you stood.

✞ ENCOURAGEMENT FOR SOMEONE ✞

But God Kept You

There are wounds that never made headlines. There are cries that never reached a microphone. There are battles fought behind closed doors, beneath forced smiles, and inside nights so heavy that language itself felt too weak to carry the pain. Abuse—whether sexual, mental, psychological, emotional, verbal, spiritual, or physical—attempts to do far more than wound the body or disturb the mind. It tries to invade identity. It tries to poison memory. It tries to attach shame to innocence, confusion to worth, silence to truth, and despair to destiny. It tries to make the survivor feel as though what happened to them now has the right to define them. But even after all that was done, one holy truth still stands above the wreckage: God kept you.

You may have asked, Where was God when it happened? Where was He when I was afraid? Where was He when I cried, and no one came? Where was He when I felt dirty, abandoned, confused, or broken? Those are not wicked questions. They are wounded questions. They are the honest cries of a soul that has walked through darkness and is still trying to find language for what was stolen, violated, or shattered. Pain should not be minimized, and hurt should never be silenced in the name of false spirituality. But even in the hardest chapter, even in the season where it looked like evil had the loudest voice, this remains undeniable: you are still here. The fact that you are still breathing, still reaching, still reading, still longing for healing, still capable of hearing truth—these are not small things. They are evidence that what tried to erase you did not win.

The enemy intended to break you, bury you in shame, and convince you that your story ended in trauma. He intended for the wound to become your name. He intended for the violation to become your identity. He intended for the silence to become your prison. He intended for the fear to become permanent, for the mistrust to become absolute, and for the pain to speak louder than the purpose of God over your life. But the sustaining hand of God preserved you when you did not even realize you were being preserved. When your strength was gone, He held what you could not hold together. When your voice was silenced,

He heard what others did not hear. When you felt abandoned, Heaven had not moved. When it looked like darkness had the final word, God was still guarding the part of you that the enemy could not fully destroy.

Survival is not accidental. It is evidence of divine interruption.

There were moments you could have collapsed beneath the weight of it. Moments when your mind was tired, your heart was shattered, your body was carrying what words could not explain, and your soul felt exhausted from trying to survive what should never have happened. Yet somehow, you are still here. That "somchow" is not an empty chance. That "somehow" is mercy. That "somehow" is the keeping power of God. You endured what should have crushed you, and yet you remain. Not untouched, not unchanged, not unscarred—but still here. Still reachable by grace. Still recoverable. Still redeemable. Still capable of healing. Still capable of joy. Still capable of purpose. Still capable of becoming more than what was done to you.

Hear this clearly: what happened to you was real, but it is not the truest thing about you. The wound is real, but it is not your identity. The violation is real, but it is not your destiny. The pain is real, but it is not your permanent residence. The shame that tried to cling to you does not belong to you. The confusion that followed what happened does not define your worth. The silence you were forced into does not mean your voice is gone forever. You are not ruined. You are not disqualified. You are not too damaged for God to heal. You are not too fractured for Him to restore. You are not beyond tenderness, beyond safety, beyond peace, beyond love, or beyond purpose. The hand of God is not intimidated by your wound.

And this must be said with tenderness and force: what was done to you was not your fault. Not because you were young. Not because you were trusting. Not because you were vulnerable. Not because you were afraid. Not because you froze. Not because you did not speak sooner. Not because you did not know how to stop it. Not because you were manipulated. Not because someone used power, fear, secrecy, pressure, confusion, or emotional control against you. The blame belongs to the one who sinned against you, not to the one who was wounded by it.

Do not carry what Heaven never assigned to you. Do not wear guilt for a crime committed against your soul. Release false responsibility. Reject false shame. Refuse the lie that what was done to you somehow became yours to bear as moral failure.

God kept more than your body. He kept your destiny. He kept the part of you that still longs for truth. He kept the part of you that still responds to compassion. He kept the part of you that still hopes healing is possible. He kept the seed of life, the possibility of joy, the future that trauma tried to convince you was gone forever. There is still something holy alive in you. There is still something recoverable in you. There is still something beautiful that abuse could not fully extinguish. The enemy may have touched your story, but he does not own your ending.

Now hear this gently but boldly: what you survived can become someone else's lifeline. There are wounds that many leaders, counselors, and clergy cannot fully articulate because they have not walked through them. But your survival carries a kind of witness that polished language alone can never produce. That does not mean you owe the world your story before you are ready. It does not mean pain must immediately become public ministry. It does mean this: your life still carries purpose. Your testimony still carries weight. Your healing still has meaning. God does not waste pain. He redeems it. The very place where the enemy tried to mark you with shame can become the place where God reveals His keeping power, His restoring mercy, and His refusal to let darkness have the final word over your life.

You are not defined by what happened to you—you are defined by the One who kept you through it.

That means your future does not have to mirror your worst moment. That means your identity does not have to bow to the memory of violation. That means your relationships do not have to remain permanently governed by fear. That means your mind can be renewed. Your heart can be tended. Your trust can be rebuilt wisely. Your voice can return. Your peace can grow again. Your joy can rise in places you thought were permanently buried. Healing may be a process, and it may come in layers, but do not mistake process for impossibility. The God who kept you is still able to restore you.

So breathe again. Not because the wound was small, but because grace is greater. Cry if you need to. Grieve what was taken. Tell the truth. Refuse shame. Reach for help. Let safe people walk with you. Let God love you in the places that still ache. Let truth confront the lies that trauma planted. Let compassion touch the places where fear tried to settle permanently. Let your soul hear this until it sinks beneath the scar tissue: you were not abandoned. You were kept.

And if all you can hold onto right now is one sentence, let it be this: What tried to destroy me did not have the final word. God kept me.

✞ A POWERFUL WORD FROM THE LORD ✞

You were not forgotten in the darkness. You were not abandoned in the pain. You were not erased by what tried to break you. I saw what others did not see. I heard what others did not hear. I kept you when the weight of it should have crushed you. I covered you when confusion surrounded you. I preserved the part of you the enemy wanted destroyed. What tried to shame you will not own you. What tried to silence you will not define you. What tried to bury your voice, fracture your identity, and poison your future will not have the final word over your life.

The hand of evil was real, but My hand was greater. The wound was real, but My keeping power was greater. The night was long, but My mercy was longer. You thought you were only surviving, but I was preserving. You thought you were barely making it, but I was carrying what you could not hold together. You thought the story had become only pain, but I was guarding a purpose beneath the ashes. What hell meant as destruction, I will answer with redemption. What the enemy marked for ruin, I will rear with meaning. What was done to you will not become the master of who you are.

Hear the Word of the Lord through Genesis 50:20 (KJV):
"But as for you, ye thought evil against me; but God meant it unto good, to bring to pass, as it is this day, to save much people alive."

Stand in that truth. Evil was intended. Harm was real. The betrayal was not imaginary. The suffering was not small. But even what was meant for evil does not escape the sovereignty of God. The Lord is able to take what was meant to crush you and make it serve a holy purpose it never intended to produce. He does not call evil good—but He is so great that He can overrule evil, outlast evil, expose evil, heal what evil wounded, and bring forth life where darkness thought it had ended everything.

So hear this with power: your survival is not survival alone—it is an assignment. Not because the pain was good, but because the God who kept you is greater than the pain. Not because what happened was acceptable, but because what happened will not be wasted in the hands of a Redeemer. There is oil in what you endured. There is authority in what you survived. There is a voice rising out of what tried to bury you. There is comfort you will carry for others. There is discernment being forged in you. There is a testimony that will speak where polished words cannot reach. There are broken people who will one day breathe again because God kept you alive long enough to become proof that survival is possible, healing is real, and shame does not get the final word.

You are still here.
And because you are still here—God is not finished.
He is not finished healing.
He is not finished restoring.
He is not finished rebuilding.
He is not finished speaking life into places that still ache.
He is not finished turning mourning into strength, confusion into clarity, and survival into purpose.

So rise in the truth of what God has spoken over you.
You were not overlooked.
You were preserved.
You were kept for a reason.
And what tried to end you will become evidence that the keeping power of God is stronger than the darkest thing you survived.

✞ A FINAL PRAYER FOR PARENTS AND GUARDIANS ✞

Heavenly Father,

We come before You with humility, sobriety, and gratitude, acknowledging that every child is a gift, a trust, and a sacred assignment placed in human hands by divine wisdom. We thank You for the lives You have entrusted to parents, guardians, grandparents, mentors, pastors, and caregivers. We confess that this responsibility is far greater than human strength alone can carry, and so we look to You—the Keeper of Israel, the Defender of the innocent, the God who neither slumbers nor sleeps.

Lord, grant us eyes that see beyond appearances. Sharpen our discernment so that we will not be lulled into complacency by familiarity, reputation, or routine. Teach us to recognize what is healthy, what is harmful, what is pure, and what is attempting to disguise itself as harmless. Deliver us from passivity. Deliver us from denial. Deliver us from the kind of fear that remains silent when courage is required.

Father, protect the children under our care—physically, emotionally, mentally, spiritually, and relationally. Guard their bodies from harm, their minds from corruption, their hearts from distortion, and their identity from confusion. Let no predatory influence gain foothold in their lives. Let no secret take root in silence. Let no manipulation flourish where truth should stand. Let Your hand rest heavily upon them, and let Your presence surround them wherever they go.

Cover our homes with Your peace. Let prayer live in our rooms, truth govern our conversations, and holiness shape our atmosphere. Expose what needs to be exposed. Correct what needs to be corrected. Strengthen what needs to be strengthened. Heal what has been wounded. Restore what has been fractured. Rebuild what has been broken.

Lord, help us to parent and lead with wisdom. Teach us when to speak, when to listen, when to confront, when to wait, and when to act without hesitation. Let our love be more than sentiment. Let it be watchful. Let it be courageous. Let it be disciplined. Let it be faithful.

Keep us from reacting in anger, speaking carelessly, or dismissing what should be investigated. Make us stable, present, prayerful, and teachable.

For every child who has already been wounded, we ask for healing. Bind up the brokenhearted. Silence every lie trauma has spoken into their identity. Restore trust where it has been shattered. Restore peace where fear has settled. Restore hope where sorrow has lingered. Let Your mercy meet them in the deepest places of pain. Surround them with wise help, compassionate care, and unwavering love.

And for us, as parents and guardians, let us never forget that this assignment is not casual. It is sacred. Help us to stand faithfully at the gate of our homes. Help us to remain awake when the world grows sleepy. Help us to guard what cannot guard itself. And when our day of stewardship is measured before You, let it be said that we did not abandon our post.

We submit our homes to You.
We submit our children to You.
We submit our fears, our limitations, and our responsibilities to You.

Strengthen our hands.
Sharpen our discernment.
Deepen our compassion.
And establish our homes as places of safety, truth, healing, and holy protection.

In the mighty name of Jesus Christ, we pray.

Amen.

✞ A PARENT'S COVENANT OF PROTECTION ✞

The Sacred Agreement Before God

—————— ✦ ——————

What is a covenant?

A covenant is not a casual agreement, nor is it a temporary arrangement built on convenience or emotion. A biblical covenant is a solemn, binding commitment established before God, governed by truth, sustained by faithfulness, and enforced by accountability. It is not merely words spoken—it is a life submitted.

Throughout Scripture, a covenant defines a relationship. God does not deal with humanity through suggestion—He deals through covenant. And every covenant carries responsibility, relationship, and requirement.

Covenant is not a feeling—it is a binding obligation.

When a child is placed into the hands of a parent, that moment is more than biological—it is covenantal.

The child is not merely given for care—they are entrusted for covering.

Parenthood is not ownership—it is stewardship before God.

To enter into a covenant with God as a parent is to accept that:

You are accountable for what enters your child's life.

You are responsible for what influences their development.

You are assigned to guard what has been entrusted.

This covenant is not activated by words alone—it is activated by alignment with God's order.

A Covenant Parent Commits To:

- Watching without becoming passive
- Guarding without becoming careless
- Questioning without hesitation
- Acting before damage occurs
- Standing firm when comfort would suggest retreat

COVENANT DECLARATION

I enter into covenant before God concerning the life entrusted to me.
I will not be passive where I am called to protect.
I will not be silent where I am called to discern.
I will not be careless where I am called to watch.

I will guard what enters.
I will question what influences.
I will confront what threatens.

I accept the weight of this assignment—
not as a burden, but as obedience.

And with the help of God,
I will stand as a faithful watchman
over the life placed in my care.

THE GUARDIAN'S OATH

A Charge to Those Entrusted With What Cannot Defend Itself

Guardianship is not assumed—it is accepted.

It is not a title given lightly, nor a role fulfilled casually. It is a sacred charge placed upon those who have been entrusted with lives that cannot yet discern danger, resist manipulation, or defend themselves against what seeks access.

To be a guardian is to stand in a position of awareness when others are unaware.

To see what others overlook.

To question what others accept.

To act when others hesitate.

This oath is not symbolic—it is binding in conviction.

As a parent, guardian, or entrusted caregiver, I acknowledge before God that the child or children under my care are not mine by ownership, but mine by stewardship. They are sacred lives entrusted to me for protection, instruction, nurture, and watchful guidance. Therefore, with sobriety, conviction, and dependence upon the Lord, I make this covenant:

THE COVENANT AGREEMENT

I covenant to remain watchful and not passive.

I will not assume safety where discernment is required. I will not confuse familiarity with purity, reputation with integrity, or comfort with wisdom. I will remain attentive to the spiritual, emotional, physical, and digital influences surrounding the children in my care.

I covenant to protect with courage.

I will not allow awkwardness, social pressure, or fear of misunderstanding to silence my sense of responsibility. If something feels misaligned, I will investigate. If boundaries are tested, I will reinforce them. If danger is detected, I will act. I will choose protection over appearance, and truth over convenience.

I covenant to create a home where honesty is safe.

I will listen without rushing, respond without cruelty, and correct without humiliation. I will strive to create an atmosphere where confession is welcomed, truth is protected, and secrecy loses its power. I will teach the children under my care that they can speak to me without fear of rejection, shame, or dismissal.

I covenant to establish and enforce clear boundaries.

I will not allow secrecy, hidden access, unexamined influence, or inappropriate familiarity to take root in the environments I am called to guard. I will set boundaries with wisdom, communicate them clearly, and uphold them consistently.

I covenant to guard the gates of my home.

I will pay attention to what enters through conversations, relationships, screens, media, attitudes, and atmosphere. I will not treat digital access casually. I will not normalize what erodes holiness, truth, dignity, or safety. I will remember that what repeatedly enters the home will eventually shape the heart.

I covenant to model what I teach.

I will not demand vigilance from children while living carelessly myself. I will seek to live with integrity, prayerfulness, consistency, and humility. I will repent where I have failed, learn where I lack wisdom, and grow where I need strengthening.

I covenant to pursue healing where wounds exist.

If a child under my care has been harmed, I will not rush their pain, shame their struggle, or silence their process. I will seek their healing with patience, truth, compassion, and wise support. I will remember that restoration is not weakness—it is holy work.

I covenant to remain spiritually alert.

I recognize that protecting a child is not merely a practical duty but a spiritual assignment. I will pray over the children under my care. I will submit my home to God. I will seek the guidance of the Holy Spirit, anchor myself in Scripture, and remain awake to the spiritual climate of the household I am called to guard.

I covenant to remember that I will answer to God for this stewardship.

Therefore, I will not carry this assignment casually. I will not abandon my post through neglect, denial, or indifference. By the help of God, I will stand, watch, pray, guard, and remain faithful.

What God entrusted… must never be left exposed.

With God as my witness, I receive this responsibility with holy seriousness and covenant to guard the children entrusted to me with love, vigilance, wisdom, and unwavering commitment.

Signed: ______________________________

Date: ________________________________

✞ SCRIPTURE DECLARATIONS ✞

Scripture Declarations for the Home

These declarations may be read aloud regularly in the home, prayed over children, or spoken during times of uncertainty, fear, or spiritual warfare.

Declaration of Divine Protection

Psalm 91:1–2 (KJV) "He that dwelleth in the secret place of the most High shall abide under the shadow of the Almighty. I will say of the LORD, He is my refuge and my fortress: my God; in him will I trust."

We declare that this home abides under the shadow of the Almighty. The Lord is our refuge, our fortress, and our defense. We place our trust in Him, and we declare that no unseen danger, hidden scheme, or corrupting influence will find easy access here.

Declaration of Wisdom and Discernment

James 1:5 (KJV) "If any of you lack wisdom, let him ask of God, that giveth to all men liberally, and upbraideth not; and it shall be given him."

We declare that God gives wisdom freely to those who ask. We ask for discernment in parenting, leadership, protection, and decision-making. We declare that confusion will not rule this home. Wisdom, clarity, and spiritual alertness will guide us.

Declaration of Spiritual Vigilance

1 Peter 5:8 (KJV) "Be sober, be vigilant; because your adversary the devil, as a roaring lion, walketh about, seeking whom he may devour."

We declare that we will remain sober and vigilant. We reject passivity, distraction, and spiritual laziness. We will stay awake to what threatens innocence, truth, peace, and safety. We will not be careless with what God has entrusted to us.

Declaration of Peace Over the Home

Isaiah 26:3 (KJV) "Thou wilt keep him in perfect peace, whose mind is stayed on thee: because he trusteth in thee."

We declare the peace of God over this home. Fear, torment, confusion, and emotional instability will not dominate this household. Our minds are stayed upon the Lord, and His peace will govern our atmosphere.

Declaration of Truth in the Home

John 8:32 (KJV) "And ye shall know the truth, and the truth shall make you free."

We declare that truth lives in this home. Lies will be exposed. Secrets that protect darkness will be broken. Truth will bring freedom, clarity, healing, and safety to every member of this household.

Declaration of Identity and Worth

Psalm 139:14 (KJV) "I will praise thee; for I am fearfully and wonderfully made."

We declare that every child in this home is fearfully and wonderfully made. They are not defined by fear, shame, confusion, or trauma. They are valuable, seen by God, and created with purpose and dignity.

Declaration Against Fear

2 Timothy 1:7 (KJV) "For God hath not given us the spirit of fear; but of power, and of love, and of a sound mind."

We declare that fear does not rule this household. God has given us power, love, and a sound mind. We reject intimidation, panic, and torment. We receive courage, stability, and spiritual strength.

Declaration of Strength for Parents and Guardians

Isaiah 41:10 (KJV) "Fear thou not; for I am with thee: be not dismayed; for I am thy God: I will strengthen thee."

We declare that parents and guardians in this home are strengthened by God. We will not shrink back in fear or weariness. God is with us, and He gives us strength to guard, lead, pray, and stand faithfully.

Declaration of Healing for the Wounded

Psalm 147:3 (KJV) "He healeth the broken in heart, and bindeth up their wounds."

We declare healing over every wounded place. God heals broken hearts and binds wounds. Trauma will not have the final word. Shame will not define identity. Healing, restoration, and hope will rise in this home.

Declaration of Household Submission to God

Joshua 24:15 (KJV) "As for me and my house, we will serve the LORD."

We declare that this house belongs to the Lord. He will govern our decisions, atmosphere, priorities, boundaries, and values. This home will serve the Lord in truth, watchfulness, and obedience.

Declaration of Resistance Against Darkness

James 4:7 (KJV) "Submit yourselves therefore to God. Resist the devil, and he will flee from you."

We declare our submission to God and our resistance to darkness. Every influence that seeks to corrupt, confuse, divide, manipulate, or harm is resisted in the name of Jesus Christ. Darkness will not rule where truth and obedience stand.

Declaration of Watchful Stewardship

Ezekiel 33:7 (KJV) “I have set thee a watchman…”

We declare that we accept our assignment as watchmen over this home. We will not sleep spiritually. We will not abandon our post. By the grace of God, we will guard what has been entrusted to us with vigilance, courage, and faithfulness.

Where There Is No Conviction, There Is No Repentance.

Where There Is No Truth, There's No Correction.

We All Can Do Better.

"I Can't Tell It All"

By the grace of God, there are depths of testimony that cannot be fully written, to place on every page. Yet what has been shared in this book is given with intention—that something within these words will meet you exactly where you are. My prayer is that even a single line will reach your spirit, awaken your discernment, and strengthen your walk with God. May what you read not only inform you, but transform you; not only speak to you, but stir you. And as God has been faithful to me, I pray you encounter that same faithfulness in your own life—real, undeniable, and life-changing.

Whatever the Child's Age May Be in Your Care
"Stay Awake"
"Stay Diligent"
"Stay Alert On The Wall"

ABOUT THE AUTHOR

"Serving the Christian Community Worldwide,"

Minister Lee Rice is a devoted servant-leader whose life and ministry have been dedicated to advancing the Gospel of Jesus Christ with conviction, integrity, and compassion. Grateful to the Lord for His abundant blessings, he also honors and cherishes his wife, Sister Catherine Rice—lovingly described as "Bone of My Bone, Flesh of My Flesh"—for her love, steadfast faithfulness, strength, and unwavering support throughout the journey of ministry and life.

As a National Evangelist, International Gospel Recording Artist, Producer, Co-Producer, Talk Show Host, Singer, Songwriter, and Multi-Award Winner, Minister Lee Rice has spent years communicating biblical truth through preaching, music, media, and mentorship. His ministry extends far beyond the pulpit, reaching individuals, families, churches, and communities through teaching that combines scriptural depth with practical application. Through every platform entrusted to him, his mission remains consistent: to strengthen believers, challenge spiritual complacency, preserve the integrity of Christian fellowship, and equip leaders with sound biblical principles.

In this work, *A Dog and His Bone*, Minister Lee Rice addresses the destructive nature of gossip, division, and undisciplined speech within Christian environments. Writing with spiritual accountability and pastoral concern, he approaches the subject not merely as an observer but as a watchman burdened to protect unity, covenant relationships, and spiritual maturity within the Body of Christ. His message is both clear and convicting: authentic faith must govern not only our worship and outward expressions of devotion, but also the words we speak and the conversations we carry.

www.ingramcontent.com/pod-product-compliance
Lightning Source LLC
LaVergne TN
LVHW040213110826
845146LV00005B/1274

9798995610410